DOING BUSINESS WITH C

DOING BUSINESS WITH C

RAY SWARTZ

Berkeley Decision Systems

PRENTICE HALL, Englewood Cliffs, New Jersey 07632

Library of Congress Cataloging-in-Publication Data

Swartz, Ray.
  Doing business with C / Ray Swartz.
    p. cm.
  Includes index.
  ISBN 0-13-217258-5
  1. C (Computer program language) 2. Business--Data processing.
I. Title.
HF5548.5.C12S95 1989
005.13'3--dc19   88-9928
                                                                                            CIP

Editorial/production supervision: Editing, Design & Production, Inc.
Cover design: Bruce Kenselaar
Manufacturing buyer: Mary Ann Gloriande

© 1989 by Prentice-Hall, Inc.
A division of Simon & Schuster
Englewood Cliffs, New Jersey 07632

The publisher offers discounts on this book when ordered
in bulk quantities. For more information, write:
    Special Sales/College Marketing
    Prentice Hall
    College Technical and Reference Division
    Englewood Cliffs, NJ 07632

All rights reserved. No part of this book may be
reproduced, in any form or by any means,
without permission in writing from the publisher.

Printed in the United Stated of America
10 9 8 7 6 5 4 3 2 1

ISBN 0-13-217258-5

PRENTICE-HALL INTERNATIONAL (UK) LIMITED, *London*
PRENTICE-HALL OF AUSTRALIA PTY. LIMITED, *Sydney*
PRENTICE-HALL CANADA INC., *Toronto*
PRENTICE-HALL HISPANOAMERICANA, S.A., *Mexico*
PRENTICE-HALL OF INDIA PRIVATE LIMITED, *New Delhi*
PRENTICE-HALL OF JAPAN, INC., *Tokyo*
SIMON & SCHUSTER ASIA PTE. LTD., *Singapore*
EDITORA PRENTICE-HALL DO BRASIL, LTDA., *Rio de Janeiro*

This book is dedicated to my mother and father.

Contents

Preface   xvii

PART 1   INTRODUCTION   1

1   Doing Business with C   1

     1.1   C Is a Portable Language   1

     1.2   C Is a Concise Language   2

     1.3   C Is a Flexible Language   2

     1.4   C Is the Language of the UNIX Operating System   3

     1.5   A Brief History   3

     1.6   Algorithms and Structured Programming   4

     1.7   Summary   8

2   Creating a C Program   11

     2.1   Summary   11

     2.2   Using a C Compiler

PART 2 THE FUNDAMENTALS OF C   12

3 First Things First   12

- 3.1 Data Types   13
- 3.2 Variable Names   14
- 3.3 Statement Format   15
- 3.4 Operators, Operands, and Expressions   16
- 3.5 Arithmetic Operators   17
- 3.6 Printing   21
- 3.7 Character Constants   22
- 3.8 Special Character Constants   23
- 3.9 Character Strings   24
- 3.10 Structured Programming with Functions   25
- 3.11 Declaring Functions   26
- 3.12 Summary   27

4 Creating C Programs   30

- 4.1 Did We Make Any Money?   30
- 4.2 Conditional Statements   34
- 4.3 Summary   42

5 Interactive Programming in C   43

- 5.1 The Standard Function Library   43
- 5.2 The Standard Library Header File   44
- 5.3 Making C Programs Interactive   45
- 5.4 String Variables   45
- 5.5 Reading Strings   48
- 5.6 Reading Numeric Data   50
- 5.7 Numeric Formatting with **printf( )**   55
- 5.8 Round-Off Error   56

Contents ix

    5.9   Expanding the P&L Statement 57

    5.10 Stepwise Refinement 59

    5.11 Summary 63

            Exercises 65

6 Creating Our Own Commands   66

    6.1   How to Write Functions 67

    6.2   Function Data Types and **void** 70

    6.3   Using "Homemade" Functions 71

    6.4   Temporarily Changing Data Types 73

            6.4.1 *Data Type Promotion and* **cast***s, 74*

    6.5   Summary 76

            Exercises 77

7 Looping Commands and the switch Statement   79

    7.1   The **while** Loop 80

    7.2   The **round( )** Function 82

    7.3   The **do while** Loop 86

    7.4   The **for** Loop 88

    7.5   Designing Programs with Loops 91

    7.6   The **switch - case** Statement 98

    7.7   Summary 102

            Exercises 103

PART 3 GENERALIZING PROGRAMS   105

8 A Need for Change   105

    8.1   Data Arrays 111

    8.2   Summary 115

            Exercises 115

9 Strings and String Arrays — 116

- 9.1 The **sprintf()** Function 127
- 9.2 The Great Escape 133
- 9.3 The **break** Command 136
- 9.4 Summary 139
    - Exercises 139

PART 4 SOME C SHORTCUTS — 141

10 The Preprocessor — 141

- 10.1 The **#define** Directive 142
- 10.2 Processing Macro Arguments 146
- 10.3 Conditional Compilation 149
- 10.4 Using **printf()** with Macros 153
- 10.5 Summary 159
    - Exercises 160

11 Making C an Efficient Operation — 161

- 11.1 Increment and Decrement Operators 161
- 11.2 Using Increment Operators in Array Indexes 166
- 11.3 Assignment Operators 169
- 11.4 The Conditional Operator 171
- 11.5 The Unary Minus Operator 174
- 11.6 Using C's Operators 178
- 11.7 Summary 178
    - Exercises 179

12 Scope Rules and Storage Classes — 181

- 12.1 Local Scope 181
- 12.2 Automatic Storage 182
- 12.3 **static** Storage 183

Contents   xi

    12.4   Global Scope   187

    12.5   Scope of Global Variables   190

    12.6   **static** Global Scope   191

    12.7   The Scope of Functions   193

    12.8   The Scope of Function Parameters   195

    12.9   Portability   197

    12.10   Using Storage to Speed Up Programs   197

    12.11   **register** Storage   198

    12.12   Initializing Variables   199

    12.13   Array Initialization in C   200

    12.14   Summary   205

               Exercises   207

PART 5   THANKS FOR THE MEMORY   208

13   *Directly Accessing Data*   *208*

    13.1   The Address Operator   210

    13.2   The Pointer Data Type   211

    13.3   The Indirection Operator   213

    13.4   Initializing Pointers   215

    13.5   A Pointed Example   215

    13.6   Pointers as Function Arguments   217

    13.7   Summary   219

              Exercises   220

14   *Arrays and Pointers*   *221*

    14.1   Arrays and Addresses   222

    14.2   Pointer Arithmetic   224

    14.3   The Array Transformation Rule   225

    14.4   Passing Arrays as Function Arguments   232

    14.5   How Pointers and Arrays Differ   234

14.6　Summary　239

　　　Exercises　240

15　Pointers and Multidimensional Arrays　241

15.1　The Two Arrays in a Two-Dimensional Array　244

15.2　Transforming Two-Dimensional Arrays　246

15.3　Arrays Bounds Checking　253

15.4　Summary　254

　　　Exercises　255

PART 6　STRINGS　256

16　Strings, Arrays, and Pointers　256

16.1　A Careful Look at **char**s　259

16.2　Writing String Functions　260

16.3　String Functions in C's Standard Library　269

16.3.1　String Handling Functions That Return an **int**, *269*
16.3.2　String Handling Functions That Return a Pointer to **char**, *271*

16.4　Summary　273

　　　Exercises　274

16.5　Addendum　275

17　Reading and Writing Strings　279

17.1　Writing Input and Output Functions　280

17.2　How **gets**( ) Works　283

17.3　Writing a Conversion Function　287

17.4　Testing and Converting Characters　288

17.5　Summary　295

　　　Exercises　295

PART 7 CREATING NEW DATA TYPES — 296

18 Data Structures — 296

- 18.1 **typedef** 297
- 18.2 Data Structures 299
- 18.3 The Member Operator (.) 303
- 18.4 Handling Structures 305
- 18.5 Pointers to Structures 306
- 18.6 Arrays of Structures 311
- 18.7 Adding Structures to the **flex-pl** Program 314
- 18.8 Structures as Structure Members 318
- 18.9 Initializing a Structure 320
- 18.10 Summary 321
  - Exercises 322

19 Dynamic Storage — 323

- 19.1 The **sizeof( )** Operator 324
- 19.2 Allocating Memory 327
- 19.3 The **realloc( )** Function 335
- 19.4 Summary 342
  - Exercises 343
- 19.5 Addendum 343
  - 19.5.1 A **realloc( )** *function,* 343

PART 8 WORKING WITH DATA FILES — 346

20 Working with Data Files In C — 346

- 20.1 The C Programming Environment 346
- 20.2 Redirecting Standard Input and Output 347
- 20.3 Accessing Files 348
- 20.4 What Is Opened Should Be Closed 351

- 20.5 Standard File I/O Functions 352
- 20.6 The **getc**( ) and **putc**( ) Functions 353
- 20.7 The **fgets**( ) Function 354
- 20.8 The **fputs**( ) Function 355
- 20.9 The **fprintf**( ) and **fscanf**( ) Functions 356
- 20.10 The **feof**( ) Macro 357
- 20.11 Making a Statement 358
- 20.12 The **get-pl** Program 358
- 20.13 The **make-pl** Program 360
- 20.14 Summary 368
  - Exercises 369

21 Command Line Arguments 370

- 21.1 *argv* and *argc* 370
- 21.2 Reading Arguments from the Commmand Line 374
- 21.3 Summary 376
  - Exercises 376

PART 9 ADDITIONAL LANGUAGE FEATURES 378

22 Additional C Features 378

- 22.1 Numeric Constants 378
- 22.2 Pointers to Functions 379
- 22.3 Enumeration Types 380
- 22.4 Unions 382
- 22.5 The **goto** Statement and Line Labels 384
- 22.6 Recursion 385
- 22.7 Bitwise Operators 385
- 22.8 One's Complement Operator 387
- 22.9 Bitwise Logical Operators 387
- 22.10 Shifting Operators 390

		22.11	Bit Fields	390	
		22.12	Summary	392	

A	The ASCII Character Set	393
B	The EBCDIC Character Set	397
C	The ANSI C Standard	401
D	A C Standard Library Reference	416
E	printf( ) Formatting Codes	429
F	General Reference Section	432
	Solutions to In-Chapter Exercises	435
	Index	437

Preface

The purpose of this book is twofold. First, it is designed to teach people how to program in the C language. The book can be used by beginning programmers who want a solid foundation in programming constructs before exploring the rocky recesses of C. In addition, more experienced programmers will find many tidbits of information that will make them better programmers as they become familiar with the C language. For readers who already know some C, I recommend that you skim the first three chapters. However, make sure that the material in Chapter 3 is understood before going on to the rest of the book.

The second purpose of this book is to demonstrate and discuss the problems associated with writing business applications. In general, a business application is one in which a user must enter data that is manipulated, stored, and printed. The key facets of business programming are printing prompts, handling data entry, verifying entered data, and output formatting. The book provides many guidelines (called *rules* in the text) for writing business application programs in C.

To achieve these two purposes, the book takes a new approach. The entire book is centered on the development of a single business application, a program that reads in a set of revenue and cost amounts and then formats a Profit and Loss Statement. This application was chosen because it provided the richness necessary to demonstrate most of C's features. In those few areas where the P&L program was inappropriate other business programs, such as an invoicing program, are used.

The P&L program begins as a small five-line program in Chapter 4 and grows into a two-program application. The first program reads data from the user and stores it in a file. The second program formats the P&L statement from the file created by the first program.

The importance of this "single-program" approach is that the reader doesn't have to learn a new example every time another programming point is described. Further, as readers become acquainted with the P&L application, advanced ideas can be discussed and demonstrated in a context that is familiar. Last, watching a program develop from a simple idea into a true application provides experience that enhances the reader's ability to program in C.

This book is a direct outgrowth of the many seminars and training sessions I have held on the C language. In live seminar, the faces of the students tell the teacher what is and isn't understood. Further, emphasis can be placed on important points through nonverbal communication such as pointing or voice inflection.

In an attempt to convey the same kind of emphasis to the reader, I have included *rules* in the text. These are special points that embody important lessons I have learned either about C, business programming, or programming in general.

The only way to learn a new skill is to practice it until the fundamentals become understood well enough to be applied with insight. To provide the reader with incentive to practice, the book contains two types of exercises. Exercises that appear in the text of chapter are focused on the material just discussed. Solutions to these exercises have been provided in the back of the book. The second type of exercise appears at the end of Chapters 5 through 21. These exercises ask the reader to apply each chapter's concept in a broader way. Solutions to these end-of-chapter exercises are left to the reader.

Writing a book is a serious committment of time and energy. There is no way this book would have been possible were it not for the love of my wife Rita, who often gave me the inspiration to go on when I didn't have the desire to do so.

A number of people freely gave their time to help me. Lance Leventhal first proposed the idea of writing a book on C to me. He helped me organize my thoughts, edited the early drafts, and provided invaluable advice. Thanks, Lance. John Wait, my editor at Prentice-Hall, showed great patience as this book grew into a three-year project. David Goldman provided detailed criticism and made innumerable improvements in the text. Rex Jaeschke's editing of Appendix C saved me a huge amount of time and effort.

Many others are to be thanked. Terry Hobart, Howard Cohen, Jay Gunter, Mel Tearle, Ray Reinhard, Kevin Carney, and Ira Pohl. Last, I'd like to thank all the students who over the past four years have helped me learn all the little facets of C that I never would have seen had I not had to explain it to someone else.

I have tried to produce an error-free book. However, I know that books, like programs, always have bugs. I take full, complete, and final responsibility for any and all errors that appear in this book. If you find an error, no matter how slight, please send a "bug report" to Ray Swartz, P.O. Box 2528, Santa Cruz, CA 95063.

PART 1
Introduction

1

Doing Business with C

As the title indicates, this book is about writing business-related programs using C. Before we begin, we should ask a question. Is C a good language for business applications?

Business programs perform a wide variety of tasks in a number of different environments. For this reason, one important component of a good business programming language is transportability. First, it should be hardware independent. No business wants to be tied to a specific machine sold by only one vendor!

C is a good business programming language because it is portable, concise, flexible, and the language of the UNIX operating system, which is available on a number of different computer systems. These points are discussed in detail below.

1.1 C IS A PORTABLE LANGUAGE

Since their creation in the late 1940s, electronic digital computers, called just computers these days, have developed with unbelievable rapidity. As they get smaller and faster they also get cheaper. The result is that more and more we are working with computers to get our jobs done. In most cases this allows us to work more effectively.

While computer costs have dropped, the comparable investment in software development has increased dramatically. As a business integrates computers into its everyday activities, the programs that process data and print reports become irreplaceable. Without computers and programs a business is likely to stop functioning entirely.

One unfortunate side effect of the explosive growth in computers is the lack of accepted standards. On any given day we are liable to interact with several different computers manufactured by different companies for different reasons, each requiring different commands to do the same things! Thus, we want to use a business programming language that is as independent as possible from the underlying computer. This frees us from the burden of redesigning our software when it is moved from one machine to another. Lack of independence can be a serious problem when a company outgrows its computer and must migrate to a larger one.

C was specifically designed so that programs written in C could be moved from one computer to another with little or no modification. The most important reason for doing our business programming in C is to save the costs, problems, and time associated with transporting existing applications between computers.

1.2 C IS A CONCISE LANGUAGE

Many programming languages were developed to cover as many contingencies as possible. The result was languages with many commands, data types, and programming options. Programmers who work with "large" languages tend to become familiar with only the subset of commands that they use. Thus, a programmer may be unable to work with programs that use all the available commands or unfamiliar options.

C's designers were aware of these problems and specifically created a small language. C contains very few commands (less than 30)[1] and some of these are rarely used. Anyone who uses C knows the *entire* language. This helps avoid confusion and is another good reason to write business programs in C.

1.3 C IS A FLEXIBLE LANGUAGE

Most programming languages, even those specifically designed for business data processing, impose restrictions on those who use them. The restrictions might be how something has to be printed, the kinds of numbers that have to be used, the way data must be represented, or the types of files that can be accessed. What seems like a nice feature may someday "get in the way."

In contrast, C provides the tools needed for writing computer programs and little else. It makes no assumptions about the problem at hand or the best way to solve it. This flexibility frees us to approach both the problem and its solution in the best way. Further, the C language is *extensible*. That is, we can extend the language by adding features when we need them and ignoring them the rest of the time.

---

[1] ANSI C contains 32 keywords.

Flexibility is one of the most important needs of today's business programmers. No longer are computers used for accounting applications only. C is a language that can work scientific, accounting, and data processing problems with equal effectiveness.

1.4 C IS THE LANGUAGE OF THE UNIX OPERATING SYSTEM

Although acknowledged computing standards are few and far between, one bright spot on the horizon is the UNIX operating system. Developed at Bell Labs by the same people who invented C, its use has spread widely. In addition, the computer industry is embracing it as a standard operating system.

The UNIX system is written primarily in C and virtually all installations of it make available the C programming language. For applications developed on UNIX systems, C is the language of choice.

C is not a perfect language. It has its shortcomings and they should be discussed too. It was designed by programmers to be used to write programs. Although this is not necessarily a problem, it does mean that C can be hard to learn by those not experienced with computer programming. Also, the language is very permissive. Many times, outright programming mistakes are legal constructs! Executing programs with such faults can cause truly spectacular errors, such as overwriting valid information on the disk or corrupting the operating system. Be advised that testing raw C programs without system backups is dangerous!

Because of C's flexibility, advanced programmers can perform what seems like magic in a few lines of C. Obscure constructs are a problem in any language, but the problem can be worse in C. Fortunately, confusion can be avoided by carefully documenting these tricky passages and restraining the urge to be *too* creative.

If asked about C, other programmers might cite different weaknesses and bring up additional advantages. After spending years as a professional programmer, the author believes that the advantages of C far outweigh its drawbacks. In any case, C is a popular language at present and all indications are that its use will only grow in the forseeable future. This, if no other reason, should make learning to use C worthwhile.

1.5 A BRIEF HISTORY

The history of the C programming language began in the late 1950s when a small group of Europeans and Americans met in Zurich, Switzerland to design an international programming language. They named this language ALGOL (ALGOritmic Language). As it happened, ALGOL 60 "lost out" to the IBM-supported FORTRAN as the first programming language in general use.

Fortunately, this wasn't the end of the story for ALGOL. The ideas embodied in its design were powerful enough to be used as the basis for a number of other languages. In fact, PL/1, Pascal, SIMULA, ADA, C, and many others are called ALGOL-like languages because they use ideas first introduced in ALGOL.

The computer programs that manage computer systems are called *systems programs*. Many of the earliest computer programs were systems programs. A number of computer languages were created for developing such programs. C was developed in 1972 by Dennis Ritchie at Bell Laboratories as the systems language of the UNIX operating system, then under design as well.

C is a direct descendant of the B programming language. B was created by Ken Thompson, Ritchie's colleague and developer of the UNIX operating system. B was used to write the early versions of UNIX. B was based on BCPL (British Combined Programming Language) an earlier systems programming language. Many of C's features come directly from BCPL.

The world found out about C in 1978 when Brian Kernighan and Dennis Ritchie published a book called *The C Programming Language*. It contained a complete definition of the language that quickly became the de facto standard. It was adherence to this language definition that made C a portable language. In 1983, the American National Standards Institute (ANSI) convened the X3J11 committee to create an ANSI standard for the C language. It is expected that an ANSI C standard will be ratified in 1988. For the most part, ANSI C will match Kernighan and Ritchie C. However, several extensions have been added to C. Where appropriate, mention will be made of these additions. See Appendix C for a full discussion of the proposed ANSI C standard.

1.6 ALGORITHMS AND STRUCTURED PROGRAMMING

A computer program is nothing more than a set of instructions. When executed in the proper order, these instructions accomplish the task or set of tasks intended. Unfortunately, correctly translating these instructions into statements the computer understands can be a difficult job.

The first step in writing a computer program is to design how it will work. One design technique is creating an *algorithm* first, before writing the program in a specific computer language. An algorithm is an ordered set of steps that accomplish a specified task, for example, a cooking recipe. It lists the proper preparation steps to create a meal. To write a correct computer program requires that we know what to do, as well as the order to do it in. By designing an algorithm that describes the task at hand, we can decrease the time and effort required to make our programs work. Algorithms will be used extensively throughout this book.

It has been shown that every algorithm can be produced with only three basic patterns. These are

1. Two or more instructions carried out one after the other
2. One of two sets of instructions executed as the result of a logical (i.e., true or false) test
3. A set of instructions repeated

These three constructs are called *control structures* because they control the order of execution of the steps in an algorithm. They have been given appropriate names:

Sec. 1.6   Algorithms and Structured Programming

1. *Sequence* structure
2. *Selection* structure
3. *Repetition* or *looping* structure

The sequence structure represents a series of instructions that are executed sequentially. Once begun, all the statements in the sequence are performed in the order they are listed. Figure 1-1 shows a sequence structure graphically. The lines inside the box represent the individual programming statements that comprise the sequence. The structure is entered at the top, the statements are executed, and the structure is exited at the bottom.

The selection structure allows the computer to decide which instructions to perform next. The choice is determined by the result of a logical test. If the test is true, one set is performed; if the test is false, the other. In Figure 1-2, the sequence on the

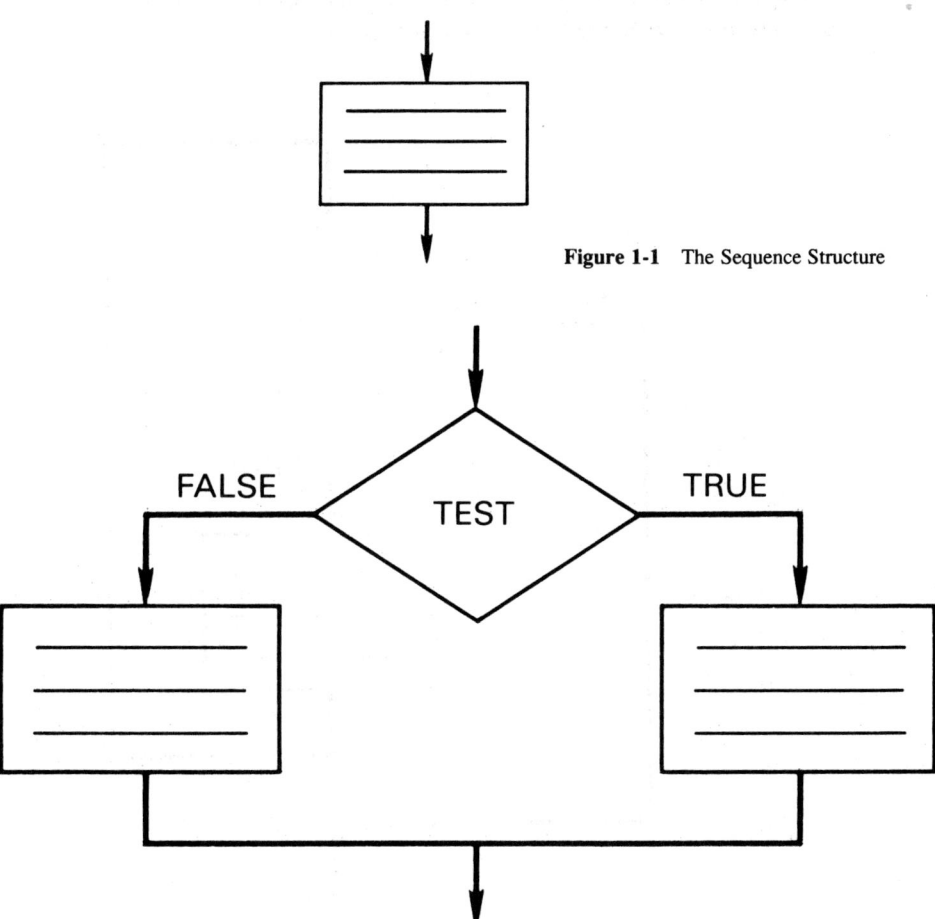

Figure 1-1   The Sequence Structure

Figure 1-2   The Selection Structure

right is executed if the test is true. The one on the left is chosen if the test is false. In either case, the entire structure is exited at the bottom.

The repetition or looping structure provides the ability to repeat a set of instructions. Generally, this structure is called a *loop*. The instructions being repeated are called the *body* of the loop. Like the selection structure, loops, too, are controlled by a logical test. The program remains in the loop, repeating the loop's body, as long as the test is true. We exit out of the loop when the test is false. For this reason, the test in a loop is called a *stopping condition*.

Loops are divided into two types, those that test at the top, called **while** loops, and those that test at the bottom, called **do while** loops. Figure 1-3 shows a **while** loop and Figure 1-4 a **do while** loop. The main distinction between them is that **while** loops test the stopping condition *before* the body of the loop is executed. If the test evaluates to false the first time, the body of a **while** loop is not performed at all! **do while** loops, on the other hand, test after the loop's body has been performed. This means **do while** loops always execute the loop's body at least once.

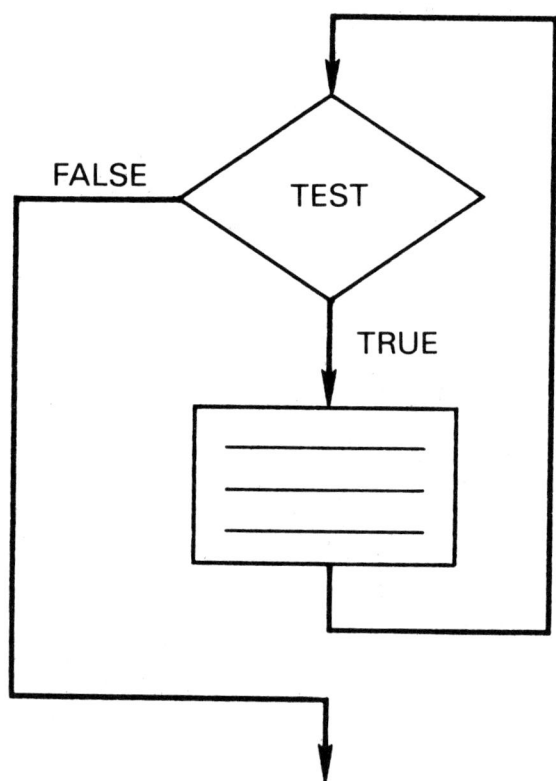

Figure 1-3 The **while** Loop

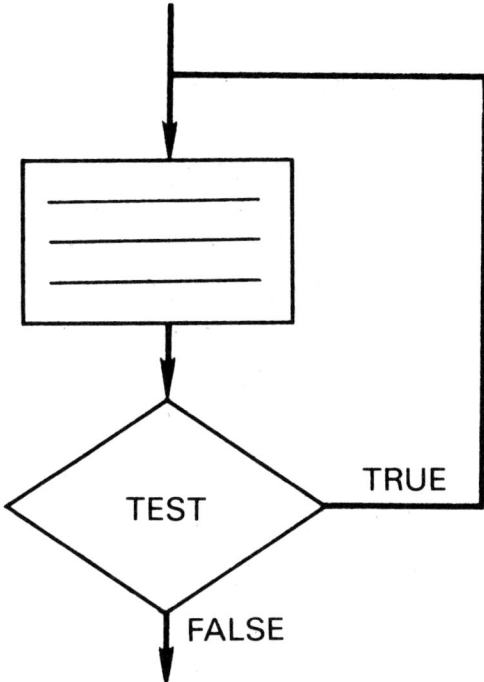

Figure 1-4 The **do while** Loop

Rule   Use the correct loop.

Up to now, we have only shown sequences being selected (Figure 1-2) or repeated (Figures 1-3 and 1-4). However, any of the three structures can be used in conjunction with the selection and loop structures. In reality, algorithms "weave" these structures together to provide a solution to the problem. Figure 1-5 shows a typical combination.

Exercise 1-1[2]   Describe what is going on in Figure 1-5.

ALGOL was designed to use these three structures to translate algorithms into computer programs. Since then a number of languages have implemented these structures as part of the language and, as a result, are called *structured programming languages*. C is one of them.

The essence of structured programming is to use the structures as "building blocks" to assemble algorithms that can be directly translated into a programming language. This not only makes designing correct programs less difficult but also makes them more understandable. The development of structured programming has had a significant impact on computers and those who program them. The programs presented throughout this book demonstrate the use of structure programming techniques.

---

[2] The solutions to in-text exercises are in the back of the book.

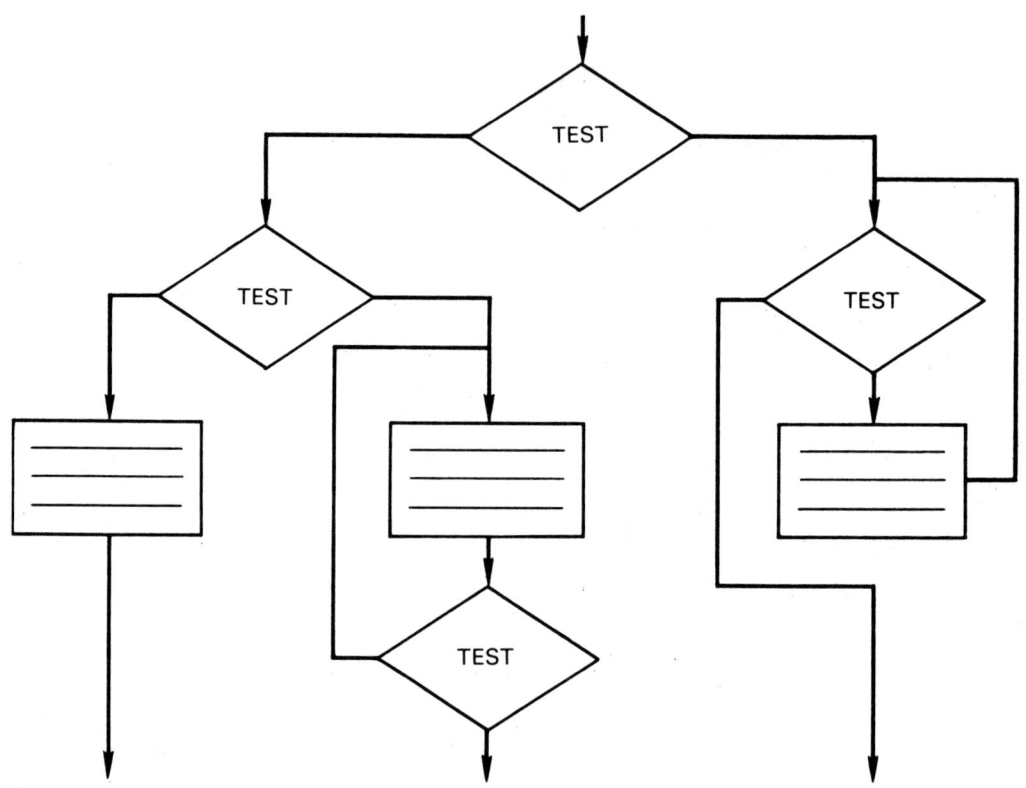

Figure 1-5 Combining Programming Structures

1.7 SUMMARY

1. C is a good business programming language because it is portable, concise, flexible, and the language of UNIX.

2. An algorithm is an ordered set of steps that accomplish a specified task.

3. An algorithm can be built from three control structures: a sequence, a selection, and a loop.

4. By weaving together these three control structures, we can create programming solutions to our programs.

5. The essence of structured programming is using the three control structures to create computer programs.
6. A structured language is one that implements the control structures as part of the language.

2

Creating a C Program

At the lowest level, a computer is nothing more than a series of complex electrical circuits. When electricity is pulsed through them, the computer performs a preset "instruction." Computers are not unique in their ability to do this—the same could be said of refrigerators and toasters. Computers are set apart from these "dumb" machines because they can be told which instructions to execute and in what order, that is, they can be programmed.

Most of today's computers can perform between 50 and 200 instructions. Each instruction is assigned a unique numeric code. Before a command can be executed, it must be expressed as one or more of these instruction codes. These codes are the only "language" understood by a computer and have become know as *machine language*.

The earliest computers could be programmed only in machine language. This is a long, tedious, and error-prone process. To ease this burden, *higher-level languages* were developed. Higher-level languages are much easier to understand because they have "English-like" commands instead of numeric codes. BASIC, Pascal, FORTRAN, and C are all higher-level languages.

One difficulty with using higher-level languages is that before the computer can execute a program, the program must be translated into machine language. This process is called *compilation*.

This translation is done by sophisticated computer programs that read commands written in a particular language and then create the equivalent instruction codes. They are called *compilers*.

There are two steps to writing a C program. First, the C statements must be entered into the computer, as text. This is done with a text editor, the text is called the *source code*. Next, we invoke the C language compiler, which translates the program we just entered into machine language.

It sounds easy and, in theory, it is. However, a compiler can only translate correct C statements. When it sees incorrect syntax, illegal operations, or unknown constructs the compiler will print error messages and stop. Thus, what actually happens is that the compiler finds errors in our program the first time we try it. We then repair these problems and compile again. This process is repeated until the compiler is able to translate our entire program without trouble.

When this has been done, we have an *executable* program. However, it doesn't end here. Just because the compiler was successful in no way means that the program works as designed. We now must begin the complex task of verifying that the program we wrote and compiled does what we want it to do! The vast majority of programming time is spent in this phase of the process, known as *debugging*.

2.1 USING A C COMPILER

The C language is portable, but this doesn't mean that the compilation procedure is the same on all systems. There are some general guidelines, however. As a rule, the name of the file that holds the source code should end with a **.c**. Also, a common name of the C compiler is **cc**. As an example, to compile the source code in the file *example.c* would require this command:

```
cc example.c
```

The name of the resulting executable program file varies. On Unix systems, the compiler creates a file called *a.out*, which we could then execute. Compilers run on other systems tend to put the compiled code in a file appropriately named for execution on that system. For example, if we compiled *example.c* on an MS-DOS computer, it would deposit the executable code in the file *example.exe* or *example.com*. If this process is unfamiliar, check the compiler's documentation or ask the system administrator for specific information.

2.2 SUMMARY

1. A computer can only execute machine language instructions.
2. A C program must be translated into machine language to execute.
3. To create a C program, we have to enter the text (source code) of the program onto the computer and then compile it into an executable program.
4. By convention, C source code files end in *.c*.

PART 2
The Fundamentals of C

3
First Things First

Computers are useful because of their ability to store huge amounts of information. This information might be numbers, such as a financial report, or alphabetic characters, such as names and addresses. Once data has been stored on a computer system, it can be manipulated in whatever ways are dictated by the user's needs. However, managing computerized information requires the proper *tools*. On a computer, the basic tools are programming languages.

One of the most important responsibilities of a programming language is to identify what kind of information it is manipulating. This prevents the computer from performing meaningless operations, like

```
"Apples" - "Oranges" + 4
```

To be available, data must be stored in the computer's memory. Computer memory consists of uniquely numbered cells, each of which can hold a piece of information. These unique cell numbers are called *memory addresses*. We need to know the address where something is stored in order to manipulate it.

A programming language, such as C, frees us from keeping track of memory addresses by substituting names for them. These names are called *variables*. Variables make computer programming much easier by allowing us to use descriptive names instead of meaningless numeric address to refer to stored data. In fact, we will say that information is stored *in* a variable.

Before we can use a variable, we must tell C something about it. This is called *defining* a variable. Specifically, we must identify what kind of information the variable will store. C can manage only certain types of data. Thus, a variable must be defined to be one of the legal C *data types* before it can be used in a C program.

3.1 DATA TYPES

A variable's data type identifies the kind of information the variable will hold, such as a number or a string of alphabetic characters. C provides several data types. The most commonly used are

    int   (integer)
    char   (alphabetic character)
    float   (floating point number)
    double[1] (double precision floating point number)

The main difference amongst these data types is how they are stored inside the computer. In fact, we define a variable to be a specific data type so the computer can allocate the proper amount of memory for it. The **int** variables store integers (numbers which have no fractional part or decimal point). The **char** variables store single alphabetic characters (e.g., ASCII characters). The **float** and **double** variables store numbers with decimal points that "move around" as their sizes change. These use floating point notation. Typically, **float**s have a precision (number of significant digits) of six digits and **double**s of ten digits.

In addition to **char**, **int**, **float**, and **double**, C contains other data types. These are

    short   (short integer)
    long   (long integer)
    unsigned (unsigned integer)

A **short** variable can only store integers of limited size. Should we need to use a number larger than an **int** can handle, we can employ a **long** variable. **int**, **short**, and **long** values can be either positive or negative. The **unsigned** variables can only hold positive integers. The words **short**, **long**, and **unsigned** are called *qualifiers* because they specify what kind of **int** a variable will hold. Further, since **short**, **long**, and **unsigned** variables always must be integers, we can leave **int** off such definitions. Thus,

```
long int
```

---

[1] The ANSI standard introduces a new data type, **long double**. It has twice the precision of **double**.

and

```
long
```

are equivalent ways to define a **long** variable. In practice **int** is rarely used with **short**, **long**, or **unsigned**.

The amount of memory allocated for each data type dictates how much information such a variable can store. While the exact maximum and minimum values vary with the C version and the computer being used, typical integer limits are

DATA TYPE	MAXIMUM	MINIMUM
int	32767	-32768
unsigned int	65535	0
short	32767	-32768
unsigned short	65535	0
long	2147483647	-2147483648
unsigned long	4294967295	0

Incorrectly typed variables can cause programming errors that are difficult to identify.

RULE   Use the appropriate data types when defining variables.

3.2 VARIABLE NAMES

When we define a variable, we instruct C to connect a descriptive name to a portion of computer memory. Thus, all variable definitions must specify two things: a variable name and its data type.

C places some limits on how variables can be named. Variables names must start with a letter and can contain letters, underscores, and digits.[2] For example,

   total_value
   size3
   first_one
   counter
   x

are all valid C variable names. The following names are not legal for the reason given:

---

[2] It is legal for variable names to start with underscores, as well as letters. However, variables beginning with underscores are reserved by the compiler and should never be used.

Sec. 3.3   Statement Format   15

3_big	Starts with a number
largest-one	The - is not legal
sum total	Space not allowed
long	A word reserved by C

Both capital and lowercase letters can be used, but be careful; C distinguishes between them. For example, C interprets

```
                         VALUE
```

and

```
                         value
```

as two different variables.

The maximum length of a variable name varies between different versions of the C language. Typically, only the first eight characters are significant to C. Thus, a typical C version will take the names

```
                       income_tax
```

and

```
                     income_tax_pct
```

as the same variable since they both begin with the same eight characters.[3] Generally, this limitation is specified in the documentation for the C compiler being used. To maintain compatibility, we will assume that only the first eight characters of a variable name are significant. Notice that using the underscore overcomes C's intolerance of spaces within variable names.

When we write programs, it is vitally important that we not confuse the information stored in different variables. This problem is commonly caused by poorly chosen variable names. Our variable names should describe the data represented by the variable.

RULE   The names given a variable should be descriptive of what the variable stores. Do not use single-letter variable names.

3.3 STATEMENT FORMAT

A C program consists of C *statements*. All C statements must end with a semicolon. This means a variable definition is not valid unless it is terminated with a semicolon, for instance,

---

[3] The ANSI standard limits the significant number of characters in a variable name to the first thirty one.

```
                    int counter;
                    unsigned long grand_total;
                    float sqr_root;
                    double revenue;
                    char answer;
```

In a variable definition, the data type precedes the variable's name.

3.4 OPERATORS, OPERANDS, AND EXPRESSIONS

C provides a number of operations that we can use to manipulate stored data. These operations are represented by special characters called *operators*. For example, if *count* is defined

```
                         int count;
```

then we can store an integer in *count* with the *assignment* operator, the equal sign. Thus,

```
                         count = 5;
```

stores five in *count*.

An operator must have data to work on. The data evaluated by an operator are called *operands*. For example, in

```
                         count = 5;
```

the variable *count* and the number five are the operands used by the assignment operator.

```
                         operator
                            ↓
                         count = 5;
                           ↑     ↑
                          operands
```

The concept of operators evaluating operands is an important one in C programming.

Before C can evaluate an operator, it must have the proper amount of data. The assignment operator requires two operands, the value being assigned and the variable that will hold this value. Operators that require two operands are called *binary* operators. C also contains *unary* operators, which need only one operand. An example is the *negation operator*, the minus sign, which evaluates to the negative of its single operand. Thus,

- 3

is an expression that evaluates to negative three. There even is a *ternary operator*, one that takes three operands. This operator classification will come in handy later.

Whenever an operator is combined with operands, the result is called an *expression*. Notice that a semicolon was placed at the end of the above assignment expression. We put a semicolon at the end of the expression to make it a legal C statement. In fact, that's all that's needed to create a legal C statement—a semicolon at the end of a legal expression. Thus, these are legal statements in C:

```
4 + value;
3 * nbr1;
nbr1 * nbr2 + nbr3;
```

However, they are meaningless because nothing is done with their results. This is an example of C's permissiveness.

C contains 44 different operators. In fact, much of the rest of this book will be spent explaining what these operators do and how to use them!

3.5 ARITHMETIC OPERATORS

One common task asked of computer programs is to perform arithmetic operations, such as addition, subtraction, multiplication, and division, on numeric data. C uses the same arithmetic operators as virtually all other computer languages:

+   Addition
−   Subtraction
*   Multiplication
/   Division

All arithmetic operators are binary operators.

C also provides a *modulo* operator as well. The modulo operator is represented by the percent sign and evaluates to the *remainder* when one integer is divided by another. For example,

```
 9 % 3 = 0
10 % 3 = 1
```

Described in words, this example says that 9 is evenly divided by 3 (i.e., there is no remainder) and that 1 is left over when 10 is divided by 3.

C allows us to combine several operators within a single expression. Thus,

```
value = nbr1 + nbr2 * nbr3;
```

is a legal C statement (again, notice the semicolon). C follows a specific evaluation procedure when an expression contains more than one operator. This is important because we want the same expression to always give the same answer! These rules are called *operator precedence* and they are summarized in Table 3-1. In an expression that contains two or more operators, C calculates the one with the highest precedence first, then proceeds to the next highest one until all the operators have been evaluated.

TABLE 3-1 Precedence of Arithmetic and Assignment Operators

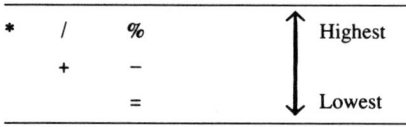

For example, the statement

```
value = nbr1 + nbr2 * nbr3;
```

contains three operators, the +, *, and =. Since multiplication has the highest precedence of the three, it is performed first. Further, multiplication is a binary operator, so the expression

```
nbr2 * nbr3
```

is evaluated. Addition is the next highest operator so the result of the multiplication is added to *nbr1*. The right side of the statement is now a single numeric value which is assigned to *total*. Notice how the rules of precedence dictated which operands were evaluated by each (binary) operator and how the results of higher precedence expressions become operands for the remaining operators.

Unfortunately, precedence doesn't always provide the solution. For example, in this statement

```
total = nbr1 / nbr2 * nbr3;
```

do we multiply or divide first? If *nbr1* equals 20, *nbr2* equals 10, and *nbr3* equals 2, the result is

```
total = 20 / (10 * 2) = 20 / 20 = 1
```

if we multiply first or

```
total = (20 / 10) * 2 = 2 * 2 = 4
```

if we divide first. Such a statement must always result in the same value or else our computer programs will be of no use.

Sec. 3.5 Arithmetic Operators

Evaluating expressions containing operators of the *same* precedence requires a second operator attribute, called *associativity*. Associativity identifies which operands are associated with which operators. A set of operators associate either *left to right* or *right to left*.

Left-to-right associativity says that we begin on the left of the expression (*nbr1*) and move to the right. The first operator we encounter (division) is evaluated with the two operands it separates (*nbr1 / nbr2*). The next operator uses this result as one of its operands and so on until there are no more operators with the same precedence in the expression. Left-to-right associativity results in assigning 4 to *total*. Right to left associativity, on the other hand, says to start on the right side the expression and move left. This evaluates the multiplication first and then the division which would assign 1 to *total*.

All arithmetic operators associate from left to right. Thus, this code

```
nbr1 = 20;
nbr2 = 10;
nbr3 = 2;
total = nbr1 / nbr2 * nbr3;
```

stores 4 in *total*. As we can see, associativity is an important part of operator evaluation. Table 3-2 lists the associativity of the operators introduced so far.

TABLE 3-2 Precedence and Associativity of Arithmetic Operators

*	/	%	Left to right
+	–		Left to right
		=	Right to left

Since storing a value in a variable is done by an operator, we can have multiple assignments in a single C statement. For example, the statement

```
nbr1 = nbr2 = nbr3 = 0;
```

is legal in C. Because the assignment operator associates from right to left, this expression stores 0 into *nbr3*, then into *nbr2*, and then into *nbr1*.[4]

Exercise 3-1   If

---

[4] With left-to-right associativity, this statement would try to assign the value in *nbr3* to the constant 0, which makes no sense.

```
nbr1 = 6;
nbr2 = 2;
nbr3 = 4;
```

what value results from these expressions?

```
a)    nbr1 + nbr2 / nbr3 * 2;
b)    nbr1 / nbr2 * (nbr3 / 2);
c)    48 / (nbr2 * nbr3) / nbr1;
d)    nbr1 % nbr3 / nbr2;
```

Precedence seems to imply that C always forces us to multiply before adding. However, C contains a special operator, represented by parentheses, whose sole purpose is to disrupt the order of precedence. Any expression enclosed in parentheses, regardless of the operators involved, has the highest precedence. As an example, in the statement

```
nbr1 + nbr2 * nbr3;
```

we know that the multiplication is done first. But in this one

```
(nbr1 + nbr2) * nbr3;
```

the addition is performed first. If an expression contains more than one set of parentheses, then the order of evaluation is left to right. Expressions enclosed in parentheses are evaluated according to the order of precedence. Thus, in

```
(nbr1 * nbr2 + nbr3) / nbr4;
```

nbr1 is multiplied by *nbr2* first, then *nbr3* is added to the result before it is divided by *nbr4*.

Parentheses have been added to the precedence table in Table 3-3. To work properly, parentheses must have the highest precedence, which they do.

TABLE 3-3 Precedence Table with Parentheses

( )				Left to right
*	/	%		Left to right
	+	−		Left to right
		=		Right to left

3.6 PRINTING

Operators allow us to manipulate data, but we need a way to display the results of these operations. In C, output is printed and formatted with the same instruction. It is **printf( )**, which stands for **print f**ormatting.

The instruction **printf( )** will display whatever is sent to it enclosed in double quotation marks. An example is

```
printf("Quarterly Profit and Loss Report");
```

which prints

```
Quarterly Profit and Loss Report
```

printf( ) is not really a C instruction, but a special printing routine (called a *function*) that is invoked whenever we want to print something. This is why we have enclosed the message being printed in parentheses. In addition, invoking the **printf( )** function is a C statement so it is terminated with a semicolon.

printf( ) can do far more than just print messages. It also can format what it prints. To do this, **printf( )** must be told what format to use. For example, suppose we want to print

```
Total profit this year is ###
```

where **###** is stored in the **int** variable *profit*. This would be done by

```
printf("Total profit this year is %d", profit);
```

Here we must tell **printf( )** two things: the complete message to be printed (called the *format string*) and the value to be included in it. The **%d** tells **printf( )** to substitute an integer value at exactly that spot in the format string. **printf( )** inserts the value stored in the variable following the format string. **%d** is called a *formatting specification*.

In this instance, we have to send **printf( )** two things: the format string and the variable to substitute. These are separated by a comma in the **printf( )** statement. **printf( )** uses the format string to tell it what other information has been sent to it.

Suppose a program contains

```
int profit;

profit = 10000;
printf("Total profit this year is %d", profit);
```

When executed, it prints

```
Total profit this year is 10000
```

To print a dollar sign before the profit, we merely add one in the format string:

```
printf("Total profit this year is $%d", profit);
```

While **printf( )** lets us insert variable values into text, it will not format the numbers inserted (e.g., provide commas). We will have to write a special function to add commas to numbers. This is done in Chapter 17.

printf( ) recognizes other formatting specifications. All **printf( )** formatting specifications are two- or three-character sequences that always begin with a percent sign. The most common are

%d **int**
%ld **long**
%f **float** and **double**
%c **char**

Additional formatting specifications will be introduced later.

3.7 CHARACTER CONSTANTS

Because of its design, a computer can only store numbers. For computers to be useful to humans, however, they also must be able to manipulate and store alphabetic characters. To do this, computers utilize numeric codes to represent alphabetic characters (e.g., ASCII or EBCDIC). In fact, the data type **char** informs the computer that a number stored in memory represents a character, not the equivalent number. These codes are called the computer's *character set*.

Oddly enough, there is no standard character set used by all computers. Further, many programming situations require us to access, read, write, or test individual characters, forcing the inclusion of specific character codes in our programs. Putting numeric character codes in a program can cause problems when we want to transport that program from one computer to another, especially if the machines employ different character sets.

To prevent character set differences from limiting C's transportability, C's designers decided to isolate the language from any computer technique for representing characters. In C, we refer to individual characters directly by enclosing them in *single* quotation marks. Characters inside single quotation marks are called *character constants*. A constant is the opposite of a variable. That is, the value of a constant *never* changes. As an example, the single letter R would be represented by

```
'R'
```

and the plus sign by

```
'+'
```

Sec. 3.8   Special Character Constants

When the program is compiled, each character constant is stored as the proper numeric code for that specific computer. This frees us from concern about how R is represented inside the computer.

RULE   A character inside single quotation marks represents that single character.

3.8 SPECIAL CHARACTER CONSTANTS

Certain characters important in computer programming are not used by humans in either written or spoken language. Typically, these "special" characters represent mechanical instructions to the computer or the machines it controls. An example is the *carriage return* character that goes at the end of a text line and instructs the computer to create a new line of text. In C, we call this a *newline* character and represent it as

$$'\backslash n'$$

The quotation marks indicate that it is treated as a character constant. That is, '\n' represents a single character, even though it takes two (a backslash and an **n**) to specify it! All special character constants are represented by a two-character sequence beginning with a *backslash*. Table 3-4 lists C's special character constants.

TABLE 3-4   Special Character Constants

'\t'	Horizontal tab
'\v'	Vertical tab
'\b'	Backspace
'\f'	Formfeed character (i.e, on printers)
'\a'	Alarm (either visible or audible; ANSI only)
'\\'	The backslash character
'\''	The single quotation mark character
'\"'	The double quotation mark character

The use of character constants hides the underlying hardware from us. This is required for us to create transportable programs.

RULE   A character preceded by a backslash and enclosed in single quotation marks is a special character constant.

We will make extensive use of character constants throughout our C programs. For example, consider the **printf( )** example shown earlier:

```
            int profit;

            profit = 10000;
            printf("Total profit this year is %d", profit);
```

What do we want **printf( )** to do after it prints the value stored in *profit*? Most likely, we would want a newline printed. However, **printf( )** only prints what we tell it to print. Specifically, this **printf( )** command

```
            printf("Total profit this year is %d", profit);
```

won't put a newline after the text because we didn't include a **\n** in the format string! Thus, to print a newline after *profit*'s value, we must add a **\n**:

```
            printf("Total profit this year is $%d\n", profit);
```

Whenever **printf( )** encounters a **\n**", it prints a newline. Single quotation marks are not necessary here because the line is already enclosed in double quotation marks.

Exercise 3-2   What will this statement do?

```
            printf("\n\tTotal profit this year is $%d\n\n",profit);
```

Using special character constants with **printf( )** is very common in C. This is another reason why C is popular. Most other languages require several different commands to do what a single **printf( )** combined with special character constants can do!

3.9 CHARACTER STRINGS

In addition to representing single characters, we will need to refer to several characters as a group (e.g., an English word). This requires a way for C to store many characters together and also to ensure that these characters remain in the proper order. Such a set of characters is called a *character string* and is just what the name implies, a sequence of characters strung together. We usually refer to a character string simply as a *string*. Generally, strings are words, phrases, sentences, or other text. They may also, however, contain special character constants as well.

Strings are different than single characters. Strings are made up of characters, and a string represents all of the characters arranged in the specified order. To denote a string requires double quotation marks. For example, the message

```
                    "ABC Computer Company"
```

is a string that might be a company's name. Whenever we use **printf( )**, we have to send it a string that tells **printf( )** what to do. Much of the time, we mix regular characters with special ones. For example,

Sec. 3.10   Structured Programming with Functions   25

```
"Total profit this year is %d\n"
```

is also a string. The **%d** and **\n** are interpreted by **printf( )** before it prints the string.

3.10 STRUCTURED PROGRAMMING WITH FUNCTIONS

One component of good programming style is breaking a task down into a series of smaller steps and then constructing a program from these parts. In C, we refer to these parts as *functions*. C programs mainly consist of functions.

A function is a separate section of C statements that performs a specialized task (e.g., one of the steps that make up our program). The program gives a function a unique name, following the same restrictions as for naming a variable. Every time we refer to the function's name, the statements that are associated with that name are executed. This is referred to as *calling* a function.

When a function is called, the related C statements are performed. When all the statements have been executed, the function terminates and *returns* to the spot in the program where the function was called. When a function returns, the program continues by executing the statement following just after the spot where the function was called. Since the instructions that makeup a function are legal C statements, anything that can be done in C can be done in a function!

Often, a function needs data before it can do its job. We can pass a function information in the form of variables or constants. Information is passed to a function as *arguments*.

Functions are powerful programming tools because they allow us to "create" our own commands. In fact, we've already seen a C function in action: **printf( )**. **printf( )** is a function that is provided with the C language.

Previously, we demonstrated **printf( )** with

```
printf("Total profit this year is %d\n", profit);
```

In this case, we passed two arguments to **printf( )**: a format string and the variable *profit*. Notice that the arguments are separated by a comma. Further, both arguments are enclosed in parentheses. In C, function calls are identified by parentheses.

printf( ) simply prints its arguments and returns. However, some functions return an "answer" when they are done processing. An example is a function that determines which of two arguments is the largest, such as

```
max(nbr1, nbr2)
```

The **max( )** function, which we would have to write, tells us which variable of the two sent as arguments holds the larger value. C allows a function to **return** a value back to the routine that called it.

To make use of the information returned by a function, we might do this:

```
large = max(nbr1, nbr2);
```

which assigns *large* either the value in *nbr1* or *nbr2*, whichever is larger. However, before we can use the variables *nbr1*, *nbr2*, and *large* they must be defined:

```
long large;
long nbr1;
long nbr2;

large = max(nbr1, nbr2);
```

This means that the data type returned by **max( )** must be a **long**, as well. How does C know this?

3.11 DECLARING FUNCTIONS

Since functions can return values, they must be declared before they can be used. This is how C knows what kind of data is returned by **max( )** in the previous example. Thus, because the arguments passed to **max( )** are **long**s, **max( )** will return a **long** (either the **long** value *nbr1* or *nbr2*). This means the declaration

```
long max();
```

must appear before the **max( )** function can be used properly.[5] We must tell C that **max( )** is a function that returns a **long** value. The parentheses in the declaration identify **max( )** as a function. Without them, C would think we were defining a variable named *max*! In addition, a corresponding declaration would be required if **max( )** returned an **int**, **float**, **double**, or another data type. The correct sequence for using **max( )** would be

```
long large;
long nbr1;
long nbr2;
long max();

large = max(nbr1, nbr2);
```

While all functions must be declared, not all must be declared *explicitly*. C will assign a data type of **int** to any function that is not declared before it is used. Not having to declare functions may be convenient for the programmer, but it makes understanding exactly what a program does difficult.

---

[5] The ANSI standard allows a more informative function declaration called a *prototype*. Function prototypes are discussed in Appendix C.

Sec. 3.12   Summary   **27**

RULE   All functions should be declared before use, even when declaring is not strictly required.

The **max( )** function demonstrates the real reason behind C functions. Instead of using **max( )**, we could have written the C statements required to determine if *nbr1* is larger than *nbr2*. However, by creating a function, we save ourselves the trouble of rewriting these same statements every time we need to do this. Once **max( )** has been written, we just call it whenever we need it! Functions are used extensively in C.

Two more introductory comments need to be made about functions. First, not all functions return a value. In some programming languages, functions that don't return values are refered to as *subroutines* or *procedures*. In C, whether a function returns a value or not, it is still called a function. A special data type is reserved for functions that don't return a value: **void**.

In addition to functions that don't return values, some functions may return information that is of no use in a particular program. An example is **printf( )**. **printf( )** returns the number of characters printed. Thus, **printf( )** is a function that returns an **int**. This mean that even if we don't declare **printf( )** (which we haven't yet!) by

```
int printf();
```

C will assume that **printf( )** returns an **int**. In fact, this is common practice!

While **printf( )** returns the number of characters printed, in the vast majority of situations we have no need to know this. In these instances, we can ignore what **printf( )** returns simply by not storing it anywhere. As an illustration, in a previous example, we used

```
printf("Total profit this year is %d\n", profit);
```

Since **printf( )**'s return value isn't used anywhere, C simply ignores it.

3.12 SUMMARY

1. In C, all variables must be defined before they can be used.
2. The data types available in C are
   - **char**   Character
   - **int**   Integer
   - **short**   Short integer
   - **long**   Long integer
   - **unsigned**   Positive integers only
   - **float**   Floating point number
   - **double**   Double precision floating point number
3. Variable names must start with a letter and can contain only letters, digits, and underscores.
4. C distinguishes between upper and lower case letters in variable names.

5. Typically, only the first eight characters of a variable's name are significant to the C compiler.
6. All C statements end with a semicolon.
7. An operator represents operations that can be performed on data.
8. An operator needs data to evaluate. Data evaluated by an operator are called operands.
9. An operator that needs only one operand is called a unary operator. An operator that needs two operands is called a binary operator. An operator that needs three operands is called a ternary operator.
10. Whenever one or more operators is combined with operands an expression is formed.
11. A statement is formed when an expression is terminated with a semicolon.
12. C's arithmetic operators are

    +   addition
    −   subtraction
    *   multiplication
    /   division
    %   modulo (remainder)
    =   assignment

13. Operators are evaluated according to a preset order of precedence. Operators with higher precedence are evaluated before operators with lower precedence if both appear in the same statement.
14. If two operators with the same precedence appear in the same statement, the operators' associativity determines which one is evaluated first. Operators associate either right to left or left to right.
15. The **printf( )** function is used for printing in C.
16. Some of the formatting characters understood by **printf( )** are

    %d   **int**
    %ld   **long**
    %f   **float** and **double**
    %c   **char**

17. Any character enclosed in single quotation marks is a character constant.
18. Special character constants are preceded by a backslash, such as

    \n   newline
    \t   tab
    \b   backspace
    \f   formfeed

19. A character string is a sequence of characters strung together and treated as a single construct.
20. A string constant is declared by enclosing it in double quotation marks.
21. A function is a separate section of C statements that are referred to by a unique name.

Sec. 3.12   Summary

22. When a function's name is referenced inside a program, the statements associated with the function are executed.
23. A function can be sent information in the form of arguments.
24. A function can return information to the routine that called it.
25. A function has to be declared as the data type of information it returns.
26. A function that does not return information must be declared **void**.
27. **printf( )** returns an **int**, the number of characters printed.

4
Creating C Programs

The best way to learn how to program in C is by writing C programs. We now know enough about C to begin creating some business programs.

4.1 DID WE MAKE ANY MONEY?

One of the most important questions a business owner must answer is "Did we make any money?" The banker wants to know, the employees are curious about it, and so are we. If we aren't making any profits, maybe it's time to begin looking for a real job!

Unfortunately, the term "profits" means different things to different people. To us it means cash in our pockets; to the bank, it means money to pay back our loans; to the government, it means tax revenues; and to our investors, it means dividends. Because so many people are interested in a business's profitability, a profit and loss statement must be produced regularly. Essentially, a profit and loss statement (called a P & L statement by accountants) lists what we made minus what we spent.

Program 4-1 is a simple C program that prints this year's profit by finding the difference between our revenues and costs.

Sec. 4.1   Did We Make Any Money?

```
main()     /* In C, we must identify the main routine   */
{
    int revenue;
    int cost;
    int profit;
    int printf();

    revenue = 25098;
    cost = 23987;
    profit = revenue - cost;     /* calculate profit */
    printf("Total profit this year is $%d\n", profit);
    exit(0);
}
```

Program 4-1

Program 4-1 introduces some other features of C. First, all programs must have a **main()** routine designated by

```
main()
```

This tells C where to start executing the program. Note that it does not end with a semicolon. When a function is defined (i.e., its commands are listed), no semicolon is put after the name.

In-line comments (text the computer ignores) are surrounded by markers (/* and */) as in

```
/*   calculate profit   */
```

This allows us to insert explanatory comments in our code. Here, we used a comment to introduce the meaning of

```
main().
```

As we write more programs, we will develop some commenting conventions.

The C language makes heavy use of braces ({ }). They are used specifically to mark where programming segments *begin* and *end*. In the example program, braces are used to mark where **main()** begins and ends.

Program 4-1 also contains the C function **exit()**. **exit()** tells C to quit executing the program and return to the operating system. The argument passed to **exit()**, in Program 4-1 a zero, is returned to the operating system as a message. On many computers, the operating system can make use of this information. An example is the *batch* files found in MS-DOS, where an *exit* value of zero means the program terminated properly. A different *exit* value might signal that an error caused the program to terminate prematurely.

When executed, a C program begins at the first statement listed in **main()**—in Program 4-1, the definition of the variable *revenue*. The program terminates when it runs out of statements to perform in **main( )** or calls **exit( )** (from anywhere in the program).

Terminating a C program with **exit( )** is not required, though it is good programming practice to do so. If the call to **exit( )** is removed from Program 4-1, it still will stop when it reaches the closing brace of **main( )**, as there are no more commands in **main( )** to execute. However, it is considered *bad* programming practice not to explicitly terminate a program.

RULE Always terminate programs with a call to **exit( )**.

Exercise 4-1 What will Program 4-1 print when executed?

Incidentally, C is not sensitive to the format of the source code file. As long as all the components are correctly placed in the program, C doesn't care where they appear on a line. For example, Program 4-1a contains the same source code as Program 4-1, but in a different format. Program 4-1a will compile correctly and produce the same output as Program 4-1.

```
main( ) /* In C, we must identify the main routine */ {
int revenue; int cost; int profit; int printf();
revenue = 25098; cost =
23987; profit = revenue
- cost; /*
calculate
profit */
printf("Total profit this year is $%d\n", profit); exit(0);}
```

Program 4-1a

While the C compiler doesn't care about appearance of a program's source code, humans do! It is far easier to understand Program 4-1 than Program 4-1a. One source code formatting rule we will use is to indent all the statements inside a pair of braces. In Program 4-1, all of the statements in **main( )** are indented. Throughout this book, we will develop other formatting rules into a consistent programming style. This will make our programs easy to read and understand.

In Program 4-1, the variable *profit* is not necessary because we can send **printf( )** *arithmetic expressions* as arguments. Instead of passing the variable *profit* to **printf( )**, we can send the expression

```
revenue - cost.
```

The subtraction is performed and the result sent to **printf( )** as an argument. The **printf( )** statement in Program 4-1 could be written as

```
printf("Total profit this year is $%d\n", revenue - cost);
```

Sec. 4.1 Did We Make Any Money?

This would allow us to delete the variable *profit* from the program altogether. This has been done in Program 4-2.

```
main()
{
    int revenue;
    int cost;
    int printf();

    revenue = 25098;
    cost = 23987;
    printf("Total profit this year is $%d\n", revenue - cost);
    exit(0);
}
```

Program 4-2

In addition to assigning the values for revenues and costs inside *main( )*, this program has another, more serious limitation. It uses an inappropriate data type. Both *revenue* and *cost* are defined as type **int**. On many computer systems, **int** can represent values in the range of +32767 to −32768 only. This is not a problem in our example program because of the numbers chosen for *revenue* and *cost*. However, it could mean that this program could handle revenues and costs no larger than $32,767!

If a value assigned to an **int** is too large the result is unpredictable and system dependent. In fact, the program may fail, should such an assignment occur. It is hard enough to make money in business without these kinds of problems!

A related and equally important question is whether the cost and revenue values are best represented by integers at all (i.e., no cents are displayed). Would **float** be more suitable?

If it is acceptable to display dollar values only, the program should define *revenue* and *cost* to be **long** integers. On most systems, this provides a much larger range of acceptable values.[1] To utilize **long** integers in Program 4-2, we must make two changes. First, the variable definitions for *revenue* and *cost* must be changed to **long** from **int**. Second, the **%d** in the **printf**( ) format string must be converted to **%ld**. Program 4-3 is the result.

```
main()
{
    long revenue;
    long cost;
    int printf();
```

---

[1] On many systems, the storage allocated for **int** is the same size as that allocated for **long**. On these systems, defining a variable as data type **long** is the same as defining it **int**.

```
        revenue = 25098;
        cost = 23987;
        printf("Total profit this year is $%ld\n", revenue - cost);
        exit(0);
}
```

Program 4-3

Exercise 4-2   Rewrite Program 4-3 to use **float**s.

4.2 CONDITIONAL STATEMENTS

Program 4-3 reports the same message whether we had a profit or a loss for the year. This could lead to mistakes if a user were to see the word "profit" and miss the negative sign (−) in front of the reported value. One of the biggest problems in business applications is miscommunication between computer program and user. It would be better for the program to display specifically whether we had a profit or loss. For a profit, the message would be the same as above. For a loss, however, the computer should report

```
        Total loss this year is ($###)
```

where ### is the amount of the loss. The parentheses are included because of accounting convention.

To print a *results-sensitive message* such as the one above, the program must be able to determine when a profit has been earned. Obviously, this happens when revenue is greater than cost. Like almost all higher-level languages, C uses an **if** - **else** statement to select what to do based on a logical test (e.g., is revenue greater than cost?). This is C's equivalent to the selection structure.

An **if** - **else** statement identifies a segment of a C program that contains commands that may or may not be performed. If a logical test is true, the section following the keyword **if** is performed. Otherwise, the section following **else** is executed. Which commands belong to which section is identified by enclosing braces:

```
        if (test) {
                commands executed only if test is true
        }
        else {
                commands executed only if test is false
        }
        rest of program
```

There are two things to note about **if** - **else** statements. First, there is no semicolon after the **if** test. This is because it is only the first part of the statement. An **if** statement contains two parts: a test and what to do if the result of the test is true. Second, the logical test is enclosed in parentheses.

Sec. 4.2   Conditional Statements   35

It is not required to have an **else** clause in an **if** - **else** statement. When there is only an **if** section, the brace-enclosed commands are executed if the test is true and skipped otherwise. The sections following the keywords **if** and **else** must contain at least one statement. As a result, the braces are optional for sections that contain a single statement only.

RULE   Enclosing braces are optional for **if** - **else** sections that contain only one statement.

C contains a number of operators that evaluate to true or false. This is required for the **if** - **else** construct to work properly. The operators fit into three categories: *relational*, *equality*, and *logical* operators. These operators are listed in Table 4-1.

TABLE 4-1   C's Relational, Equality, and Logical Operators

	Relational Operators
Symbol	Test
revenue > cost	true if revenue is *greater than* cost
revenue >= cost	true if revenue is *greater than or equal to* cost
revenue < cost	true if revenue is *less than* cost
revenue <= cost	true if revenue is *less than or equal to* cost
	Equality Operators
Symbol	Test
revenue == cost	true if revenue is *equal to* cost
revenue != cost	true if revenue is *not equal to* cost
	Logical Operators
Symbol	Test
&&	logical *and*
||	logical *or*
!	logical *not*

Notice that the equality operator is == (two equal signs) and that the test for not equals is != (an exclamation point preceding an equal sign). Don't confuse the equality operator with the assignment operator = (single equal sign). This is a common C programming error that is very hard to find.

RULE   Use the proper operator to test equality (==).

The logical operators allow us to create compound logical tests. The logical *and* operator, **&&**, evaluates to true only if *all* of the logical expressions connected with **&&** are true. For example, the logical test

(tax_cat1 < income && income < tax_cat2)

will be true only if both relational expressions are true. If just one of them is false, the entire expression will be false.

The logical *or* operator, ||, is similar to the logical *and* in effect. The difference is that the logical *or* operator evaluates to true if *one* of the logical expressions connected with || are true. For example, the logical test

(revenue < cost || sales == 0)

evaluates to true if either one of the logical expressions are true.

The third logical operator is the logical *not*. The logical *not* operator, !, evaluates to true if the expression is false and to false if the expression if true. For example, the expression

!(revenue < cost)

will evaluate to true if *revenue* is not less than (i.e., greater than or equal to) *cost*. This is the same as the >= operator. Note that logical *not* is a unary operator—it only takes a single operand.

Operators evaluate to a single numeric value. Logical expressions equate to 1 if they are true and 0 if they are false. Thus,

if (revenue > cost)

is evaluated in two steps. First the expression

revenue > cost

becomes 1 (if true) or 0 (if false). Second, the **if** tests for

if (1)   *perform the "true" section*

or

if (0)   *perform the "false" section*

It might appear that an **if** test must be either 1 or 0. This is not the case. In fact, any nonzero value will be considered true by an **if** statement. Thus,

if (27)
if (-1)

and

Sec. 4.2   Conditional Statements

```
if (.01)
```

all result in the **if** section statements being executed. This also is true of the logical operators. For example,

```
! cost
```

is the same as testing

```
cost == 0
```

The expression

```
cost == 0
```

is true if *cost* is zero. But, a value of zero is equivalent to false in C. Thus,

```
! cost
```

would also evaluate to true if *cost* is zero (false). This is common usage of the logical *not* operator. The logical *and* and logical *or* operators have one additional attribute. These two operators evaluate their operands *left to right*. Further, they terminate as soon as a result is known. Thus, logical *or* evaluates operands left to right until it finds one that is true. Then the expression is determined to be true without evaluating the remaining operands.

As an example, the expression

```
revenue > cost || sales > cost_of_goods
```

first tests if *revenue* is greater than *cost*. If it is, the logical *or* expression evaluates to true. Otherwise, *sales* is compared to *cost-of-goods*. If this expression is true, the logical *or* evaluates to true; otherwise, it evaluates to false. Note that in a logical *or* expression, a test is only evaluated if the ones to its left are false.

The same is true of logical *and* expressions. However, a logical *and* expression is only true if *all* of its tests are true. Thus, the logical *and* stops and reports false at the first false result it obtains.

Table 4-2 shows an updated precedence table. Note that the left-to-right evaluation of logical *and* and logical *or* overides precedence. Thus,

```
revenue > cost || sales88 > sales87
```

evaluates the logical *or* first even though it has a *lower* precedence than the other two operators in the expression.

TABLE 4-2 Precedence Table

( )				Left to right	Parentheses
!				Right to left	Logical *not*
*	/	%		Left to right	Arithmetic
+	−			Left to right	Arithmetic
<	<=	>	>=	Left to right	Relational
==	!=			Left to right	Equality
&&				Left to right	Logical *and*
||				Left to right	Logical *or*
&=				Right to left	Assignment
=					

Relational, equality, logical *and*, and logical *or* operators have a lower precedence than the arithmetic operators but a higher one than the assignment operator. As an illustration, the statement

```
p_or_l = revenue > cost
```

will first evaluate the expression

```
revenue > cost
```

to 1 or 0 and then store that value in *p_or_l*. This means we can test for a profit or loss by

```
p_or_l = revenue > cost;
if (p_or_l)
```
rest of program

Furthermore,

```
if (cost_of_goods + expenses > revenue)
```

adds *cost_of_goods* to *expenses* and then compares the sum to *revenue*. The result of the entire expression is 1 or 0.

Exercise 4-3   What numeric value is assigned when the following statements are executed?

```
Assume: nbr1 = nbr2 = 5; nbr3 = 6;
a) logical_value = nbr1 <= nbr2;
```

Sec. 4.2 Conditional Statements

```
            b) logical_value = 5 * nbr1 == nbr2;
            c) logical_value = 5 * (nbr1 < nbr2);
            d) logical_value = nbr1 == nbr2 < nbr3;
```

To make Program 4-3 print a message identifying either a profit or loss, we must add an **if - else** statement. The format of the **if - else** section is

```
if (revenue > cost)
    printf("Total profit this year $%d\n", revenue - cost);
else
    printf("Total loss this year ($%d)\n", cost - revenue);
```

Only one of the two **printf( )** statements will be executed.

Two additional points need to be made. First, braces are not required around the **printf( )** statements because there is only one statement in both the **if** and **else** sections. Also, in this **if - else** (selection) structure, we have indented the **printf( )** statements to show that they are part of a structured block. This convention will be used throughout this book. Program 4-4 lists Program 4-3 with this change. The added statements are shown in **bold print**.

```
main()
{
    long revenue;
    long cost;
    int printf();

    revenue = 25098;
    cost = 23987;
    if (revenue > cost)
        printf("Total profit this year is $%ld\n", revenue - cost);
    else
        printf("Total loss this year is ($%ld)\n", cost - revenue);
    exit(0);
}
```

Program 4-4

Since the values stored in *revenue* and *cost* are the same in both Programs 4-3 and 4-4, their outputs are the same.

In Program 4-4, the **printf( )** statements inside both the **if** and **else** clauses have been indented. This is another component of our programming style. All statements inside any structure will be indented. This makes identifying the structures in our program much easier.

In many cases, a structured block will contain more than one statement. We must tell C that a section contains multiple statements by enclosing the multiline section in braces. Suppose we want to display *revenue* if there are profits and *cost* if there are losses in order to print more information on our report. We could do this by adding a

printf( ) statement to each section. The resulting **if** - **else** structure is shown in Segment 4-1.

```
if (revenue > cost) {
    printf("Total profits this year $%d\n", revenue - cost);
    printf("Total revenue this year $%d\n", revenue);
}
else {
    printf("Total loss this year ($%d)\n", cost - revenue);
    printf("Total costs this year $%d\n", cost);
}
```

Segment 4-1 Multiline **if** - **else** statement

In Segment 4-1, both the **if** and **else** sections contain more that one statement and must be enclosed by braces.

At first glance, our placement of the braces in Segment 4-1 may appear odd. However, this is the style introduced by Kernighan and Ritchie in their book *The C Programming Language*. The beginning brace goes at the end of the line that starts the structure. The ending brace is on a line by itself after the last statement in the structure. The ending brace is aligned vertically with the keyword that started the structure. We will use this convention throughout the remainder of this book.

Exercise 4-4 Segment 4-1 shows two **printf( )** statements in each **if** - **else** section. Combine the two **printf( )** statements into one.

What happens in Program 4-4 if *revenue* equals *cost*? The **if** test is false and the program prints

```
Total loss this year ($0)
```

Since we didn't lose any money, this output could be misleading. The same can be said for this message:

```
Total profit this year $0
```

For clarity, the program should identify this special situation with

```
Revenues equal costs for the year.
```

The problem is that we are assuming only two outcomes (profit or loss) when in fact there are three (profit, loss, or neither). We will have to do more testing in our program before we can determine which of the three outcomes has occurred. If there isn't a profit (the **if** test is false), we then must test for a loss (*revenue* < *cost*). If there isn't a profit or a loss, we don't have to test explicitly with

Sec. 4.2   Conditional Statements

```
                    if (revenue == cost)
```

Since both the profit and loss tests were false, the third outcome *must* be true.

In computer programming, it is common to have several logical tests. C allows us to combine the **if** and the **else** to create a new selection: one that is tested (the **if** part) only if the previous test was false (the **else** part). Appropriately, this section is called an **else if** section and it only can appear after an **if** or another **else if**.

If the **else if** test is true, the commands listed in that section are executed. If the **else if** test is false, the program continues with the next **else** or **else if** in the structure. As with an **if** test, the test in an **else if** is enclosed in parentheses, too. For example,

```
               if (revenue > cost)
                  /* a profit for the year */
               else if (cost > revenue)
                  /* a loss for the year */
               else
                  /* revenues equal costs */
```

While there can only be one **if** clause in an **if** - **else** statement, there is no limit to the number of **else if**s we can use. Adding an **else** - **if** to Program 4-4 results in Program 4-5.

```
    main()
    {
        long revenue;
        long cost;
        int printf();

        revenue = 25098;
        cost = 23987;
        if (revenue > cost)
            printf("Total profit this year is $%ld\n", revenue - cost);
        else if (cost > revenue)
            printf("Total loss this year ($%ld)\n", cost - revenue);
        else
            printf("Revenues equal costs for this year\n");
        exit(0);
    }
```

Program 4-5

The output for Program 4-5 is the same as Program 4-4 since the values stored in *revenue* and *cost* are the same.

4.3 SUMMARY

1. A C program must have a **main( )** routine.
2. Comments inside a C program are marked with /* at the beginning and */ at the end.
3. The **exit( )** function terminates C programs and returns control of the computer back to the operating system.
4. C is not sensitive to the format of the source code file.
5. Functions can be sent expressions as well as variables for arguments.
6. C uses an **if** - **else** statement to implement the selection structure.
7. C provides a set of operators that evaluate to 1 if true and 0 if false.
8. Multiple logical tests can be made by using the **else if** part of the **if** statement.

5

Interactive Programming in C

One of the primary design objectives of C was to create a language that was transportable between computers. More precisely, what was desired was a language that would allow us to compile the same source code without modification on different machines. Thus, the goal of transportability can be restated as making C *machine independent.* This is a problem because one type of computer tends to be incompatible with all the others.

Some computers can only handle a single user while others are multiuser systems. Some machines have built-in terminal screens and keyboards while others require separate ones. This litany could go on to include storage devices, external interfaces, and operating systems. As a result, there is very little that can be assumed about the nature of the computer executing a C program. The uncertainties include how the program receives input from and sends output to the computer, handles the machine's memory, and deals with data files, among other problems.

5.1 THE STANDARD FUNCTION LIBRARY

The real problem is how to create a truly machine-independent programming language and at the same time incorporate the features necessary to make the language useful. The approach chosen by Dennis Ritchie is an elegant one. The C language is composed of two parts. The first part is the language itself, which consists of data types, operators, and control structures only. The second part is a standard collection of functions that provide the capabilities that are machine specific. These functions make up C's *standard function library*.

Each function in the standard library has an assigned name, a specific number of arguments that are always listed in the same order, an assigned data type, and a precise description of what the function does. The machine-specific details are added to the program when it is compiled (and the library functions are added to the program). This combination of programming features and standard functions provides us with a complete language that is, in fact, computer independent.

We've already used a standard library function: **printf( )**. This is why **printf( )** was available to us even though we didn't write it. Standard functions perform input and output, string manipulation, and other formatting tasks, as well as provide a number of additional features. We will describe other standard functions as we use them. Appendix D describes a common subset of standard library functions.

5.2 THE STANDARD LIBRARY HEADER FILE

Having a library of standard functions is not enough to create a machine-independent language. There also must be a way to identify individual machine characteristics so the compiler can account for them. For example, different computers address their memory in different ways.

C has set aside a special file to account for attributes unique to a particular computer: **stdio.h**. *stdio* stands for **stand**ard **i**nput and **o**utput. The *.h* denotes that this is a *header* file. A header file contains information that goes at the top or head of a program. The *stdio.h* file holds declarations and other specifications that are required for the computer that will execute our program.

The contents of the *stdio.h* file should be placed at the very beginning of any program that uses a standard library function. This way, no matter what machine we execute our programs on, they will able to run properly.

But, how do we go about getting the information in *stdio.h* for some computer? As it turns out, we don't have to—the compiler will do it for us! Part of C's compilation procedure is a *preprocessor* that changes our source code according to certain *directives* that can be placed in our programs. One of the most useful of these is **#include**. **#include** is always followed by a file name enclosed in double quotes.[1] An example of usage is

```
#include "stdio.h"
```

Preprocessor directives always begin with the # character. This must be the first character on the line and no space can be inserted between the # and the word "include."

---

[1] On Unix systems, < > should be used instead of double quotes. This tells the preprocessor to look for the file in the directory that normally contains the library files.

Sec. 5.4   String Variables   45

But, because preprocessor directives are not C statements, they do not end with a semicolon. The C preprocessor capabilities will be fully discussed in Chapter 10.

RULE   Preprocessor directives always begin with a **#** in the first column and do not end with a semicolon.

#include instructs the preprocessor to replace the **#include** line in the program with the contents of the file whose name is enclosed in double quotes. The result is the same as if we had actually typed the statements contained in the *stdio.h* file directly into our program. However, by using **#include**, the preprocessor gets the appropriate information from the computer system itself! Thus, by putting

```
#include "stdio.h"
```

at the top of our programs, we help insure that our code will be transportable from one computer to another.

5.3 MAKING C PROGRAMS INTERACTIVE

So far, our programs have had fixed data. This means we would have to rewrite them every time the data changed—in business applications, this will be every time we use them! This is not acceptable.

A better approach is write our programs to be independent of the data they process. That is, the programs would stay the same, regardless of the data values involved. We can do this by having the program ask the user to enter the data values. We refer to this method as *interactive programming* since the program appears to carry on a conversation with the user.

Before entering data into a program, the user must know what information the program needs. A key ingredient of interactive programming is unambiguously identifying the information to be entered. To do this, an interactive program prints a message called a *prompt* each time data is requested. We can easily create specific prompts with **printf( )**.

After printing a prompt, the program must get what the user types and store it somewhere so we can refer to it later. C can easily handle all kinds of numeric data, but what if the information entered is a string of characters, like a name or an address? C doesn't have a special data types to handle strings.

5.4 STRING VARIABLES

To store strings, we need special variables capable of holding all the characters in the string in the proper order. Although C doesn't provide such a data type, we can create *string variables* using an existing data type: **char**.

In order to define a string variable, C must know that it will hold characters. Since each character in a string is itself stored as an individual number (from the character set), C must set aside enough space in the computer's memory to hold all of the characters in the string. String definitions must include two things, the data type **char** and a number stating the *maximum* length of the string. For example,

```
char co_name[31];
```

defines *co_name* to be a string variable that can hold a maximum of thirty-one characters. It is important to notice that the string's length is enclosed in *brackets*. This is required.

RULE   A string variable's maximum length must be declared inside brackets.

The brackets are the only distinction between character variables, which only store a single character, and string variables. In fact, this is how C tells the two data types apart!

A string variable can store a string of any size up to its maximum declared length. Thus, *co_name* could hold "Smith's Garage" eventhough this name only uses fourteen of the thirty-one characters set aside. But, how does C know that the other sixteen character slots in *co_name* are empty? This is a problem because computer memory cannot be "empty"; it always holds some value. Further, the values randomly stored in the empty spots in *co_name* represent some character in the computer's character set.

One solution to this problem would be to put 0s in the seventeen unused character locations. This isn't a good idea because it requires that the computer store thirty-one characters, many of which are empty characters, everytime we store anything into *co_name*, no matter how short. This simply takes too long.

A better idea is to use a special character constant to mark the end of a string stored in a variable. This character is the *end of string (eos)* character and is represented by

```
'\0'
```

Recall that the single quotation marks denote a single character and the backslash identifies a special character constant. The end of every string in C is marked by **\0**. The *eos* character is represented in memory by the value zero.

If we stored "Smith's Garage" in the string variable *co_name*, we would have to use 15 characters, the 14 in the actual name and the **\0** at the end. This is shown in Figure 5-1.

Figure 5-1   Storing strings in memory

Sec. 5.4 String Variables

Anything stored after the **\0** in *co_name* is ignored by C.

  RULE Every string ends with a **\0**.

Forgetting the **\0** at the end of a string is a common programming error in C. Further, since *co_name* was defined to hold thirty-one characters, it really can store only 30 because the last one must be **\0**!

Previously, we noted that single characters constants were enclosed in single quotation marks. String constants, on the other hand, are surrounded by double quotation marks. Thus,

```
'R'
```

and

```
"R"
```

have different meanings! **'R'** is a single character while **"R"** is a two-character string that includes the character **R** followed by **\0**.

  RULE Use the proper constant when referencing characters. Letters within single quotation marks represent single characters and letters within double quotation marks are strings that end with **\0**.

To print the string stored in *co_name*, we would use **printf( )** with the string format specification **%s**:

```
printf("Profit and Loss Statement for %s\n", co_name);
```

When referencing the entire string stored in *co_name*, we just use the string variable's name. However, to specifically refer to one of the characters stored in *co_name*, we have to identify which one we want.

Since *co_name* was defined

```
char co_name[31];
```

the computer set aside enough space for thirty-one characters. Each slot in *co_name* is numbered from 0 to 30. Thus,

```
co_name[0]
```

identifies the first character stored in *co_name* and

```
co_name[8]
```

the *ninth* one. Thus, individual characters in a string are referred to by combining the string variable's name with a position number enclosed in brackets.

A common C programming error is using **[1]** to refer to the first character in a string. Another problem is trying to use the maximum length of a string as an index. For example, *co_name* is defined as a thirty-one-character string, but

```
co_name[31]
```

is an indexing error because the characters stored in *co_name* are numbered from 0 to 30.

RULE The characters stored in a string array are referred to by number, starting at 0.

The formatting specification, **%c**, tells **printf( )** to print a single character. This means that

```
printf("%c", co_name[0]);
```

will print the first character in the company's name.

5.5 READING STRINGS

How do we read a string entered in response to a prompt? In C, this is done with the

```
gets()
```

function. **gets( )** stands for **get** string and is part of the standard library. **gets( )** must be declared as a *pointer to* **char**:

```
char *gets();
```

The "*****" declares **gets( )** to be a function that returns a pointer.[2]

gets( ) obtains a string of characters typed at the keyboard up to a newline and stores the entered data in the string variable sent to **gets( )** as an argument. When the user enters information and presses the *return* key, **gets( )** reads the characters and stores them in the specified string (including an **\0**) and returns to the calling routine.

Consider Segment 5-1, which obtains the company name from the user.

---

[2] Pointers are discussed in detail in Part 4. Pointer notation is required to declare **gets( )**. This is its only usage until Part 4.

Sec. 5.5   Reading Strings

```
char co_name[31];    /* input string */
char *gets();
int printf();

printf("Enter Company Name: ");
gets(co_name);
rest of program
```

Segment 5-1

When executed, Segment 5-1 prompts with

```
Enter Company Name:
```

and waits for the user to respond. The cursor is left at the end of the prompt string. This is why we included a space to the right of the colon. Recall that without a \n, **printf( )** leaves the cursor at the end of the line. Then, whatever the user enters will be read by **gets( )** and stored in *co_name*.

Segment 5-1 has a potential problem: the string *co_name* was defined to be thirty-one characters long. Will the company name always be less than thirty characters long (remember the \0 that goes at the end)? Probably not—an example is a company named International Business Machines!

What happens if more characters are entered than will fit in the string variable sent to **gets( )**? **gets( )** doesn't check if the string variable sent is large enough to hold what is entered. Further, neither does C. **gets( )** simply tacks the extra characters onto the end of the string *as if* it were large enough, writing over whatever is located in the computer's memory just past the string sent to **gets( )**. This is called an overwriting error. What results when an overwriting error occurs is unpredictable, but most likely the program will fail (usually in some odd way).

Because neither C nor **gets( )** checks for overwriting errors, we must keep this problem in mind when writing our programs. With our present understanding of C, there is nothing we can do about it. For now, our program simply will inform the user of this limitation, allowing him or her to abbreviate the name if necessary.

RULE   Tell the user exactly what input the program expects, including any limitations.

To satisfy this rule the prompt for company name should be changed to

```
printf("Enter Company Name (30 characters maximum): ");
```

Remember that we need a place for the terminating \0. This doesn't solve the problem, it just alerts the user to it.

Another idea is to make *co_name* large enough to handle very long company names. An arbitrary size is eighty-one characters—the length of a line on most terminal screens plus one for the \0. To be safe, we could use an even larger string variable. A safe length would depend on what kind of information the user was entering.

Exercise 5-1   Change Segment 5-1 to allow an eighty-character company name.

One reason interactive programs fail is faulty input data. A primary cause of incorrect data entry is confusion on the part of the user. Because of this, we should include some key that uniquely identifies a prompt from other messages we display. Our prompts always will end with a colon followed by a space.

RULE   Be consistent.

5.6 READING NUMERIC DATA

By making our profit and loss program interactive, that is, having it ask the user to enter this year's revenues and costs, we can make it more useful. To make Program 4-5 interactive, we must read numeric values entered by the user. Unfortunately, there is no

```
getnum()
```

function in the standard library. However, the standard library does contain a set of *conversion* functions[3] that change strings of digits into their corresponding numeric values. These are listed in Table 5-1.

TABLE 5-1   Numeric Conversion Function in the Standard Library

atoi(numstr)	converts *numstr* to an **int**	declared: int atoi();
atol(numstr)	converts *numstr* to a **long**	declared: long atol();
atof(numstr)	converts *numstr* to a **double**	declared: double atof();

In C, reading a number is a two-step process:

Step 1:   Read the number entered as a string of numeric characters with **gets( )**.

Step 2:   Convert the string to a number using the appropriate conversion function.

Program 5-1 demonstrates this by reading an entered value with **gets( )**, converting the string *instr* to an integer, and then printing it.

---

[3] C functions can return only one data type. This is why three conversion functions are required.

Sec. 5.6 Reading Numeric Data

```c
#include "stdio.h"

main()
{
    char instr[81];    /* input string */
    char *gets();      /* reads string */
    int nbr;           /* holds converted value */
    int atoi();        /* converts string to int */
    int printf();

    printf("Enter an Integer: ");
    gets(instr);
    nbr = atoi(instr);    /* convert instr to int */
    printf("The number you entered is %d\n", nbr);
    exit(0);
}
```

Program 5-1

We have **#include**d *stdio.h* because Program 5-1 uses standard library functions. We will **#include** *stdio.h* in all the programs in the rest of this book. The output of Program 5-1 is shown in Output 5-1.

```
Enter an Integer: 334
The number you entered is 334
```

Output 5-1

The conversion functions return when they encounter a non-numeric character in the string. This is demonstrated in Output 5-1a, which is the output of Program 5-1 with different input.

```
Enter an Integer: 234abc
The number you entered is 234

(re-run)

Enter an Integer: abcdefg123
The number you entered is 0

(re-run)

Enter an Integer: -123.34
The number you entered is -123
```

Output 5-1a

Characters that are not digits but have a numeric meaning are interpreted properly by these conversion functions. This means, a '+' or '−' is understood as the beginning character. The first '.' in a string is treated properly by *atof( )*, though ignored by *atoi( )* and *atol( )* (as shown in Output 5-1a).

Exercise 5-2 Revise program 5-2 to read and display a floating point number.

Making Program 4-5 (the last P&L program) interactive may seem simple, but we should design the program completely before we begin writing code. This is an important first step that many programmers skip, believing they can quickly write the program at hand. On most occasions, writing a program without designing it first requires much more time and effort. In this book, we will always create an algorithm before writing our programs. The algorithm for an interactive P&L program is listed in Algorithm 5-1.

1. Prompt and **gets( )** revenue as a string of digits
2. Convert input string to a numeric value and store in *revenue*
3. Prompt and **gets( )** cost as a string of digits
4. Convert input string to a numeric value and store in *cost*
5. If *revenue > cost*
    print amount of profit
   otherwise if *revenue < cost*
    print amount of loss
   otherwise
    print "revenue equals cost"

Algorithm 5-1

Before our design is complete, we must decide on the data type of the variables *revenue* and *cost*. If we were only concerned with dollar values (i.e., no cents), **long** would be the logical choice. However, we want to account for every cent, so we will use **double**. In this case, we change steps 2 and 4 to use the **atof** function as follows:

1. Prompt and **gets( )** revenue as a string of digits
2. Convert input string to a **double** with **atof( )** and store in *revenue*
3. Prompt and **gets( )** cost as a string of digits
4. Convert input string to a **double** with **atof( )** and store in *cost*
5. If *revenue > cost*
    print amount of profit
   otherwise if *revenue < cost*
    print amount of loss
   otherwise
    print "revenue equals cost"

Sec. 5.6 Reading Numeric Data

Program 5-3 is the program written from Algorithm 5-1.

```
/*              *****   PL-REPT    *****
 * This program prompts the user for revenues and costs
 * (both double) and prints profit if revenue > cost,
 * loss if cost > revenue, or a breakeven message if
 * neither.
 *
 * Written by Ray Swartz for "Doing Business with C"
 */

#include "stdio.h"

main()
{
    double revenue;    /* holds total revenue - entered by user */
    double cost;       /* holds total cost - entered by user */
    double atof();
    char instr[81];    /* input string */
    char *gets();
    int printf();

    printf("Enter this year's REVENUES: ");
    gets(instr);                    /* Read revenue */
    revenue = atof(instr);          /* Convert revenue to double */
    printf("\n\nEnter this year's COSTS: ");
    gets(instr);                    /* Read costs */
    cost = atof(instr);             /* Convert costs to double */
    if (revenue > cost)             /* Test for profit */
        printf("\nTotal profit this year $%f\n", revenue - cost);
    else if (cost > revenue)        /* Test for loss */
        printf("\nTotal loss this year ($%f)\n", cost - revenue);
    else                            /* Neither profit or loss */
        printf("\nRevenues equal costs for this year\n");
    exit(0);
}
```

Program 5-2

The comments (surrounded by /* and */) in Program 5-2 fall into three separate categories. First, an introduction gives the name of the program (**pl-rept**) and describes what it does. Second, what each variable represents is described. Third, program statements are explained in English by *in-line comments*. In this program, the in-line comments simply list the algorithm steps that correspond to specific statements. A well-written program should contain all three types of comments.

An introduction should describe what the program does, who wrote (or modified) it, and list any additional information that may prove useful. Additional information might be who authorized the program, where it will be used, a reference to external design documents, or anything else that will make maintenance and modification easier.

Describing each defined variable begins by choosing meaningful variable names. Further, what data will be stored in each one is described. If the variable's data will be entered by the user, this too is noted. Standard library functions need not be detailed.

In-line comments are used to make the code more obvious to someone not familiar with our programming style or what the program does. Unfortunately, there is no general rule for determining when a C statement won't be "obvious" to someone. When in doubt, include a comment. At the very least, the steps in the algorithm should be noted. However, there is no need to comment on those statements that are already clear, such as simple assignments or straightforward **printf( )** statements.

All the programs and functions written in this book will be well-documented by this definition. As the book progresses, we will expand these categories to include other information.

The output from Program 5-2 is shown in Output 5-2.

```
Enter this year's REVENUES: 65248.04

Enter this year's COSTS: 47268.94

Total profit this year $17979.100000

(re-run)

Enter this year's REVENUE: 652014.37

Enter this year's COSTS: 765842.66

Total loss this year ($113828.290000)

(re-run)

Enter this year's REVENUE: 27341.95

Enter this year's COSTS: 27341.95

Revenues equal costs for this year
```

Output 5-2

There is a problem with the output of Program 5-2—it does not look the way most people would expect. Instead of cents, we get six decimal places!

RULE   Program output must be in a format the user can understand easily.

Since the program is reporting dollars and cents, it should print only two decimal places.

5.7 NUMERIC FORMATTING WITH printf( )

Print formatting involves much more than simply printing strings, numbers, tabs, and the like. We also must be able to control the precise format of the output, such as the number of digits and decimal places displayed.

printf( ) can handle such demands. To change our program to print dollar values correctly, we need only specify that the floating point value is always to have exactly two decimal places. This is done with the following **printf( )** command:

```
printf("\nTotal profit this year $%.2f\n", revenue - cost);
```

The **%.2f** tells **printf( )** to print the value to exactly two decimal places. We also can tell **printf( )** how many characters should be printed. For example, the specification

```
%8.2f
```

tells **printf( )** to print a **float** or **double** value with a *minimum* of eight spaces and exactly two decimal places. As an illustration, this code fragment

```
profit = 2514.2;
printf("Total profit this year $%8.2f\n",profit);
...
```

produces this output

```
Total profit this year $ 2514.20
```

The numeric field is a total of eight characters wide (note the space between the dollar sign and the first number) and has two decimal places. The specification **%8.2f** guarantees the printing of at least eight characters (including spaces if necessary), one of which will be a decimal point. Also, two decimal places will be printed, filled with zeros if necessary. Thus, **%8.2f** describes a number having the form

```
#####.##
(12345678)
```

where **#** could be a digit or a leading space when positioned to the left of the decimal point and represents only a digit when placed to the right of it. We can specify widths for all other **printf( )** formats in the same way. For example, the specification **%10d** (for **int**s) or **%10ld** (for **long**s) guarantees the printing of at least ten characters. This will include leading blanks if the number has less than ten digits—nine and a minus sign if the number is negative. A field width specifier is a *minimum* only. A number that is longer than the specified width will still be printed in full.[4]

---

[4] A full description of **printf( )**'s format specifications is contained in Appendix E.

RULE A field width specifier in a **printf( )** format only specifies a minimum field size. If necessary to display a variable's full value, the field will be expanded.

Exercise 5-3 Revise Program 5-2 to display dollars and cents.

5.8 ROUND-OFF ERROR

The accuracy of the computer's memory is limited and, as a result, not all floating point numbers can be represented exactly inside a variable. It is common that **float** and **double** variables store only a close approximation of the values assigned to them, that is, the values have been "rounded off" to fit inside the space reserved for them. If these approximate values are added together the result is an approximate answer. The difference between the true answer (one found by doing an exact calculation) and the computer's answer is known as *round-off error*. Round-off error can occur whenever we manipulate **float** or **double** variables in any way.

In Program 5-2, we enter two **double** values, compare them, and then, in most cases, print out the result of one subtracted from the other. When Program 5-2 is executed, round-off error might cause inaccuracy in the calculations, making the final total off by a cent. As an illustration of the effect of round-off error, consider the addition of two values: .514 and .494.

```
    .514
  + .494
  ------
   1.008
```

If these values are rounded when they are printed, the sum won't look correct.

```
    .51       .514 rounded
  + .49       .494 rounded
  ------
   1.01      1.008 rounded
```

This is not a problem with C but an inherent problem with floating-point numbers. Round-off error doesn't occur with every value in every program that uses **float**s or **double**s. It depends on the compiler and the machine being used.

Incidentally, this is why we defined our variables as **double** instead of **float**. Round-off error is smaller with **double** variables than with **float**s since **double**s have twice the precision of **float**s. However, round-off error is a persistent problem that can make transactions involving dollars and cents inaccurate.

Fortunately, there are several ways to handle the problems associated with round-off error. One is to store all dollar values in cents. This is a integer quantity that can be stored exactly. To display the answer in familiar dollar and cents format, we simply divide by 100.[5] Another approach is to deal with round-off error explicitly in those

---

[5] This approach does require some specialized functions to perform the transformation from dollar-and-cents format to internal-cents-only format.

Sec. 5.9   Expanding the P&L Statement   57

expressions where it might be introduced. This will be done later, when C's mechanisms for doing this have been introduced.

For now, we will fall back on accounting convention to skirt the round-off error problem entirely. Most P&L statements display dollar amounts only, ignoring cents altogether. By doing this, we don't introduce any error in our calculations because exact dollar amounts can be stored as **int**s or **long**s.

Exercise 5-4   Modify Program 5-2 to use **long** variables and to print the numeric results in a field ten characters wide.

5.9 EXPANDING THE P&L STATEMENT

With the addition of proper formatting commands, Program 5-2 prints a minimally acceptable P&L statement. In general, of course, a single "bottom-line" figure is not enough. Bankers, stockholders, and tax collectors want to know where the revenue came from and how the money was spent. A *real* P&L statement must divide the costs and revenues into major categories and report the totals for each category in addition to the profit or loss figure.

We can enhance Program 5-2 to create just such a P&L statement by having the user enter the totals for the revenue and cost components. The program then can format the P&L report to include figures for each revenue and cost category as well as totals for revenue, cost, and the final profit or loss figure.

For example, suppose we run Johnson's Books, a retail bookstore. Our revenues consist of retail sales and rebates from book distributors. Our costs are the cost of the goods we sell, employee wages, store rent, advertising, and miscellaneous expenses. Figure 5-2 lists these.

The output of this new program will be more complex than that of the Program 5-2. We must detail both revenues and costs and total them. Figure 5-3 shows what such a detailed P&L statement should look like.

This may appear to be much more complicated then our previous efforts, but it is only a straightforward extension of Program 5-2. Instead of entering just revenues and costs, the program must prompt for and store additional information. While the output is more sophisticated, it still uses only a series of **printf( )** statements.

Revenue	**Cost**
Sales	Cost of goods sold
Rebates	Wages
	Rent
	Advertising
	Miscellaneous expenses

Figure 5-2   Breakdown of Revenues and Costs for Johnson's Books

```
                REVENUES

                Sales                        $  38987
                Rebates                      $   5000
                                             --------
                TOTAL REVENUE                          $  43987



                COSTS

                Cost of goods sold           $  14247
                Wages                        $   5501
                Rent                         $   3600
                Advertising                  $    250
                Miscellaneous Expenses       $   4761
                                             -------
                TOTAL COST                             $  28359

                PROFIT                                 $  15628
```

Figure 5-3 Profit and Loss Statement for Johnson's Books

We will assume that the maximum for each revenue or cost item is six digits, a limit of $999,999. To handle all possible input, we must allow the totals to handle up to seven digits, a limit of $9,999,999. Both of these are beyond the capacity of **int**s on some computers, so in this program we will use **long**s. The algorithm for this program is listed as Algorithm 5-2.

1. Read (**gets( )**) and convert (**atol( )**) revenue components.
2. Read (**gets( )**) and convert (**atol( )**) cost components.
3. Print values for each revenue component and total revenue
4. Print values for each cost component and total cost
5. If total revenue >= total cost
      print profit
   otherwise
      print loss

Algorithm 5-2

To maintain the format of this report, we will print the special case of

```
                total revenue = total cost
```

as

```
                PROFIT                                 $      0
```

Although Algorithm 5-2 may suffice for some programmers, others may want more details before they begin coding. As a rule, the more detailed the algorithm, the easier the program is to write. For this reason, a design approach called *stepwise refinement* was developed.

5.10 STEPWISE REFINEMENT

The idea behind stepwise refinement is to examine each step in an algorithm and to refine it by adding more detail. As an example, we can "refine" steps 1 and 2 in Algorithm 5-2 as shown in Algorithm 5-3.

From
    1. Read (**gets( )**) and convert (**atol( )**) revenue components
    2. Read (**gets( )**) and convert (**atol( )**) cost components

to
    1. a. Read (**gets( )**) and convert (**atol( )**) Sales
       b. Read (**gets( )**) and convert (**atol( )**) Rebates
    2. a. Read (**gets( )**) and convert (**atol( )**) Cost of goods sold
       b. Read (**gets( )**) and convert (**atol( )**) Wages
       c. Read (**gets( )**) and convert (**atol( )**) Rent
       d. Read (**gets( )**) and convert (**atol( )**) Advertising expenses
       e. Read (**gets( )**) and convert (**atol( )**) Miscellanous expenses

Algorithm 5-3   An Example of Stepwise Refinement

Refining algorithm steps is an important programming design tool. How far should each step be refined? A good rule of thumb is to add detail to an algorithm until the necessary C code for each step becomes obvious.

Every cost and revenue component entered must be stored in a separate variable. Thus, we need to define a **long** variable for each value to be read. Further, we will need two additional variables, one for total revenue and one for total cost. Table 5-2 lists the variables we will use.

Since these variables will be defined as **long**s, our code must convert the strings of digits entered into **long** values. While we need a **long** variable for each amount entered, we do not need what is stored in the entry string—the argument sent to **gets( )**—after we have converted what it contains into a **long**. This means we need only a single "input string" that can be "reused" every time we read in a value. This will save us from having to define a new input string for each data value.

We now have all the information needed to write the data entry part of Program 5-3, the enhanced P&L report.

TABLE 5-2 Variable List for Revenue and Cost Components

Value to be entered	Variable
Total Retail Sales	sales
Total Rebates	rebates
Cost of Goods Sold	cgs
Total Wages Paid	wages
Total Store Rent Paid	rent
Total Advertising Expenses	ads
Total Miscellaneous Expenses	misc
Total Revenue	revenue
Total Cost	cost

```c
/*              *****  PL-REPT1  *****
 * This program prompts the user for revenue and cost
 * components and builds a Profit and Loss statement
 * from them.  The components are stored as longs.
 *
 * Written by Ray Swartz for "Doing Business with C"
 */

#include "stdio.h"

main()
{
    char instr[81];     /* general input string */
    char *gets();
    int printf();
    long atol();
    long sales;         /* total retail sales */
    long rebates;       /* total rebates */
    long cgs;           /* cost of goods sold */
    long wages;         /* total wages paid */
    long rent;          /* total store rent paid */
    long ads;           /* total advertising expense */
    long misc;          /* total miscellaneous expense */
    long revenue;       /* total revenue */
    long cost;          /* total cost */
```

Sec. 5.10 Stepwise Refinement

```
/* Get revenues first */

printf("\nRevenue for Johnson's Books\n");
printf("\nEnter dollar amounts only - no cents\n\n");
printf("Enter Total Sales: ");
gets(instr);        /* get and convert total sales */
sales = atol(instr);
printf("Enter Total Rebates Received: ");
gets(instr);        /* get and convert total rebates */
rebates = atol(instr);

/* Now get costs */

printf("\n\nCosts\n\n");
printf("Enter Cost of Goods Sold: ");
gets(instr);        /* get and convert costs of goods sold */
cgs = atol(instr);
printf("Enter Total Wages Paid: ");
gets(instr);        /* get and convert total wages paid */
wages = atol(instr);
printf("Enter Total Store Rent Paid: ");
gets(instr);        /* get and convert rent */
rent = atol(instr);
printf("Enter Total Advertising Expenses: ");
gets(instr);        /* get and convert advertising */
ads = atol(instr);
printf("Enter Total Miscellaneous Expenses: ");
gets(instr);        /* get and convert misc. exp. */
misc = atol(instr);
rest of program
```

Program 5-3 Data Entry Section (input)

The output section of Program 5-3 is little more than a series of **printf( )** statements. The biggest problem in formatting the output section is getting the columns to line up properly. Putting **printf( )** statements one after the other will help us align the columns. We can now write the output section of Program 5-3.

```
data entry section
printf("\n\tProfit and Loss Statement for Johnson's Books\n\n");
printf("          REVENUES\n\n");
printf("          Sales                   $%6ld\n", sales);
printf("          Rebates                 $%6ld\n", rebates);
printf("                                  ------\n");
revenue = sales + rebates;    /* total revenues */
printf("          TOTAL REVENUE                    $%7ld\n",
       revenue);
```

```c
        printf("\n\n");
        printf("          COSTS\n\n");
        printf("          Cost of Goods Sold      $%6ld\n", cgs);
        printf("          Wages                   $%6ld\n", wages);
        printf("          Rent                    $%6ld\n", rent);
        printf("          Advertising             $%6ld\n", ads);
        printf("          Miscellaneous Expenses  $%6ld\n", misc);
        printf("                                   ------\n");
        cost = cgs + wages + rent + ads + misc;   /* total costs */
        printf("          TOTAL COST                       $%7ld\n\n",
                cost);
        if (revenue >= cost)
            printf("          PROFIT                           $%7ld\n",
                revenue - cost);
        else
            printf("          LOSS                            ($%7ld)\n",
                cost - revenue);
        exit(0);
}
```

Program 5-3 Output Section

One inconvenience of computer programming is the limited size of the terminal screen. This makes some **printf( )** statements too long to be displayed by the terminal screen on a single line. C allows us to split a statement into two or more lines, since it recognizes the end of a statement only when it sees a semicolon. However, we must be careful where we split a **printf( )** statement. Do not split the format string. A **printf( )** statement should be split between arguments only. For example, the following **printf( )** statement appeared in the output section of Program 5-3.

```c
        printf("          TOTAL COST                       $%7ld\n\n",
                cost);
```

We split this **printf( )** statement after the format string. Since **printf( )** interprets the format string literally, this **printf( )** would NOT work properly:

```c
        printf("          TOTAL COST                       $%7
                ld\n\n", cost);
```

We have now written both halves of Program 5-3, data entry and report formatting. The entire program is created by putting these halves together. The output of Program 5-3 recreates the P&L report in Figure 5-2 and is shown as Output 5-3.

```
        Revenue for Johnson's Books

        Enter dollar amounts only - no cents
```

```
Enter Total Sales: 38987
Enter Total Rebates Received: 5000

Costs

Enter Cost of Goods Sold: 14247
Enter Total Wages Paid: 5501
Enter Total Store Rent Paid: 3600
Enter Total Advertising Expense: 250
Enter Total Miscellaneous Expenses: 4761

   Profit and Loss Statement for Johnson's Books

      REVENUES

      Sales                        $  38987
      Rebates                      $   5000
                                   --------
      TOTAL REVENUE                             $   43987

      COSTS

      Cost of Goods Sold           $  14247
      Wages                        $   5501
      Rents                        $   3600
      Advertising                  $    250
      Miscellaneous Expenses       $   4761
                                   --------
      TOTAL COST                                $   28359

      PROFIT                                    $   15628
```

Output 5-3

5.11 SUMMARY

1. The C language consists of two parts, the language and a standard library of functions.
2. When a C program is moved from one computer to another and recompiled, that machine's versions of the standard library functions are made part of the program.
3. Many of the functions in the standard library need information that must be made part of our programs. This machine specific-data is stored in a header file called *stdio.h*.
4. To make *stdio.h* part of our programs, we can use the preprocessor's **#include** directive. This makes the contents of a file part of our program.

5. A variable that can hold a string of characters is defined as data type **char** and must contain an integer constant that states the maximum number of characters the variable can store. The string length is enclosed in brackets:

```
char co_name[31];
```

6. In C, character strings stored in variables are terminated with a special character constant called the end of string (eos) character represented by \0.
7. To refer to the entire string, we just use the variable's name. To identify a character stored in the string requires the variable name and the number of the character inside brackets:

```
co_name[3]
```

8. The first character in a string is numbered 0.
9. A string entered from the keyboard can be read by a C program using the **gets( )** function. **gets( )** is sent the string variable that is to store the entered string as an argument.
10. **gets( )** is a standard library function that is declared

```
char *gets();
```

11. **gets( )** stores all the characters entered up to a newline into the string sent as an argument. The function does not check if the string is large enough to handle all the characters entered. A program will fail if too many characters are stored in a string variable.
12. Whenever information is requested from the user, a message should be displayed that describes what information is to be entered. This message is called a *prompt*. A prompt should list any program limitations on the data to be entered, such as maximum string length or largest number.
13. There is no C function to read a number from the user. Instead, a string of digits is read and then converted to the proper data type using one of these three standard library functions:

atoi(instr)	Converts *instr* into an **int**
atol(instr)	Converts *instr* into a **long**
atof(instr)	Converts *instr* into a **double**.

14. A program should contain three types of documentation: an introduction, variable description, and in-line comments.
15. The standard library function **printf( )** can format the numbers it prints. We can specify the minimum width of a field as well as how many decimal places to print.
16. Round-off error occurs because a computer only stores a close approximation of a decimal number.

Sec. 5.11   Summary

17. **printf( )** can be used to create formatted reports.
18. An algorithm step should be expanded until the C code for that step becomes obvious. This process is called stepwise refinement.

E X E R C I S E S

5-5. Write a program that gets a series of sales amounts for each week and then prints the total sales for the month (assume each month has four weeks).

5-6. Write a program that reads in a date by getting the month, day, and year as **int**s and then verifies that the date specified is a valid one.

5-7. The owner of Johnson's Books wants a program to print an inventory report. The report is to prompt for the dollar amount held in each of six inventory categories. The report is to print each category, the amount, and then a total. The six inventory categories are

Paperbacks
Hardbacks
Magazines
Used Books
On-sale Books
Nonbook items

5-8. After reviewing the P&L statement produced by Program 5-3, the accountant says that rebates should not be listed as revenue but instead as reductions in the cost of goods sold. The accountant suggests that the P&L statement separately list cost of goods sold and rebates and then report the difference as the "actual" cost of goods sold. For example,

```
         Cost of Goods Sold              $ 14247
              Rebates                    $  5000
                                         ───────
         Actual Cost of Goods Sold       $  9247
```

Implement this suggestion.

5-9. At present, Program 5-3 prints the P&L statement with revenues first then costs. Modify Program 5-3 to print the P&L statement with revenues in one column and costs in another column. The columns should be totaled with the actual profit or loss printed on a separate line. See Figure 5-2 for the statement format.

6
Creating Our Own Commands

In Chapter 5, we created an interactive program that read in values for a company's revenue and cost components and then printed a formatted profit and loss statement. This was listed as Program 5-3.

In Program 5-3, every value was entered with the same three statements. For example, these statements are used to read in total sales:

```
printf("Enter Total Sales: ");
gets(instr);
sales = atol(instr);
```

Except for the prompt and the variable that stores the value entered, the statements used to read each revenue and cost entry are the same.

Instead of having to repeat this series of statements every time we want the user to enter data, it would be better if we had a special input function to do it for us. Recall that the main use of functions is to generalize the commands that perform a specific task. Substituting functions for often repeated code segments not only saves us typing time but also makes our programs easier to understand and modify.

Unfortunately, there is no function in the standard library that prints a prompt and reads in some data. But that's no problem, because we can create one for ourselves!

Sec. 6.1   How to Write Functions   67

The first step in writing any function (or program, for that matter) is to design it. Thus, before we begin coding we have to know what the function will do. The input function's algorithm is shown as Algorithm 6-1.

1. Print a prompt (adding a ": " to the end)
2. Read the data entered as a string of digits
3. Convert the string to its numeric value (as a **long**)
4. Return the converted value to the calling routine so it can be stored in the proper variable

Algorithm 6-1

Since this function will read in a **long** value, let's call it the **getlong( )** function. **getlong( )** will be used to enter all kinds of information, so we must make it as general as possible.

RULE   Functions should be designed to be as general as possible.

getlong( ) has to print a specific prompt every time it is called. We can generalize **getlong( )** by passing it the specific prompt to print as an argument. An an example,

```
sales = getlong("Enter Total Sales");
```

would be used to enter the amount of total sales. When called, **getlong( )** will print

```
Enter Total Sales:
```

read the value entered by the user, with **gets( )**; convert it to a **long**, with **atol( )**; and then return the converted value (which is stored in the variable *sales*). Incidentally, we must enclose **getlong( )**'s argument in double quotation marks because we want C to treat the prompt as a string constant.

6.1 HOW TO WRITE FUNCTIONS

Although a function is a separate section of code that is distinct from **main( )**, it need not be put in a separate file. Instead, a function's source code can be listed in the same file with **main( )**. This is the method that we will use. If we were to put a function's code in another file, we would have to merge this file with the one containing **main( )** when we compiled the program.

A function definition consists of five parts:

1. Data Type
2. Function Name

3. Arguments (parameter list)
4. Argument (parameter) declarations
5. Body of the function (source code)

A function definition must contain all five parts (only 1, 2, and 5 if no arguments will be sent to the function) before the function can be used. A function's data type specifies the data type of the value returned by the function. The rules for naming functions are the same as naming variables—they must start with an alphabetic character and can contain characters, digits, and the underscore. We also must identify how many arguments (if any) this function expects to receive. Since a function's arguments are really just variables, the data type of each argument must be declared, as well. Lastly, the statements to be executed when the function is called must be written.

We've already named our input function **getlong( )** and know that it will return a **long**. **getlong( )** will be passed a single argument: the prompt to print. The first line of the **getlong( )** function definition is

```
long .getlong(prompt)
 (1)     (2)    (3)     ← Function Parts
```

Because **getlong( )** is a function, we must enclose the argument list in parentheses—just as we would when calling it. If more than one argument is to be passed, the arguments would have to be arranged in the exact order they will be sent to the function and separated by commas. Out-of-order function arguments are a main cause of C programming errors. Also, since a function definition is a programming structure, we don't put a semicolon at the end of the definition line. Putting a semicolon after a function name in its definition is another common programming error.

RULE   List a function's arguments in the proper order.

RULE   A function definition does not end with a semicolon.

The argument sent to **getlong( )** is represented in the function definition by the variable *prompt*. *prompt* is called a *formal parameter name* and is declared like any other C variable. Within **getlong( )**, *prompt* assumes the value of the argument passed to the function.

Before we can use *prompt*, it needs to be declared. To declare *prompt* as a string, we must specify its length. However, we don't know how long *prompt* is going to be! Further, *prompt* will be different lengths depending on the message **getlong( )** is asked to print.

The solution to this dilemma is that the string represented by *prompt* has already been stored somewhere else. In Program 5-3, it is a string constant in **main( )**. In fact, our declaration of *prompt* is not a storage allocating definition. Instead, *prompt* is

Sec. 6.1   How to Write Functions   69

declared as a formal parameter which allows it to use information stored elsewhere on the system.[1]

Formal parameters that are strings require a special declaration:

```
char prompt[];
```

In essence, this tells C that *prompt* represents a string that will be passed to this function. The key feature is the empty brackets, which tell C that *prompt* is a string and not just a single character. We refer to parameters declared like this as *dummy variables*. Also, since this is a variable declaration, it ends with a semicolon.

We now have created four of the five parts of **getlong( )**:

```
long getlong(prompt)     /* parts 1, 2, and 3 */
char prompt[];           /* part 4 */
```

The last part is the actual C code to be performed when the function is called. The algorithm for this function is listed as Algorithm 6-1. The C translation of Algorithm 6-1 is shown as Segment 6-1.

```
{
    char instr[81];      /* input string */
    char *gets();
    int printf();
    long atol();
    long nbr;            /* value returned */

    printf("%s: ",prompt);    /* no newline */
    gets(instr);
    nbr = atol(instr);
    return(nbr);         /* returns nbr to calling routine */
}
```

Segment 6-1 C Code For **getlong( )** Function

When **getlong( )** is called, this code will be executed. We've introduced a new keyword in Segment 6-1, **return**. **return** instructs C to terminate the function and to continue the program just after the function call in the calling routine. **return** is used in functions only.

In Segment 6-1, the variable *nbr* is returned by **getlong( )**. This means the value represented by *nbr* will replace **getlong( )** in the calling routine. This is done because *nbr* is enclosed in parentheses in a **return** statement. For functions that don't return a value, we use **return** without parentheses:

```
return;
```

---

[1] This isn't quite true, but for our present purposes it is true enough.

The full definition of **getlong( )** is shown as Function 6-1.

```
long getlong(prompt)        /* parts 1, 2, and 3 */
char prompt[];              /* part 4 */
{
    char instr[81];         /* input string */
    char *gets();
    int printf();
    long atol();
    long nbr;               /* number converted from instr */

    printf("%s: ",prompt);  /* part 5 */
    gets(instr);
    nbr = atol(instr);
    return(nbr);
}
```

Function 6-1 Full Definition of **getlong( )** Function

6.2 FUNCTION DATA TYPES AND void

Incidentally, we do not have to **#include** *stdio.h* in Function 6-1 because **getlong( )** is not a C program. Instead, *stdio.h* will be **#include**d by the program using **getlong( )**.

As we now know, a function is a separate section of code. What does this mean for the variables defined inside a function? As with the function itself, the variables defined inside the braces of a function only exist while the function is executing. These variables are created when the function is called and disappear when the function terminates. A variable defined in a function cannot be refered to outside the confines of that function. Variables defined inside a function are called *local* variables. Further, changes made to local variables are only seen inside the function.[2]

Not all functions return a value. A new data type was recently added to C to identify such functions, **void**. **void** tells the compiler that this function doesn't return a value. Once a function is defined as type **void**, the compiler will ensure that it is not used in an expression or in any place a returned value is expected.

RULE   Functions that don't return a value are declared as data type **void**.

C also allows the data type to be omitted from function definitions and declarations. Without an explicit data type, a function is defined as **int** by the compiler. Before **void** was introduced into C, functions that didn't return information were left undeclared in calling routines. Even today, it is quite common in C programs to use undeclared functions. This is particularly true of some standard library functions like **printf( )**, whose return values are generally ignored.

---

[2] There are exceptions. See Chapter 12.

Sec. 6.3 Using "Homemade" Functions

Although a mechanism exists that allows the use of undeclared functions, the author considers it to be bad programming style. It hinders thorough documentation and can lead to mistakes through oversight and cause problems when a program is moved from one machine to another, if the move requires recompilation. As a result, we will declare the data types of functions whenever we use them.

Some versions of C haven't yet implemented the **void** data type. In this case, **int** should be used instead of **void**.

6.3 USING "HOMEMADE" FUNCTIONS

Now that we have defined the **getlong( )** function, the next step is to integrate it into Program 5-3. To do this, we simply replace each data input sequence with a call to **getlong( )**. For example, this statement is used to read in the value for total sales:

```
sales = getlong("Enter Total Sales");
```

Remember that before we can use a function, we must declare it.[3] This requires

```
long getlong();
```

The empty parentheses indicate that **getlong( )** is a function. Program 6-1 integrates these changes into Program 5-3.

```
/*              *****  PL-REPT2  *****
 * This program prompts the user for revenue and cost
 * components and builds a Profit and Loss statement
 * from them.
 *
 * Written by Ray Swartz for "Doing Business with C"
 */

#include "stdio.h"

main()
{
    int printf();
    long getlong();    /* prompt and return value entered */
    long sales;        /* total retail sales */
    long rebates;      /* total rebates */
    long cgs;          /* cost of goods sold */
    long wages;        /* total wages paid */
    long rent;         /* total store rent paid */
    long ads;          /* total advertising expense */
    long misc;         /* total miscellaneous expense */
    long revenue;      /* total revenue */
    long cost;         /* total cost */
```

---

[3] The ANSI standard introduces a new format for function declarations, called function prototypes. See Appendix C for more information.

```c
        /* Get revenues first */

        printf("\nRevenue for Johnson's Books\n\n");
        printf("\nEnter dollar amounts only - no cents\n\n");
        sales = getlong("Enter Total Sales");
        rebates = getlong("Enter Total Rebates Received");

        /* Now get costs */

        printf("\n\nCosts\n\n");
        cgs = getlong("Enter Cost of Goods Sold");
        wages = getlong("Enter Total Wages Paid");
        rent = getlong("Enter Total Store Rent Paid");
        ads = getlong("Enter Total Advertising Expense");
        misc = getlong("Enter Total Miscellaneous Expenses");

        /* print P&L report */

        printf("\n\tProfit and Loss Statement for Johnson's Books\n\n");
        printf("        REVENUES\n\n");
        printf("        Sales              $%6ld\n", sales);
        printf("        Rebates            $%6ld\n", rebates);
        printf("                           ------\n");
        revenue = sales + rebates;     /* total revenue */
        printf("        TOTAL REVENUE              $%7ld\n",
                revenue);
        printf("\n\n");
        printf("        COSTS\n\n");
        printf("        Cost of Goods Sold  $%6ld\n", cgs);
        printf("        Wages               $%6ld\n", wages);
        printf("        Rent                $%6ld\n", rent);
        printf("        Advertising         $%6ld\n", ads);
        printf("        Miscellaneous Expenses $%6ld\n", misc);
        printf("                           ------\n");
        cost = cgs + wages + rent + ads + misc;  /* total costs */
        printf("        TOTAL COST                 $%7ld\n\n",
                cost);
        if (revenue >= cost)
            printf("        PROFIT                     $%7ld\n",
                revenue - cost);
        else
            printf("        LOSS                       ($%7ld)\n",
                cost - revenue);
        exit(0);
    }
```

Sec. 6.4 Temporarily Changing Data Types

```
long getlong(prompt)    /* print prompt and read in a long */
char prompt[];
{
    char instr[81];     /* input string */
    char *gets();
    int printf();
    long atol();
    long nbr;           /* converted value */

    printf("%s: ",prompt);
    gets(instr);
    nbr = atol(instr);
    return(nbr);
}
```

Program 6-1 Integrating a Function into a Program

The output of Program 6-1 is the same as Output 5-3.

Exercise 6-1 Johnson's Books actually has two sales sources, mail-order and retail sales. Modify Program 6-1 to reflect this.

6.4 TEMPORARILY CHANGING DATA TYPES

A very useful extension to our Profit & Loss statement would be the printing of percentages for each category. For planning purposes, it is valuable to know what percentage sales is of total revenue, or what percentage rent is of total costs. Further, it helps bring the information in the P&L statement into perspective.

Adding percentages to our P&L report requires us to sum each section's categories into a total and then divide each amount by that total. Segment 6-2 illustrates how we might plan to add percentages to the sales category on the P&L report.

```
revenue = sales + rebates;   /* total for percentages */
printf("    Sales              $%6ld    %4.2f%%\n",
       sales, sales / revenue * 100);
```

Segment 6-2

Because **printf( )**'s format specifications begin with a percent sign, **printf( )** will get confused if we simply list a percent sign in the format string to be printed literally. To prevent this confusion, **printf( )** uses a special formatting specification for the percent sign: %%. Since we are printing percents, we have included %% in the **printf( )** in Segment 6-2.

Unfortunately, the approach in Segment 6-2 won't work. The variables *sales* and *revenue* are both **long**s, that is, they are integers. In C, the division of one integer by another results in an integer answer. In this case, **printf( )** will print either 100 (if *sales* = *revenue*) or 0 (if *revenue* > *sales*).

The problem arises because C only evaluates an operator when all its operands are the same data type.[4] The expression then evaluates to that data type. This is why an integer results when *sales* is divided by *revenue*. To get the proper output, we must somehow *coerce* the division of two **long**s to produce a **float** result.

6.4.1 Data Type Promotion and casts

This problem suggests a more basic question: How does C resolve an expression that contains variables of different data types? Since an expression can be evaluated only if the operands are the same data type, C must have a way of changing a value's data type to get the operands in an expression to match. To get data type agreement, C *temporarily* will change the data type of a variable within that single expression only. This process is called *promotion*.

C promotes "small" data types to "larger" ones. Table 6-1 lists C's data types in promotion order. Data types are promoted down the list until all the values in an expression are the same. The result of the expression will be of that data type.

TABLE 6-1 Promotion List

short	
int	
unsigned	Direction of Promotion
long	
unsigned long	↓
float	
double	

Since *sales* and *revenue* are both **long**s, the expression

```
sales / revenue
```

results in a 0 or 1 expressed as a **long**. Given these rules, our problem stems from the fact that we have stored all data as **long**s.

At first glance, one solution would be to define *revenue* a **double**. Then, in the expression

```
sales / revenue
```

sales is first promoted to a **double** (see Table 6-1) and the division is performed in data type **double**. A similar solution is to define *revenue* a **double**.

We also can solve this data type problem without redefining any variables. We can *coerce* the calculation to give its result as a **double** even though only integers are

---

[4] The assignment operator is an exception. Operand values on the right of an assignment operator are *converted* into the data type of the operand on the left of the operator.

Sec. 6.4 Temporarily Changing Data Types

involved! We do this by using another C operator called a **cast**. Casts allow us to explicitly change a variable's data type within a single expression.

A variable is cast into a specific data type by enclosing that new data type in parentheses and placing this next to the target variable. For example, we could **cast** *revenue* to be a **double** by

```
(double) revenue
```

If this change is made in the expression

```
sales / (double) revenue * 100
```

then the promotion rules take over and make *sales* and the constant 100 into **double**s. The division is then performed with a **double** result. Incidentally, the same would occur if *sales* were **cast** to a **double**:

```
(double) sales / revenue * 100
```

Either of these would accomplish our goal without requiring us to change any variable's definition. Thus, the best way to add percentages to our P&L program is to use **cast**s. This code prints the sales percentage:

```
revenue = sales + rebates;    /* total for percentages */
printf("    Sales              $%6ld    %4.2f%%\n",
       sales, sales / (double) revenue * 100);
```

Note that a **cast** is an operator just like division or multiplication. However **cast** has higher precedence than the arithmetic operators and the **cast** is done first (see precedence table in Appendix F).

It may seem as if we could **cast** *revenue* into a **double** in the assignment statement:

```
(double) revenue = sales + rebates;
```

and that this would work, too. However, an assignment statement changes memory. As a result, a variable on the left-hand side of an assignment operator cannot be **cast** to a different data type.

RULE A variable on the left side of an assignment operator cannot be cast to a different data type.

Do not get confused when promotion is involved in assignment statements. For example, if the variable *percent* is a **double** and *sales* and *revenue* are **long**s, then

```
percent = sales / revenue;
```

would first evaluate

$$\text{sales / revenue}$$

to a **long**. The integer result would then be *converted* into a **double** and stored in *percent*. Recall that division has a higher precedence than assignment and in this expression the division is performed as integer division. A conversion then must occur across the assignment operator to ensure that the proper data type is stored in memory.

On the other hand, in this expression

$$\text{percent = (double) sales / revenue;}$$

the division is performed as **double** and the correct percentage is stored in *percent* as a **double**. This means that the rules of promotion are used on the right-hand side of an assignment statement and then the expression's result is converted into the data type of the variable on the left-hand side of the assignment, if necessary.

What is the data type of a constant? A constant is assigned a data type based on two rules. First, if the constant has a decimal point, it is stored as a **double**. Second, if it is an integer, it is stored as an **int** unless it is too big to fit into an **int**, in which case it is stored as a **long**. If an integer constant is followed by the letter l or L, it is stored as a **long** no matter what its value. Table 6-2 shows the data types assigned to the listed constants.

TABLE 6-2 Constant Data Types

Constant	Data type
0, 82, 9876	**int**
984756474, 1L, 98761	**long**
0.3, 1.0, 432.987	**double**

Be careful when using l (lower-case L), as in 9876*l*, to convert an integer constant to a **long**—in many character sets it closely resembles the digit 1. For this reason, we always use **L** with integer constants.[5]

6.5 SUMMARY

1. Sections of repeated code should be replaced by a function.
2. When designing a function, be sure to make it as general as possible so that it can be used in a wide variety of similar circumstances.
3. Before a function can be used in a program, it must be defined. A function definition has five parts: a data type, name, parameter list, parameter declarations, and the body of the function.

---

[5] The ANSI standard includes additional numeric constant type specifiers. See Appendix C for more information.

4. A dummy variable can be used to pass a string to a function as an argument. A dummy variable identifies the name of the string but not its length. For example,

```
char prompt[];
```

5. The **return** statement signals the end of a function and tells C to continue the program at the spot following where the function was called.
6. A function can send information back to the routine that called the function. This is done by the **return** statement.
7. Functions that don't return information are declared as type **void**.
8. An operator only evaluates its operands when they all have the same data type.
9. In expressions containing different data type, C promotes one or more of the operands until all operands have the same data type.
10. Promotion occurs according to a set pattern where "smaller" data types are promoted into larger ones. An operand higher on the following list is promoted to match the data type of one farther down the list.

TABLE 6-1   Promotion List

short	
int	
unsigned	Direction of Promotion
long	
unsigned long	↓
float	
double	

11. In some expressions, the data type of an operand must be temporarily changed to get the desired results. An operand's data type can be changed inside an expression by using the **cast** operator. A **cast** is represented by listing the desired data type inside parentheses.
12. The data type of a numeric constant is determined by its value. All numbers containing a decimal point are stored as type **double**. Integers too large to be stored as **int** are stored as **long**. An integer constant can be **cast** as a **long** by putting an L or l after it.

E X E R C I S E S

6-2. Every category line in the P&L statement is printed by the **printf( )** function. Create a separate function called **print_line( )** that accepts a descriptive string and an amount and prints the line in the proper format.

6-3. Sometimes components of revenues or costs may be zero. This is especially true if the P&L statement is printed weekly or monthly, as many businesses prefer. Change the **print_line( )** function written in Exercise 6-2 to not print lines with a zero amount.

6-4. Revise Program 6-1 to print percentages on the P&L statement. A category's percentage should be calculated on the total for that section (i.e., either revenues or costs).

6-5. The sales department issues a report every month that lists sales by week. Write a program to implement the monthly sales report. Assume that every month has four weeks. The program should include an input function that is sent a week number and returns the sales amount entered for that week.

6-6. The accounting department wants to extend the monthly sales report (see Exercise 6-5) into a monthly profit report. The report lists weekly sales, weekly costs, weekly profit or loss, and the percentage that the profit or loss is of weekly revenue. The report printing should be done by a function.

6-7. Revise the program written for Exercise 6-6 to list the revenue and cost totals for all the months preceding this one (a "to date" total, i.e., one total for all the preceding months). Have the monthly sales report list the profit/loss at the beginning of the month and at the end of the month. As an extension, have the report show the percent change in the profit/loss.

6-8. Add budget figures to the P&L report. Each category line should list the actual amount and the amount budgeted for that category.

7
Looping Commands and the *switch* Statement

In previous chapters, we have described what constitutes a C statement and how C executes a sequence of statements and implements the selection structure with the **if** - **else** statement. In this chapter, we will introduce the third programming structure, the loop.

A loop structure controls the repeated execution of a segment of code. How many times the loop's body (the repeated segment) is performed depends on the result of a logical test. In C, a loop repeats as long as the associated test is true. When the test equates to false, the statements inside the loop are no longer executed and the loop terminates.

Many large business data-processing problems are nothing more than the repeated application of a single task. An illustration is the payroll. To print checks for all the employees in a business requires the code to print a check for a single employee and a loop to ensure it is done once for each employee. There are numerous other business examples that demonstrate this fundamental programming concept.

This is why loops are essential in computer programming. They allow us to solve enormous problems with a minimum of code. In fact, it usually isn't any more difficult to do something 10,000 times as it is to do the same thing two times!

The loop structure can be implemented in two different ways. The key distinction is whether the logical test is performed at the "top" or "bottom" of the loop. Put another way, the body of the loop can be executed either before or after the logical test. As was mentioned in Chapter 2, loops that test at the top (before) are called **while** loops and those that test at the bottom (after) are called **do while** loops.

7.1 THE while LOOP

To demonstrate how loops are used in C, let's solve a problem at Johnson's Books. In trying to expand their business, Johnson's Books has offered discounts to certain good customers, as well as to businesses who want to resell books. Making sure the proper discount is charged to each customer has caused some problems in the order department. We have been asked to print a table with 9%, 12%, 15%, 18.5%, and 22% discounts on the top and the dollar amounts from $15.95 to $39.95 on the side. The entries in the table will be the per-book prices of books, where the row is the book's retail price and the column is the discount percentage. Figure 7-1 shows some sample entries in such a table.

	Discount Percentage				
Retail Price	9%	12%	15%	18.5%	22%
15.95	14.51	14.04	13.56	13.00	12.44
16.95	15.42	14.92	14.41	13.81	13.22
		rest of table			

Figure 7-1 Johnson's Books Discount Table

Writing a program to print this discount table is a good example of using a loop to solve a large problem by repeatedly applying a single solution. In this case, the code that will print one line in the table will print all the others, too! The algorithm for this program is listed in Algorithm 7-1.

1. Print table heading
2. Set retail = 15.95
3. If retail <= 39.95, go to (4)
   else go to (7)
4. Print line in table
5. Retail = retail + 1.0
6. Go to (3)
7. End

Algorithm 7-1 Printing a Discount Table

The program depicted in Algorithm 7-1 implements a **while** loop. The logical test (step 3) is executed *before* the body of the loop (steps 4, 5, and 6).

In C, a **while** loop has the format

```
while ( logical test ) {
body of the loop
}
```

Sec. 7.1 The while Loop

The logical test is enclosed in parentheses and uses the same operators as the **if - else** statement. Recall that a logical test evaluates to 1 (true) or 0 (false). The **while** loop will repeat the loop's body if a *nonzero* value is found as the result of the logical test. As with the **if - else** statement, the braces are required only if they enclose more than 1 statement. This is because a loop's body must contain at least one statement.

Unlike previous programs, we must deal directly with decimal numbers here. As a result, we will use data type **double**. Program 7-1 implements this program.

```
/*        *****   DISC-TBL   *****
 *
 *    This program prints a table with retail prices
 *    for the rows and discount percentages as the
 *    columns.  The prices range from 15.95 to 39.95
 *    and the discounts are 9%, 12%, 15%, 18.5%, 22%
 *
 *    Written by Ray Swartz for "Doing Business with C"
 */

#include "stdio.h"

main()
{
    double retail;      /* retail price being discounted */
    int printf();

    printf("Retail              Discount Percentage\n");
    printf("Price        9%%     12%%    15%%    18.5%%    22%%\n");
    printf("------------------------------------------\n");
    retail = 15.95;     /* first value in table */
    while (retail <= 39.95) {
        printf("%.2f    %.2f    %.2f    %.2f    %.2f    %.2f\n",
                retail,
                retail * .91,
                retail * .88,
                retail * .85,
                retail * .815,
                retail * .78);
        retail = retail + 1.0;
    }
    exit(0);
}
```

Program 7-1

C doesn't care how many lines a statement spans—as long as it ends with a semicolon. Thus, the **printf( )** statement that prints the table entries in Program 7-1 is perfectly legal. When Program 7-1 is executed, the result is Output 7-1.

```
           Retail            Discount Percentage
           Price      9%     12%    15%   18.5%   22%
           ---------------------------------------------
           15.95     14.51  14.04  13.56  13.00  12.44
           16.95     15.42  14.92  14.41  13.81  13.22
           17.95     16.33  15.80  15.26  14.63  14.00
           18.95     17.24  16.68  16.11  15.44  14.78
           19.95     18.15  17.56  16.96  16.26  15.56
           20.95     19.06  18.44  17.81  17.07  16.34
           21.95     19.97  19.32  18.66  17.89  17.12
           22.95     20.88  20.20  19.51  18.70  17.90
           23.95     21.79  21.08  20.36  19.52  18.68
           24.95     22.70  21.96  21.21  20.33  19.46
           25.95     23.61  22.84  22.06  21.15  20.24
           26.95     24.52  23.72  22.91  21.96  21.02
           27.95     25.43  24.60  23.76  22.78  21.80
           28.95     26.34  25.48  24.61  23.59  22.58
           29.95     27.25  26.36  25.46  24.41  23.36
           30.95     28.16  27.24  26.31  25.22  24.14
           31.95     29.07  28.12  27.16  26.04  24.92
           32.95     29.98  29.00  28.01  26.85  25.70
           33.95     30.89  29.88  28.86  27.67  26.48
           34.95     31.80  30.76  29.71  28.48  27.26
           35.95     32.71  31.64  30.56  29.30  28.04
           36.95     33.62  32.52  31.41  30.11  28.82
           37.95     34.53  33.40  32.26  30.93  29.60
           38.95     35.44  34.28  33.11  31.74  30.38
           39.95     36.35  35.16  33.96  32.56  31.16
```

Output 7-1

7.2 THE round( ) FUNCTION

In Program 7-1, we used **%.2f** as the **printf( )** format specification. This says to print a **double** value with two decimal places. As Output 7-1 shows, this is what **printf( )** did. However,

$$39.95 * .91 = 36.3545$$

and **printf( )** "rounded" the answer![1] This is how **printf( )** works.

Incidentally, rounding off means to approximate a value by increasing or decreasing it to the next *closest* acceptable amount. Rounding follows a simple rule. If the digit is 5 or greater in the location being rounded, we take the next higher value; otherwise, we take the next lower one.

---

[1] Be careful here. **printf( )** doesn't always round off the answer correctly. As an example, on the author's computer, the value 39.95 * .9 (a 10% discount) was printed as 35.95. Yet, the actual answer is 35.955 and it should be rounded to 35.96.

Sec. 7.2 The round( ) Function

For example, to round to the nearest hundred, we look at the tens digit. The number 11045 would become 11000, and 11055 gets rounded to 11100. The same thing works for fractional values. To print out dollar and cents means rounding to the nearest hundredth. In this case, we look at the thousandths digit (the third decimal place). Thus, 36.3545 becomes 36.35, and 36.3555 becomes 36.36.

This is the second time we've dealt with printing cents. The first time we ignored the problems associated with round-off error by recording only dollars. In many business applications, it isn't possible to simply ignore cents. As a result, we must find a way for dealing with cents that guarantees that our programs *always* get the exact answer "to the penny."

What we will do is implement our own rounding-off function, called **round( )**, which is sent a **double** argument and returns that value rounded off to two decimal places (dollars and cents). Thus, the call

```
round(36.3545)
```

returns

```
36.35
```

and

```
round(36.3555)
```

returns

```
36.36
```

Rounding a number to the nearest cent is implemented by representing all values within a specific range by a single value. For example, all amounts between 36.3450 and 36.3549 get rounded to 36.35. Put another way, if *amt* is a **double** and

```
36.3450 <= amt < 36.3550
```

then we can approximate *amt* with 36.35.

We can't implement rounding directly because of the inexact way computers store floating-point values. Instead, we have to perform this operation by shifting and converting numbers. The basic idea is that numbers between 36.3500 and 36.35499 are rounded by chopping off the digits after the cents (second decimal place). Another word for "chopping off" is *truncation*. Truncation is what happens to the fractional parts when a **float** or **double** is stored into an integer data type.

To round off to the nearest cent requires us to multiply the value by 100 first, since truncation will occur at the decimal point. Thus, if

```
36.3500 <= amt < 36.3550
```

then

$$\text{(long) (amt * 100.0) / 100.0}$$

is 36.35. Recall that a data type enclosed in parentheses is a *cast* which temporarily converts a value into that data type. In this case, the multiplication is performed as a **double**, since *amt* is a **double** and the multiplication is enclosed in parentheses. Converting that result to a **long** truncates the fractional part smaller than cents (hundredths). In effect, this converts *amt* to cents. By dividing by 100.0, we convert *amt* back to dollar and cents.

This works fine if

$$36.3500 <= \text{amt} < 36.3550$$

but if

$$36.3550 <= \text{amt} < 36.3599...$$

then this calculation would round down when it should round up! The same is true if

$$36.3450 <= \text{amt} < 36.3500$$

The "lower" half of the rounding range can be accounted for by adding .005 to *amt* before truncation. Arithmetically, if

$$36.3450 <= \text{amt} < 36.3550$$

then

$$36.35 <= \text{amt} + .005 < 36.36$$

To round up properly, we simply have to add .5 after the multiplication. This is implemented by the expression

$$\text{(long) (amt * 100.0 + .5) / 100.0}$$

Note that **cast**s have higher precedence than arithmetic operators, which is why the expression contains parentheses.

The **round( )** function is nothing more than this expression inside a function. Function 7-1 implements **round( )**.

Sec. 7.2   The round( ) Function

```
/* ***** ROUND *****
 *
 * This function rounds a double value to the nearest
 *  hundredth (cents).
 *
 * Written by Ray Swartz for "Doing Business with C"
 */
    double round(amt)
    double amt;
    {
        double round_amt;     /* the result of the rounding calculation */

        round_amt = (long) (amt * 100.0 + .5) / 100.0;
        return(round_amt);
    }
```

Function 7-1   The **round( )** Function

The whole purpose of *round_amt* in Function 7-1 is to store the rounded value so it can be returned in the next statement. *round_amt* is what's called a *temporary variable*, that is, a variable that holds a value until something else is done to it. In this case, it is unnecessary, since **return** can evaluate an expression before passing back the result. Thus, Function 7-2 is another way to write **round( )**

```
/* ***** ROUND *****
 *
 * This function rounds a double value to the nearest
 *  hundredth (cents).
 *
 * Written by Ray Swartz for "Doing Business with C"
 */
    double round(amt)
    double amt;
    {
        return( (long) (amt * 100.0 + .5) / 100.0);
    }
```

Function 7-2   The Revised **round( )** Function

Exercise 7-1   Modify Program 7-1 to use the **round( )** function. Does the resulting output differ from Output 7-1?

Undoubtedly, there will be values that should round up that, in fact, get rounded down. Such is the nature of floating-point numbers and digital computers. Virtually all floating-point calculations in C should be accurate enough to add numbers with two decimal places together without significant error. Although these precautions help

7.3 THE do while LOOP

A **do while** loop tests at the bottom. To demonstrate, we will rewrite Program 7-1 to use a **do while** loop. The algorithm for the **do while** version of Program 7-1 is listed as Algorithm 7-2.

1. Print table heading
2. Set retail = 15.95
3. Print line in table
4. Retail = retail + 1
5. If retail <= 39.95 go to (3)
6. End

Algorithm 7-2 Printing the Discount Table with a **do while** Loop

A **do while** loop has this format

```
do {
    body of the loop
} while ( logical test );
```

Again, the braces are not required if the loop's body consists of only one statement. Also, notice the semicolon at the end of the logical test. This is required.

RULE   A **do while** loop ends with a semicolon.

Program 7-1 has been rewritten to use a **do while** loop and the result is Program 7-2.

```
/*      ***** DISC-TBL2 *****
 *
 * This program prints a table with retail prices
 * for the rows and discount percentages as the
 * columns. The prices range from 15.95 to 39.95
 * and the discounts are 9%, 12%, 15%, 18.5%, 22%
 *
 * Written by Ray Swartz for "Doing Business with C"
 *
 * Modified to use a do while loop.
 */
```

Sec. 7.3 The do while Loop

```
#include "stdio.h"

main()
{
    double retail;      /* retail price being discounted */
    int printf();

    printf("Retail                Discount Percentage\n");
    printf("Price          9%%    12%%    15%%    18.5%%    22%%\n");
    printf("-------------------------------------------------\n");
    retail = 15.95;     /* first value in table */
    do {
    printf("%.2f    %.2f    %.2f    %.2f    %.2f    %.2f\n",
            retail,
            retail * .91,
            retail * .88,
            retail * .85,
            retail * .815,
            retail * .78);
    retail = retail + 1.0;
    } while (retail <= 39.95);
    exit(0);
}
```

Program 7-2 Using a **do while** loop

Program 7-2's output is the same as Output 7-1.

If the output is the same when we use a **while** and **do while** loop, why does C need both of them? In the case of Programs 7-1 and 7-2, it in fact makes no difference which one we use. However, with a small modification, it would.

Suppose we changed these programs to read the beginning price for the discount table from the user (see Exercise 7-2). The prices in the table would begin at the entered value and go up to $39.95. Let's further suppose that we have made the appropriate changes to both Programs 7-1 and 7-2. Program 7-1a will refer to the modified Program 7-1 and Program 7-2a to the modified Program 7-2.

Now, what happens if the user enters a value larger than $39.95? Program 7-1a (the **while** loop) tests *before* it enters the loop and since the test is false, Program 7-1a exits without executing the loop's body at all. Program 7-2a (the **do while** loop), on the other hand, executes the loop's body once before it tests the logical statement. As a result, Program 7-2a would print an entry in the table before it exited the program.

This succinctly demonstrates the difference between **while** and **do while** loops. **do while** loops are guaranteed to perform the statements in the loop at least once. It is possible that the statements in a **while** loop won't be executed at all.

This is an important distinction that often comes in handy. Program 7-1a actually did the right thing: It didn't print an entry in the table larger than 39.95. This is how the program should act. In this case, the **while** loop would be the correct one to use. However, in many programs it simply doesn't matter which loop is used. This was the case in the actual Programs 7-1 and 7-2, both resulted in the same output.

We must be careful to use the proper looping construct in our programs. Using the wrong loop is the source of hard to find programming errors that only occur under certain circumstances.

Exercise 7-2   Modify Program 7-1 to prompt for and read the beginning and ending prices to put in the discount table. NOTE: Since the user will be entering amounts expressed in dollars and cents, the program should use the function **atof( )** to perform the conversion of the entered string.

7.4 THE for LOOP

One of the main tasks performed by loops is to control a counter. That is, the loop counts the number of times the loop's body is executed, stopping when the limit set in the logical test is met. The loops in both Programs 7-1 and 7-2 do this, printing lines in the tables from $15.95 to $39.95.

Counting a loop's repetitions requires a variable to act as the counter. In Programs 7-1 and 7-2, we used *retail* to do the counting. When a counter is used in a loop, three steps must be performed. First, the counter must be *initialized* to the starting value. Second, the counter must be *tested* to see if the loop's limit has been reached. Third, the counter must be *incremented* to account for the just completed repetition. The first step (initialize) is done once, before the loop starts. Steps two and three are performed at the end of each loop iteration.

As an illustration, in Program 7-1 *retail* is the counting variable and it is initialized with the statement:

```
retail = 15.95;
```

It is tested in the **while** loop by

```
while (retail <= 39.95)
```

and incremented by

```
retail = retail + 1.0;
```

In a **do while** loop, the same steps occur, but the test occurs at the bottom of the loop (see Prog 7-2). The order in a **do while** loop is *initialize–increment–test*. In both the **while** and **do while** loops, the increment is done before the next test is performed. This is a common attribute of counting loops. Without the increment, the loop couldn't count its repetitions!

Counting loops are so common in programming that C contains a special looping construct to represent them. We could use either a **while** or **do while** to control a counting loop. However, the **while** and **do while** loops only provide a way to test for the loop's stopping condition. The initialize and increment statements must be

Sec. 7.4 The **for** Loop

performed elsewhere. This can cause a documentation problem by separating the three steps involved in controlling the loop. One of the steps could be overlooked or misinterpreted if is it "buried" inside the program somewhere—especially, if the steps are not obvious.

To make counting loops easier to write, control, and document, C contains the **for** loop. A **for** loop provides a way to put all of a loop's controlling information in one place where it is easily found and altered, if necessary.

The **for** loop format is

```
for (initialize; test; increment) {
   body of the loop
}
```

The **for** loop contains three sections separated by semicolons. The first section holds one or more initializing statements; the second section, the logical test that controls the loops; and the third section is made up of one or more increment statements. It works like this: The statement(s) in the initialize section are executed only when the loop is entered. The test is then performed. If it is false, the loop's body is not performed and the loop is skipped (however, the initializing steps have been taken). If the test is true, the statements in the body are executed and after the last statement in the loop is done, the statement(s) in the increment section is performed. The sequence of logical test, body of the loop, and increment is repeated until the test evaluates to false.

Since a **for** loop tests *before* it performs the loop's body, it really is just a specialized **while** loop. **for** loops simply provide some additional structure. In fact, for every **for** loop, there is an equivalent **while** loop. Program 7-3 shows the discount table program with a **for** loop.

```
/*       ***** DISC-TBL *****
 *
 * This program prints a table with retail prices
 * for the rows and discount percentages as the
 * columns.  The prices range from 15.95 to 39.95
 * and the discounts are 9%, 12%, 15%, 18.5%, 22%
 *
 * Written by Ray Swartz for "Doing Business with C"
 *
 * Modified to use a for loop
 */

#include "stdio.h"

main()
{
    double retail;      /* retail price being discounted */
    int printf();
```

```
        printf("Retail              Discount Percentage\n");
        printf("Price      9%%     12%%    15%%    18.5%%   22%%\n");
        printf("-------------------------------------------------\n");
        for (retail = 15.95; retail <= 39.95; retail = retail + 1.0)
        printf("%.2f    %.2f   %.2f   %.2f   %.2f   %.2f\n",
                retail,
                retail * .91,
                retail * .88,
                retail * .85,
                retail * .815,
                retail * .78);
        exit(0);
}
```

Program 7-3 Using a **for** Loop

The sections of a **for** loop are separated with semicolons. A very common programming error is to use commas instead of semicolons.

RULE   The sections of a **for** loop are separated by semicolons.

Substituting a comma for a semicolon is not an error that will be reported by the compiler. This is why it is such a difficult problem to find and debug.

In C, the comma is an operator that allows more than one independent expression to be contained in a single statement. This is useful if our loop initialization requires more than one step. For example, this **for** loop will set *total* and *count* to zero before beginning the loop:

```
for (total = 0, count = 0; count < 10; count = count + 1) {
    rest of loop
```

The comma also can be used to perform two or more increment statements.

We can leave one or more of a **for** loop's sections empty. An empty section is ignored entirely. For example, this implementation of a **for** loop

```
for (retail = 15.95; retail <= 39.95; retail = retail + 1.0) {
    rest of loop
}
```

is equivalent to

```
retail = 15.95;
for ( ; retail <= 39.95; retail = retail + 1.0) {
    rest of loop
}
```

Sec. 7.5 Designing Programs with Loops

An empty section is left blank but the separating semicolon must be included in the **for** statement.

This **for** loop is an infinite loop:

```
for (;;){
    rest of loop
}
```

so is this **while** loop

```
while (1) {
    rest of loop
}
```

as is this **do while** loop

```
do {
    rest of loop
} while (1);
```

Obviously, infinite loops should be avoided if at all possible and they are shown here for completeness only.

7.5 DESIGNING PROGRAMS WITH LOOPS

We've learned how to represent all three structures in C: sequence, selection, and repetition. We know how to call functions and how to create them. Now, we will learn how to combine these into a meaningful programming application.

The order department has thanked us for the discount pricing tables. They say it has lessened the pricing mistakes on the orders. To supplement the tables, they have asked for a program to verify the discount applied and the final invoice total.

A Johnson's Books' invoice consists of number of lines. Each invoice line lists the number of books purchased, the retail price of the book, and the total for this invoice line (number of books multiplied by retail price). See Figure 7-2 for a sample invoice line.

Books	Title	Price	Total
12	Title1	24.95	299.40

rest of invoice

Figure 7-2 Sample Johnson's Books Invoice

The total for each line is summed to get the retail total. The customer's discount is applied to the retail total to get the invoice total.

The program we've been asked to write should read in the number of books and the retail price from an invoice line and then display the line total. This checks the accuracy of each invoice line. The user will continue to enter invoice lines until all have been entered and checked. A 0 entry for number of books will signal that the invoice doesn't contain any more lines. After the last invoice line is read, the program prints the retail total. The program then gets the customer's discount code and figures the invoice total. The algorithm for this program is listed as Algorithm 7-3.

1. Set total to 0
2. Prompt for and read number of books on this line
3. If books == 0, go to (8)
   else go to (4)
4. Prompt for and read retail price
5. Print line total
6. Add line total to retail total
7. Go to (2)
8. Print the retail total (prediscounted price)
9. Prompt for and read customer's discount code
10. Calculate invoice total
11. Print invoice total
12. Exit

Algorithm 7-3

Note that the title of each book isn't entered because this program only checks the dollar amounts entered and the discount applied.

Although the program described by Algorithm 7-3 could be written as one long **main( )** routine, it is better to create specific functions to do different parts of the program. Several small, one-task functions are easier to write, test, repair, and modify than a single large program that does many things. In fact, this is another tenet of structured programming.

RULE A program should be constructed of functions and each function should do only one thing.

We will follow this rule throughout this book.

The **main( )** routine's job is to define variables that are used by the program and to call the functions in the proper order and with the correct arguments. In fact, **main( )** should resemble an algorithm with the function calls corresponding to each step in the algorithm. This should not be taken to extremes, however. **main( )** should perform any simple data manipulation for which a function is unnecessary. An example is step 5 in

Sec. 7.5 Designing Programs with Loops

Algorithm 7-3 which simply performs an addition. Program 7-4 is the main routine that implements Algorithm 7-3. The name of this program is **chk-inv**.

```
/*      *****   CHK-INV   *****
 *
 *   This program reads all the lines on an invoice.
 *   After entry of a line, it prints the line total.
 *   It totals and prints the invoice lines,
 *   reads in the customer's discount code
 *   and then prints out the discounted invoice total.
 *   Input terminates when 0 is read for number of books.
 *
 *   Written by Ray Swartz for "Doing Business with C".
 */

#include "stdio.h"

main()
{
    double getdbl();
    double getdisc();    /* read in customer code, return discount */
    double price;        /* retail price of books ordered */
    double total;        /* invoice total */
    double disc_pct;     /* customer's discount percentage */
    int getint();
    int books;           /* number of books ordered */

    total = 0;           /* initialize invoice total */

    /* First get all the invoice lines */

    while ((books = getint("Number of books ordered")) != 0) {
        price = getdbl("Retail price of books ordered");
        printf("\nTotal of %d books at $%.2f is %.2f\n\n",
                books, price, books * price);
        total = total + books * price;
    }

    /* Now, get customer discount and figure invoice total */

    disc_pct = getdisc();
    printf("\nPre-discount Invoice total: $%.2f\n");
    printf("\nDiscount percentage: %.2f%%\n", disc_pct);
    printf("Invoice total: $%.2f\n", total * (1 - disc_pct));
    exit(0);
}
```

Program 7-4 The chk-inv main( )

total is used to accumulate the invoice total. It must be initialized before its stored value can be used. This is the purpose of the program's first statement

```
total = 0;
```

The functions **getint( )** and **getdbl( )** are the integer and floating-point equivalents of the **getlong( )** function. **get_disc( )** prints a specialized prompt of possible discount codes and then returns the discount percentage that is allowed to this customer based on the code entered.

Program 7-4 uses a **while** loop to control the entry of invoice lines. The **while** loop's stopping test is

```
while ((books = getint("Number of books ordered")) != 0) {
    rest of loop
}
```

At first glance, this combination of an assignment and a logical test may seem incorrect. However, recall the definition of a C expression: *any* combination of operators and operands. In fact, the **while**'s stopping test is a legal (and quite useful) expression.

As Figure 7-3 shows, the loop's stopping test contains three sets of parentheses.

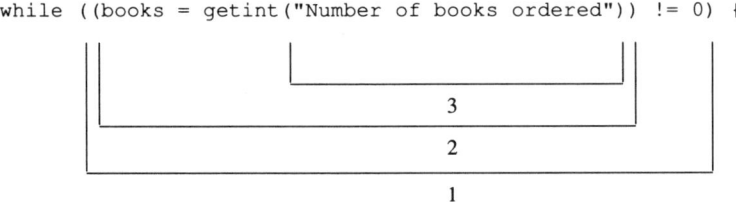

Figure 7-3 Complex Stopping Test

The value returned by **getint( )** is assigned to *books* (1 in Figure 7-3) and then tested for being 0 (2 in Figure 7-3). This way, if 0 is entered, we terminate the invoice line entry loop. Otherwise, we enter the loop with *books* set to the proper value (1 in Figure 7-3). In essence, we are doing two things with one statement—this is a common occurrence in C! For the loop to work properly, the test must occur after the assignment. To make this happen requires the use of parentheses to "rearrange" the operators' precedence. In Figure 7-3, the parentheses labeled 2 enclose the assignment, which is performed before the inequality. Without parentheses the inequality, which has higher precedence, is done first.

This ability to mix operators in an expression in any fashion required by the program at hand is one of the real strengths of the C language. The usage in Figure 7-3 is common; in fact, it soon becomes indispensable!

Sec. 7.5 Designing Programs with Loops

getint( ) and **getdbl( )** are very similar to **getlong( )**. The differences are

1. The data type of the function
2. The conversion function used

getlong( ) is shown as Function 7-3 (same as Function 6-1). Function 7-4 lists **getint( )** and Function 7-5, **getdbl( )**.

```
int getlong(prompt)       /* print a prompt and read in an int */
char prompt[];            /* prompt to print */
{
    char instr[81];       /* input string */
    char *gets();
    int printf();
    long atol();
    long nbr;             /* converted value */

    printf("%s: ",prompt);
    gets(instr);
    nbr = atol(instr);
    return(nbr);
}
```

Function 7-3 The **getlong( )** Function

```
int getint(prompt)        /* print a prompt and read in an int */
char prompt[];            /* prompt to print */
{
    char instr[81];       /* input string */
    char *gets();
    int printf();
    int atoi();

    printf("%s: ",prompt);
    gets(instr);
    return(atoi(instr));
}
```

Function 7-4 The **getint( )** Function

```
int getdbl(prompt)          /* print a prompt and read in a double */
char prompt[];              /* prompt to print */
{
    char instr[81];         /* input string */
    char *gets();
    int printf();
    double atof();

    printf("%s: ",prompt);
    gets(instr);
    return(atof(instr));
}
```

Function 7-5 The getdbl( ) Function

A "cosmetic" change has been made to both **getint( )** and **getdbl( )**. In **getlong( )**, the variable *nbr* is assigned the converted value that then is returned by the function. *nbr* has no other use in **getlong( )**.

In C, a function can be an argument to another function. When this happens, the argument-function is called and its return value then is sent as an argument to the original function. The same is true of the **return** statement. Thus,

```
nbr = atol(instr);
return(nbr);
```

can be replaced with

```
return(atol(nbr));
```

The value returned by **atol( )** is then returned by **getlong( )**. This change has been made to both **getint( )** and **getdbl( )**.

We only need to write the **get_disc( )** function to complete the **chk-inv** program. **get_disc( )** is not sent any arguments. Instead, it prints a specialized prompt, reads the response, and then converts the number entered into the appropriate discount percentage which is returned to **main( )**. The algorithm is listed in Algorithm 7-4.

1. Print prompt of customer classes
2. Prompt for and read the code representing this customer's classification
3. If the code entered is valid, go to (4)
      else print "Invalid Customer Code" and go to (1)
4. Determine the appropriate discount for the code entered
5. Return customer's percentage discount

Algorithm 7-4 The get_disc( ) Algorithm

Sec. 7.5   Designing Programs with Loops

The order department has supplied us with a list of customer classifications and their discounts. These are shown in Table 7-1.

TABLE 7-1   Customer Classes and Related Discounts

Customer type	Discount
High volume retail	9%
Wholesale	12%
High volume wholesale	15%
Mail order company	18.5%
High volume mail order	22%

The **get_disc( )** prompt will identify each available customer class with a number. The prompt displayed by **get_disc( )** is shown in Figure 7-4.

```
1. High volume retail
2. Wholesale
3. High volume wholesale
4. Mail order company
5. High volume mail order

Enter this Customer's Classification Code:
```

Figure 7-4   The **get_disc( )** prompt

The actual discount percentage is left out of the prompt for two reasons. First, the user does not need to know this information and it could cause confusion. Second, discounts often change and keeping them out of the prompt makes implementing such changes easier.

When a number is entered, **get_disc( )** must verify that it is a valid customer code. This means it must be a 1, 2, 3, 4, or 5. If it isn't, the user has made a mistake and **get_disc( )** reports that an invalid response has occurred and then reprompts. It will continue this loop until a valid code is entered.

Assigning the proper discount percentage can be done with a series of **if** - **else if** - **else** tests:

```
if (code == 1)
    discount = .09;      /* high volume retail */
else if (code == 2)
    discount = .12;      /* wholesale */
else if (code == 3);
    discount = .15;      /* high volume wholesale */
else if (code == 4)
    discount = .185;     /* mail order company */
else
    discount = .22;      /* high volume mail order */
```

Incidentally, we don't have to test explicitly if *code* equals 5, because we know *code* is valid (we tested it before we got here) and if *code* is not 1, 2, 3, or 4, it must be 5.

Function 7-6 lists the first version of **get_disc( )**.

```
double get_disc()          /* prompt for and return customer discount % */
{
    int printf();
    int getint();          /* prompts for and reads an int */
    int code;              /* number entered as customer code */
    double discount;       /* percent discount for this customer */

    /* Print prompt and get a valid customer code */

    do {
        printf("\n1. High Volume Retail\n");
        printf("2. Wholesale\n");
        printf("3. High Volume Wholesale\n");
        printf("4. Mail Order Company\n");
        printf("5. High Volume Mail Order\n\n");
        code = getint("Enter this Customer's Classification Code");
        if (code < 1 || code > 5)      /* valid code? */
            printf("\nInvalid Response\n");
    } while ( code < 1 || code > 5);   /* loop until valid */

    /* Assign discount for this customer code */

    if (code == 1)
        discount = .09;    /* high volume retail */
    else if (code == 2)
        discount = .12;    /* wholesale */
    else if (code == 3)
        discount = .15;    /* high volume wholesale */
    else if (code == 4)
        discount = .185;   /* mail order company */
    else
        discount = .22;    /* high volume mail order */
    return(discount);
}
```

Function 7-6 Version 1 of **get_disc( )** Function

7.6 THE switch - case STATEMENT

Function 7-6 uses an **if** - **else** structure to determine which code was entered. All we are doing, however, is repeatedly testing if the variable *code* is equal to a specific integer constant. It is common, especially in interactive programming, to have the user enter an integer code that then is interpreted by successive comparisons.

Sec. 7.6 The **switch-case** Statement

C contains a special construct to handle the specific situation just described, the successive comparison of a variable to a set of integer constants. It is called the **switch** statement. The **switch** statement contains any number of options, called **case**s, that are labeled by an integer.

A **switch** compares an integer variable or expression against each **case** label, executing the section whose label matches the variable's value. If none match, a special optional section, labeled **default**, is executed. If none match and there is no **default** label, all options are skipped and the **switch** statement has no effect. Segment 7-1 shows the **switch** statement that would replace the **if - else** section in Function 7-6.

```
switch (code) {
   case 1: discount = .09;    /* high volume retail */
           break;
   case 2: discount = .12;    /* wholesale */
           break;
   case 3: discount = .15;    /* high volume wholesale */
           break;
   case 4: discount = .185;   /* mail order company */
           break;
   default: discount = .22;   /* high volume mail order */
}
```

Segment 7-1 An Example **switch** Statement

Note that the entire list of **switch** options is enclosed in braces.

As Segment 7-1 shows, each option in a **switch** statement is labeled with the **case** keyword and an integer value followed by a colon. The **case** labels are just that, labels. Once the **switch** statement locates the section to execute, it will continue through the remaining statements (regardless of whether they are labeled or not) until one of two things occurs—the closing brace of the **switch** statement is found or a **break** command is encountered. If the closing brace is found, the **switch** statement terminates and the program continues at the statement following the **switch**. If the keyword **break** is encountered, the rest of the **switch** is skipped and the program immediately continues at the statement following the end of the **switch**.

RULE   All the option sections in a **switch** statement should end with **break**.

Each **case** section in Segment 7-1 ends with **break** because we only want to assign a percentage to *discount* once, that is, when the proper **case** option is executed, we want to exit the **switch** statement. This is accomplished by the **break** statements. The **default** section doesn't end with **break**, because the entire **switch** statement ends after that option, anyway.

A **switch** option can have more than one label. For example, if all wholesale purchasers, whether high-volume or not, received the same discount of 12 percent, the options

```
                case 2: discount = .12;
                        break;
                case 3: discount = .12;
                        break
```

could be combined into one option with 2 **case** labels:

```
                case 2:
                case 3:  discount = .12;
                         break;
```

In addition, the **case** labels can be any value that is an integer constant. Thus, character and special character constants are legal. As an illustration, these are all valid **case**s:

```
                        case 'a':

                        case '\n':

                        case '*':
```

Incidentally, this label

```
                        case 1:
```

and this one

```
                        case '1':
```

are different. The first one matches the value 1 and the second the numeric value in the character set that represents the digit one as a character.

The **case** keyword must precede every integer constant used to label an option. There is no way to specify a *range* of integer values. Each one in the range would have to be listed individually.

The value tested by a **switch** statement must be an integer. It can be an integer variable or an expression that evaluates to an integer. Further, every **case** label must evaluate to a unique integer.

A second version of **get_disc**( ), one containing the **switch** statement in Segment 7-1, is listed as Function 7-7.

```
    double get_disc()      /* prompt for and return customer discount % */
    {
        int printf();
        int getint();      /* prompts for and reads and int */
        int code;          /* number entered as customer code */
        double discount;   /* percent discount for this customer */
```

Sec. 7.6 The switch-case Statement

```
    /* Print prompt and get a valid customer code */

    do {
        printf("\n1. High Volume Retail\n");
        printf("2. Wholesale\n");
        printf("3. High Volume Wholesale\n");
        printf("4. Mail Order Company\n");
        printf("5. High Volume Mail Order\n\n");
        code = getint("Enter this Customer's Classification Code");
        if (code < 1 || code > 5)       /* valid code? */
            printf("\nInvalid Response\n");
    } while ( code < 1 || code > 5);   /* loop until valid */

    /* Assign discount for this customer code */

    switch (code) {
    case 1: discount = .09;     /* high volume retail */
            break;
    case 2: discount = .12;     /* wholesale */
            break;
    case 3: discount = .15;     /* high volume wholesale */
            break;
    case 4: discount = .185;    /* mail order company */
            break;
    default: discount = .22;    /* high volume mail order */
    }
    return(discount);
}
```

Function 7-7 Version 2 of **get_disc( )** Function

By combining the **main( )** listed as Program 7-4 with the **getint( )**, **getdbl( )**, and **get_disc( )** functions, we get the **chk-inv** program. To demonstrate the **chk-inv** program, we will enter the test invoice listed as Figure 7-5.

Customer type: Mail order

Books	Title	Price	Total
12	Title1	24.95	299.40
6	Title2	24.95	149.70
	Total		449.10
	Discount: 18.5%		82.08
	Invoice total		367.02

Figure 7-5 Test Invoice for **chk-inv** Program

The output of the **chk-inv** program is shown in Output 7-2.

```
Number of books ordered: 12
Retail price of books ordered: 24.95

Total of 12 books at $24.95 is 299.40

Number of books ordered: 6
Retail price of books ordered: 24.95

Total of 6 books at $24.95 is 149.70

Number of books ordered: 0

1. High Volume Retail
2. Wholesale
3. High Volume Wholesale
4. Mail Order Company
5. High Volume Mail Order

Enter this Customer's Classification Code: 4

Pre-discount Invoice Total: $449.10

Discount percentage: 18.5%

Invoice total: $366.02
```

Output 7-2

As Output 7-2 shows, the invoice total listed in Figure 7-5 is incorrect. **chk-inv** was written to catch just this kind of error!

7.7 SUMMARY

1. A loop controls the repeated execution of a segment of code.
2. A loop continues to execute a segment of code (called the body of the loop) as long as a logical test evaluates to true.
3. There are two types of loops, those that test at the top of the loop and those that test at the bottom.
4. A **while** loop tests at the top. If the logical test is false the first time, the body of the loop isn't performed at all.
5. The **printf( )** function rounds values printed to a specified number of decimal places.

Sec. 7.7   Summary

6. To round off a value, it is multiplied or divided by a factor of 10 until the spot in the number to be rounded is just to the right of the decimal place. Then, .5 is added to this value and the decimal part is truncated (the number is converted to an integer) and the number adjusted back to its previous size.
7. A **do while** loop tests at the bottom of the loop, after the body has been executed.
8. The main difference between **while** and **do while** loops is that if the logical test is false the first time it is tested **while** loops do not perform the loop's body and **do while** loops do (since the first test will be after the body is performed the first time).
9. The **for** loop is a type of **while** loop. The **for** loop is designed for loops that are to repeat a set number of times. **for** loops have the form

```
for (initialize; test; increment)
    body of loop
```

10. A program's **main( )** should define needed variables, call functions, and perform only simple data manipulation.
11. Loops are commonly controlled by logical expressions that contain several operators.
12. The **switch** statement tests an integer expression against a set of integer values, denoted by the **case** keyword. If the result of the expression matches one of the listed **case** values, the statements following the **case** are executed.
13. The **case** labels are meaningful only while the **switch** expression is being matched against the **case** labels. Once a **case** section is chosen, C will continue down though the rest of the statements that make up the **switch** statement, ignoring the **case** labels entirely.
14. The **break** statement tells C to halt execution of a **switch** statement and to continue after the **switch**'s ending brace. Typically, each **case** section ends with **break**.
15. **case** labels have to be integer or character constants. Several **case** labels can identify the same section of C statements.

E X E R C I S E S

7-3. Write a program that prints a table of the sales tax on a dollar amount. The table should show 5%, 6%, and 6.5% sales tax. The dollar amounts should go from 0 to 10 by 25 cents:

Amount	Tax Amount		
	5%	6%	6.5%
0.25	.02	.02	.02

7-4. Write a general function, called **round( )**, that rounds a **double** value at a spot specified by an integer. If the integer is positive, it is the number of digits to the left of the decimal point. If it is negative, it is the number of digits to the right of the decimal point. For example,

    round(1456.64531, -3)   Rounds to 1456.645
    round(1456.64531, 1)   Rounds to 1460

7-5. The company has decided to implement a pension plan. The required pension contribution for each employee is listed in the following table (the percentages are of gross salary):

Salaried	6%
Full-time	4.2%
Part-time	2.3%
Others	0%

Write a program that calculates the total pension contribution required to cover all employees for a payroll period. The program should prompt the user for how many entries are to be entered and then loop that many times. NOTE: There is no need to read employee names. This is a summary report only.

7-6. Change the program in Exercise 7-5 to stop when 0 is entered as the payroll amount.

7-7. Write a program that calculates the total pension contribution made for a single employee over the lifetime of his or her employment. Assume that the pension percentages remain the same (see Exercise 7-5) and that an employee gets paid the same amount for an entire year.

7-8. Rewrite the program in Exercise 7-7 to read in a payroll amount and the length of time (in months) the employee earned that amount.

7-9. Change the **chk-inv** program to read in the names of each book purchased and print this information in the report.

PART 3
Generalizing Programs

8
A Need for Change

After using **pl-rept2,** Program 6-1, to create profit and loss statements, Johnson's Books needs to change the statement's format. Recently, they began receiving interest on their checking accounts. As a result, they earned interest that must appear on their P&L statement. While this change is simple for us to make, it points out a problem with the program. It must be changed whenever a change is needed in the P&L format.

Businesses are dynamic organizations that require flexible accounting and financial reporting systems. Our business application programs must be easy to adapt to different situations. We cannot expect users to modify the source code of a program, no matter how simple such a change seems to us as programmers.

One way to make our P&L statement program more flexible is to have users enter both the category name and amount of a revenue or cost. Then, changing or adding a category is done easily by the user. This approach differs significantly from Program 6-1 (the current P&L program) that allows entries in specified categories only. In essence, we must make the program produce a *generalized* P&L statement instead of a specific one.

The only change needed is to allow the entry of a revenue or cost category, as well as an amount. This involves three steps.

1. Print a prompt for a category
2. Read the category
3. Prompt for and read this category's amount

We can read the category with **gets( )** and the dollar amount with our **getlong( )** function. Since our program must read several categories, we will create a function called **getcat( )** that is passed a string variable to hold the entered name and returns the amount entered.

Before we write **getcat( )**, we must resolve a problem. How will **getcat( )** know whether it is getting a revenue or cost category? This is important so **getcat( )** can prompt the user correctly. For revenues the prompt is

```
               Enter a Revenue Category:
```

and for costs

```
               Enter a Cost Category:
```

The simplest solution is sending **getcat( )** an additional argument that is the string *Revenue* or *Cost*. This argument will be inserted into **getcat( )**'s prompt. **getcat( )** is shown as Function 8-1.

```
long getcat(catstr, class)
char catstr[];     /* string variable for entered category */
char class[];      /* category classification (Revenue or Cost) */
{
    char *gets();
    int printf();
    long getlong();    /* prints a prompt and reads long */

    printf("\nEnter a %s Category (30 Character Maximum): ", class);
    gets(catstr);                 /* read category name */
    return(getlong(catstr));      /* return amount entered */
}
```

Function 8-1 The **getcat()** Function

getcat( ) is sent two arguments. As required, both are declared as formal parameters. The formal parameter *catstr* represents the string to store the entered category name and *class* represents the string *Revenue* or *Cost*. In Function 8-1, these two parameters are declared *outside* the braces that enclose the statements executed by **getcat( )** but below the definition of the function's name. This is how formal parameters are declared. If more arguments were sent to the function, more parameters would be listed here.

We chose thirty characters as the maximum for a category name. This is an arbitrary length, but some reasonable limit is necessary to preserve the format of the P&L statement. This limitation must be reflected in category name variables, as well. Also, the prompt sent to **getlong( )** is a string variable rather than a string constant. This does not require any changes in **getlong( )** because it handles either alternative in the same way. In fact, **getlong( )** won't even know the difference!

Chap. 8 A Need for Change

The **getcat( )** function reads the entered category name into *catstr*, a local variable. For **getcat( )** to work properly, the name put into *catstr* must get stored in the argument *represented* by *catstr*, as well. We know that local variables get created each time the function is called and disappear when it terminates. But, what happens when we modify a formal parameter, the local variable that represents one of the function's arguments? Does the category name entered vanish when **getcat( )** returns?

As written in Function 8-1, **getcat( )** does store the category name into the string variable represented by *catstr* (i.e., the argument passed to **getcat( )**). Is this a contradiction? No, because *catstr* is declared as a **char** *dummy variable* (i.e., a string variable). This alerts C that *catstr* identifies the contiguous memory locations where the string variable sent to **getcat( )** as an argument stores characters. Storing characters "in" *catstr* actually puts them in the original string's memory locations. Since *catstr* is a dummy variable, using *catstr* is like using the actual string argument itself. This is why **getcat( )** works properly!

However, it must be emphasized that the changes made to local variables are local to the function where they are made. The only exception to this rule is when we are modifying a dummy variable. This will be discussed in depth in Part 4.[1]

Exercise 8-1   At present, **getcat( )** prints that the maximum number of characters allowed in a category name is thirty. Modify **getcat( )** to take this limit as an argument.

Before we can write a P&L program to read both the categories and amounts, we must know the number of revenue and cost categories, so we can define the variables required to store them. Let's assume that the P&L statement has three revenue and five cost categories. This is the format of the P&L statement needed by Johnson's Books.

Each category requires two variables: a string for the name and a **long** for the amount. Figure 8-1 shows the variables we will use.

```
char rv_cat1[31];       /* revenue category 1 */
char rv_cat2[31];       /* revenue category 2 */
char rv_cat3[31];       /* revenue category 3 */
char cs_cat1[31];       /* cost category 1 */
char cs_cat2[31];       /* cost category 2 */
[char cs_cat3[31];      /* cost category 3 */
char cs_cat4[31];       /* cost category 4 */
char cs_cat5[31];       /* cost category 5 */
long rev1;              /* amount in revenue category 1 */
long rev2;              /* amount in revenue category 2 */
long rev3;              /* amount in revenue category 3 */
long cost1;             /* amount in cost category 1 */
long cost2;             /* amount in cost category 2 */
```

---

[1] In reality, this is not an exception at all. We simply don't know enough about C's features at this point to understand what's really happening. Explanation of this is deferred until Part 4, where *pointers* are discussed.

```
long cost3;         /* amount in cost category 3 */
long cost4;         /* amount in cost category 4 */
long cost5;         /* amount in cost category 5 */
long totalrev;      /* total revenue */
long totalcost;     /* total cost */
```

Figure 8-1 Variables for a General P&L Program

This program is called **gnrl-pl**. The entry section for **gnrl-pl** calls **getcat( )** once for each category. All we must do is substitute the proper variables as shown in Segment 8-1.

```
/*  ***** GNRL-PL *****
 *
 * This program formats a profit and loss statement
 * with 3 revenue and 5 cost categories.  The user
 * enters both the category name and the amount
 *
 * Written by Ray Swartz for "Doing Business with C"
 */

#include "stdio.h"

main()
{
    int printf();
    char rv_cat1[31];     /* revenue category 1 */
    char rv_cat2[31];     /* revenue category 2 */
    char rv_cat3[31];     /* revenue category 3 */
    char cs_cat1[31];     /* cost category 1 */
    char cs_cat2[31];     /* cost category 2 */
    char cs_cat3[31];     /* cost category 3 */
    char cs_cat4[31];     /* cost category 4 */
    char cs_cat5[31];     /* cost category 5 */
    long getcat();        /* read in category name and amount */
    long rev1;            /* amount in revenue category 1 */
    long rev2;            /* amount in revenue category 2 */
    long rev3;            /* amount in revenue category 3 */
    long cost1;           /* amount in cost category 1 */
    long cost2;           /* amount in cost category 2 */
    long cost3;           /* amount in cost category 3 */
    long cost4;           /* amount in cost category 4 */
    long cost5;           /* amount in cost category 5 */
    long totalrev;        /* total revenue on P&L report */
    long totalcost;       /* total cost on P&L report */

    printf("Enter Dollars amounts only -- no cents\n");
    printf("\n\nREVENUES\n\n");
```

Chap. 8 A Need for Change

```
        rev1 = getcat(rv_cat1, "Revenue");
        rev2 = getcat(rv_cat2, "Revenue");
        rev3 = getcat(rv_cat3, "Revenue");
        printf("\n\nCOSTS\n\n");
        cost1 = getcat(cs_cat1, "Cost");
        cost2 = getcat(cs_cat2, "Cost");
        cost3 = getcat(cs_cat3, "Cost");
        cost4 = getcat(cs_cat4, "Cost");
        cost5 = getcat(cs_cat5, "Cost");
        report printing section

/*      ***** GETCAT *****
 *
 * This function prompts for a revenue or cost category
 * name (depending on the string stored in the argument
 * class), reads the name entered, then calls getlong()
 * to read the amount for this category.
 * Written by Ray Swartz for "Doing Business with C"
 */

long getcat(catstr, class)
char catstr[];      /* string variable for entered category */
char class[];       /* category classification (Revenue or Cost) */
{
    char *gets();
    int printf();
    long getlong();   /* prints a prompt and reads long */

    printf("\nEnter a %s Category (30 Character Maximum): ", class);
    gets(catstr);                   /* read category name */
    return(getlong(catstr));        /* return amount entered */
}
```

Segment 8-1 The Data Entry Section of the **gnrl-pl** Program

We did not use a loop because no two statements are the same. Each category requires different variables.

The P&L report can be printed in much the same way as in previous programs. The only difference is that string variables are used instead of string constants to print category names. To print each category requires one **printf( )** statement.

At first glance, we might use this **printf( )** statement to print the first revenue line:

```
            printf("%30s   $%6ld\n",rv_cat1, rev1);
```

Recall that

```
                                %6ld
```

tells **printf( )** the minimum width for the listed **long** value. Should the printed value be less than 6 digits, the computer will fill with blanks on the left if necessary. We call this *right-justified* output because the numbers (or characters) are printed against the right side of the print field. The specification

```
                         %30s
```

tells **printf( )** the same thing, except for a string, not a number. This will display a string in a right-justified 30 character field. For example, suppose the first revenue category is SALES and the amount is 43660. The above **printf( )** displays

```
              SALES  $  43660
```

This right-justifies the category name, but we want them left-justified, that is, with the name to the left, in the P&L report. To make **printf( )** *left-justify* an argument, place a hyphen before the width specifier, as in

```
                         %-30s.
```

For example, the statement

```
           printf("%-30s  $%6ld\n",rv_cat1, rev1);
```

prints

```
              SALES                        $43660
```

We can use this **printf( )** statement for each category line in the P&L report. The only changes required are in the arguments.

To complete the P&L report, we must total the revenue and cost amounts and print this year's profit/loss. We also must provide section headings. Segment 8-2 contains the program segment that prints the P&L statement.

```
data entry section
printf("\tProfit and Loss for Johnson's Books\n\n");
printf("          REVENUE\n\n");
printf("%-30s  $%6ld\n", rv_cat1, rev1);
printf("%-30s  $%6ld\n", rv_cat2, rev2);
printf("%-30s  $%6ld\n", rv_cat3, rev3);
totalrev = rev1 + rev2 + rev3;   /* total revenue amounts */
printf("                              ------\n");
printf("        TOTAL REVENUE            $%7ld\n",
        totalrev);
printf("\n\n");
printf("          COSTS\n\n");
printf("%-30s  $%6ld\n", cs_cat1, cost1);
printf("%-30s  $%6ld\n", cs_cat2, cost2);
```

```
              printf("%-30s     $%6ld\n", cs_cat3, cost3);
              printf("%-30s     $%6ld\n", cs_cat4, cost4);
              printf("%-30s     $%6ld\n", cs_cat5, cost5);

                     /* total cost amounts */

              totalcost = cost1 + cost2 + cost3 + cost4 + cost5;
              printf("                                    ------\n");
              printf("          TOTAL COSTS            $%7ld\n\n",
                     totalcost);
              if (totalrev >= totalcost)
                  printf("          PROFIT                 $%7ld\n",
                         totalrev - totalcost);
              else
                  printf("          LOSS                  ($%7ld)\n",
                         totalcost - totalrev);
              exit(0);
```

Segment 8-2 Report Printing Section of **gnrl-pl** Program

Although this program lets us enter both categories and amounts, it doesn't provide any flexibility. The user is locked into a three-revenue, five-cost profit and loss statement. This is unacceptable.

A better design is to allow a variable number of revenue and cost categories and corresponding amounts. This is not difficult to achieve.

8.1 DATA ARRAYS

By creating **getcat( )**, we have reduced reading a revenue or cost component's name and category amount to a single function call. Unfortunately, to hold all the data entered, each call to **getcat( )** needs two unique variables—one for the name and one for the amount. At present, individual variables are defined specifically to hold the information entered in a single category. This approach offers no flexibility. Every program produces a single P&L format only. Once compiled, these P&L programs always read and print the same number of revenue and cost categories.

We could eliminate this restriction if we had a general way to assign unique variable names. Then, a single statement, a generalized **getcat( )** call, could be repeated inside a loop to enter any number of revenue or cost components. Generalized variable names exist and are called an *array*.

An array is a block of memory that is given a *single name*. It contains a specific number of *elements*, each of which is identified by a number called an *index*. Arrays add flexibility to a program because an individual array element can be indexed with a variable. This allows us to write compact code that performs very large tasks!

In Segment 8-1, three variables are needed to store the revenue amounts entered: *rev1*, *rev2*, and *rev3*. These variables are stored in memory as three individual **long**s that must be specifically named in a C statement. This is pictured in Figure 8-2.

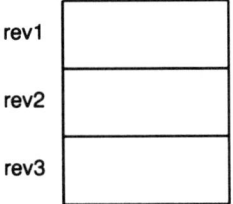

Figure 8-2 Three Individual **long** Variables

Using an array to represent these values requires the same space (three **long**s). However, all of an array's members are identified by the same name. A particular element is refered to by an integer index combined with the array's name. The array index is enclosed in *brackets* and the first member of an array is element number 0. As an example, if *rev_amt* is an array that contains three **long** elements, the three elements are identified by

rev_amt[0]	the first array element
rev_amt[1]	the second array element
rev_amt[2]	the third array element

The *rev_amt* array is pictured in Figure 8-3.

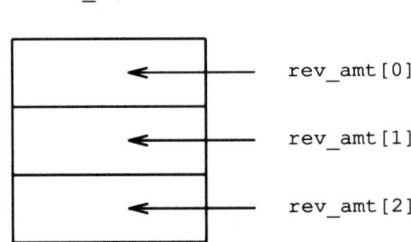

Figure 8-3 An Array with Three **long** Elements

RULE An array element's index is enclosed in brackets.

RULE The first element in an array is element number 0.

Once an array's elements are created (i.e., defined), a single element can be used in place of a variable. Thus,

```
rev1 = getcat(rv_cat1, "Revenue");
```

and

```
rev_amt[0] = getcat(rv_cat1, "Revenue");
```

Sec. 8.1 Data Arrays

are equivalent statements. Further,

```
rev_total = rev1 + rev2 + rev3;
```

can be replaced by

```
rev_total = rev_amt[0] + rev_amt[1] + rev_amt[2];
```

As with any variable, we must define an array before using it. Besides the standard information (data type and name), array definitions must supply the number of elements, also.

The first step in converting the **gnrl-pl** program to use arrays is creating the revenue and cost data arrays. Let's call the revenue array *rev_amt* and the cost array *cost_amt*. Both arrays store **long** values. In **gnrl-pl**, three revenue categories are entered. *rev_amt* is defined by

```
long rev_amt[3];
  ↑       ↑       ↑
 Type   Name   Number of Elements
```

Note the square brackets in this array definition. The brackets identify the number of elements in the array. Further, the definition of array elements must be specified with an integer constant.

RULE   Arrays must be defined before they can be used.

RULE   The number of elements listed in an array definition must be an integer constant.

Exercise 8-2   Rewrite Segment 8-1 to use the *rev_amt* and *cost_amt* arrays.

Substituting *rev_amt* and *cost_amt* into Segment 8-1 has no meaningful effect (see the answer to Exercise 8-2). The same number of statements is required to read the same number of revenue and cost categories. Further, the program still has no flexibility because we still need a unique statement for each category entered.

At first glance, it seems that arrays don't add anything to the **gnrl-pl** program. This is because we haven't yet taken full advantage of arrays. Our previous array example only used integer constants to index the *rev_amt* array. However, an array index can be any integer expression, that is, an expression that contains integer constants, variables, or both. (This includes **short**s, **long**s, and **unsigned**s, as well as **int**.) For example, if *count* is defined as an **int**, then

```
count = 0;
rev_amt[count] = getcat(rv_cat1, "Revenue");
```

performs the same as

```
rev_amt[0] = getcat(rv_cat1, "Revenue");
```

If an expression is used, the expression is evaluated and the resulting integer is used as the array index. Thus,

```
count = 0;
rev_amt[count + 1] = getcat(...);
```

is the same as

```
rev_amt[1] = getcat(...);
```

For this to work properly, the expression inside the brackets must always be evaluated before the array element is referenced. Put another way, brackets must have very high precedence. In fact, brackets have the highest precedence and are just like parentheses. The only distinction between brackets and parentheses is that brackets are used with arrays and parentheses are used everywhere else!

RULE Brackets are operators that represent array elements. Brackets have the highest precedence, equivalent to parentheses. Any expression inside brackets is evaluated before that array element is indexed.

The ability to index array elements with variables is the key to creating flexible application programs. It also allows us to use a minimum of code when writing these programs. By combining a **for** loop and an array, we can refer to an almost unlimited amount of information. For example, this **for** loop

```
for (count = 0; count < 3; count = count + 1)
    rev_amt[count] = getcat(...);
```

gets three revenue categories. By changing the test value to 5, the same code reads five revenue categories:

```
for (count = 0; count < 5; count = count + 1)
    rev_amt[count] = getcat(...);
```

We can use this powerful combination of arrays and loops to provide the flexibility needed in the **grnl-pl** program.

Unfortunately, there is a complication. Each category is represented by both a name and an amount. Before we can use a **for** loop to enter revenue (or cost) categories, we must create arrays to hold the category names, as well as the amounts. So far, we only know how to define numeric arrays, that is, arrays that store numbers. Strings and arrays of strings act a bit differently than arrays that hold numeric values. As a result, we must know more about string arrays before we add them to **gnrl-pl**. This is the focus of the next chapter.

8.2 SUMMARY

1. Business programs need to be flexible and easily adapted to different situations.
2. Changes made to formal parameters declared as dummy variables (i.e., string variables) are made to the variables passed to the function and represented by the formal parameters.
3. One way to generalize a program is to use string variables instead of string constants.
4. **printf( )** normally right justifies strings when a field width is specified. **printf( )** will left justify a string if a minus sign is put in front of the field width specifier.
5. An array is a block of memory with a single name. Each variable element inside this block of memory can be accessed by the array name and an index enclosed in brackets.
6. The first element in an array is element number 0.
7. An array index must be an integer but need not be a constant. Indexing an array with an integer variable greatly increases a program's flexibility.
8. The real power of arrays comes when they are combined with loops. In this way, the same set of statements can handle virtually any amount of data.

E X E R C I S E S

8-3. Write a program that reads in the daily sales for a period. The program should ask the user how many day's sales are to be entered and then prompt for that much data. The program prints a report that lists the sales for the period in the order they were entered, the total sales for the period, and the daily average (mean). Assume no more than fifty day's data will be entered.

8-4. Change the program in Exercise 8-3 to get a beginning date and then to prompt by date for each day's sales (be sure to handle dates that span months and years). The program should also print a title on the report that lists the days covered.

8-5. The accounts receivable department (the people who collect money owed by customers) has requested an account aging report. The report is to show the "age" of the accounts receivables. The age of a receivable is the number of days between the present date and the date of the invoice. Write a program that reads in a number of days since an invoice was issued and the amount of an invoice, stores the amount into one of these four aging categories: 0-30 days, 31-60 days, 61-90 days, and 91+ days. Write the program so that this is done until some quit signal is entered and then the program prints a report of the totals in each aging category.

8-6. In Exercise 8-5, the four aging categories are set to 0-30, 31-60, 61-90, and 91+. Rewrite the program in Exercise 8-5 to allow the user to enter the number of days in each aging category. Allow four aging categories. Be sure to verify that the categories are consistent.

8-7. Modify the program in Exercise 8-5 or 8-6 to prompt for the current date when the program begins and then to read the date and amount of each receivable. The program is to identify which category is appropriate for each receivable.

9

Strings and String Arrays

The definition of a string variable is similar to the definition of a numeric array. For example,

```
char rv_cat1[31];
```

creates a variable to hold the name of a revenue category and

```
long rev_amt[3];
```

defines an array to hold the values entered in three revenue categories. As this similarity suggests, string variables are actually *character arrays* and

```
char rv_cat1[31];
```

defines *rv_cat1* to be an array of thirty-one character elements.

However, character arrays are different than numeric arrays in one important way. The elements in a numeric array are treated as individual variables, but a character array's elements are handled as part of an entire string. Whenever we use the variable *rv_cat1*, we refer to all the characters stored in the *rv_cat1* array as a single string. As an illustration, suppose that the user entered

Sales

as the first revenue category. C stores the string as

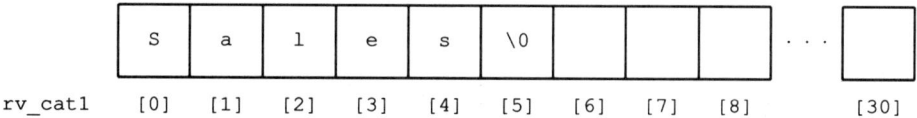

Now, when we use only the array name, as in

```
printf("%s\n", rv_cat1);
```

we refer to the entire string.

In addition to using the entire string, we also can refer to the individual characters that make up the string. Since a string variable is a character array, we can use an index to identify one of the array's elements. Thus,

```
rv_cat1[1]
```

is the second character in *rv_cat1* (remember C's arrays begin with element 0). In this case, it is the "a" in *Sales*.

In Chapter 8, this **for** loop was listed as a way to enter any number of revenue categories:

```
for (count = 0; count < 3; count = count + 1)
    rev_amt[count] = getcat(...);
```

However, before this example will work properly, we must be able to refer to strings the same way we identify array elements. That is, we need an *array of strings*. This requires us to create an *array of character arrays*. This is why an ellipsis (the ...) is shown for **getcat( )**'s arguments.

This reference,

```
rv_cat1[count]
```

is to a single character, not an entire string. Thus,

```
rev_amt[count] = getcat(rv_cat1[count], "Revenue");
```

won't work properly.

We will call an array of character arrays a *string array*. A string array is just what it sounds like, an array of strings. In an array of strings, each element is a string!

In an array, all elements are the same data type. This is required. For a string array, this means each string in the array is the same length. Thus, defining a string array requires one more piece of information besides data type, array name, and number of array elements (strings, in this case). We also must specify the length of the string elements. The following definition establishes a string array named *rev_cat* that holds five strings of 31 characters each:

```
char rev_cat [5] [31];
```

    ↑   ↑   ↑   ↑
Type Array Number Length of
        name   of   each string
                strings

Note that we use two sets of square brackets—one for the number of strings in the array and one for the number of characters in each string—and that no comma is placed between them.

    RULE A string array is defined with two sets of brackets. The first is how many strings the array holds and the second is the number of characters in each string. The two sets of brackets are *not* separated by a comma.

Since array indexes begin at 0, *rev_cat* stores five strings, numbered 0 through 4. Like other arrays, each element (string) in *rev_cat* is refered to by the array name and the string's index.

    The first string is *rev_cat[0]*.

    The second string is *rev_cat[1]*.

    The third string is *rev_cat[2]*.

    The fourth string is *rev_cat[3]*.

    The fifth and last string is *rev_cat[4]*.

Thus, the variable

```
rev_cat[0]
```

refers to a thirty-one-character string, which is the first element in the string array *rev_cat*. As does this,

```
count = 0;
rev_cat[count]
```

We could read a string into this element with

```
gets(rev_cat[0]);
```

Chap. 9 Strings and String Arrays

or print it with

```
                printf("%s\n", rev_cat[0]);
```

An individual character in one of the strings in a string array must be refered to with two indexes. The first index identifies the string and the second one the character in that string. For example,

```
                        rev_cat[0][5]
```

is the sixth character of the first string in the *rev_amt* array.

As an illustration, let's rewrite the **gnrl-pl** program to use arrays. At present, this version reads three revenue and five cost categories (see Segments 8-1 and 8-2).

To store the revenue and cost information, we will use these arrays:

```
        long rev_amt[3];         /* revenue amounts */
        long cost_amt[5];        /* cost amounts */
        char rev_cat[3][31];     /* revenue category names */
        char cost_cat[5][31];    /* cost category names */
```

Since we now have arrays for both parts of a category entry, the input of each section can be done with loops. This loop will read three revenue categories

```
        for (count = 0; count < 3; count = count + 1)
            rev_amt[count] = getcat(rev_cat[count], "Revenue");
```

The cost entry loop is quite similar:

```
        for (count = 0; count < 5; count = count + 1)
            cost_amt[count] = getcat(cost_cat[count], "Cost");
```

Segment 9-1 shows the data input section of **gnrl-pl** written to use arrays and loops.

```
/*   ***** GNRL-PL *****
 *
 * This program formats a profit and loss statement
 * with 3 revenue and 5 cost categories.  The user
 * enters both the category name and the amount.
 *
 * Written by Ray Swartz for "Doing Business with C"
 *
 * Modified to use arrays
 */

#include "stdio.h"
#include "getcat.c"    /* source code for the getcat function */
```

```
main()
{
    int printf();
    int count;                  /* loop counter */
    long getcat();              /* read in category name and amount */
    long rev_amt[3];            /* revenue amounts */
    long cost_amt[5];           /* cost amounts */
    long totalcost;             /* total of all cost amounts */
    long totalrev;              /* total of all revenue amounts */
    char rev_cat[3][31];        /* revenue category names */
    char cost_cat[5][31];       /* cost category names */

    printf("Enter Dollar amounts only -- no cents\n");
    printf("\n\nREVENUES\n\n");
    for (count = 0; count < 3; count = count + 1)
        rev_amt[count] = getcat(rev_cat[count], "Revenue");
    printf("\n\nCOSTS\n\n");
    for (count = 0; count < 3; count = count + 1)
        cost_amt[count] = getcat(cost_cat[count], "Cost");
    report printing section
```

Segment 9-1 Data Input Section of **gnrl-pl** Using Arrays

The variables *totalcost* and *totalrev* are used in the report printing section of the program. Also, we have chosen to **#include** the source code of the **getcat( )** function instead of listing it in this program file. Recall that the **#include** directive tells C to replace the **#include** line with the contents of the file listed in quotes. Function 9-1 lists the file **getcat.c**.

```
/*      ***** GETCAT *****
 *
 * This function prompts for a revenue or cost category
 * name (depending on the string stored in the argument
 * class), reads the name entered, then calls getlong()
 * to read the amount for this category.  The amount entered
 * is returned by getcat.
 *
 * Written by Ray Swartz for "Doing Business with C".
 */

#include "getlong.c"    /* source code of getlong function */

long getcat(catstr, class)
char catstr[];          /* string variable for entered category name */
char class[];           /* category classification (Revenue or Cost) */
{
    char *gets();
    int printf();
```

```
            long getlong();      /* prints a prompt and reads long value */

            printf("\nEnter a %s Category (30 Character Maximum): ", class);
            gets(catstr);                /* read category name */
            return(getlong(catstr));     /* return amount entered */
        }
```

Function 9-1   Contents of **getcat.c** File

The **getcat.c** file contains more than the source code for the **getcat( )** function. It also **#include**s the **getlong.c** file, which holds the source code for the **getlong( )** function. Since **getcat( )** calls **getlong( )**, when the code for **getcat( )** is **#include**d in a program the **getlong( )** function must get **#include**d too. This is another feature of the **#include** command—**#include**s can be nested, that is, an **#include**d file can direct the compiler to **#include** other files (which can contain **#include** directives as well). The nesting level of **#include** files is limited by each compiler. Check the compiler's documentation for this limitation.[1] Function 9-2 lists the contents of the **getlong.c** file.

```
        /* ***** GETLONG *****
         * This function prints a prompt (passed in as an argument)
         * and reads and converts the value entered.  The converted
         * value is returned by getlong.
         *
         * Written by Ray Swartz for "Doing Business with C"
         */

        long getlong(prompt)   /* print prompt and read a long */
        char prompt[];
        {
            char instr[81];    /* input string */
            char *gets();
            int printf();
            long atol();

            printf("%s: ", prompt);
            gets(instr);
            return(atol(instr));
        }
```

Function 9-2   Contents of the **getlong.c** File

Because we are using arrays to read the revenue and cost information, we must rewrite the part of the program that formats the report. The same changes are necessary here as in the data entry section—substituting array elements for individual variables and using **for** loops to print array data. Much of the program's printing simply labels

---

[1] The ANSI standard sets this nesting level at 8.

the report. These lines need not be changed. However, we must update the **printf( )** statements responsible for displaying the individual categories and amounts.

All category entries, whether revenue or cost, are printed in the same format:

```
printf("%-30s $%6ld\n", category name, amount);
```

With arrays, we only need one general **printf( )** statement enclosed in a controlling **for** loop. To print the revenue categories, we use this loop

```
for (count = 0; count < 3; count = count + 1)
    printf("%-30s $%6ld\n", rev_cat[count], rev_amt[count]);
```

Printing cost entries is done with

```
for (count = 0; count < 5; count = count + 1)
    printf("%-30s $%6ld\n", cost_cat[count], cost_amt[count]);
```

The output section of **gnrl-pl** does more than print the names and amounts entered. It also totals revenues and costs to determine if we earned a profit or not. In the previous version of **gnrl-pl**, the revenue and cost amounts were summed in one statement, such as

```
totalrev = rev1 + rev2 + rev3;
```

This approach forces us to decide how many revenue and cost categories are entered before we compile the program. This removes all flexibility from this program.

A better idea is to sum the revenue and cost components inside the printing **for** loops. The loops perform one iteration for each element in the revenue and cost arrays. During each iteration we can add the element indexed by the loop counter to the total variable, either *totalrev* or *totalcost*. These variables *accumulate* the totals as the loop progresses and, as a result, they are called *accumulators*.

For example, this statement adds the revenue category indexed by *count* to whatever is stored in *totalrev* at present:

```
totalrev = totalrev + rev_amt[count];
```

When *count* has indexed all the loop's elements, *totalrev* will store the total of the revenue amounts. Thus, to add the category amounts, we only have to insert this addition into the output printing **for** loops. The revenue printing loop becomes

```
for (count = 0; count < 3; count = count + 1) {
    printf("%-30s $%6ld\n", rev_cat[count], rev_amt[count]);
    totalrev = totalrev + rev_amt[count];
}
```

Chap. 9 Strings and String Arrays

The cost loop becomes

```
for (count = 0; count < 5; count = count + 1) {
   printf("%-30s  $%6ld\n", cost_cat[count], cost_amt[count]);
   totalcost = totalcost + cost_amt[count];
}
```

Note that we enclosed the loop body in braces. This is required because the loop consists of more than one statement.

Summing the revenue and cost entries in the printing loops works properly only under one condition, that the accumulating variable is set to 0 before the loop begins. Otherwise, whatever value is stored in the accumulator will be added to the category totals. This is critical in C because local variables are not set to any value when they are created; they simply contain whatever value happens to be in memory at the time. Thus, we must explicitly initialize both *totalrev* and *totalcost* to 0 before each print loop. This is done by

```
totalrev = 0;
```

and

```
totalcost = 0;
```

RULE Local variables are not initialized to any value.

RULE Accumulator variables must be initialized to 0 before use.

Segment 9-2 lists the report printing section of the **gnrl-pl** program that uses arrays.

```
data entry section
printf("\tProfit and Loss for Johnson's Books\n\n");
printf("          REVENUE\n\n");

/* Loop to print and total the revenue categories */

totalrev = 0;
for (count = 0; count < 3; count = count + 1) {
   printf("%-30s  $%6ld\n", rev_cat[count], rev_amt[count]);
   totalrev = totalrev + rev_amt[count];
}
printf("                                ------\n");
printf("      TOTAL REVENUE           $%7ld\n\n\n",
       totalrev);
```

```
    /* Loop to print and total the cost categories */

    totalcost = 0;
    for (count = 0; count < 5; count = count + 1) {
        printf("%-30s   $%6ld\n", cost_cat[count], cost_amt[count]);
        totalcost = totalcost + cost_amt[count];
    }
    printf("                                    ------\n");
    printf("         TOTAL COST                  $%7ld\n\n\n",
            totalcost);
    if (totalrev >= totalcost)
        printf("         PROFIT                      $%7ld\n",
                totalrev - totalcost);
    else
        printf("         LOSS                       ($%7ld)\n",
                totalcost - totalrev);
    exit(0);
}
```

Segment 9-2 Report Printing Section of **gnrl-pl** Using Arrays

The **gnrl-pl** program that results from combining Segments 9-1 and 9-2 prints a profit and loss statement after reading exactly three revenue and five cost categories. This means that Segments 9-1 and 9-2 perform the same task as Segments 8-1 and 8-2. However by employing arrays in Segments 9-1 and 9-2, we have set the stage for creating a flexible P&L formatting program.

All the P&L programs we have written so far are limited to a specific number of revenue and cost entries. The problem is that the components of a business's profit and loss statement change all the time. Thus, our program must adapt to whatever number of revenue and cost categories the user presently needs. As we shall see, this is a straightforward extension of Segments 9-1 and 9-2.

The first step in extending Segments 9-1 and 9-2 to handle any number of revenue and cost entries is determining how the **gnrl-pl** program is limited. First, the arrays that hold the information entered are defined with a specific number of elements. Second, the data entry loops are controlled by constants. As a result, the arrays can't store more information nor can the loops read it.

One way to solve these problems is to define the arrays to a set maximum size (say twenty elements) and then have the user specify the number of revenue and cost categories to be entered. We then use these values to control the entry and printing loops. This change adds the flexibility we are seeking. The algorithm for this new program, called **flex-pl**, is listed as Algorithm 9-1.

1. Define arrays to hold twenty elements
2. Prompt for and read number of revenue categories to be entered and store this value in *rev_count*
3. Read *rev_count* number of revenue entries

4. Prompt for and read number of cost categories to be entered and store this value in *cost_count*

5. Read *cost_count* number of cost entries

6. Print the P&L statement

Algorithm 9-1 Algorithm for **flex-pl**

As usual, **main( )** will call a separate function to perform each step in Algorithm 9-1. The **main( )** that implements Algorithm 9-1 is shown as Program 9-1.

```
/* ***** FLEX-PL *****
 *
 * This program reads the category and amount of a set of
 * revenues and costs and prints a formatted P&L statement.
 * The program prompts the user for how many revenue
 * and cost categories will be entered.
 * The program then prompts for and reads that number
 * of entries.
 *
 * Written by Ray Swartz for "Doing Business with C"
 */

#include "stdio.h"
#include "getcat.c"       /* source code for getcat function */
#include "getint.c"       /* source code for getint function */
                          /* getint is used in cat_nbr() */
main()
{
    char rev_cat[20][31]; /* revenue categories entered */
    char cost_cat[20][31]; /* cost categories entered */
    int rev_count;        /* number of revenue categories */
    int cost_count;       /* number of cost categories */
    int cat_nbr();        /* get number of category entries */
    long cost_amt[20];    /* cost amounts entered */
    long rev_amt[20];     /* revenue amounts entered */
    void getrev();        /* read all revenue entries */
    void getcost();       /* read all cost entries */
    void print_pl();      /* print the P&L statement */
```

```
    rev_count = cat_nbr("Revenue", 20);   /* get number of revenue entries */
    getrev(rev_cat, rev_amt, rev_count);  /* get revenue entries */
    cost_count = cat_nbr("Cost", 20);     /* get number of cost entries */
    getcost(cost_cat, cost_amt, cost_count); /* get cost entries */
    print_pl(rev_cat, rev_amt, rev_count,
         cost_cat, cost_amt, cost_count);
    exit(0);
}
```

Program 9-1 main( ) Routine of **flex-pl**

The *rev_cat*, *rev_amt*, *cost_cat*, and *cost_amt* arrays are sent as arguments to several of the functions in **flex-pl**. This process is explained below. Also, as called for in the algorithm, we have increased the number of array elements to twenty. However, we have maintained the maximum string length at thirty-one characters to preserve the format of the P&L statement.

flex_pl contains three functions, **getrev( )**, **getcost**, and **print_pl( )**, which perform a task but have no need to return information back to **main( )**. Recall that such functions are defined as data type **void**. **void** tells the compiler to insure that these functions are never used on the right side of an assignment statement or in an expression.

The **cat_nbr( )** function takes two arguments, a category type and a maximum. It prompts the user for the number of categories of the specified type to be entered. The user's response is tested against the maximum argument before **cat_nbr( )** returns this number to the calling routine. If the number entered is too large, **cat_nbr( )** loops, reprompting for a valid entry. The **cat_nbr( )** function is listed as Function 9-3.

```
/* ***** CAT_NBR *****
 *
 * This function prompts the user to specify the number
 * of categories to be entered.  This value is tested
 * against the max argument for size and, if valid,
 * is returned to the calling routine.
 *
 * Written by Ray Swartz for "Doing Business with C"
 */

int cat_nbr(type, max)
char type[];       /* Revenue or Cost */
int max;           /* maximum number of entries allowed */
{
    int printf();
    int getint();
    int nbr;       /* number entered */

    do {
        printf("\n%s categories to enter: ", type);
```

```
            if ((nbr = getint("")) > max)
                printf("\nOnly %d categories allowed\n", max);
        } while (nbr > max);    /* loop until a valid number is entered */
        return(nbr);
}
```

Function 9-3   The **cat_nbr( )** Function

To ensure a valid number of categories is entered, what **getint( )** returns is first stored in *nbr* and then tested against *max*. If the value entered is too large, an error message is displayed and the **do while** loop repeats.

cat_nbr( ) calls the **getint( )** function to read and convert the number of categories entered by the user. **getint( )** expects a prompt to be sent as an argument. However, **cat_nbr( )** gets the number of both revenue and cost categories. The prompt required by **cat_nbr( )** changes. As a result, in Function 9-3, we print the prompt with **printf( )**, by combining a set message with the *type* argument. **getint( )** can't create the prompt for us because it only takes a single argument. Since the prompt is displayed before we call **getint( )**, we don't want **getint( )** to print anything. This is why **getint( )** is sent an empty string ("") as an argument in Function 9-3.

9.1 THE sprintf( ) FUNCTION

This is the second time we've needed to create a prompt by inserting one string into another. The other one was in the **getcat( )** function where *Revenue* or *Cost* was inserted into a prompt, as well.

Business applications make heavy use of prompts. As a result, we often need to create a prompt by combining several strings together. Further, our utility functions, such as **getlong( )** and **getint( )**, expect a single string as the prompt to print.

It may appear that we have made a design error. However, the standard library contains a very useful function that allows us to create custom prompts whenever we need them. It is the **sprintf( )** function. As the name implies, **sprintf( )** is a close relative of the **printf( )** function. In fact, **sprintf( )** works just like **printf( )**, with one exception.

printf( ) combines the format string with the listed arguments to create a string that is printed on the computer screen. **sprintf( )** also merges the format string with the other arguments, however, **sprintf( )** stores the result in a string sent as an argument, instead of printing it at a terminal.

A sample call to **sprintf( )** is

```
        sprintf(prompt, "\n%s categories to enter", type);
```

sprintf( ) inserts the string stored in *type* into the format string and puts the result in *prompt*. If *type* holds *Revenue*, then the string

```
                    Revenue categories to enter
```

is stored in the variable prompt by **sprintf**. Now, we can send **getint( )** the prompt in a single string:

```
    sprintf(prompt, "\n%s categories to enter", type);
    getint(prompt);
```

This is a better way to display **cat_nbr( )**'s prompt than to print it and then send **getint( )** an empty string. These lines make what is happening more obvious.

Like **printf( )**, **sprintf( )** is an **int** function. **sprintf( )** returns the number of characters stored in the string that holds the formatted result. An important point is that **sprintf( )** *doesn't* check that the receiving string is large enough to hold the number of characters that will be put in it. If this string is not large enough to store all these characters, the program will fail in some unpredictable way.

Exercise 9-1   Rewrite the **getcat( )** function, to tell the user to enter dollars only (no cents). Use **sprintf( )**.

The data entry functions **getrev( )** and **getcost( )** read in all the information associated with every category of a specific type, either revenues or costs, respectively. The information entered must be stored in the designated arrays. For this scheme to work properly, the functions must have access to all the elements in these arrays. Thus, we must pass an entire array to the function, as an argument. Incidentally, the same is true of the printing function **print_pl( )**, which must access the data in these arrays as well.

We've passed entire arrays as function arguments before. We did this with character arrays (i.e., strings). *single dimension* numeric arrays, those arrays defined with a single index, are treated the same as character arrays. We send only the array name as an argument and the function declares this argument as a dummy variable. The array's elements can then be identified inside the function in the normal manner, that is, with an array name and an index.

For *multidimension* arrays, those with two or more indexes, we still send only the array name as an argument, but the function must provide some specific information for this argument. The function must declare the sizes of all the array's dimensions (indexes), except the first one.

As an illustration, the *rev_cat* array has two dimensions

```
            char rev_cat[20] [31];
```

To send **getrev( )** the entire *rev_cat* array, we simply list *rev_cat* as one of **getrev( )**'s arguments. In this case, it is the first one.

```
            getrev(rev_cat, rev_amt, rev_count);
```

Sec. 9.1   The sprintf( ) Function

In **getrev( )**, the formal parameter that represents the first argument, *cat_name*, must be defined

```
                       char cat_name[] [31];
```

This tells **getrev( )** that each string element in the *cat_name* array has thirty-one characters. This is important when a string in the array is refered to in the function. Without knowing the length of each string element, the function wouldn't know where an array's elements started (i.e., how many characters from the beginning of the array).

This isn't a problem with single dimension arrays because each element refers to only one value the size of the array's data type. To find an array element we simply count over the number of elements specified by the index. Each element in a multidimension array is composed of smaller arrays. To properly index such arrays when passed as a function argument requires knowing the exact sizes of the array's elements. As with single dimension arrays, the function need not know the first index, since it starts at the beginning of the array and increases by the declared amount.

The **getrev( )**, and **getcost( )** functions are taken from Segment 9-1. **print-pl** is from Segment 9-2. The main change is that the loops are controlled by a variable instead of a constant. **getrev( )** is listed as Function 9-4, **getcost( )** as Function 9-5, and **print-pl( )** as Function 9-6.

```c
/* ***** GETREV *****
 *
 * This function prompts for and reads revenue categories
 * and amounts.  The category name and amount arrays
 * are passed to the function as arguments, as is
 * the number of categories to enter.
 *
 * Written by Ray Swartz for "Doing Business with C"
 */

void getrev(cat_name, cat_amt, cat_nbr)
char cat_name[][31];         /* category names */
long cat_amt[];              /* amounts */
int cat_nbr;                 /* number of categories to enter */
{
    int printf();
    long getcat();           /* read category and return amount */
    int count;               /* loop counter */

    printf("\nEnter Dollar amounts only -- no cents\n");
    printf("\n\nREVENUES\n\n");
    for (count = 0; count < cat_nbr; count = count + 1)
        cat_amt[count] = getcat(cat_name[count], "Revenue");
    return;
}
```

Function 9-4   The **getrev( )** Function

```
/* ***** GETCOST *****
 *
 * This function prompts for and reads cost categories
 * and amounts.  The category name and amount arrays
 * are passed to the function as arguments, as is
 * the number of categories to enter.
 *
 * Written by Ray Swartz for "Doing Business with C"
 */

void getcost(cat_name, cat_amt, cat_nbr)
char cat_name[][31];         /* category names */
long cat_amt[];              /* amounts */
int cat_nbr;                 /* number of categories to enter */
{
    int printf();
    long getcat();           /* read category and return amount */
    int count;               /* loop counter */

    printf("\nEnter Dollar amounts only -- no cents\n");
    printf("\n\nCOSTS\n\n");
    for (count = 0; count < cat_nbr; count = count + 1)
        cat_amt[count] = getcat(cat_name[count], "Cost");
    return;
}
```

Function 9-5 The **getcost( )** Function

```
/* ***** PRINT_PL *****
 *
 * This function prints a formatted Profit and Loss
 * statement.  It is sent two category name arrays
 * and two category amount arrays--one set for
 * revenues and one for costs.  The number of entries
 * of each type is sent to the function as arguments, also.
 *
 * Written by Ray Swartz for "Doing Business with C"
 */

void print_pl(rev_cat, rev_amt, rev_count,
              cost_cat, cost_amt, cost_count)
char rev_cat[][31];          /* revenue category names */
long rev_amt[];              /* revenue amounts */
int rev_count;               /* number of revenue entries */
char cost_cat[][31];         /* cost category names */
long cost_amt[];             /* cost amounts */
int cost_count;              /* number of cost entries */
{
    int printf();
    int count;               /* loop counter */
```

Sec. 9.1 The sprintf() Function

```
        long totalrev;           /* revenue amounts total */
        long totalcost;          /* cost amounts total */

        printf("\n\tProfit and Loss for Johnson's Books\n\n");
        printf("          REVENUE\n\n");

        /* Loop to print and total the revenue categories */

        totalrev = 0;
        for (count = 0; count < rev_count; count = count + 1) {
            printf("%-30s   $%6ld\n", rev_cat[count], rev_amt[count]);
            totalrev = totalrev + rev_amt[count];
        }
        printf("                                          ------\n");
        printf("          TOTAL REVENUE                   $%7ld\n\n\n",
             totalrev);
        printf("\n\n         COSTS\n\n");

        /* Loop to print and total the cost categories */

        totalcost = 0;
        for (count = 0; count < cost_count; count = count + 1) {
            printf("%-30s   $%6ld\n", cost_cat[count], cost_amt[count]);
            totalcost = totalcost + cost_amt[count];
        }
        printf("                                          ------\n");
        printf("          TOTAL COST                      $%7ld\n\n\n",
             totalcost);
        if (totalrev >= totalcost)
            printf("          PROFIT                       $%7ld\n",
                totalrev - totalcost);
        else
            printf("          LOSS                        ($%7ld)\n",
                totalcost - totalrev);
        return;
}
```

Function 9-6   The **print_pl( )** Function

The **flex-pl** program results from combining Program 9-1 with Functions 9-4, 9-5, and 9-6. **flex-pl** allows the entry of up to twenty revenue and cost categories and then formats a P&L statement based on those entries. Also, the program has been built using functions to perform its major components. Thus, changing the P&L statement's format or modifying the data entry functions can be done by working with a single function only. This makes program maintenance much easier.

Exercise 9-2   At present **flex-pl** uses **getrev( )** to read revenue entries and **getcost( )** to read cost entries. Combine these two functions into one that can read in either revenue or cost categories, depending on the arguments sent. Call this new function **getent**( ).

We were asked to make these changes to the **gnrl-pl** program because Johnson's Books received some interest on their checking accounts and needed to update their P&L statement. Let's run **flex-pl** with this new category to see how it works. Johnson's Books received $2,457 in interest this year. The rest of the information comes from Figure 5-3, the previous P&L statement. The program run and output are shown in Output 9-1.

```
Revenue categories to enter: 3

Enter Dollar amounts only -- no cents

REVENUES

Enter a Revenue Category (30 Character Maximum): Sales
Sales: 38987

Enter a Revenue Category (30 Character Maximum): Rebates
Rebates: 5000

Enter a Revenue Category (30 Character Maximum): Interest
Interest: 2457

Cost categories to enter: 5

Enter Dollar amounts only -- no cents

COSTS

Enter a Cost Category (30 Character Maximum): Cost of Goods Sold
Cost of Goods Sold: 14247

Enter a Cost Category (30 Character Maximum): Wages
Wages: 5501

Enter a Cost Category (30 Character Maximum): Rents
Rents: 3600

Enter a Cost Category (30 Character Maximum): Advertising
Advertising: 250

Enter a Cost Category (30 Character Maximum): Miscellaneous Expenses
Miscellaneous Expenses: 4761
```

```
            Profit and Loss for Johnson's Books

            REVENUE

Sales                           $  38987
Rebates                         $   5000
Interest                        $   2457
                                   ------
       TOTAL REVENUE                 $   46444

            COST$

Cost of Goods Sold              $  14247
Wages                           $   5501
Rents                           $   3600
Advertising                     $    250
Miscellaneous Expenses          $   4761
                                   ------
       TOTAL COST                    $   28359

       PROFIT                        $   18085
```

Output 9-1

9.2 THE GREAT ESCAPE

Up to this point, we've refered to the elements of the *rev_cat* and *cost_cat* arrays as strings only. However, many times we need to evaluate the individual characters that make up a string. In this section, we explore how to do this.

The **flex-pl** program requires the user to specify the number of revenue and cost categories (up to a preset maximum) contained on a profit and loss statement. To do this, **flex-pl** asks the user how many categories to read.

After the number of categories to read has been entered, **flex-pl** prompts for exactly that many entries. If the user discovers that either more or less categories need to be entered, there is no way to do it. Once the number of categories has been specified, nothing can be done about it.

However, experience shows that data entry is a dynamic process, that is, how much information needs to be entered can change while the program is running. After specifying the amount of data to read, people may see shortcuts in the data or find out that more is to be entered. As an example, a user might count five revenue categories in this month's P&L statement and tell the program to get five revenue entries, but later notice that one of the categories has an amount of zero and decide not to enter it.

The **flex-pl** program is unforgiving in these instances; exactly the number specified must be read. A better design would allow the user to enter information until told to stop up to a preset maximum, in this case twenty categories. This approach requires less of the data entry person (no need to count the entries) and provides even more flexibility.

How will the user tell the program to stop reading data? We have to create a special code to act as the *quit signal*. Since data entry terminates when the quit signal is entered, we must choose a code that doesn't occur in the data set. Thus, it would be foolish to use *Sales* as the word that terminates data entry. In a program like **flex-pl**, where the amounts entered can be positive, negative, or zero and the category names are unlimited, it is difficult to choose a unique code that won't interfere with possible data.

To minimize confusion, the quit signal should be entered at the first possible prompt in the data entry sequence. In **flex-pl**, this is the category name. For a quit signal, we will use 'Q' (a capital Q) entered by itself as the category name.

RULE If a program allows a quit signal, that signal should be entered at the first possible prompt.

When "Q" is entered as a string, it actually is represented by two characters, a 'Q' followed by a '\0' in the category name. The expression

```
if (cat_name[count][0] == 'Q' && cat_name[count][1] == '\0')
```

tests if the quit signal is entered. The variable *cat_name* is the parameter in the data entry functions that represents the category name and *count* represents the loop counter controlling the data entry loop.

Before we start changing the **flex-pl** program, we need to design how the program will handle unlimited data entry. One required change is to remove the code that gets the number of categories to enter. This is done by deleting the two calls to the **getcat( )** function.

Next, **main( )** needs to know how many categories are entered so the entry count can be passed to **print_pl( )**. The entry functions **getrev( )** and **getcost( )** can pass the category count back to **main( )**. The new **main( )** is shown as Program 9-2.

```
/* ***** FLEX-PL *****
 *
 * This program reads the category and amount of a set of
 * revenues and costs and prints a formatted P&L statement.
 * The program reads entries until a Q only is entered
 * as a category name (the quit signal) or until 20 categories
 * have been entered.
 *
 *   Written by Ray Swartz for "Doing Business with C"
 */
```

Sec. 9.2 The Great Escape

```
#include "stdio.h"
#include "getcat.c"       /* source code for getcat function */

main()
{
    char rev_cat[20] [31];   /* revenue categories entered */
    char cost_cat[20] [31];  /* cost categories entered */
    int rev_count;           /* number of revenue categories */
    int cost_count;          /* number of cost categories */
    int getrev();            /* read all revenue entries */
    int getcost();           /* read all cost entries */
    long cost_amt[20];       /* cost amounts entered */
    long rev_amt[20];        /* revenue amounts entered */
    void print_pl();         /* print the P&L statement */

    rev_count = getrev(rev_cat, rev_amt);         /* get revenues */
    cost_count = getcost(cost_cat, cost_amt);     /* get costs */
    print_pl(rev_cat, rev_amt, rev_count,
             cost_cat, cost_amt, cost_count);
    exit(0);
}
```

Program 9-2 The New **main( )** for **flex-pl**

To ensure that too many entries aren't read, the functions will read in a maximum of twenty names. Further, both **getrev()** and **getcost()** are presently defined as **void** functions. They must be changed to functions that return **int**s.

The only additional modifications required are to the data entry functions themselves. Note that **print_pl( )** is unaffected by our new design. This is the strength of modular programming. We only have to work on the functions that perform the tasks being changed!

In the **getrev( )** function, data entry is performed inside this **for** loop:

```
for (count = 0; count < 20; count = count + 1)
    cat_amt[count] = getcat(cat_name[count], "Revenue");
```

After **getcat( )** returns, we have to check *cat_name* for the quit signal. This is done with the **if** statement shown previously:

```
if (cat_name[count][0] == 'Q' && cat_name[count][1] == '\0')
```

What do we do if the **if** test is true? Since the test is done inside the **for** loop, we want to terminate the loop immediately and return.

9.3 THE break COMMAND

C provides a special command that terminates loops. It is **break**. Earlier, we used **break** to skip over options in a **switch** statement. When **break** is encountered inside a loop, the program is transferred to the statement following that loop's closing brace.

RULE   The **break** command causes the immediate termination of a loop.

The resulting **for** loop is

```
for (count = 0; count < MAX_CATEGORIES; count = count + 1) {
    cat_amt[count] = getcat(cat_name[count], "Revenue");
    if (cat_name[count][0] == 'Q' &&
        cat_name[count][1] == '\0')  /* test quit signal */
            break;   /* Quit signal entered */
}
```

If the test for the quit signal is true, we execute the **break** and terminate the loop. Incidentally, **break** has the same effect no matter what kind of loop it is in. Thus, **break** terminates **for**, **while**, or **do while** loops.

The variable *count* will hold the number of categories entered when the loop terminates. It may seem that *count* will be one too large because *count* is incremented before the entry that is the quit signal. However, since *count* starts at 0, it equates to the actual number entered. Thus, when the loop terminates, we simply

```
return(count);
```

Function 9-7 lists the new **getrev( )** function.

```
/* ***** GETREV *****
 *
 * This function prompts for and reads revenue categories
 * and amounts. The category name and amount arrays
 * are passed to the function as arguments.
 *
 * Written by Ray Swartz for "Doing Business with C"
 *
 * Modified to check for a quit signal (Q) and return
 * the number of categories entered.
 */

int getrev(cat_name, cat_amt)
char cat_name[][31];         /* category names */
long cat_amt[];              /* amounts */
{
    int printf();
    long getcat();           /* read category and return amount */
```

Sec. 9.3 The break Command

```
        int count;              /* loop counter */

        printf("\nEnter Dollar amounts only -- no cents\n");
        printf("\n\nREVENUES\n\n");
        for (count = 0; count < 20; count = count + 1) {
            cat_amt[count] = getcat(cat_name[count], "Revenue");
            if (cat_name[count][0] == 'Q' &&
                cat_name[count][1] == '\0')  /* test for quit signal */
                break;    /* Quit signal entered */
        }
        return(count);
    }
```

Function 9-7 A **getrev( )** Function that Tests for a Quit Signal

Incidentally, if the quit signal is not entered, the entry loop terminates when *count* is 20 (*count* < 20 is false), which is the number of categories entered. The code for **getcost( )** is quite similar and won't be shown here.

Our new **flex-pl** program contains an odd inefficiency. If the quit signal is entered, the **getcat( )** function still prompts for the amount to put in category *Q*. For this to work properly, we must modify the **getcat( )** program also to test for the quit signal and not prompt for amount if the quit signal is found.

Exercise 9-3 Write a new **getcat( )** function that checks for the quit signal (a *Q* only) and doesn't prompt for category amount if the quit signal is found. Store the result back in the file **getcat.c**.

break is not a structured programming command since it transfers control of the program from inside a block to outside that block without using the loop control mechanism. For this reason, some people think it is poor programming style to use **break**. They argue that it is easily overlooked. This is why we documented the **break** command with the comment

```
            /* Quit signal entered */
```

RULE Clearly document the **break** statement whenever it is used to terminate a loop.

Another argument against **break** is that it is unnecessary. Instead of using **break** we could have introduced a special variable called *quit_flag* that is initialized to 0 (false) and is set to 1 (true) if the quit signal is found. We can test for the quit signal in the loop control with

```
            count < 20 && quit_test == 0
```

Now, when the quit signal is entered, the loop terminates normally.

If we use *quit_flag* one other change must be made. The variable *count* is increment before the loop test is performed. Now, if the quit signal is entered, *count* is one too large and has to be decrement before its value is returned:

```
return(count - 1);
```

However, if all twenty categories are entered, *count* is the proper size. Function 9-8 shows this version of **getrev( )**.

```
/* ***** GETREV *****
 *
 * This function prompts for and reads revenue categories
 * and amounts.  The category name and amount arrays
 * are passed to the function as arguments.
 *
 * Written by Ray Swartz for "Doing Business with C"
 *
 * Modified to check for a quit signal (Q) and return
 * the number of categories entered.
 * Modified to remove break statement.
 */

int getrev(cat_name, cat_amt)
char cat_name[][31];          /* category names */
long cat_amt[];               /* amounts */
{
    int printf();
    long getcat();            /* read category and return amount */
    int count;                /* loop counter */
    int quit_flag;            /* set to 1 if quit signal found */

    quit_flag = 0;    /* set to initial value */
    printf("\nEnter Dollar amounts only -- no cents\n");
    printf("\n\nREVENUES\n\n");
    for (count = 0; count < 20 && quit_flag == 0; count = count + 1) {
        cat_amt[count] = getcat(cat_name[count], "Revenue");
        if (cat_name[count][0] == 'Q' &&
            cat_name[count][1] == '\0')   /* test for quit signal */
                quit_flag = 1;    /* terminate loop */
    }
    if (count < 20)
        return(count - 1);
    else
        return(count);
}
```

Function 9-8 A **getrev( )** Function that Tests for a Quit Signal and Doesn't Use **break**

Whether we use **break** or not is a question of personal style. However, it is best to be consistent whatever our preference might be.

9.4 SUMMARY

1. A string variable is actually a character array.
2. Because a string variable is an array, an array of strings is actually an array of character arrays.
3. An array of strings is defined with two indexes. The first identifies how many strings are in the array and the second the maximum number of characters in each string.
4. To refer to one of the strings in a string array, use the array name and a single index.
5. To identify a character in one of the strings in the array, use the array name, the index of the string, and the index of the character in that string.
6. **#include** files can contain **#include** directives.
7. Local variables are not initialized when the function they belong to is called.
8. The **sprintf( )** function is a relative of the **printf( )** function. **sprintf( )** takes an additional argument, a string variable to hold the results of combining the formatting string with the listed arguments.
9. To pass an array with more than one dimension to a function we simply list the name. However for a function to use the array properly, the function must declare the sizes of all the array's dimensions except the first one, which is unnecessary.
10. Data entry is a dynamic process and programs should allow users to change their minds in the middle of the program.
11. The **break** command causes the immediate termination of a loop.
12. Whenever **break** is used to terminate a loop, it should be clearly documented.

E X E R C I S E S

9-4. At present, the **flex-pl** program only prints a P&L statement for Johnson's Books. Change it to read the company name from the user. Write a function called **getname( )** to handle the input.

9-5. The **flex-pl** program provides no opportunity for a user to correct a mistake made entering a category's information. Modify the program to print the category data entered and then to ask the user if this is correct. If not, the user should be allowed to re-enter the data.

9-6. Constantly typing **y** after a category is entered can get to be bothersome. Modify Exercise 9-5 to verify the categories entered after each section's (either revenue or cost) data has been entered. Be sure to allow the user to correct any errors made.

9-7. Write a program that reads a customer's name, invoice number, and invoice total and then prints a daily sales report which lists all the invoices written that day and the total sales.

Be sure to have the user verify that the data entered is correct. Assume that no more than thirty invoices are written a day.

9-8. Write a program to print an invoice. An invoice includes customer's name and address, one line for each item purchased (with description, cost, amount of this item purchased, and total for this item), and an invoice total. Assume that an invoice can handle thrity items. If a customer purchases more than thirty items, the second invoice can have the total from the first invoice as the first item!

PART 4
Some C Shortcuts

10
The Preprocessor

C provides a special tool to help us write programs that can be modified, tested, and transported more easily. It is the *preprocessor*. The C preprocessor does just what its name implies, it processes our source code *before* it gets compiled. Using special *directives*, we instruct the preprocessor to change our source code into a form acceptable by the compiler.

Preprocessor directives have a special syntax. They always begin with # as the first character. In addition, because the preprocessor works before the compiler, its lines are *not* terminated with semicolons.

We've already used one preprocessor directive, **#include**. The preprocessor replaces the line containing the **#include** directive with the contents of the file whose name appears enclosed in double quotation marks after **#include**.[1]

#include is a convenient way to add important information to our programs without knowing anything but where it is stored. We've used the **#include** directive to make the source code of the **getcat( )** function available to the **flex-pl** program. It also allows us to put required, system-specific information in our programs. By using the contents of a file, called *stdio.h*, which can be changed from system to system, we are able to transport our programs without making any changes to them. All we have to do is recompile our programs on the new system. The preprocessor does the rest!

---

[1] On Unix systems, < > can be used in place of double quotation marks.

10.1 THE #define DIRECTIVE

In Chapter 4 we wrote our first P&L program, Program 4-1. Although it provided a good example at the time, it was useless as a business tool. In the intervening five chapters, we have improved this program by reading category names and using loops to read information that is stored in easily indexed arrays. In addition, the program continues to request information until the user is through entering data.

While the **flex-pl** program no longer asks how many categories are to be entered, we still have to set an arbitrary maximum for the number of categories. This is because an array's dimensions must be defined by integer constants. Constants, be they numeric or string, always place a limitation on a program. As a result, we should endeavor to eliminate all constants from our programs.

We set the maximum number categories at twenty. However, suppose we need to extend the maximum number of categories to thirty, to meet the demands of this year's P&L statement. To do this, we must adjust the definitions of all the data arrays, the two category string arrays, and the two amount arrays. The original definitions are

```
char rev_cat[20][31];      /* revenue categories */
char cost_cat[20][31];     /* cost categories */
long cost_amt[20];         /* cost amounts */
long rev_amt[20];          /* revenue amounts */
```

They must become

```
char rev_cat[30][31];
char cost_cat[30][31];
long cost_amt[30];
long rev_amt[30];
```

We also have to change the constants that implement this maximum. In **flex-pl**, the **getrev( )** and **getcost( )** functions control the entry loop with this limit:

```
for (count = 0; count < 20; count = count + 1)
```

We must substitute 30 for 20 in this loop.

Adjusting a constant doesn't cause any problem if we change *all* instances of that constant. If we miss just one, the program will not always work properly. Further, this kind of error is often difficult to find since it affects the results only when the previous maximum is exceeded.

C has a simple solution to this problem, *macro substitution*. A macro is an identifier associated with a text string. Before the program gets compiled, the text string is substituted for the macro identifier wherever the macro appears in the program's source code. Put another way, a macro is a *symbolic name* that is replaced by a text string. C's preprocessor performs the substitution.

Macros are created by the **#define** preprocessor directive. The **#define** command has the form

Sec. 10.1 The #define Directive 143

```
#define macro_identifier text_to_substitute
```

A **#define** line contains three parts, the **#define** directive, the macro name, and the text to substitute. Spaces or tabs separate each part. The replacement text string is all the characters after the macro's name to the end of the line. The same restrictions apply to macro names that apply to variable names. By convention, macros that represent constants are all uppercase characters.

An important thing to note is that *no* semicolon ends the **define** directive. In fact, only include a semicolon if the program element that results after substitution requires one.

RULE Do not end a **#define** directive line with a semicolon unless the semicolon is part of the replacement string.

Macro substitution allows us flexibility when we must use constants. To adjust a constant's value, we simply change its macro definition. When we recompile the program, the preprocessor will substitute the new value in all the right spots!

For example, let's define MAX_CAT as the maximum number of categories a user can enter. Presently, we define it with

```
#define MAX_CAT 20
```

Now, we can use MAX_CAT to refer to the maximum number of categories. Actually, MAX_CAT is replaced by the numeric characters 2 and 0. The preprocessor deals with our source code as text only. The compiler, on the other hand, will treat these characters as an integer constant.

To define the data arrays in the **flex-pl** program, we use

```
char rev_cat[MAX_CAT] [31];
char cost_cat[MAX_CAT] [31];
long cost_amt[MAX_CAT];
long rev_amt[MAX_CAT];
```

We also must change the **getrev( )** and **getcost( )** functions:

```
for (count = 0; count < MAX_CAT; count = count + 1)
```

To increase the maximum number of categories, we only have to make a single change: redefine MAX_CAT from

```
#define MAX_CAT 20
```

to

```
#define MAX_CAT 30
```

A macro must be defined before it can be used. By convention, macro definitions appear either at the beginning of the program file or in a separate header file that is **#include**d.

As an extended example of how macros work, let's suppose we've been asked to write a program that, among other things, calculates the sales tax on a purchase. Since the actual sales tax percentage changes from time to time, we will use this macro:

```
#define SALES_TAX_PCT .065
```

If

```
float purchase;    /* total amount of purchase */
float total;       /* purchase plus sales tax */
```

then

```
total = purchase * (1 + SALES_TAX_PCT);
```

Sales taxes vary depending on where a good or service is bought. Many times, local taxes are added to the state's sales tax. This would require a second macro

```
#define LOCAL_SALES_TAX_PCT .005
```

Will this new macro cause a problem for the preprocessor because it contains the name of another macro (SALES_TAX_PCT)? There are three places were no macro substitution occurs—inside a keyword or identifier, inside comment lines, and inside string constants (between double quotes).

RULE A macro is substituted for an entire word only. No substitution occurs *inside* a keyword or identifier, inside comment lines, and inside string constants.

Thus, the actual sales tax calculation can be written

```
total = purchase * (1 + SALES_TAX_PCT + LOCAL_SALES_TAX_PCT);
```

This is a bit cumbersome. However, we can compact this statement because C's preprocessor allows macros to contain other macros. Put another way, a macro is expanded until no more macros are contained in the expanded result. As an example, we can use this macro

```
#define SALES_TAX  SALES_TAX_PCT + LOCAL_SALES_TAX_PCT
```

Now, SALES_TAX can be used instead of the expression. Recall that a macro must be **#define**d before it can be used. Thus, SALES_TAX_PCT and

Sec. 10.1   The **#define** Directive   **145**

LOCAL_SALES_TAX_PCT must be **#define**d before SALES_TAX. Now, to figure sales tax, we use

```
total = purchase * (1 + SALES_TAX);
```

After the SALES_TAX macro is replaced, the line is rescanned by the preprocessor for any additional macros and

```
total = purchase * (1 + SALES_TAX);
```

becomes

```
total = purchase * (1 + SALES_TAX_PCT + LOCAL_SALES_TAX_PCT);
```

which becomes

```
total = purchase * (1 + .065 + .005);
```

RULE   The preprocessor expands macros until no more macros are found in the replacement text.

Be careful not to define circular macros, such as

```
#define FOOLISH_MACRO   REAL_BAD_IDEA
#define REAL_BAD_IDEA   FOOLISH_MACRO
```

Although some compilers will spot the redundancy, many will do what we've asked and eventually fail.

Macros inside double quotation marks are not expanded. Above, we defined MAX_CAT as the maximum number of categories that can be entered into the **flex-pl** program. We might be tempted to tell the user:

```
printf("The maximum number of categories is MAX_CAT\n");
```

However, no substitution is done because the entire format string is enclosed in quotes. The correct way to do this is

```
printf("The maximum number of categories is %d\n", MAX_CAT);
```

Exercise 10-1   Replace the constant used to define the length of the strings (thirty-one) in the category name arrays in **flex-pl** with a macro. Be sure to replace all instances of this constant.

10.2 PROCESSING MACRO ARGUMENTS

In addition to direct text substitution, we can define macros that take arguments. These arguments are inserted into the macro's replacement string before the text is put into the program. This means we can create macros that resemble functions in style.

For example, instead of using a macro to represent the sales tax percentage, we can define a macro that substitutes the proper calculation. In other words, we can replace

```
total = purchase * (1 + SALES_TAX);
```

with

```
total = FIGURE_TAX(purchase);
```

The FIGURE_TAX macro is defined by

```
#define FIGURE_TAX(AMOUNT)   AMOUNT * (1 + SALES_TAX)
```

Before substitution, the argument sent to FIGURE_TAX, represented by AMOUNT in the definition, is inserted into the replacement text. Then, the modified text string is put into the source code. (Incidentally, notice that we did not end the text string with a semicolon.)

Macros that take arguments have two syntax requirements. First, the arguments are "declared" by enclosing them in parentheses as part of the macro's identifier. Second, no spaces are allowed between the macro name and the opening (left) parenthesis. Macros can be sent more than one argument by separating the arguments by commas. Space is allowed between arguments. Commas inside double or single quotation marks (i.e., inside a string sent as an argument) are ignored.

The preprocessor enforces argument number conformity in macros. If a macro is defined with two arguments, the preprocessor will report an error if that macro is listed with other than two arguments.

Our definition of FIGURE_TAX works properly in this statement

```
total = FIGURE_TAX(purchase);
```

However, in this one

```
total = FIGURE_TAX(item1 + item2);
```

there is a problem. After substitution, this becomes

```
total = item1 + item2 * (1 + .065 + .005);
```

The resulting statement only calculates tax on *item2*.

The problem originates in our definition of FIGURE_TAX. Because the argument is replaced directly into the text string, we must be careful to ensure that all arguments are treated properly. What we want is for the macro to expand to

```
total = (item1 + item2) * (1 + .065 + .005);
```

Thus, in the replacement string, we must enclose the macro's argument in parentheses:

```
#define FIGURE_TAX(AMOUNT)    (AMOUNT) * (1 + SALES_TAX)
```

To figure the percent discount, including tax, we might use this statement

```
disc = list_price / FIGURE_TAX(purchase);
```

After macro expansion, this becomes

```
disc = (list_price) / (purchase) * (1 + .065 +.005);
```

In the resulting statement, the division is performed first and this calculation has no real meaning.

Again, the problem is improper grouping in the macro definition. We want the entire text string treated as a single value. To ensure this, we must enclose the entire replacement string in parentheses:

```
#define FIGURE_TAX(AMOUNT)    ((AMOUNT) * (1 + SALES_TAX))
```

Now,

```
disc = list_price / FIGURE_TAX(purchase);
```

becomes

```
disc = list_price / ((purchase) * (1 + .065 +.005));
```

which evaluates properly.

RULE   Enclose the macro argument and the entire substitution string in parentheses.

The substitution performed with the **#define** facility is direct text replacement. Unlike the compiler, the preprocessor does not know anything about C. As a result, we must exercise extra caution when using macros, especially macros that take arguments. As we saw, perfectly correct C code can be "broken" by an ill-conceived macro. These kinds of bugs are painfully difficult to locate.

Macros with arguments are called *in-line functions* because they have the ability to take arguments but avoid the overhead of a function call. In addition, since macros become part of the program, they work with all of C's data types without modification. Functions, on the other hand, must be passed arguments with specific data types. This means several sales tax calculating functions would be required to replace the FIGURE_TAX macro, depending on the data type used.

Macros have some drawbacks as well. First, macros expand into C code which can make the program much larger. Also, because macros are not functions, any changes in a macro's definition will change our source code. Lastly, macros can have unwanted side effects when substituted into our programs.

Exercise 10-2 Write a printing macro called **PRd** that takes an **int** variable argument and expands into a **printf( )** statement that displays the argument's value followed by a newline. For example, this call to **PRd**

```
int value;

value = 12;
PRd(value);
```

should print

```
12
```

A macro's replacement text is what appears between the macro name and the end of the **#define** line. Does this limit us to one-line macros only? Yes, but the preprocessor provides a way around it. The preprocessor will ignore a newline that is "quoted" by a backslash (\). This allows us to imbed newlines in the replacement text.

As an illustration, this statement prints the amount of profit on the P&L statement:

```
printf("       PROFIT                  $%7ld\n",
    totalrev - totalcost);
```

This can be turned into the **PRINT_RESULT** macro.

```
#define PRINT_RESULT(result, total1, total2) \
    printf("       %s                  $%7ld\n",\
        result, total1 - total2)
```

The "end of the line" that terminates the macro is the unquoted newline (the one not preceded by \).

PRINT_RESULT is a good example of a space-saving macro. It can print either the profit line

```
PRINT_RESULT("PROFIT", totalrev, totalcost);
```

or loss line

```
PRINT_RESULT("LOSS", totalcost, totalrev);
```

Exercise 10-3 Modify the **print_pl( )** function to use the PRINT_RESULT macro.

Exercise 10-4 Create a macro called PRINT_CAT which is sent a category name and amount and implements the **printf( )** statement that prints a category's entry in the P&L statement:

```
printf("%-30s  $%6ld\n", category name, amount);
```

10.3 CONDITIONAL COMPILATION

In addition to including files and defining macros, the preprocessor can control what statements get compiled in a program, that is, the preprocessor can control what sections of a program are passed to the compiler. This feature, called **conditional compilation**, allows a programmer to "switch" parts of a program "on" or "off" as needs dictate. However, because this is done prior to compilation, to activate or remove a section of code requires recompiling the program.

There are times when we want to execute "extra" statements in a program. One example is when we are debugging a newly written program. It would be nice if we could add special debugging statements to the source code during this process and then, when they're no longer needed, take them out of the program without having to physically remove them. Now, if a problem arises or we have to modify this program, the debugging statements are already part of the source code.

Conditional compilation works by adding or deleting lines from the program's source code *before* it is passed onto the compiler. A set of preprocessor control lines act as *true/false* tests. A true result means the following code is inserted into the program. If the test is false, those statements are removed from the source code.

There are three different preprocessor tests. Like all preprocessor commands, they begin with a #.

#if
#ifdef
#ifndef

The **#if** control line tests a *constant expression*. If it evaluates to nonzero (true), all the statements following it up to a

```
#endif
```

control line are included in the program. Should the expression equal zero (false), the lines are not compiled. A constant expression can contain certain operators but must have numeric or single-character constant operands only. These binary operators are allowed:

```
    *       /
    %       +
    -       ==
    !=      <
    <=      >
    >=      &&
    ||
```

as are these unary operators

```
    -
    !
```

as is the conditional operator (described in the next chapter).[2] Macros can be used too, as long as they are replaced by constants.

Both the **#ifdef** and **#ifndef** control lines test whether or not a symbolic name has been **#define**d. **#ifdef** is true if the listed macro has been **#define**d. The **#ifndef** directive is true for macros that have *not* been **#define**d. **#ifdef** and **#ifndef** ignore any value assigned to the macro they are evaluating. No matter which conditional compilation directive is used, the preprocessor directive

```
                    #endif
```

marks the end of the section.

As an example, Program 10-1 shows how we would add some debugging **printf( )**s to the **flex-pl main( )** routine. Here, we are printing out the value returned by the **getrev( )** and **getcost( )** functions.

```
/* ***** FLEX-PL *****
 *
 * This program reads the category and amount of a set of
 * revenues and costs and prints a formatted P&L statement.
 * The program reads entries until a Q only is entered
 * as a category name (the quit signal) or until 20 categories
 * have been read.
 *
 * Written for Ray Swartz for "Doing Business with C"
 */

#include "stdio.h"
#include "getcat.c"         /* source code for getcat function */
```

---

[2] Additional operators that can be used in a constant expression are the bitwise operators: <<, >>, &, ^, |, ~. However, we haven't discussed them yet so they aren't included in the text. See Chapter 22.

Sec. 10.3 Conditional Compilation

```c
#define MAX_CAT 20
#define DEBUG 1          /* if set to 1, debugging stmt included */

main()
{
    char rev_cat[MAX_CAT][31];   /* revenue categories entered */
    char cost_cat[MAX_CAT] [31]; /* cost categories entered */
    long cost_amt[MAX_CAT];      /* cost amounts entered */
    long rev_amt[MAX_CAT];       /* revenue amounts entered */
    int rev_count;               /* number of revenue categories */
    int cost_count;              /* number of cost categories */
    int getrev();                /* read all revenue entries */
    int getcost();               /* read all cost entries */
    void print_pl();             /* print the P&L statement */

    rev_count = getrev(rev_cat, rev_amt);      /* get revenues */
#if DEBUG == 1
    printf("rev_count = %d\n", rev_count);
#endif
    cost_count = getcost(cost_cat, cost_amt);  /* get costs */
#ifdef DEBUG
    printf("cost_count = %d\n", cost_count);
#endif
    print_pl(rev_cat, rev_amt, rev_count,
             cost_cat, cost_amt, cost_count);
    exit(0);
}
```

Program 10-1 Using Conditional Compilation

Both **#ifdef** and **#if** were used to demonstrate usage. However, in Program 10-1, they could have different effects. If *DEBUG* is set to 0, the **#if** tests to false and the **#ifdef** is true. Be sure to use the proper preprocessor directive when performing conditional compilation. Incidentally, the **#ifndef** control line was not demonstrated; its usage is similar.

Like the **if** statement in C, the **#if** preprocessor directive tests for 0 or non-0. Since *DEBUG* is **#defin**ed as one,

```
#if DEBUG
```

performs the same as

```
#if DEBUG == 1
```

With C, it is not uncommon to write a program designed to run on a number of different computers. In this case, we may need to include special commands for each target machine. We can handle this with conditional compilation and the **#if** - **#elif** - **#else** - **#endif** construct. The **#elif** and **#else** control lines mirror the **else if** and **else** aspects of C's **if** statement. As an example, suppose we were writing a program to be executed on computers running under CPM, MS-DOS, and UNIX. We can customize the program to take advantage of specific system features by segregating the machine-specific commands like this:

```
#define CPM 1
#define MSDOS 2
#define UNIX 3
#define MACHINE_TYPE the appropriate macro

#if MACHINE_TYPE == CPM
    ...     /* CPM specific code */
#elif MACHINE == MSDOS
    ...     /* MS-DOS specific code */
#elif MACHINE_TYPE == UNIX
    ...     /* UNIX specific code */
#else
    ...     /* generic code */
#endif
```

On certain occasions, we may want to remove a symbolic name that has been previously **#define**d. We can do this with the **#undef** preprocessor control line. The preprocessor will only allow a token to be **#define**d once. As an example, suppose we wanted to use a replacement string for NULL, other than the one included in the *stdio.h* file. Once we

```
#include "stdio.h"
```

we can't say

```
#define NULL 0
```

since *NULL* has been **#define**d in the *stdio.h* file.[3] First we would have to **#undef** it:

```
#include "stdio.h"

#undef NULL
#define NULL 0
```

Many C compilers make conditional compilation even more flexible by allowing symbolic names to be **#define**d when the compiler is invoked. On the UNIX operating system, the C compiler is named **cc**. By specifying a special argument, **−D**, we can tell the compiler to **#define** a macro. As an illustration, to compile a debugging version of **flex-pl**, Program 10-1, we could invoke the compiler with

---

[3] The ANSI standard allows *benign redeclaration* of macros. See Appendix C for more information.

Sec. 10.4   Using **printf( )** with Macros   153

```
cc flex-pl.c -DDEBUG=1
```

This will compile the **flex-pl** source code file as if the line

```
#define DEBUG 1
```

were placed at the top of the program. For completeness, the –U compiler option performs as the –D option except it **#undef**s a macro. Any one version of the C compiler may have additional or different options. Check the system documentation for details.

10.4 USING printf( ) WITH MACROS

In Program 10-1, we used the macro MAX_CAT as the maximum number of categories that could be read by the program. However, we did not substitute a macro for the maximum length of each category name. At first glance, creating a macro call MAX_LEN and inserting it in all the right places should do the trick. Unfortunately, this won't work.

The problem is the **printf( )**s used to print the category lines in the P&L statement. The format specification for both revenue and cost categories is

```
"%-30s    $%6ld\n"
```

The length of the category name is listed as 30. The preprocessor won't see a macro inside the double quotation marks. Further, if we remove the constant and just use

```
"%-s    $%6ld\n"
```

then the category names are printed to their exact length only and the amounts aren't printed in a column, unless all of the names are the same length.

The solution is to use yet another of **printf( )**'s formatting tools. The formatting problem arises because we have to specify the length of the category name to format the P&L statement properly. However, **printf( )** doesn't require field width specifiers to be *listed as constants in the format specification.* If an *asterisk* is placed between the % and the data type code, **printf( )** will read the field size from its argument list. Thus, the format specification

```
"%-*s    $%6ld\n"
```

tells **printf( )** that the first argument (following the format specification) holds the field width for the string specified by %s. As an example,

```
printf("%-30s    $%6ld\n", rev_cat[count], rev_amt[count]);
```

is the same as

```
        printf("%-*s   $%6ld\n", 30, rev_cat[count], rev_amt[count]);
```

Further, if

```
        #define MAX_LEN 31    /* length of the category name string */
```

this **printf( )** works too

```
      printf("%-*s   $%6ld\n", MAX_LEN - 1, rev_cat[count], rev_amt[count]);
```

All three **printf( )** calls print the category name in a left justified thirty-character field. Incidentally, we subtract one from MAX_LEN to account for the \0 at the end of the string.

One more change is required before we can replace *all* the constants that refer to category name length. Both **getrev( )** and **getcost( )** use the **getcat( )** function to read the category name and amount. **getcat( )** prints a prompt with

```
      printf("\nEnter a %s Category (30 Character Maximum): ", class);
```

class is a formal parameter that represents the kind of category being read (*Revenue* or *Cost*).

We could change the prompting **printf( )** to

```
          printf("\nEnter a %s Category (%d Character Maximum): ",
                 class, MAX_LEN);
```

However, the **getcat( )** function is **#include**d in the **flex-pl** program with

```
              #include "getcat.c"
```

To make the macro MAX_LEN available to **getcat( )**, we must **#define** MAX_LEN before we **#include** the function's source code.

```
                   #define MAX_LEN 31

                   #include "getcat.c"
```

Using MAX_LEN in the **getcat( )** function provides us with flexibility in setting the size of the category names, but it also forces us to have a macro called MAX_LEN in every program that uses **getcat( )**. This may cause more problems than it solves.

A better solution is to rewrite **getcat( )** using conditional compilation to determine if MAX_LEN has been **#define**d and to take appropriate action in either case. To implement a macro-definable string length, we will **#define** another macro called *STRING_LEN* that is set to MAX_LEN − 1 if MAX_LEN is **#define**d and to 30 if it isn't. Function 10-1 lists this version of **getcat( )**. Incidentally, note that **getcat( )** now

Sec. 10.4 Using **printf( )** with Macros

checks for the quit signal ("**Q**" only) and doesn't prompt for category amount if it is found.

```
/*     ***** GETCAT *****
 *
 * This function prompts for a revenue or cost category
 * name (depending on the string stored in the argument
 * class), reads the name entered, then calls getlong
 * to read the amount for this category.  The amount entered
 * is returned by getcat.
 *
 * Written by Ray Swartz for "Doing Business with C"
 *
 * Modified to test for the quit signal (Q only)
 * entered as category name.  If the quit signal is
 * found, the function does not prompt for amount.
 *
 * Modified to use a macro (STRING_LEN) for the maximum
 * category name length.
 */

#include "getlong.c"      /* source code of getlong function */

#ifdef MAX_LEN
#define STRING_LEN MAX_LEN - 1
#else
#define STRING_LEN 30
#endif

long getcat(catstr, class)
char catstr[];       /* string variable for entered category name */
char class[];        /* category classification (Revenue or Cost) */
{
    char *gets();
    int printf();
    long getlong();      /* prints a prompt and reads long value */

    printf("\nEnter a %s Category (%d Character Maximum): ",
           STRING_LEN, class);
    gets(catstr);                  /* read category name */
    if (catstr[0] == 'Q' && catstr[1] == '\0')
        return(0);     /* quit signal -- don't prompt for amount */
    else
        return(getlong(catstr));   /* return amount entered */
}
```

Function 10-1 Putting a Macro in **getcat( )**

156 The Preprocessor   Chap. 10

Program 10-2 lists the entire **flex-pl** program modified to use macros for both the length of category names and the maximum number of categories that can be entered.

```
/* ***** FLEX-PL *****
 *
 * This program reads the category and amount of a set of
 * revenues and costs and prints a formatted P&L statement.
 * The program reads entries until a Q only is entered
 * as a category name (the quit signal) or until MAX_CAT
 * categories have been read.
 *
 * Written for Ray Swartz for "Doing Business with C"
 *
 * Modified to use MAX_CAT and MAX_LEN macros for maximum
 * number of categories and category length, respectively.
 */

#define MAX_LEN 31      /* Length of category name strings */
#define MAX_CAT 20      /* maximum number of category names */

#include "stdio.h"
#include "getcat.c"     /* source code for getcat function */

main()
{
    char rev_cat[MAX_CAT] [MAX_LEN];    /* revenue categories */
    char cost_cat[MAX_CAT] [MAX_LEN];   /* cost categories */
    long cost_amt[MAX_CAT];             /* cost amounts */
    long rev_amt[MAX_CAT];              /* revenue amounts */
    int rev_count;          /* number of revenue categories */
    int cost_count;         /* number of cost categories */
    int getrev();           /* read all revenue entries */
    int getcost();          /* read all cost entries */
    void print_pl();        /* print the P&L statement */

    rev_count = getrev(rev_cat, rev_amt);       /* get revenues */
    cost_count = getcost(cost_cat, cost_amt);   /* get costs */
    print_pl(rev_cat, rev_amt, rev_count,
             cost_cat, cost_amt, cost_count);
    exit(0);
}
```

Sec. 10.4 Using **printf( )** with Macros

```
/* ***** GETREV *****
 *
 * This function prompts for and reads revenue categories
 * and amounts.  The category name and amount arrays
 * are passed to the function as arguments.
 *
 * Written by Ray Swartz for "Doing Business with C"
 *
 * Modified to check for a quit signal (Q) and return
 * the number of categories entered.
 */

int getrev(cat_name, cat_amt)
char cat_name[][MAX_LEN];    /* category names */
long cat_amt[];              /* amounts */
{
    int printf();
    long getcat();           /* read category and return amount */
    int count;               /* loop counter */

    printf("\nEnter Dollar amounts only -- no cents\n");
    printf("\n\nREVENUES\n\n");
    for (count = 0; count < MAX_CAT; count = count + 1) {
        cat_amt[count] = getcat(cat_name[count], "Revenue");
        if (cat_name[count][0] == 'Q' &&
            cat_name[count][1] == '\0')   /* test  for quit signal */
               break;     /* possible loop exit */
    }
    return(count);
}

/* ***** GETCOST *****
 *
 * This function prompts for and reads cost categories
 * and amounts.  The category name and amount arrays
 * are passed to the function as arguments, as is
 * the number of categories to enter.
 *
 * Written by Ray Swartz for "Doing Business with C"
 *
 * Modified to check for a quit signal (Q) and return
 * the number of categories entered.
 */

int getcost(cat_name, cat_amt)
long cat_name[] [MAX_LEN];   /* category names */
long cat_amt[];              /* amounts */
```

```
{
    int printf();
    long getcat();           /* read category and return amount */
    int count;               /* loop counter */

    printf("\nEnter Dollar amounts only -- no cents\n");
    printf("\n\nCOSTS\n\n");
    for (count = 0; count < MAX_CAT; count = count + 1) {
        cat_amt[count] = getcat(cat_name[count], "Cost");
        if (cat_name[count][0] == 'Q' &&
            cat_name[count][1] == '\0')  /* test for quit signal */
                break;       /* possible loop exit */
    }
    return(count);
}


/* ***** PRINT_PL *****
 *
 * This function prints a formatted Profit and Loss
 * statement.  It is sent two category name arrays
 * and two category amount arrays--one set for
 * revenues and one for costs.  The number of entries
 * of each type is sent to the function as arguments, also.
 *
 * Written by Ray Swartz for "Doing Business with C"
 *
 * Modified to use the MAX_LEN macro for string length.
 */

void print_pl(rev_cat, rev_amt, rev_count,
              cost_cat, cost_amt, cost_count)
char rev_cat[] [MAX_LEN];    /* revenue category names */
long rev_amt[];              /* revenue amounts */
int rev_count;               /* number of revenue entries */
char cost_cat[] [MAX_LEN];   /* cost category names */
long cost_amt[];             /* cost amounts */
int cost_count;              /* number of cost entries */
{
    int printf();
    int count;               /* loop counter */
    long totalrev;           /* revenue amounts total */
    long totalcost;          /* cost amounts total */

    printf("\tProfit and Loss for Johnson's Books\n\n");
    printf("        REVENUE\n\n");

    /* Loop to print and total the revenue categories */
```

```
            totalrev = 0;
            for (count = 0; count < rev_count; count = count + 1) {
                printf("%-*s   $%6ld\n", MAX_LEN - 1, rev_cat[count],
                       rev_amt[count]);
                totalrev = totalrev + rev_amt[count];
            }
            printf("                                         ------\n");
            printf("          TOTAL REVENUE              $%7ld\n\n\n",
                    totalrev);

            /* Loop to print and total the cost categories */

            totalcost = 0;
            for (count = 0; count < cost_count; count = count + 1) {
                printf("%-*s   $%6ld\n", MAX_LEN - 1, cost_cat[count],
                       cost_amt[count]);
                totalcost = totalcost + cost_amt[count];
            }
            printf("                                         ------\n");
            printf("          TOTAL COST                 $%7ld\n\n\n",
                    totalcost);
            if (totalrev >= totalcost)
                printf("          PROFIT                   $%7ld\n",
                        totalrev - totalcost);
            else
                printf("          LOSS                    ($%7ld)\n",
                        totalcost - totalrev);
            return;
        }
```

Program 10-2   The Macro Version of **flex-pl**

10.5 SUMMARY

1. C contains a preprocessor that looks at the source code before the compiler does and makes certain requested changes.
2. All preprocessor directives begin with # in the first location on a line.
3. The **#define** directive creates a macro. All macros are substituted for prior to compilation.
4. Macros are very useful in making our programs more general by providing a single place to define a program's constants.
5. The preprocessor doesn't know C. It does direct text substitution. This can cause some unintended expressions.
6. We can define macros that take arguments. The arguments are made part of the text that is substituted by the preprocessor.

7. Care must be exercised when writing macros that take arguments because where these macros are used can change the meaning of a poorly written macro.
8. The preprocessor can control which parts of a program get compiled through conditional compilation.
9. Conditional compilation allows us to insert debugging statements into our programs or modify our programs to work on different machines without changing the source code.
10. The **printf( )** function will take the field width specifier from the argument list if an asterisk is put into the formatting code.

E X E R C I S E S

10-5. Define a macro called *round* which rounds its argument to the nearest unit.

10-6. Define a macro, CAT_PROMPT, that displays the prompt for a revenue or cost category, including the maximum category size.

10-7. Rewrite the **getcat( )** function to use the CAT_PROMPT macro created in Exercise 10-5.

10-8. Modify the **flex-pl** program to use **double**s or **long**s to hold the category amounts. Do this by conditional compilation.

10-9. Write a macro that takes a category index as an argument and then tests for the quit entry signal ("**Q**" only). Add this macro to the **getrev( )** and **getcost( )** functions.

11
Making C an Efficient Operation

Although C's preprocessor allows us to write programs more quickly, it doesn't speed up our programs at all. Another set of C shortcuts actually make our program execute faster. This is the result of special operators that implement *efficient* versions of standard programming commands.

11.1 INCREMENT AND DECREMENT OPERATORS

One of the most common operations performed by a computer is adding 1 to a stored value. This is done when we count through a loop, index an array, record an occurrence, or as part of another command. We can speed up our programs significantly if we can find a more efficient way to increment a variable by 1. C contains just such a special operator. It is called the *increment* operator.

The increment operator tells C to add 1 to a stored value. This operator is denoted by two plus signs placed next to the variable being incremented. As an example,

```
count++;
```

does the same thing as

$$\text{count} = \text{count} + 1;$$

C also has a special *decrement* operator designated by two minus signs. The statement

$$\text{count} - -;$$

is equivalent to

$$\text{count} = \text{count} - 1;$$

The increment and decrement operators execute faster than the expanded versions. To understand why, we must take a look at how a computer actually executes the two different statements.

In virtually all of today's computers, the part that stores data (*memory*) is separate from the part that manipulates it (the *processing unit*, often called the CPU). The CPU cannot operate on information in memory, which must first be brought into the CPU. Inside the CPU are a few specialized storage locations called *registers*.

Before a stored value is available to the CPU, it must be brought into one of the CPU's registers by special *load* instructions. After processing, the results, also held in a CPU register, are put back into memory with special *store* instructions.

To implement the C statement

$$\text{total} = \text{nbr1} + \text{nbr2};$$

where all three variables are the same integer data type, requires the steps listed in Table 11-1.

TABLE 11-1 How a Computer Adds Two Numbers

1. Bring the value stored in *nbr2* into a CPU register
2. Bring the value stored in *nbr1* into another CPU register
3. Add the values together (store the sum in a "result" register)
4. Store the contents of the "result" register into the variable *total* (in memory)

In this example, we are using variables with the same data type. If type conversions are required, the CPU must do much more before step 3 is performed.

These same steps are executed to evaluate

$$\text{count} = \text{count} + 1;$$

with the exception that step 1 loads a constant into a CPU register, not a value from memory (generally, this takes less time). Since *count* appears on both sides of the equal sign, steps 2 and 4 access the same memory location.

Sec. 11.1   Increment and Decrement Operators   163

Because incrementing a value by one is such a common command, CPUs contain a special *one-step* instruction that simply adds 1 to a value stored in memory. Because special CPU circuitry is used to implement this instruction, it executes very quickly. The increment operator represents this specific instruction! Thus,

```
count++;
```

tells C to use the increment instruction whereas

```
count = count + 1;
```

uses the four-step procedure in Table 11-1. Incidentally, the same analysis holds for the decrement operator.[1]

The two programs listed as Programs 11-1 and 11-2 were timed to determine the difference in execution speeds.

```
main()
{
    int i = 0;

    while (i < 50000)
        i++;
    exit(0);
}
```

Program 11-1   Timing Program with Increment Operator

```
main()
{
    int i = 0;

    while (i < 50000)
        i = i + 1;
    exit(0);
}
```

Program 11-2   Timing Program with Addition Operator

On the author's home computer, Program 11-1 executed in .58 seconds and Program 11-2 took .82 seconds—a savings of about 30 percent! As a result, we will use increment and decrement operators whenever we can. Increment and decrement operators cannot be applied to variables on the left side of an assignment statement. As a result, this statement

---

[1] The increment instruction is faster because two of the four steps are combined into a single *add 1* instruction. This takes less time than storing the constant 1 into a register (step 2) and then adding it to another value (step 3).

```
                    total++ = nbr1 + nbr2;
```

is illegal.

Increment and decrement are *unary* operators, that is they require a single operand only, the variable being incremented (decremented). All unary operators have the same high precedence—one below the highest.

The real power of increment and decrement operators comes from their flexibility. Because they are implemented with a single CPU instruction, increment and decrement operators can be used almost anywhere, even in the middle of another expression! Further, *how* they are used changes how they are evaluated.

As we know, variables must be loaded into the CPU before any of the requested processing can occur. The CPU can operate on information stored in CPU registers only. Thus, once the CPU has loaded the value from memory, the data *in memory* no longer has an effect on the CPU's calculation. As a result, any changes made to the value in memory *after* it is loaded into the CPU have no effect on the processing done by the CPU. In contrast, any changes that occur before the CPU loads a value are reflected in the CPU's processing.

Increment and decrement operators take advantage of this distinction between memory and the CPU in a very interesting way. We can have the increment (decrement) take effect either *before* the value is loaded into the CPU or *after*. The increment (decrement) is reflected in an expression's evaluation if done before being loaded and is not part of the calculation if done after!

If the operator appears to the left of (before) the variable, the increment is performed *before* the variable's value is loaded into the CPU. In this case, the CPU's value and the variable's value are the same. For example, if

```
                    int nbr;

                    nbr = 2;
```

then the statement

```
                    total = ++nbr * 2;
```

increments *nbr*'s value by 1 before it is loaded into the CPU. Even though *nbr* equals 2 when the expression starts, 3 is the value loaded into the CPU. Once there, it is multiplied by 2. This occurs because the ++ is to the left of *nbr* in the expression. Thus,

```
                    ++nbr * 2
```

is the same as

```
                    nbr = nbr + 1;
                    total = nbr * 2;
```

Sec. 11.1 Increment and Decrement Operators

The increment operator has higher precedence than the multiplication operator and

```
++nbr * 2
```

becomes

```
3 * 2
```

and 6 is stored in *total*.

If we move the increment operator to the other side of the variable, for example,

```
nbr++
```

the increment takes place *after* the variable's value is loaded into the CPU. Again, if

```
int nbr;

nbr = 2;
```

then the statement

```
total = nbr++ * 2;
```

stores 4 in *total*, even though *nbr* holds 3 after the statement has been executed. Thus,

```
total = nbr++ * 2;
```

is the same as

```
total = nbr * 2;
nbr = nbr + 1;
```

When a variable's value is loaded into a CPU register, that variable's value is *fixed* in the expression being evaluated. Increment (decrement) operators that take effect before the value is fixed are called *prefix* operators. Those that increment (decrement) after the value is fixed are called *postfix* operators.

Exercise 11-1   Consider this program:

```
#define TAX_CALC(dlr) ((dlr) * (1 + .065))

#include "stdio.h"
```

```
main()
{
    int count = 0;      /* loop counter */

    while (++count < 10)
        printf("Tax on $%d is %.2f\n", count, TAX_CALC(count));
    exit(0);
}
```

Which of the following does it print out tax calculations for?

a. 0 to 11
b. 1 to 11
c. 0 to 10
d. 1 to 10
e. 0 to 9
f. 1 to 9?

Incidentally, if we only want to add one to a variable, either

```
++count;        /* prefix operator */
```

or

```
count++;        /* postfix operator */
```

will do. Some people suggest that

```
++count;
```

is easier to "see" in a program. Throughout this text, however, we will use

```
count++;
```

in these situations, from force of (author's) habit.

11.2 USING INCREMENT OPERATORS IN ARRAY INDEXES

In the **print_pl( )** function (Program 9-4), this loop is used to print each cost entry and then add this category's amount to the total cost:

```
for(count = 0; count < cost_count; count = count + 1) {
    printf("%-*s  $%6ld\n", MAX_LEN - 1, cost_cat[count],
                            cost_amt[count]);
    totalcost = totalcost + cost_amt[count];
}
```

Sec. 11.2 Using Increment Operators in Array Indexes

There are several ways to "speed up" this loop with an increment operator.
First, we can substitute

```
count++
```

for

```
count = count + 1
```

in the **for** loop

```
for(count = 0; count < cost_count; count++)
```

We even can do away with the loop increment statement entirely by inserting an increment operator into the cost totaling statement:

```
totalcost = totalcost + cost_amt[count++];
```

We use a postfix operator here so that the increment occurs after the array element is indexed. This ensures that the element just printed is the one added to *totalcost*. With this change, the loop becomes:

```
for(count = 0; count < cost_count;) {
    printf("%-*s $%6ld\n", MAX_LEN - 1, cost_cat[count],
                    cost_amt[count]);
    totalcost = totalcost + cost_amt[count++];
}
```

Note the empty increment section in the **for** loop.
Another approach is to use a **while** instead of a **for** loop:

```
count = 0;
while (count < cost_count) {
    printf("%-*s  $%6ld\n", MAX_LEN - 1, cost_cat[count],
                    cost_amt[count]);
    totalcost + totalcost + cost_amt[count];
    count++;
}
```

By incrementing the loop counter in one of the loop's statements, we even can shorten the loop as shown in Segment 11-1.

```
        count = 0;
    while (count < cost_count) {
        printf("%-*s   $%6ld\n", MAX_LEN - 1, cost_cat[count],
                                 cost_amt[count]);
        totalcost =  totalcost + cost_amt[count++];
    }
```

Segment 11-1   Exchanging a **for** with a **while**

It is very common in C programs to increment a loop counter inside a statement in the loop's body.

Exercise 11-2   Rewrite the **while** loop in Segment 11-1 to increment the counter as part of the logical test:

```
              count < cost_count
```

With so many possibilities, which loop should we use? As a rule, we should use **for** when the loop contains a counting variable that is explicitly initialized and incremented. After all, **for** loops were specifically designed for these kinds of loops. Since it is best to be obvious when programming, we will use the **for** loop listed in Segment 11-2.

```
    for (count = 0; count < rev_count; count++) {
        printf("%-*s   $%6ld\n", MAX_LEN -1, cost_cat[count],
            cost_amt[count]);
        totalcost =  totalcost + cost_amt[count];
    }
```

Segment 11-2

When evaluated as part of an expression, the increment and decrement operators cause a change to occur in the computer's memory. This is called a *side effect* because the state of the computer changes (i.e., memory is modified). This is unusual. The only other operator that does this is an assignment operator. Further, it means that we must be very careful of the side effects caused by our use of these operators.

As an illustration, it might appear that we can rearrange the statements in the **for** loop in Segment 11-2 to increment the counting variable in the **printf( )** statement:

```
    for (count = 0; count < rev_count;) {
       totalcost =  totalcost + cost_amt[count];
       printf("%-*s   $%6ld\n", MAX_LEN -1, cost_cat[count],
            cost_amt[count++]);
    }
```

However, this may not work since we don't know the order of evaluation of **printf( )**'s arguments. If the second argument is referred to first, the increment operator's side

Sec. 11.3   Assignment Operators   169

effect occurs before the other argument is retrieved. The result is that the array indexes do not match and the wrong amount is printed! Moreover, even if it works properly on one machine, it may not work on another. It fully depends on how a particular C compiler is implemented.

RULE   Never use an increment (decrement) operator in a statement that contains another instance of the variable being incremented (decremented).

As a further example, never write

```
total = ++nbr1 + nbr1;
```

Instead, use

```
total = 2 * ++nbr1;
```

In most situations, increment and decrement operators can be applied unambiguously. However, it is best to avoid problems by not using them in any expression where their effect is questionable.

11.3 ASSIGNMENT OPERATORS

Another efficient shorthand in the C language is the *assignment operator*. Assignment operators take advantage of the same efficiency exploited by increment and decrement operators. Assignment operators can be used in expressions when the same variable appears on both sides of an equal sign. For example, in this statement

```
value1 = value1 * value2;
```

we multiply *value1* by *value2* and store the product back in *value1*. Because *value1* appears on both sides of the assignment, it must be referred to twice! This is inefficient. C allows us to shorten this to

```
value1 *= value2;
```

An assignment operator can be created for all the binary arithmetic operators by combining them with the equal sign. Thus,

```
value1 = value1 + value2     becomes     value1 += value2

value1 = value1 - value2     becomes     value1 -= value2

value1 = value1 / value2     becomes     value1 /= value2
```

and so on.

All assignment operators have the same, very low precedence (see Table 11-2, below). For example, in this assignment,

```
value1 *= value2 + value3;
```

the addition is evaluated first (since it has higher precedence) even though the assignment operator involves multiplication. As a result, the expression

```
value1 *= value2 + value3;
```

is evaluated as

```
value1 = value1 * (value2 + value3);
```

Put another way, the expression on the right hand side is fully evaluated before the assignment operator is brought into play.

Consider this statement

```
huge_array[i2+1] [c1+2] = huge_array[i2+1] [c1+2] + 5;
```

At a glance, it is not obvious that we simply are adding 5 to the listed array element. An assignment operator clarifies this statement:

```
huge_array[i2+1] [c1+2] += 5;
```

Assignment operators not only make our programs easier to read and write but can make our programs execute faster as well.

We can use an assignment operator in the **print_pl( )** function (Program 9-4). In **print-pl( )**, we total the revenue and cost amounts inside the loops that print out this information. The loop that prints the revenue categories is shown in Segment 11-3.

```
for(count = 0; count < rev_count; count++) {
    printf("%-*s  $%6ld\n", MAX_LEN - 1, rev_cat[count],
           rev_amt[count]);
    totalrev = totalrev + rev_amt[count];
}
```

Segment 11-3   Revenue Printing Loop

The value of *totalrev* is accumulated by the last statement in the loop

```
totalrev = totalrev + rev_amt[count];
```

By using an assignment operator, we can shorten this to

```
totalrev += rev_amt[count];
```

11.4 THE CONDITIONAL OPERATOR

C contains an unusual operator that implements the **if** - **else** structure, that is, evaluates to different values based on a logical test. This is why is it called the *conditional* operator.

Consider this code segment:

```
if (nbr1 > nbr2)
    max = nbr1;
else
    max = nbr2;
```

It compares *nbr1* to *nbr2* and stores the larger of them into *max*. In fact, storing one of two values into another variable is a common use of the **if** - **else** structure. However, to do so requires two separate assignment statements.

In C, we can replace such conditional statements with the conditional operator. Transforming a programming structure into an operator allows us to use a single assignment statement. Again, our code gets smaller and faster.

The conditional operator is represented by the two characters **?** and **:**. The operator evaluates one of two expressions depending on the outcome of a logical test. This operator is illustrated by the expression

```
(nbr1 > nbr2) ? nbr1 : nbr2
```

The expression evaluates to *nbr1* (whatever is between the **?** and the **:**) if the logical test

```
nbr1 > nbr2
```

is true and to *nbr2* (whatever is after the **:**) if the test is false. This is shown graphically in Figure 11-1.

```
(nbr1 > nbr2) ? nbr1 : nbr2
    ↑             ↑      ↑
Logical test      ↑      Value of entire expression
                          if test is false
         Value of entire expression
            if test is true
```

Figure 11-1 Evaluation of Conditional Operator

We can replace the previous **if** - **else** structure with this expression:

```
max = (nbr1 > nbr2) ? nbr1 : nbr2;
```

If *nbr1* is larger than *nbr2*, this statement becomes

```
max = nbr1;
```

otherwise it evaluates to

```
max = nbr2;
```

Parentheses are not required around the expression's logical test. This is because the conditional operator has very low precedence, just above the assignment operator. Thus, most operators have higher precedence anyway! However, the intent of the operator is much clearer if parentheses are used (and sometimes even that doesn't help).

As we know, before an operator is evaluated, all operands must have the same data type; the result of the operation is that data type. The same is true of the conditional operator. Consider this example

```
max = (max <= 1) ? 1 : max * .5;
```

This statement either stores 1 in *max* (max <= 1) or multiplies *max* by 0.5. The data type of the constant 1 is **int** and of

```
max * .5
```

is **double**. Before the expression is evaluated, the 1 is converted to 1.0, so that the data types match.

Exercise 11-3   What does this do?

```
result = (totalrev >= totalcost) ? totalrev - totalcost :
                                   totalcost - totalrev;
printf("      %s           %ld\n",
       (totalrev >= totalcost) ? "PROFIT" : "LOSS", result);
```

By far the most common use of the conditional operator is in macro expressions. An obvious example is

```
#define max(a,b)   (((a) > (b)) ? (a) : (b))
```

which evaluates to the maximum of the two arguments. Incidentally, the parentheses are necessary to ensure proper evaluation if either macro argument is an expression or **maxi** is used in a larger expression.

The **if** - **else if** - **else** structure can be simulated by nesting conditional operators. For example, suppose we want to compare total revenues to total costs and get the result as follows:

Sec. 11.4 The Conditional Operator

Test	Result	
totalrev > totalcost	1	(Profit)
totalrev == totalcost	0	(Breakeven)
totalrev < totalcost	-1	(Loss)

We can do this with an expression that contains two conditional operators. This expression is listed in Segment 11-4.

```
(totalrev > totalcost) ? 1 : (totalrev == totalcost) ? 0 : -1
```

Segment 11-4 Nested Conditional Operators

If the logical test

```
totalrev > totalcost
```

is true, the expression evaluates to 1. If it is false, C tests

```
totalrev == totalcost
```

If this test is true, the expression becomes 0; otherwise, it evaluates to −1.

For the expression in Segment 11-4 to work properly, the conditional operator must associate from right to left, which it does. In this expression, the operators associate as shown in Figure 11-2.

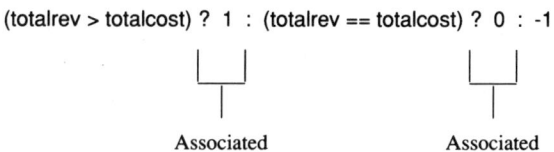

Figure 11-2 Associating Conditional Operators

Put another way, ? and : are like right and left parentheses. They can be matched up (from the inside out).

Exercise 11-4 Write an **if** - **else if** - **else** statement that matches this expression:

```
v3 = (v1 > v2) ? (v2 > 0) ? v2 : 0 : (v1 > 1) ? v2 : v1;
```

As the preceding paragraph and Exercise 11-4 demonstrate, the conditional operator can be confusing. It is recommended that the conditional operator be used sparingly and only that one appear in any single expression.

11.5 THE UNARY MINUS OPERATOR

The last operator we will discuss in this chapter is the *unary minus operator*. This is the familiar negation sign from arithmetic, as in -3. It is the sign of a variable or expression and can be used with all arithmetic types. All unary operators have the same precedence and associativity. Thus, unary minus falls in the same precedence level as increment, decrement, and cast operators (see Table 11-2). The expression

```
-nbr1 + nbr2
```

will be evaluated as

```
(-nbr1) + nbr2.
```

All the operators introduced in this chapter have been added to the precedence table listed in Table 11-2.

TABLE 11-2 Precedence Table

Operator	Associativity
() []	Left to right
++ -- -	Right to left
* / %	Left to right
+ -	Left to right
< <= >= >	Left to right
== !=	Left to right
?:	Right to left
= += -= *= /= %=	Right to left
,	Left to right

Program 11-3 is a listing of the **flex-p1** program rewritten to use the features discussed in this chapter. Even though **main( )** is unchanged, it is listed for continuity. As usual, each change has been highlighted in bold print.

Sec. 11.5 The Unary Minus Operator

```c
/* ***** FLEX-PL *****
 *
 * This program reads the category and amount of a set of
 * revenues and costs and prints a formatted P&L statement.
 * The program reads entries until a Q only is entered
 * as a category name (the quit signal) or until MAX_CAT
 * categories have been read.
 *
 * Modified to use operators to be more efficient.
 *
 * Written for Ray Swartz for "Doing Business with C"
 */

#define MAX_LEN 31        /* Length of category name strings */
#define MAX_CAT 20        /* maximum number of category names */

#include "stdio.h"
#include "getcat.c"       /* source code for getcat function */

main()
{
    char rev_cat[MAX_CAT] [MAX_LEN];  /* revenue categories */
    char cost_cat[MAX_CAT] [MAX_LEN]; /* cost categories */
    long cost_amt[MAX_CAT];           /* cost amounts */
    long rev_amt[MAX_CAT];            /* revenue amounts */
    int rev_count;        /* number of revenue categories */
    int cost_count;       /* number of cost categories */
    int getrev();         /* read all revenue entries */
    int getcost();        /* read all cost entries */
    void print_pl();      /* print the P&L statement */

    rev_count = getrev(rev_cat, rev_amt);       /* get revenues */
    cost_count = getcost(cost_cat, cost_amt);   /* get costs */
    print_pl(rev_cat, rev_amt, rev_count,
            cost_cat, cost_amt, cost_count);
    exit(0);
}

/* ***** GETREV *****
 *
 * This function prompts for and reads revenue categories
 * and amounts.  The category name and amount arrays
 * are passed to the function as arguments.
 *
 * Written by Ray Swartz for "Doing Business with C"
 *
 * Modified to check for a quit signal (Q) and return
 * the number of categories entered.
 */
```

```c
int getrev(cat_name, cat_amt)
char cat_name[][MAX_LEN];   /* category names */
long cat_amt[];             /* amounts */
{
    int printf();
    long getcat();          /* read category and return amount */
    int count;              /* loop counter */

    printf("\nEnter Dollar amounts only -- no cents\n");
    printf("\n\nREVENUES\n\n");
    for (count = 0; count < MAX_CAT; count++) {
        cat_amt[count] = getcat(cat_name[count], "Revenue");
        if (cat_name[count][0] == 'Q' &&
            cat_name[count][1] == '\0')    /* test for quit signal */
                break;      /* possible loop exit */
    }
    return(count);
}

/* ***** GETCOST *****
 *
 * This function prompts for and reads cost categories
 * and amounts.  The category name and amount arrays
 * are passed to the function as arguments, as is
 * the number of categories to enter.
 *
 * Written by Ray Swartz for "Doing Business with C"
 *
 * Modified to check for a quit signal (Q) and return
 * the number of categories entered.
 */

int getcost(cat_name, cat_amt)
long cat_name[] [MAX_LEN];  /* category names */
long cat_amt[];             /* amounts */
{
    int printf();
    long getcat();          /* read category and return amount */
    int count;              /* loop counter */

    printf("\nEnter Dollar amounts only -- no cents\n");
    printf("\n\nCOSTS\n\n");
    for (count = 0; count < MAX_CAT; count++) {
        cat_amt[count] = getcat(cat_name[count], "Cost");
        if (cat_name[count][0] == 'Q' &&
            cat_name[count][1] == '\0')    /* test for quit signal */
                break;      /* possible loop exit */
    }
    return(count);
}
```

Sec. 11.5 The Unary Minus Operator

```c
/* ***** PRINT_PL *****
 *
 * This function prints a formatted Profit and Loss
 * statement.  It is sent two category name arrays
 * and two category amount arrays--one set for
 * revenues and one for costs.  The number of entries
 * of each type is sent to the function as arguments, also.
 *
 * Written by Ray Swartz for "Doing Business with C"
 *
 */

void print_pl(rev_cat, rev_amt, rev_count,
              cost_cat, cost_amt, cost_count)
char rev_cat[] [MAX_LEN];   /* revenue category names */
long rev_amt[];             /* revenue amounts */
int rev_count;              /* number of revenue entries */
char cost_cat[] [MAX_LEN];  /* cost category names */
long cost_amt[];            /* cost amounts */
int cost_count;             /* number of cost entries */
{
    int printf();
    int count;              /* loop counter */
    long totalrev;          /* revenue amounts total */
    long totalcost;         /* cost amounts total */

    printf("\tProfit and Loss for Johnson's Books\n\n");
    printf("          REVENUE\n\n");

    /* Loop to print and total the revenue categories */

    totalrev = 0;
    for (count = 0; count < rev_count; count++) {
        printf("%-*s   $%6ld\n", MAX_LEN - 1, rev_cat[count],
               rev_amt[count]);
        totalrev += rev_amt[count];
    }
    printf("                                  ------\n");
    printf("          TOTAL REVENUE       $%7ld\n\n\n",
           totalrev);
```

```
        /* Loop to print and total the cost categories */

        totalcost = 0;
        for (count = 0; count < cost_count; count++) {
            printf("%-*s  $%6ld\n", MAX_LEN - 1, cost_cat[count],
                   cost_amt[count]);
            totalcost += cost_amt[count];
        }
        printf("                                          ------\n");
        printf("          TOTAL COST                  $%7ld\n\n\n",
               totalcost);
        if (totalrev >= totalcost)
            printf("          PROFIT                      $%7ld\n",
                   totalrev - totalcost);
        else
            printf("          LOSS                       ($%7ld)\n",
                   totalcost - totalrev);
        return;
}
```

Program 11-3 The Modified **flex-pl** Program

11.6 USING C'S OPERATORS

C has a large number of operators to do a multitude of tasks. At first, it will probably seem awkward to use many of these operators, especially the conditional, assignment, and increment/decrement operators. You may even be thinking, "Surely these operators make our programs more difficult to change and document!"

In reality, the usefulness of these operators becomes more obvious with repeated use. In many cases, it isn't long before other languages are viewed as "limited" because they don't offer many of C's features! Further, the effective use of operators is one idiom of the C language. It simply makes no sense to program in C without using them. Finally, we must get acquainted with all of C's operators because we will come across them often as we encounter C programs written by others.

RULE   When programming in C; do as C programmers do!

11.7 SUMMARY

1. C contains several operators that make C programs more efficient.
2. Increment (decrement) operators allow us to add 1 (subtract 1) from an integer variable without using an assignment operator.

Sec. 11.7   Summary

3. Increment and decrement operators identify a single instruction inside the computer.

4. Increment and decrement operators are unary and can be used to change the values of operands in other expressions.

5. If an increment (decrement) operator appears to the left of its operand, the variable is incremented (decremented) before that operand is evaluated in a larger expression. If the operator appears to the right of its operand, the variable is incremented (decremented) after the operand is evaluated in the larger expression.

6. Increment and decrement operators have side effects, that is, they cause memory to be changed. As a result, an expression should not use the increment (decrement) operator on a variable that appears more than once in an expression.

7. Assignment operators combine an operator with an assignment to create a more efficient operation. The expression

$$a = a \; op \; b$$

becomes

$$a \; op= \; b.$$

8. The conditional operator implements an **if** - **else** structure as an operator. This operator evaluates to different values based on the result of a logical test.

9. The unary minus operator implements negation and is used to make positive numbers negative and vice versa.

E X E R C I S E S

11-5. Write this program as concisely (as short) as possible:

```
#include "stdio.h"

#define TAX_RATE .065

main()
{
    int amount = 1;
    float tax_amt;
    float total;
```

```
        printf("Amount\tSales Tax\tTotal\n");
        while (amount < 20) {
            tax_amt = amount * TAX_RATE;
            total = tax_amt + amount;
            printf("%6d\t%9.2f\t%.2f\n", amount, tax_amt, total);
            amount = amount + 2;
        }
        exit(0);
    }
```

11-6. Write the following statements as a single statement.

a.
```
count = count + 1;
total = value * count * .065;
```

b.
```
if (count != 0)
    total = cost / count;
else
    total = 0;
```

c.
```
if (district = 1) {
    tax = .065;
    total = total + cost * tax;
}
else {
    tax = .07;
    total = total + cost * tax;
}
```

11-7. Define a macro, called *max3*, that evaluates to the maximum of its three arguments. Use conditional operators.

12

Scope Rules and Storage Classes

In the program **flex-pl**, a variable named *count* is defined in both the **get_entry( )** and **print_pl( )** functions. Is this necessary or can we use *count* anywhere in a program once it is defined? To answer this question, we must learn more about what information C stores on the variables we define in our programs.

In addition to name and data type, C provides two additional attributes for each defined variable: *scope* and *storage class*. A variable's scope determines when a variable or function is *visible* to (can be referred to by) the current routine.

A variable's storage class identifies how long the memory associated with that variable remains active (stores information).

C provides two kinds of scope and two types of storage. A variable can have *block* or *file* scope and *automatic* or *static* storage.

12.1 BLOCK SCOPE

A variable defined between a set of braces is in scope only between those braces. Variables are unknown outside the block where they are defined. Thus, all of the variables defined in **main( )** can be used in **main( )** only. The same goes for those defined in **get_entry( )**, **print_pl( )**, and the other functions in **flex_pl**. In fact, this separation is so strong that we can even use the same variable names in different functions without problem, as we did with *count*.

Variables can be defined whenever a new block of code begins, that is, after any opening brace. This means an **if** statement or **while** loop can define and use its own set of variables. While it is uncommon to create new variables inside such blocks, it is possible to do so. In most instances, a function block is where new block scope variables are defined.

Variables defined inside a function or block are often called *local* variables because such variables can only be referred to within that function (or block). If two variables with the same name are in scope at the same time, the scope rules identify which variable is being referred to when a reference is made to this variable name. Put another way, if the statement

```
count = count + 1;
```

is encountered, we can use the scope rules to determine which variable named *count* gets incremented.

12.2 AUTOMATIC STORAGE

In addition to having a specific scope, all variables belong to a *storage class*. A variable's storage class indicates when and for what duration the variable's memory is active. The default storage class for block scope variables is *automatic*.

Automatic variables only "exist" while the function block they are part of is being executed. For example, when the **getlong( )** function (Program 6-1) is called, the local variables *instr* and *nbr* are created. These variables are available until **getlong( )** returns, at which point they disappear. This is why such variables are called automatic—they automatically appear inside their function (or block) and disappear when the function (or block) terminates. As a result, any changes made to automatic variables have effect only within a single invocation of a function (or block). Automatic variables are said to provide temporary storage.

C reserves the keyword **auto** to define the storage class of automatic variables. However, automatic storage is the default for local (block scope) variables and, by convention, **auto** is left out of the definition. Thus,

```
auto char instr[81];
```

and

```
char instr[81];
```

are equivalent. In fact, the author has never seen the keyword **auto** used in a C program! We shall continue to omit **auto** from our variable definitions.

Sec. 12.3   **static** Storage   183

C does not initialize automatic storage. Further, since automatic variables are created anew each time the function is called, these variables store *random* values (i.e., garbage) when they are first used in a function. We cannot assume anything about their values at the beginning of a function. Automatic variables must be initialized before the value stored in them is referred to. A common C programming error is to assume that automatic variables are initialized to 0.

RULE   Initialize automatic variables before referring to the value stored in them.

12.3 static STORAGE

In addition to automatic storage, C also allows **static** storage. Static variables provide permanent storage. C allows block scope variables to have **static** storage. While **static** local variables can only be referred to inside a particular block, they do not disappear when the block terminates. Instead, their storage remains active, even though the variables can only be accessed inside the block where they are defined.

The effect of **static** variables is that the programs "remember" the values stored in them across function invocations. For example, consider the **getlong( )** function. Many times, **getlong( )** is used to enter a series of values that are totaled somewhere in the program. A useful variation of **getlong( )** might actually keep track of the total of all values read so far. The function could then report the accumulated total at the appropriate time.

As we know, a legal data type is required to define a variable. In addition, a variable's storage class must be defined, too. For a block scope (local) variable, if no storage class is listed it is assumed to be automatic. Since most block scope variables have automatic storage, their definitions list data type only.

Creating a **static** variable requires putting the keyword **static** as the first word in that variable's definition. To define *total* to be a **static long** requires

```
static long total;
```

Although there is a default storage class, no such default exists for data type. Thus, this definition

```
static total;
```

will cause a compiler error.

To illustrate the use of **static** local variables, we will write a function called **tgetlong( )**. **tgetlong( )** performs just like **getlong( )** with the exception that it keeps a running total of all values entered by the function. A **static** local variable will be used to accumulate this total.

Like **getlong( )**, **tgetlong( )** is sent a single argument, the prompt to print, and returns the value entered as a **long**. To make the totaling feature useful, **tgetlong( )** must be able to report this total as well as reset the **static** accumulator to 0.

Normally, the argument sent to **tgetlong( )** is a string of characters. However, when **tgetlong( )** sees a specific argument, it will return its stored total and then reset its total to 0.

The "reset" argument has to be something that cannot be used as a prompt. C contains just such a special value, **NULL**. **NULL** represents a string with *no* storage. This is the value we will send to **tgetlong( )** when we want to know the total of values entered since the total was reset. Incidentally, the value **NULL** is defined in the file *stdio.h* and we need not concern ourselves with what **NULL** equals or how it is defined.

A **NULL** string (one with no storage) is different than an *empty* string. Specifically, the string represented by

" "

holds one character, the '\0'. **NULL**, on the other hand, is equivalent to a string with no storage capability. The key point is that **NULL** is distinguishable from all other strings.

RULE **NULL** represents a string without storage capacity. It is distinguishable from all other strings.

When **tgetlong( )** receives **NULL** as an argument, it returns the stored total and resets its accumulator to 0. For all other arguments, the function prints the string as a prompt and returns the number entered, adding to the **static** accumulator before it does so. The **tgetlong( )** function is listed as Function 12-1.

```
/*  ***** TGETLONG *****
 * This function prints a prompt (sent in as an argument) and
 * reads a long value which is returned by the function.
 * The function accumulates the total of all values entered.
 * This accumulated total is returned and the accumulator is reset
 * to zero when NULL is the argument passed.
 *
 * Written by Ray Swartz for "Doing Business with C"
 */

long tgetlong(prompt)
char prompt[];    /* prompt to print or NULL signal */
{
    static long total;   /* block scope - static storage */
    long value;          /* converted value */
    long atol();
    char *gets();
    char instr[30];      /* input string */
```

Sec. 12.3　static Storage

```
        if (prompt == NULL) {
           value = total;
           total = 0;          /* reset the accumulator */
        }
        else {  /* read and convert a value */
           printf("%s: ", prompt);
           gets(instr);
           value = atol(instr);
           total += value;     /* accumulate total entered */
        }
        return(value);
    }
```

Function 12-1　The **tgetlong**() Function

To test if the argument sent to **tgetlong**() is a real string or not, we simply compare the formal parameter *prompt* to the defined term **NULL**.[1]

At first glance, it may seem as if we have ignored the important rule, always to initialize accumulator variables before using them. However, this advice specifically mentions *automatic* variables as requiring initialization. **static** variables, unlike *automatic* ones, have permanent storage and are initialized by the compiler. **static** numeric variables are set to 0 and static **char** or string variables to '\0'.

RULE　　**static** variables are initialized to 0 ('\0' for strings) when they are defined.

As a result, **tgetlong**() works properly, even though the accumulator, *total*, is not explicitly set to 0. Program 12-1 is a test program for **tgetlong**() and Output 12-1 shows the test performed.

```
#include "stdio.h"
#include "tgetlong.c"   /* code for tgetlong function */

main()
{
   long tgetlong();
   long test_total;    /* to test tgetlong total */
   int count;          /* loop counter */

   test_total = 0;  /* test_total is an automatic local variable */
   for (count = 0; count < 5; count = count + count++)
      test_total += tgetlong("Enter an integer number");
   printf("\ntest_total = %ld, tgetlong's total = %ld\n\n",
          test_total, tgetlong(NULL));
```

---

[1] Why and how this works will be explained fully in Part 4.

```
    test_total = 0;   /* to test that tgetlong resets total */
    for (count = 0; count < 5; count = count + count++)
        test_total += tgetlong("enter number");
    printf("\ntest_total = %ld, tgetlong's total = %ld\n\n",
           test_total, tgetlong(NULL));
    exit(0);
}
```

Program 12-1 Test Program for **tgetlong( )** Function

```
tgetlong test program run

Enter an integer number: 5662
Enter an integer number: 33221
Enter an integer number: 254
Enter an integer number: 1
Enter an integer number: 334

test_total = 39472, tgetlong's total = 39472

Enter an integer number: 3487
Enter an integer number: -148
Enter an integer number: 2214
Enter an integer number: 669
Enter an integer number: 457

test_total = 6679, tgetlong's total = 6679
```

Output 12-1 Test of the **tgetlong( )** Function

In addition to testing the **tgetlong( )** function, Program 12-1 demonstrates an important point. In almost every instance where a **static** variable is used, the same effect can be achieved by storing the same information in an automatic variable in the routine that calls the function. In Program 12-1 this is done by *test_total*. If necessary, this data can be passed to the function as an argument.

This is not to say that **static** storage should not be used. However, it is important not to *overuse* **static** storage. **static** local storage is appropriate in three instances. First, **static** local storage is necessary if a function must store information across function calls and the function is called by different routines. This is the case with **tgetlong( )**. Second, **static** storage is necessary if the information being stored is used only inside the function and must be kept across function calls. The typical example is a random number generator that needs the previous value to generate the next one. Third, **static** local storage allows certain variables to be initialized. Initialization is discussed in detail later in this chapter.

static local storage is one of the special features of C. However, it can cause problems if used without thoughtful planning. We are accustomed to getting a "clean"

Sec. 12.4   File Scope   187

set of variables when we enter a function. Since **static** local variables don't automatically reset, such variables can wreak havoc if not used properly. In all cases, be careful when using **static** local variables.

12.4 FILE SCOPE

In addition to block scope, C provides a kind of scope that is not limited by function boundaries. Such variables are said to have file scope and are often called *global* variables. File scope variables can be referenced anywhere from their definition to the end of the source code file that contains them.

File scope variables have **static** storage. This cannot be changed and **static** should not be used when defining file scope variables (see section 12.6).

Variables defined inside a function's beginning and ending braces are local to that function.

To illustrate global variables, we will rewrite the **tgetlong** function to store its total in a global variable. The purpose of the **tgetlong( )** function is to make the total of all values entered available without forcing the programmer to total them explicitly. **tgetlong( )** uses **static** storage to do this. The same trick can be performed with a global variable.

In fact, using a global variable makes the programming much simpler—we don't have to bother defining it in the function, it is there already! In addition, there is no need to reset the total inside the function. Resetting it can be done anywhere, since a global variable can be referred to throughout the source code file.

File scope introduces a complication, however. What happens if two variables with the same name have overlapping scope? As an illustration, suppose our program defines *total* to be a **double** variable with file scope. In addition, suppose one of the program's functions defines *total* to be an **int** variable. Now, what happens when the variable *total* is referenced? Does the block scope or file scope variable get used?

When two variables have overlapping scope, the one with "more general" scope is *hidden* by the one with "less general" scope. Thus, file scope variables are not available in functions that define variables (either automatic or **static**) with the same names. In the previous example, whenever *total* is used inside the function, the variable with block scope is referenced.

What is necessary to allow a function to access a global variable? There are two ways for a function to define its intention to use a global variable. One is simply to use the variable in a statement. This is called *declaration by inclusion*. The other is to declare the variable to be *external* to the function with the **extern** keyword. Variables defined *outside* the confines of a function are said to be *external* to that function.

The **gtgetlong( )** function (the "g" stands for global) is just like **tgetlong( )** except it adds the value read to the global variable *total*. Function 12-2 shows a version of **gtgetlong( )** using declaration by inclusion. Function 12-3 demonstrates **extern** declaration.

```
    long total;         /* defines total to have file scope */

    long gtgetlong(prompt)
    char prompt[];
    {
        long atol();
        long value;         /* converted value */
        char *gets();
        char instr[30];     /* input string */

        printf("%s: ", prompt);
        gets(instr);
        value = atol(instr);
        total += value;     /* declaration by inclusion */
        return(value);
    }
```

Function 12-2 The **gtgetlong( )** Function with Declaration by Inclusion

```
/* assume that total was defined to have file scope */

long gtgetlong(prompt)
char prompt[];
{
    extern long total;    /* declares total to be external */
    long atol();
    long value;           /* converted value */
    char *gets();
    char instr[30];       /* input string */

    printf("%s: ", prompt);
    gets(instr);
    value = atol(instr);
    total += value;       /* adds value to external total */
    return(value);
}
```

Function 12-3 The **gtgetlong( )** Function with an **extern** Declaration

As an example of usage, Program 12-2 shows a program that tests the **gtgetlong( )** function. Compare Program 12-2 with Program 12-1 to see the difference between block scope and file scope variables. The lines in Bold are those lines changed from Program 12-1.

```
long total;       /* defines total to have file scope */

#include "stdio.h"
#include "gtgetlong.c"   /* code for gtgetlong function */
```

Sec. 12.4 File Scope

```
main()
{
    extern long total;
    long etgetlong();
    long test_total;   /* to test tgetlong total */
    int count;         /* loop counter */

    test_total = 0;    /* test_total is an automatic local variable */
    for (count = 0; count < 5; count = count + 1)
        test_total += gtgetong("Enter an integer number");
    printf("\ntest_total = %ld, extern total = %ld\n\n",
            test_total, total);
    test_total = 0;    /* reset both test_total */
    total = 0;         /* and total to 0 */
    for (count = 0; count < 5; count = count + 1)
        test_total += gtgetlong("enter number");
    printf("\ntest_total = %ld, extern total = %ld\n\n",
            test_total, total);
    exit(0);
}
```

Program 12-2 Test Program for **gtgetlong( )** Function

Given the same input as that used in Output 12-1, Program 12-2 would give the same results as Program 12-1.

Since global variables have static storage, global variables are initialized to 0 if numeric and '\0' if **char** when defined. Note that the declaration

```
extern long total;
```

does not affect the value stored in *total*. Declaring a variable **extern** tells the compiler that this function will access a variable external to the function. Note that the data type of *total* is part of the external declaration.

RULE   Global (file scope) variables are initialized to 0 (\0 for strings) when defined.

It should be emphasized that the keyword **extern** does nothing more than state a function's intention to use an external variable. The keyword has no effect on this variable's storage.

A distinction must be made between *defining* a global variable and *declaring* an external one. Defining a global variable means to allocate storage for it. In essence, this creates it. Declaring an external variable notifies the compiler that this function will use a variable defined externally. A global variable can be declared many times (with the **extern** keyword) but defined only once. As an illustration, in Program 12-2, *total* is defined by the statement

```
                       long total;
```

that appears above the start of **main( )** and is declared inside **main( )** by

```
                    extern long total;
```

Automatic variables, are defined and declared by the same statement. Thus, in talking about automatic variables, we will use the term *define* to mean both definition and declaration. With file scope variables, we will be more selective in our use of these terms.

Global variables provide a great deal of flexibility to C programmers. Because global variables are visible everywhere (from their definition down), they make passing information between functions easy. This can be useful if a large number of variables must be passed amongst several functions. Instead of listing all these variables in the function call, we can define the variables to be global and then have the functions access them directly.

In addition, global variables provide a straightforward method for sharing information between functions that don't call one another. Instead of contriving a way to pass the information to both functions, it may be better to store this data in variables with file scope. For example, an input function and an output function don't call one another but may need to share information.

Global variables are a two-edged feature. The same attributes that make global variables attractive allow them to cause incredible problems. First, they disrupt the structure of our programs by allowing interdependencies between functions that are not obvious. Maintaining or debugging programs that make heavy use of global variables is very difficult and sometimes virtually impossible.

One major feature of structured programming is the creation of general functions that can be reused whenever needed. If we rely on global variables to pass information between functions, our programs will be forced to define a set of global variables just to make these functions work together. Eventually, similarly named variables will occur and some or all of these functions will have to be rewritten to resolve this naming conflict. In the end, indiscriminate use of global variables will make programs hard to write, debug, document, and maintain.

RULE   Global variables should be used with caution and only after other approaches have been considered.

12.5 EXTERNAL SCOPE

So far, the programs shown in this book have been small enough to fit into a single source code file. However, the source code for fully featured applications might be too large to fit comfortably into one file. Instead, the program might be split into several source code files that are compiled together to form the executable image. Further, when developing large systems, different programmers might work on entire sections of

Sec. 12.6 **static** File Scope

a program's source code. In addition, each one of these sections could be split into several files.

File scope variables are accessible to functions in other source code files if these variables are declared to be *external* to those files. As we know, the statement

```
extern long total;
```

declares *total* as a global variable defined elsewhere. If it appears in a file, the declaration makes *total* available to every function in that source code file, as a global variable.

Global variables provide a linkage between source code files. Suppose a change is to be made to just one of the functions in a program that has several source code files. Once that change is made, do we have to recompile the entire program?

Recall that compilation of a C program into an executable file is a two-step process. First, the source code commands are translated into machine language (compiling) and then the functions in the standard library are combined with this machine language file (linking) to create an executable file.

Thus, a single change in a program can be made without having to compile the entire program again. We simply have to compile the source code file that contains the change and then relink it with the compiled versions of the other (unchanged) source code files. This saves a lot of time, since compilation can be a lengthy process.[2]

Variables declared external to a function or a code file are noted by the compiler. It is up to the linker to resolve external references. This is why we can recompile only one of many source code files and then relink the entire program together.

In addition to declaring external variables in source code files that use them, we have to *define* external variables somewhere in the program. At present, differences exist amongst compilers as to how this is done. Some compilers require exactly one definition of a global variable. Others allow any number of definitions of a global variable, so long as they are all the same. Still others require the defining instance of a global variable to initialize the variable.[3] Clearly, the compiler's documentation must be checked before using global variables in a program with several source code files.

In most cases, a special header file is created that contains definitions for all the external variables. This file is then **#includ**ed in one of the program files, usually the one containing **main( )**. Global variables can be defined and declared in the same header file using conditional compilation.

12.6 static FILE SCOPE

Many of the problems associated with file scope variables arise in programs with multiple source code files. For this reason, C provides a way to limit the scope of global variables. Normally, global variables, if declared properly, can be seen in other program files.

---

[2] The entire program must be recompiled if the data type of a global variable is changed.

[3] The ANSI standard requires exactly one global definition.

It is external visibility that can cause naming conflicts amongst global variables. Using yet another C feature, we can limit a global variable's scope to the source code file where it is defined. This is done by defining a global variable to be **static**. **static** global variables have file scope but cannot be seen outside the source code file that defines them. That is, they are external to all functions in a specific file and out of scope everywhere else.

As an example, one common approach with programs that contain multiple source code files is to put all the input functions in a separate file. Let's suppose that this program uses **getint( )**, **getlong( )**, and **getdbl( )**. All three programs need a string variable to hold the value entered by the user. Instead of defining a separate string in each function, we can use a globally defined string.

However, to avoid naming conflicts, we want this input string to be visible in this program file only. Function 12-4 shows the source code file containing these entry functions.

```
/* instr is a static variable with file scope */
static char instr[30];   /* input string for all three input functions */

int getint(prompt)
char prompt[];
{
    extern char instr[30];
    char *gets();
    int printf();
    int atoi();

    printf("\n%s: ", prompt);
    gets(instr);
    return(atoi(instr));
}

long getlong(prompt)
char prompt[];
{
    extern char instr[30];
    char *gets();
    int printf();
    long atol();

    printf("\n%s: ", prompt);
    gets(instr);
    return(atol(instr));
}

double getdbl(prompt)
char prompt[];
```

```
{
    extern char instr[30];
    char *gets();
    int printf();
    double atof();

    printf("\n%s: ", prompt);
    gets(instr);
    return(atof(instr));
}
```

Function 12-4 Program File Containing Input Functions

instr is a character array. When declaring global arrays, it isn't necessary to include the array size in the declaration. Thus,

```
extern char instr;
```

is perfectly acceptable.

12.7 THE SCOPE OF FUNCTIONS

In addition to using the same input string, the functions in Function 12-4 all use **gets( )** and **printf( )**. If these functions could be declared globally, we wouldn't have to list them inside each entry function.

Unless otherwise stated, every function declaration is assumed to be external. That is, when we declare **printf( )** with

```
int printf();
```

it's as if we had written

```
extern int printf();
```

In fact, this is what makes **printf( )** available to the function that declares it.

This means we can declare **gets( )** and **printf( )** globally and then access them inside the entry functions. Function 12-5 shows this.

```
static char instr[30];    /* input string for all three input functions */
int printf();
char *gets();

int getint(prompt)
char prompt[];
```

```
{
    extern char instr;   /* array size is not required */
    int atoi();

    printf("\n%s: ", prompt);
    gets(instr);
    return(atoi(instr));
}

long getlong(prompt)
char prompt[];
{
    extern char instr;
    long atol();

    printf("\n%s: ", prompt);
    gets(instr);
    return(atol(instr));
}

double getdbl(prompt)
char prompt[];
{
    extern char instr;
    double atof();

    printf("\n%s: ", prompt);
    gets(instr);
    return(atof(instr));
}
```

Function 12-5 Program File Containing Input Functions

Incidentally, we also could declare **atoi( )**, **atol( )**, and **atof( )** externally. However, since these functions are only used once and in different places, it is best to include them in the function where they are called.

As with global variables, declaring functions is different than defining them. A function definition is where the code for the function is listed. The scope of a function's definition is assumed to be global.

There may be times when we want to restrict a function's scope to just the program file that contains the function definition. As with global variables, this can be done with the keyword **static**. Putting **static** in front of the function's name and data type in the definition does just this. As an example, Function 12-6 shows how to make **getint( )** a **static** function.

Sec. 12.8   The Scope of Function Parameters   195

```
    static char instr[30];    /* input string for all three input functions */

    static int getint(prompt)    /* can be used in this file only */
    char prompt[];
    {
        extern char instr;
        char *gets();
        int printf();
        int atoi();

        printf("\n%s: ", prompt);
        gets(instr);
        return(atoi(instr));
    }
```

Function 12-6   Making a Function **static**

12.8 THE SCOPE OF FUNCTION PARAMETERS

Even though a function's formal parameters are listed outside a function's braces, formal parameters have block scope. This is because formal parameters aren't separate variables; instead, they represent a local version of the function's arguments. Because function parameters have local scope, any changes made to them have only local effect, that is, changes made to formal parameters won't be seen outside the function's invocation.

To maintain local function parameters, C passes all function arguments by *value*. This means a function receives a *copy* of the the data stored in each of its arguments. Any changes to this data affect this copy, not the original. When the function terminates, the formal parameters, like the automatic variables, disappear, as do the modifications made to them.

An example will help illustrate this point. Suppose we've been asked to write a function that calculates sales tax for a region that has several different percentages. The function is passed two arguments: *price*, which holds the amount to be taxed, and *region*, which represents the area whose sales tax rate applies. The function, called **taxcalc( )**, must do two things, determine the appropriate tax percentage and then add the appropriate amount of tax to *price*. The function is to return the tax percentage used.

For this example, let us assume there are three possible tax rates in either of four regions:

    Region 1   6.00%
    Region 2   5.75%
    Region 3   6.00%
    Region 4   6.50%

A version of the **taxcalc( )** function is shown as Function 12-7. Because changes made to formal parameters are local, Function 12-7 *doesn't* work properly.

```
/*   ***** TAXCALC *****
 *
 * This function determines the amount of sales tax required
 *   for a particular region and adds that amount of sales
 *   tax to the price.
 *
 * NOTE: This function doesn't do what it is supposed to
 *       because function parameters have local scope.
 *
 * Written by Ray Swartz for "Doing Business with C".
 */

double taxcalc(price, region)
double price;
int region;
{
    double rate = 0;    /* tax percentage charged */

    switch(region) {
        case 1:
        case 3:
            rate = .06;
            break;
        case 2:
            rate = .0575;
            break;
        case 4:
            rate = .065;
    }
    price += rate * price;  /* error - this change is local */
    return(rate);
}
```

Function 12-7 The **taxcalc( )** Function

The **taxcalc( )** function receives copies of the value stored in the variables represented by the formal parameters *price* and *region*. The statement

$$\text{price += rate * price;}$$

modifies the function's *copy* of *price* but makes no change to the true value of the actual variable passed to the function. As a result, **taxcalc( )** doesn't work correctly because the *price* argument has the same value after the function returns as it does before the function is called.

Sec. 12.10   Using Storage to Speed Up Programs   197

RULE   A function's formal parameters have local scope. Any changes made to a parameter have no effect on the argument's true value.

There is a way to make global changes to a function's parameters; it involves concepts not yet discussed, however. These are introduced in Part 5. A working version of the **taxcalc( )** function is written in Chapter 13.

12.9 PORTABILITY

As was mentioned earlier, different C compilers handle the defining of global variables in different ways. This raises the question: How portable is the use of global variables?

The answer involves the linking phase of compilation. Some C implementations use a linker supplied with the compiler. Some computer operating systems supply a linking program. Still others use commercially available linkers that are designed to create executable programs from the compilers of many different languages.

This variety, too, has caused some confusion about the correct usage of global variables. Specifically, there is no agreement on how many characters are significant in a global variable name. Further, some linkers are *case-insensitive*, that is, they make no distinctions between upper and lower case characters. To such linkers,

```
int TOTAL;
```

and

```
long total;
```

are seen as conflicting definitions of the same variable.

The best available advice (the ANSI C standard) says to assume that global variable names will be limited to six significant characters and that the case of these characters will be ignored. This does not mean we only can use six character global variable names. It simply means that the *first* six must be different in every global name we use.

A specific implementation may offer more flexibility when naming global variables. However, to insure source code portability, it is best to stick to these limitations. In either case, check with the system's documentation to be sure.

RULE   To ensure portability of global variable names, limit them to six significant characters and assume that the case will be ignored.

12.10 USING STORAGE TO SPEED UP PROGRAMS

Automatic local variables are created when a function is called. Thus, the time required to execute a function's commands includes the time it takes to allocate enough memory to store its automatic variables. This is done every time the function is called. Clearly, the more automatic local variables defined in a function, the longer that function takes to complete.

static variables, on the other hand, have permanent storage allocated by the compiler. Thus, functions that use **static** variables in place of automatic ones will run faster! In most cases, the increase in speed will be insignificant. However, careful substitution of permanent (**static**) for automatic storage can make a meaningful difference in execution speed.

When turning automatic variables into ones with permanent storage, be careful not to introduce problems. Specifically, only variables that are initialized before use are candidates for permanent storage.

12.11 register STORAGE

Another way to speed up functions is by taking advantage of special high-speed memory. Data stored in memory have to be brought into the computer's CPU to be processed. Most CPUs contain a small number of memory locations, called *registers*. Since data in CPU registers are already inside the CPU, no time is spent fetching them from memory. Thus, another way to speed up programs would be to store often used data inside one of these registers. This would save us the time required to locate information in the memory and move it into the CPU.

C contains a special storage class specifier, **register**, that *asks* the compiler to store a variable in a CPU register, if possible. One problem with using CPU registers to store data is that many times the CPU doesn't have any available! Even large computers have only a few CPU registers. If no registers are available, the **register** keyword is ignored and the variable is stored as an automatic.

There are some restrictions on what can be stored in a register. First, only automatic variables and a function's formal parameters can be **register**. Also, most compilers will store only integer data in registers. Integer data types include **char**, **int**, **unsigned**, **short**, and **long**. Other restrictions may apply, as well. Check the compiler's documentation for specifics.

As an example, to request that the compiler put the variable *total* in a register, this definition is required:

```
register int total;
```

If *total* was a formal parameter in a function, this is required:

```
int funct(total)    /* funct is name of function */
register int total;
{
    ...
```

Sec. 12.12   Initializing Variables

As this chapter shows, one area where C has few standards is in dealing with a variable's storage class. This especially is true when dealing with global and **register** variables. An extra measure of care should be exercised when such variables are used.

12.12 INITIALIZING VARIABLES

Automatic local variables are not initialized when they are created. As a result, many local variables must be assigned a beginning value before we can use them properly. An example is the *totalrev* and *totalcost* variables used in the **print_pl( )** function to accumulate the revenue and cost totals, respectively. Since they are accumulators, they must be initialized to 0.

To save time, C allows us to define a variable and assign it a value in the same statement. We do this by adding an assignment to the definition statement. For example,

```
long totalrev = 0;
```

defines *totalrev* to be a **long** variable and initializes it to 0.

In addition to constants, we can initialize automatic local variables with expressions or even function calls. However, if we use variables in an initializing expression, they must be *previously defined* variables. As an illustration, this is legal

```
int count = 2;
int limit = count * 12;
```

as is

```
int count = 2;
int value = 3;
int maximum();      /* returns maximum of its two arguments */
int limit = maximum(count, value);
```

but this is not

```
int maximum = count * 12; /* count hasn't been defined yet */
int count = 2;
```

The above rules only apply to automatic local variables. **static** variables can be initialized when defined with constants or constant expressions only. A constant expression is one containing only constant operands.

RULE   Variables with **static** storage can be initialized when they are defined but with constant or constant expressions only.

Thus,

```
static double value = 5.097 * 2.745;
static char beg_alpha = 'a';
static int length = MAX_LEN;   /* MAX_LEN is defined macro */
```

are all legal.

Function calls and variables cannot appear as initializers in the definition of **static** variables. As a result, these *global* definitions are *not legal*:

```
int length = strlen(co_name);   /* not legal - can't */
                                /* use a function call */

int count = 5;            /* legal */
int max = count * 3;      /* not legal - can't use variables */
```

static variables are initialized only once.

Unlike automatic local variables, **static** variables are set to 0 unless explicitly initialized to some other value.

RULE   **static** variables are initialized to 0 unless they are initialized otherwise.

12.13 ARRAY INITIALIZATION IN C

In addition to single variables, certain types of arrays can also be initialized when they are defined. The determining factor is the array's storage class. Automatic local arrays *cannot* be initialized when defined. (This restriction has been lifted in ANSI C.) Instead, the elements in automatic local arrays have to be individually assigned in the body of the function.

static arrays can be initialized when defined. An array is initialized in much the same manner as a single variable. That is, we assign the values we want to be stored in the array's elements. However, the list of initial values must be enclosed with braces and the values separated by commas.

To initialize the *discount* array to a set of customer discount percentages (from Table 7-1) requires

```
static double discount[5] = {.09, .12, .15, .185, .22};
```

The result is the same as if we did

```
double discount[5];

discount[0] = .09;
discount[1] = .12;
```

Sec. 12.13   Array Initialization in C

```
discount[2] = .15;
discount[3] = .185;
discount[4] = .22;
```

We do not have to initialize every element in an array. However, array elements are initialized beginning at the first element. If there are more array elements than values in the *initializer list*, the remaining elements are set to 0 (or '\0'). Thus, in this version

```
static double discount[9] = {.09, .12, .15, .185, .22};
```

elements 5 through 8 are set to 0.

When an initializer list is present in an array definition, we do not have to list the number of elements in the array. C assumes we want as many array elements as there are initial values. This definition creates a five-element array that stores the specified values.

```
static double discount[] = {.09, .12, .15, .185, .22};
```

static character arrays can be initialized, as well. There is only one significant difference between initializing character and numeric arrays. When storing a string in a character array, we don't need to enclose the string in braces. We must use double quotation marks instead. For example, to initialize *co_name* to hold the company's name requires:

```
static char co_name[81] = "Johnson's Books";
```

As expected, this puts the listed characters in the first sixteen elements (don't forget the **\0**) in the *co_name* array. Elements 16 through 80 are set to **\0**.

Another way to initialize character arrays is on an element by element basis. For example,

```
static char co_name[81] = {'A','c','m','e',' ','I','n','c','.','\0'};
```

is completely equivalent to

```
static char co_name[81] = "Acme Inc.";
```

Note the single quotation marks. Character constants are used when initializing the individual elements in *co_name*. Also, the **\0** must be specifically included at the end of the initializing string.

We enclosed the list of single characters with braces. The braces are required when initializing array elements with single values of any data type. When initializing with string constants, we do not use braces and the **\0** is automatically assumed to be part of the constant.

As with numeric arrays, when an initializer is present, the array size can be omitted from a character array definition. In this case, the array length is set to exactly hold the initializing values. For example,

```
                static char co_name[] = "Acme Inc.";
```

defines *co_name* to be an array of ten **char**s.

Arrays with more than one dimension can be initialized in much the same way. As an example, in business applications it is common to need to know the number of elapsed days between two dates. Because the months have a varying number of days, it is difficult to calculate days between dates. One approach is to create an array containing the number of days from January 1 to the first of each month. This information simplifies the elapsed day calculations.

To account for both leap and nonleap years, we will create a two-dimensional **int** array. The array will be called *month_cnt* and the elements with 0 as the first index will hold the values for a regular year and those indexed by 1 will be for leap year. The second index will refer to the months by number. Thus, *month_cnt[0][1]* is January for nonleap years and *month_cnt[1][12]* is December for leap years.

The arrays elements store the number of days elapsed from January 1 to the first of the numbered month. Thus,

```
                month_cnt[0][1]  = 0;
                month_cnt[0][2]  = 31;     /* January has 31 days */
                month_cnt[0][3]  = 59;     /* non-leap year February */
                ...
                month_cnt[0][12] = 334;    /* December - non-leap year */
                month_cnt[1][1]  = 0;
                month_cnt[1][2]  = 31;
                month_cnt[1][3]  = 60;     /* leap year February */
                ...
                month_cnt[1][12] = 335;    /* December - leap year */
```

Incidentally, the elements *month_cnt[0][0]* and *month[1][0]* are set to 0, to ease our calculations.

A two-dimensional array can be viewed as a set of rows and columns. The array's first index represents the rows. The second index identifies the columns. When an initializer is listed for a two-dimensional array, the elements are initialized by row. Each row's values are grouped together with braces and the entire initialization list is enclosed in another set of braces and terminated with a semicolon. The *month_cnt* array is initialized by

```
                static int month_cnt[2][13] = {
                    {0,0,31,59,90,120,151,181,212,243,273,304,334},
                    {0,0,31,60,91,121,152,182,213,244,274,305,335}
                };
```

Note that the row initializing lists are also separated by commas.

As with one-dimensional arrays, if the initializer list does not contain enough values, the remaining elements are set to 0. For example, this definition

Sec. 12.13   Array Initialization in C   203

```
        static int amount[2][5] = {
            {1},           /* element [0][0] only */
            {2,3},         /* elements [1][0] and [1][1] only */
            {3,4,5}        /* first three in row 2 */
        };
```

only initializes six elements in the *amount* array. The rest are set to 0.

To continue the date example, suppose we wanted to attach the name of each month to its number. We might define a two-dimensional **char** array called **months** and initialize it:

```
            static char months[13][10] = {
                "Invalid",
                "January",
                "February",
                "March",
                "April",
                "May",
                "June",
                "July",
                "August",
                "September",
                "October",
                "November",
                "December"
            };
```

Just like the previous example, the rows, each of which is actually a string, are individually initialized. Since we are using string constants, we don't need to use braces, except around the entire list.

Program 12-3 shows the concepts introduced in this chapter integrated into the **flex-pl** program. We have declared **printf( )** globally. This allows us to use it in any function without redeclaring each time. We've also created a **static** variable, *co_name*, to represent the company's name. This allows initialization and makes modification easy. Last, the variables *totalcost* and *totalrev* are initialized in their definitions. The **main( )**, **getrev( )**, and **getcost( )** functions have not been changed and are not shown.

```
/* ***** FLEX-PL *****
 *
 * This program reads the category and amount of a set of
 * revenues and costs and prints a formatted P&L statement.
 * The program reads entries until a Q only is entered
 * as a category name (the quit signal) or until MAX_CAT
 * categories have been read.
 *
 * Written for Ray Swartz for "Doing Business with C"
 *
 */

#define MAX_LEN 31      /* Length of category name strings */
#define MAX_CAT 20      /* maximum number of category names */
```

```
#include "stdio.h"
#include "getcat.c"       /* source code for getcat function */

int printf();


/* main() doesn't change */


/* getrev() doesn't change */


/* getcost() doesn't change */


/* ***** PRINT_PL *****
 *
 *
 * This function prints a formatted Profit and Loss
 * statement.  It is sent two category name arrays
 * and two category amount arrays--one set for
 * revenues and one for costs.  The number of entries
 * of each type is sent to the function as arguments, also.
 *
 * Written by Ray Swartz for "Doing Business with C"
 *
 * Modified to use a static char array to hold the
 * company's name which it is initialized to.
 */

void print_pl(rev_cat, rev_amt, rev_count,
              cost_cat, cost_amt, cost_count)
char rev_cat[] [MAX_LEN];    /* revenue category names */
long rev_amt[];              /* revenue amounts */
int rev_count;               /* number of revenue entries */
char cost_cat[] [MAX_LEN];   /* cost category names */
long cost_amt[];             /* cost amounts */
int cost_count;              /* number of cost entries */
{
    int count;               /* loop counter */
    static char co_name[] = "Johnson's Books";   /* company name */
    long totalrev = 0;       /* revenue amounts total */
    long totalcost = 0;      /* cost amounts total */

    printf("\tProfit and Loss for %s\n\n", co_name);
    printf("        REVENUE\n\n");
```

```
        /* Loop to print and total the revenue categories */

        for (count = 0; count < rev_count; count++) {
            printf("%-*s  $%6ld\n", MAX_LEN - 1, rev_cat[count],
                rev_amt[count]);
            totalrev += rev_amt[count];
        }
        printf("                                   ------\n");
        printf("         TOTAL REVENUE             $%7ld\n\n\n",
            totalrev);

        /* Loop to print and total the cost categories */

        for (count = 0; count < cost_count; count++) {
            printf("%-*s  $%6ld\n", MAX_LEN - 1, cost_cat[count],
                cost_amt[count]);
            totalcost += cost_amt[count];
        }
        printf("                                   ------\n");
        printf("         TOTAL COST                $%7ld\n\n\n",
            totalcost);
        if (totalrev >= totalcost)
            printf("         PROFIT                    $%7ld\n",
                totalrev - totalcost);
        else
            printf("         LOSS                     ($%7ld)\n",
                totalcost - totalrev);
        return;
    }
```

Program 12-3 The Updated **flex-pl** Program

We now have two ways to initialize variables. We can use an explicit assignment in the program or combine the assignment with the definition statement. Which one should we use? Some argue that initializations are easily overlooked if part of the definition. Others say that finding a simple assignment inside a bunch of C codes can be difficult. Ultimately, it is a matter of style. In our programs, we will initialize variables in definitions with constants only.

12.14 SUMMARY

1. Where a variable is defined determines the variable's scope, that is, where the variable can referenced.
2. A variable is "visible" (usable) only within the code section that contains the variable's definition.

3. Variables defined inside a function are called local variables and have block scope.
4. In addition to having a specific scope, a variable belongs to a storage class. Storage class determines when the variable's memory is active.
5. The default storage class for local (block scope) variables is automatic.
6. Automatic storage is active only when the function that contains the variable is executing. When the function starts, the variable is created and when the function terminates, the variable disappears.
7. Automatic local variables are not initialized.
8. Another storage class is **static**. **static** variables have permanent storage.
9. Local **static** variables can only be used in the function where they are defined but do not disappear when the function terminates.
10. The macro **NULL** represents a string with no characters. It is distinguishable from all other strings.
11. A **static** variable is initialized by the compiler to 0 if a numeric variable and to '\0' if a **char** or string variable.
12. **static** storage is useful if information needs to be stored across function calls and to allow initialization of certain variables.
13. A second type of scope is file scope (usually called *global* variables). Global variables are visible throughout a source code file.
14. A global variable is one defined outside the braces of any function.
15. When two variables have overlapping scope, the one with more general scope is hidden by the one with less general scope.
16. There are two ways for a function to declare its intention to use a global variable. One is declaration by inclusion, which occurs when a global variable is used in statement. The other is declaring the variable to be storage class **extern**.
17. **static** variables are initialized by the compiler to 0 if numeric and '\0' if **char**.
18. Defining a variable means to reserve memory for that variable. Declaring a variable means notifying the compiler that that variable (which was previously defined) will be used in this program block.
19. A global variable is declared (not defined) with the keyword **extern**.
20. Defined file scope variables can be made visible to other source code files of the same program by declaring them **extern** in that program file.
21. It is recommended that global variables used in more than one source code file be defined in only one of the source code files.
22. Global variables can be limited in scope to only one source code file by defining them as having **static** file scope. **static** global variables are not visible to other source code files under any circumstances. The same is true for **static** function definitions.
23. Function definitions are global. When a function is declared, it is assumed that the declaration is **extern** in the same way that local variables are assumed to be automatic.

Sec. 12.14   Summary

24. Global variables and function are linked together during the linking phase of compilation. Different linkers can handle differently sized global names. To ensure portability of global names (function and variable), the first six characters of any global name must be unique and case-insensitive.
25. Programs will execute more quickly if permanent storage (**static**) is substituted for automatic storage.
26. Automatic variables can be initialized when they are defined. This is done by assigning them a value in the definition, for instance,

```
int total = 0;
```

27. Automatic variables can be initialized by constants, expressions, previously defined variables, or function calls.
28. **static** variables can also be initialized when they are defined. However, these variables can only be initialized with constants or constant expressions (expressions that contain only constants as operands).
29. **static** arrays can be initialized when defined, but automatic arrays cannot (although this restriction is being lifted in the ANSI standard).
30. To initialize an array, the initial values are enclosed in braces and each value is separated by commas.
31. If there are fewer initial values then array slots, the remaining elements are set to 0 (or '\0').
32. If the size of the array is left out of an initialized array definition, the array will be defined to be large enough to hold all the initial values.
33. String variables can be initialized by enclosing the initial string in double quotes.
34. Arrays of higher dimensions are initialized in the same way except each rows initial values are enclosed in braces inside the entire initializing list.

E X E R C I S E S

12-1. Modify the **getcat( )** function to use **tgetlong( )**. If **NULL** is **getcat( )**'s first argument, the function should return the total entered and reset the **static** total in **tgetlong( )**. NOTE: The *getcat.c* file must be changed to **#include** *tgetlong.c* instead of *getlong.c*.

12-2. Modify both the **getrev( )** and **getcost( )** functions to use the **getcat( )** function described in Exercise 12-1. Assume that *totalrev* and *totalcost* are global variables.

12-3. Rewrite **flex-pl** to use the **getrev( )** and **getcost( )** functions from Exercise 12-2.

PART 5
Thanks for the Memory

13

Directly Accessing Data

In Chapter 8, we learned about arrays, which store related data under one name. Arrays allow us to simplify our programs by reusing program segments to access stored information. Although using arrays helps us write concise programs, it forces us to view our data in a certain way, as a series of *numbered* elements.

To refer to an array element, we must provide the name and number of that element. This forces us to keep track of where we are in each data array, usually with an index variable. In many applications, this presents no difficulties. In fact, programs that read and store entered data or must perform repeated calculations on a set of similar values can use the array indexes to control the program's loops, as well.

In other types of programs, however, constantly updating an array's index can cause programming problems. As an example, consider a text editor, a program that allows us to enter, change, or delete text in a document. If we view the characters that make up the document as elements in an array, we have two choices. We can have either a huge array of characters, where each character is numbered from the first one, or a string array where every character is referred to from the beginning of a specifically numbered line.

In reality, the problems are not caused by how we store the data, but how we refer to the data once it has been stored! Arrays force us to view the data as a consecutively numbered set of elements *beginning with element number 0*. This viewpoint is so strong that we actually must renumber the array's elements before inserting or after deleting characters from the document. Rearranging array elements is required to maintain the numeric ordering of the data, but it takes a tremendous amount of computing time, a requirement that grows as the document gets larger.

Programming would be easier if we could choose any spot in the document as a data reference point. This allows us the flexibility to deal with individual characters, as well as large chunks of data, without constantly having to reset counters and update arrays. C provides this data access by allowing us to directly reference memory locations through the use of **pointers**. In fact, as we will discover shortly, there is no such thing as an array!

13.1 A LOOK AT COMPUTER MEMORY

To fully understand C's use of pointers and how pointers work, it is valuable to take a detailed look at the computer's memory. The data we "store" in arrays and variables are actually values the computer holds in its memory. A computer's memory is comprised of individual memory *locations*. Each memory location is identified by a unique *address*. These addresses are integers beginning at 0 and increasing by one up to the memory limit of the machine. Each memory location can store "a piece of data." It may take several physical memory locations to store a single value, depending on the data type involved. Thus, a memory location has two attributes; a numeric address and the ability to store information.

RULE   A memory location has two attributes: an address and a storage capability.

We retrieve data from the computer's memory by referring to the address where it is stored. The same is true for storing information. We have to tell the computer where to put data by providing a specific memory address.

The address of a memory location never changes. The same address always refers to the same memory location. In contrast, the value stored at a memory location is changed easily. In fact, the whole idea of computer programming is altering stored data in a systematic way!

One feature of all higher-level programming languages is the use of variable names instead of numeric addresses to refer to memory locations. The compiler converts our variable names into memory addresses. This is why we must define the data type of our variables before we use them.

A variable is a symbolic name that identifies a memory location's address. As a result, a variable is an *indirect* reference to data stored in memory. The variable directly refers to the *address* where the data is stored. Thus, to find the value represented by a variable requires us to go to the specified memory address (a direct reference) and get the value stored there (an indirect reference).

As an illustration, consider your home address. Letters properly addressed to you are delivered there. However, if you move, the address of the building remains the same, even though the inhabitants have changed. This makes your home address an indirect reference to you—it directly refers to the building itself!

The concept of indirection underlies all higher level programming languages. Further, indirection makes programming much easier by allowing the use of (meaningful) variable names instead of (meaningless) numeric addresses. In fact, most higher-level languages allow us to refer to memory using variable names only.

C, on the other hand, provides a mechanism for referring to memory locations by numeric address or by variable name, whichever is needed. Accessing memory by address provides the flexibility to refer to any value in memory without having to know its symbolic name.

To simplify the following discussion of C's memory accessing features, our beginning examples use individual variables instead of arrays. As a result, it may appear that these capabilities are of limited use. This is not the case and once the basic concepts are introduced we will demonstrate the value of the features.

13.2 THE ADDRESS OPERATOR

As an illustration of how variables and memory work together, suppose we define the variable *nbr* as an **int** and initialize it to 10.

```
int nbr = 10;
```

Further suppose, when the program is compiled, *nbr* is stored at memory location 2500. When the program is executed, location 2500 holds 10.

One way to refer to memory location 2500 is by manipulating *nbr*. The statement

```
nbr = nbr + 5;
```

results in

```
     ┌────┐
     │ 15 │
     └────┘
nbr ──────▶ 2500
```

C contains a special operator which evaluates to the address where a variable stores data. This is called the *address* operator and is represented by the **&**. In our example, the variable *nbr* is stored at location 2500. This means the expression

```
&nbr
```

evaluates to 2500.

Sec. 13.3   The Pointer Data Type

The address operator is a unary operator. Further, this operator can be applied to certain kinds of operands only—those that actually represent memory locations. This means we can't find the address of a constant or an expression because these values are not stored in a memory location. Thus, **&3** and **&(x+1)** are illegal.[1]

13.3 THE POINTER DATA TYPE

It is vitally important that a computer maintain the distinction between a memory address and a value stored at that address. To confuse these two memory attributes would wreck havoc on our programs and render the computer useless. Thus, even though the expression

```
&nbr
```

evaluates to an integer,[2] it is not same as the **int** data type. In fact, if

```
int addr;
int nbr = 10;
```

the statement

```
addr = &nbr;
```

is illegal because

```
&nbr
```

equates to a memory address which cannot be stored in an "ordinary" variable.

In addition, knowing the address where data is stored is not enough to refer to that data. We also must know how much memory it takes to hold that data.

A memory location can hold any data type, such as **char**, **int**, **long**, and **double**. However, data types require different amounts of storage space. For example, it requires several memory locations to hold a **double** value whereas it generally takes only one to store a **char**. This means the address operator must identify not only a memory location but what kind of data is stored there. Thus, if

```
int nbr = 10;
```

---

[1] In C parlance, an *object* is one or more accessible memory locations. We can assign values to an object as well as refer to values stored in one. A variable or expression that refers to an object either to assign it a value or refer to the value stored is called an *lvalue* ("ell"-value). The address operator can only be applied to *lvalues*. Incidentally, *lvalue* is so named because it describes variables and expressions that appear on the left side of an assignment.

[2] This may not always be the case. On some machines, memory addresses are expressed in other ways. However, in general, memory addresses are integers.

then

&nbr

actually evaluates to a *memory address of an* **int**. C contains a special data type to store the result of the address operator. It is called a *pointer*. Pointers store memory addresses and refer to a specific data type. Thus, the address

&nbr

could be stored in a *pointer to an* **int**.

In actuality, pointers are themselves variables. Like all other C variables, pointers must be defined before use and have a unique name. A pointer must be defined as the data type it will refer to. Put another way, a pointer *points to a specific data type*.

Pointer definitions require special syntax to distinguish them from regular variables. To define a pointer, we must precede the pointer's name with an *asterisk* in the definition. Thus,

    int *addr;

defines *addr* to be a *pointer to int*. There are three parts to a pointer definition: (1) a data type, (2) an asterisk, and (3) the pointer's name:

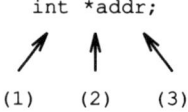

In actuality,

    int *

is a *pointer data type* which is used to define a *pointer to int*. It should be viewed as a single construct. All data types have equivalent pointers:

char *	Pointer to **char**
long *	Pointer to **long**
float *	Pointer to **float**
double *	Pointer to **double**

Incidentally, there can be space between the asterisk and the pointer's name. This means

    int *addr;

Sec. 13.4   The Indirection Operator

and

$$\text{int * addr;}$$

are both legal.

Once defined, a pointer can be assigned an address. If

```
int *addr;     /* a pointer to int */
int nbr = 10;
```

then

```
addr = &nbr;   /* assign nbr's memory address to addr*/
```

is a legal assignment that stores the address of the memory location represented by the variable *nbr* into the **int** pointer *addr*.

13.4 THE INDIRECTION OPERATOR

addr now holds the address where *nbr* stores data. However, an address indirectly identifies the data held at a memory location (an address directly refers to the location itself). Thus, *addr* only provides an indirect reference to the data stored in *nbr*. We can use *addr* to retrieve the value stored in *nbr* by using another special C operator, the *indirection* operator. The indirection operator, which is represented by an asterisk, can only be applied to pointers (addresses) and it evaluates to the value stored at that address. For example, if

```
int *addr;
int nbr = 10;

addr = &nbr;
```

then

```
*addr
```

equates to the value stored at the address referred to by *addr*, which is the same as the variable *nbr*! Continuing the previous example, if

```
int *addr;
int nbr = 10;

addr = &nbr;      /* point addr at nbr */
```

then

```
                printf("%d\n", *addr);
```

prints

10

the value stored in *nbr*. Once *addr* has been assigned *nbr*'s address, the expression ***addr** and the variable *nbr* can be used interchangeably. The same goes for *addr* and **&nbr**. Figure 13-1 shows this equivalence.

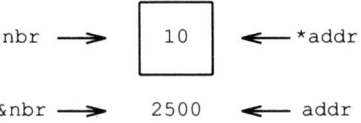

Figure 13-1 Pointers and Variables

Program 13-1 provides an example.

```
main()
{
    int *addr;
    int nbr = 10;

    addr = &nbr;    /* point addr at nbr */
    printf("*addr = %d, nbr = %d\n", *addr, nbr);
    exit(0);
}
```

Program 13-1 The Equivalence of Pointers and Variables

When executed, Program 13-1 prints

*addr = 10, nbr = 10.

In fact, once

addr = &nbr;

has been done, there is only one difference between *nbr* and *addr*: With *nbr* the computer handles the details of indirection, and with *addr* we must perform the indirection ourselves.

Both the address and indirection operators are unary and have the same precedence as the other unary operators. An updated precedence table is shown in Table 13-1.

Sec. 13.6   A Pointed Example   215

TABLE 13-1 Updated Precedence Table

Operator						Associativity
()	[]					Left to right
++	--	(type)	*	&	-	Right to left
*	/	%				Left to right
+	-					Left to right
<	<=	>=	>			Left to right
==	!=					Left to right
&&						Left to right
||						Left to right
?:						Right to left
=	+=	-=	*=	/=	%=	Right to left

13.5 INITIALIZING POINTERS

Like other variables in C, pointers can be initialized when they are defined. For example,

```
int nbr;
int *addr = &nbr;   /* point addr at nbr */
```

defines *addr* as a *pointer to* **int** and initializes it to point at *nbr*. This works properly, because the address and indirection operators have higher precedence than the assignment operator. Thus, the result of the address operation on *nbr* is stored in *addr* after *addr* is defined a *pointer to* **int**. Note that *nbr* must be defined before it can be used to initialize *addr*.

13.6 A POINTED EXAMPLE

We also can assign values into memory using pointers and the indirection operator. If

```
int nbr;
int *addr = &nbr;    /* point addr at nbr */
```

then the assignment

```
*addr = 10;
```

stores the value 10 in the memory referenced by *addr*. Since *addr* points at *nbr*,

```
*addr = 10;
```

is equivalent to

```
                    nbr = 10;
```

As an example, consider Program 13-2.

```
main()
{
    int printf();
    int nbr = 10;
    int *addr = &nbr;      /* point addr at nbr */

    printf("1. *addr = %d and nbr = %d\n", *addr, nbr);
    *addr = 3;
    printf("2. *addr = %d and nbr = %d\n", *addr, nbr);
    exit(0);
}
```

Program 13-2   Changing Memory with Pointers

In Program 13-2, the variable *nbr* is initialized to 10. Once we point *addr* at *nbr* then the expression **addr* equals 10, too. Thus, the first **printf( )**,

```
            printf("1. *addr = %d and nbr = %d\n", *addr, nbr);
```

prints

```
            1. *addr = 10 and nbr = 10
```

The next statement

```
                    *addr = 3;
```

says "store the value 3 where *addr* points." But *addr* points at *nbr*, so the second **printf( )** displays

```
            2. *addr = 3 and nbr = 3
```

We changed what was stored in *nbr* by changing ***addr**! This is a demonstration of the power of pointers.

The statement

```
                    *addr = 3;
```

works properly because the indirection operator has higher precedence than assignment. The indirection occurs first, converting *addr* from an address into the storage location at that address, then the assignment puts the value 3 there.

13.7 POINTERS AS FUNCTION ARGUMENTS

In Chapter 12, we discussed the local scope of a function's formal parameters. We said that the changes made to local variables inside a function are local to that function. Formal parameters are local because copies of the arguments get passed to the function. Changes made to the copies do not affect the original variables, and when the function terminates the argument copies disappear.

A difference exists between formal parameters and a function's automatic local variables. Automatic variables are created when the function begins executing and disappear when it terminates. Formal parameters, on the other hand, represent values stored in variables outside the scope of the function.

The variables sent to a function as arguments are stored somewhere in memory. We can't modify the memory of the original variables by using the copy passed to the function. However, using pointers and indirection, we can change what is stored in *any* memory location inside the computer. Thus, we can modify the value stored in a variable outside the function by passing a pointer to that variable as a function argument. Then, inside the function we use indirection to refer to the variable's actual memory!

RULE A function can change variable outside the function's scope through the use of pointer arguments and indirection.

If a pointer to a variable is sent to a function as an argument, the function receives a copy of the variable's memory address. Using the indirection operator with this address allows us to make changes directly to that variable's memory. As an example, consider the **taxcalc( )** function. The intention of **taxcalc( )** is to modify the value of one of its arguments, *price*, in accordance with the sales tax that applies to an area identified by the function's second argument, *region*.

The function, listed as Function 13-1, is passed a pointer to the *price* argument. This allows the variable's value to be changed from inside the function.

```
/*   ***** TAXCALC *****
 *
 * This function determines the amount of sales tax required
 * for a particular region and adds that amount of sales
 * tax to the price.
 *
 * Written by Ray Swartz for "Doing Business with C".
 */

double taxcalc(price, region)
double *price;   /* where price is stored */
int region;
{
    double rate = 0;    /* tax percentage charged */
```

```
    switch(region) {
        case 1:
        case 3:
            rate = .06;
            break;
        case 2:
            rate = .0575;
            break;
        case 4:
            rate = .065;
    }
    *price += rate * (*price);
    return(rate);
}
```

Function 13-1 The **taxcalc( )** Function

Since *price* represents a pointer, it must be declared as a pointer:

```
double *price;
```

Further, to get the value stored at this address requires indirection. This statement

```
*price += rate * (*price);
```

multiplies the tax rate by the value given by *price* and adds it to the value given by *price*. The result is stored where *price* points. When **taxcalc( )** terminates, the memory location sent as *price* has been changed to account for sales tax. Incidentally, the parentheses in this expression are not needed and are included for clarity only.

How do we pass an address argument to a function? We use the address operator. In fact, this is one of the most common uses of the address operator. If the variable *sales* holds the amount to be taxed, and *region* the location of the sale, then **taxcalc( )** is called by

```
percent = taxcalc(&sales, region);
```

The expression

```
&sales
```

evaluates to the address where *sales* is stored. Incidentally, *percent* holds the sales tax percentage returned by **taxcalc( )**.

One aspect of structured programming is the creation of small functions to perform common tasks. To make these functions applicable in a wide variety of situations requires that functions not interfere with one another. This requirement is why all the changes that occur in a function are local. However, without a way to alter arguments, a function could only communicate with its calling routine by returning a single value, which would limit the usefulness of functions.

The use of pointer arguments expands the usefulness of functions by allowing them to make changes in selected arguments *and* return a value, if necessary. Pointers let functions retain their privacy of action (changes are local) and, at the same time, modify arguments when the task warrants it. In fact, one of the most important uses of pointers is as function arguments!

13.8 SUMMARY

1. Arrays enforce a viewpoint on data, that of consecutively numbered sets of similar elements beginning with element numbered 0.
2. A computer's memory is comprised of individual memory locations. Each location has a unique address.
3. A variable is a symbolic name that identifies a memory location's address. As a result, the variable is an indirect reference to the stored data. The variable directly refers to the address where the data is stored.
4. C contains a special operator that evaluates to the address where a variable stores data. It is called the address operator and is represented by **&** (an ampersand).
5. In order to maintain a distinction between memory addresses and regular data, C only allows memory addresses (what **&** expressions evaluate to) to be stored in special variables called pointers.
6. Different data types require different amounts of memory, usually spanning more than a single memory location. In addition to knowing the address where data is stored, we also must know the data type stored at that location to insure that we retrieve all of the data.
7. Pointer variables must refer to a specific data type.
8. A pointer variable is defined by combining an asterisk with a data type:

char *	Pointer to **char**
long *	Pointer to **long**
float *	Pointer to **float**
double *	Pointer to **double**

9. The indirection operator, an asterisk, is used to retrieve data referred to by a pointer variable.
10. Once a pointer has been assigned the address of a variable, both can be used to reference the data:

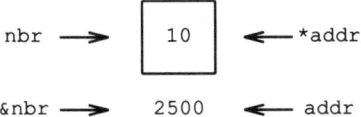

11. The address and indirection operators are unary.
12. Pointers can be passed as arguments to functions that allow changes to be made directly to data stored outside the scope of the function.

EXERCISES

13-1. At present, the **getrev( )** function returns the number of revenue categories entered. Modify the **getrev( )** function to take the number of categories entered (the local variable *count*) as an argument and then to assign this value inside the function so that it is available in the calling routine. This removes the need for **getrev( )** to return a value, and the function should be declared **void**.

13-2. Rewrite the **flex-pl main( )** to handle the **getrev( )** function written in Exercise 13-1.

13-3. Modify the **getlong( )** and **tgetlong( )** functions to assign the entered value to an argument passed to the functions instead of returning it. These functions would then become type **void**.

13-4. A previous exercise (6-2) asked for the creation of a function called **print_line( )**, which printed a line in the P&L statement and was called by **print_pl( )**. Modify that function (write it first if necessary) to take a category name, category amount, and a total to which the category amount is added.

13-5. Entering dates is common in business data processing. Write a function that is sent the date in three integers, one each for month, day, and year, and then prompts with these values as the current date. If the user responds with a newline, the function returns without modifying the date. Otherwise, the date should be entered and stored in the function's arguments.

14

Arrays and Pointers

Earlier, we made the provocative statement that there is no such thing as an array. This is true in the sense that there is no underlying computer construct called an "array." Instead, arrays are created by operations performed entirely by the programming language. To understand how this is done, let's take a closer look at how arrays work.

An array is defined as a block of memory, given a single name, that contains a specific number of elements. Each element is referred to by the array's name and an index enclosed in brackets. Thus, if

```
int nbr[5];   /* define an array called nbr with 5 elements */
```

then

```
                        nbr[1]
```

identifies the second element in the *nbr* array. Put another way,

```
                        nbr[1]
```

tells the computer to get the second **int** from the *beginning* of the *nbr* array.

Before the memory location represented by

```
nbr[1]
```

can be accessed, C must know the array's starting address. In addition, the computer must know the type of data stored in the array to account for the amount of memory required for one array element. As an illustration, the second element in a **double** array is located farther from the beginning of the array than the second element in an array of **int**s.

14.1 ARRAYS AND ADDRESSES

In C, arrays actually are implemented through the use of pointers! A pointer identifies where the array starts. Any array element can be retrieved by knowing where the array begins (a pointer).

An array definition tells C to reserve a block of *contiguous* memory locations large enough to handle the entire array. Next, the array's name is defined as a pointer that is assigned the address of this newly allocated memory. Thus, the *nbr* array starts where *nbr* points! Further, C knows how much memory each data type requires and simple multiplication and addition determine the address of each element.

RULE An array's name is really a pointer to the beginning of the memory reserved for the array's elements.

For example,

```
int nbr[5];
```

defines *nbr* to be a five-element **int** array. If an **int** is stored in two memory locations, the entire *nbr* array requires ten locations. Thus,

```
int nbr[5];
```

actually tells C to allocate ten contiguous memory locations, defines *nbr* to be a *pointer to* **int**, and then assigns *nbr* the address of where this memory begins! This is shown in Figure 14-1.

Sec. 14.1   Arrays and Addresses

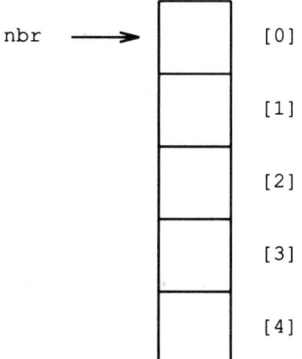

Figure 14-1   Defining an Array

When an array element is referred to, C uses the array name as a pointer to find the beginning of the array and the index to identify which memory location to use. As an example, the element

$$\text{nbr[1]}$$

is located at the address one **int** past the address stored in *nbr* or

$$\text{nbr + (the number of memory locations to store 1 \textbf{int})}$$

As it turns out, this calculation can be done easily.

Consider the expression

$$\text{nbr + 1}$$

where *nbr* is a *pointer to* **int**. Before the addition operator is evaluated, all its operands must be the same data type. This means the constant 1 is promoted to type *pointer to* **int** prior to the addition. More precisely, the constant is promoted to the *amount of memory* required to store 1 **int**. Thus, the result of

$$\text{nbr + 1}$$

is the exact memory address of the second element in the *nbr* array. Further, the rules of promotion guarantee that the result is the same no matter what data type is stored in the array!

14.2 POINTER ARITHMETIC

Expressions that combine pointers and constants in this fashion perform, what is called, *pointer arithmetic*. In pointer arithmetic, constants represent a "data-type chunk" of memory. Thus, if

`int *nbr`	then *nbr + 1* is a pointer to the next **int**
`long *nbr`	then *nbr + 1* is a pointer to the next **long**
`float *nbr`	then *nbr + 1* is a pointer to the next **float**
`double *nbr`	then *nbr + 1* is a pointer to the next **double**
`char *nbr`	then *nbr + 1* is a pointer to the next **char**
	and so on.

Figure 14-2 shows this graphically.

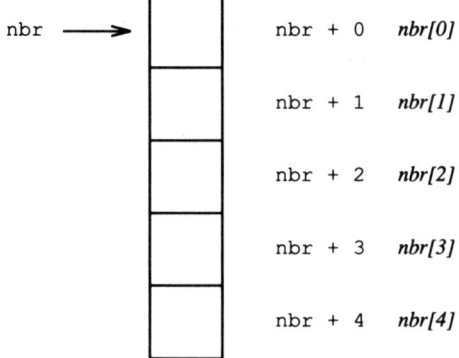

Figure 14-2 Using Pointer Arithmetic to Refer to Array Elements

If *nbr* is an array then the expression

```
nbr + 1
```

calculates the address of the second array element, regardless of *nbr*'s data type. Since

```
nbr + 1
```

is an address, we can use the indirection operator to retrieve the value held there. Thus, the expression

```
*(nbr + 1)
```

Sec. 14.3 The Array Transformation Rule   **225**

evaluates to what is stored in the array's second element. The parentheses are required because the indirection operator has higher precedence then addition and, to locate the second element, we have to add first to get its address.

14.3 THE ARRAY TRANSFORMATION RULE

In reality, the expression

```
nbr[1]
```

is converted into the equivalent pointer calculation

```
nbr + 1
```

and then indirection is applied to retrieve the stored value

```
*(nbr + 1)
```

This means that brackets represent an operator that can be replaced by an addition, a set of parentheses, and the indirection operator. We can use this *transformation* to convert any array reference to its equivalent pointer expression:

    nbr[0]   is the same as   *(nbr + 0)
    nbr[1]   is the same as   *(nbr + 1)
    nbr[2]   is the same as   *(nbr + 2)
              and so on

Incidentally, this is why the first element in a C array is numbered 0.

RULE   The brackets used in an array reference can be replaced by an addition, a set of parentheses, and the indirection operator.

This rule, called the *array transformation rule*, is the key to understanding how pointers work.

Without parentheses, the expression is something entirely different. The expression

```
*nbr + 1
```

says to get the value stored at the address referred to by *nbr* (the array's first element) and then add 1 to it. Precedence tells us to perform the indirection first (which retrieves the value) and then the addition.

As an illustration, after the statements listed as Segment 14-1 are executed the *nbr* array looks like this:

```
                int nbr[5];

                nbr[0] = 3;
                nbr[1] = 5;
                nbr[2] = 2;
                nbr[3] = 6;
                nbr[4] = 8;
```

Segment 14-1 Initializing the *nbr* Array

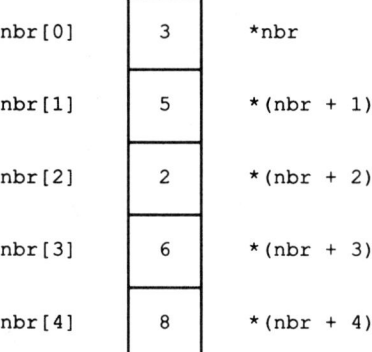

The expression

```
                *nbr + 1
```

is the same as

```
                nbr[0] + 1
```

which is 4. The expression

```
                *(nbr + 1)
```

on the other hand, is the same as

```
                nbr[1]
```

which equates to 5.

Exercise 14-1 Assume that the code in Segment 14-1 has been used to initialize the *nbr* array. Evaluate each of these expressions

Sec. 14.3   The Array Transformation Rule

a. `*nbr + 5`
b. `*(nbr + 2 * 2)`
c. `(*nbr + 3) * 2`
d. `*(nbr + nbr[2])`
e. `*(nbr + *nbr)`
f. `*(nbr + *(nbr + 2))`

Virtually all languages that implement arrays do so with pointers. However, in most languages a programmer cannot access such pointers directly and instead must use the array name–index terminology only. Since pointers are part of the C language, we can directly refer to any value stored in the computer's memory even if it is an element inside an array.

As an example of the equivalence of pointers and arrays, consider the **for** loop in Segment 14-2, which comes from the **print_pl( )** function. It prints the cost categories and amounts and totals them.

```
for (count = 0; count < cost_count; count++) {
    printf("%-*s   $%6ld\n", MAX_LEN - 1,
            cost_cat[count], cost_amt[count]);
    totalcost += cost_amt[count];
}
```

Segment 14-2   **for** Loop from **print_pl( )**

Using the array transformation rule, the reference

$$cost\_amt[count]$$

can be replaced by

$$*(cost\_amt + count)$$

Segment 14-3 shows the **for** loop in Segment 14-2 modified to use pointer arithmetic.

```
for (count = 0; count < cost_count; count++) {
    printf("%-*s   $%6ld\n", MAX_LEN - 1,
            cost_cat[count], *(cost_amt + count));
    totalcost += *(cost_amt + count);
}
```

Segment 14-3   Modified **for** Loop from **print_pl( )**

The loops in Segments 14-2 and 14-3 will perform in the same way.

Another way to refer to array elements is to establish an *alternative* pointer to the array and then "walk through" the array using this pointer. For example, the statements in Segment 14-4 define and initialize the *nbr* array. In addition, a *pointer to* **int**, *nbr_ptr*, is defined and then assigned the address of the array's third element.

```
int nbr[5];
int *num_ptr;

nbr[0] = 3;
nbr[1] = 5;
nbr[2] = 2;
nbr[3] = 6;
nbr[4] = 8;
num_ptr = nbr + 2;    /* point num_ptr at nbr[2] */
```

Segment 14-4 Creating Another Pointer to an Array

Since *nbr* is a *pointer to* **int**, this expression

```
nbr + 2
```

also evaluates to a *pointer to* **int**. Thus,

```
num_ptr = nbr + 2;
```

points *num_ptr* to the array's third element. Another way to identify an array element is with the address operator. Since

```
nbr[2]
```

is the value stored in the array's third element,

```
&nbr[2]
```

is the memory address where it is held. As a result, the two statements

```
num_ptr = nbr + 2;
```

and

```
num_ptr = &nbr[2];
```

are completely equivalent.

Incidentally, the expression

```
&nbr[2]
```

evaluates as the address where *nbr[2]* is stored because brackets have higher precedence than the address operator.

Sec. 14.3 The Array Transformation Rule

Figure 14-3 graphically shows the results of executing the statements in Segment 14-4.

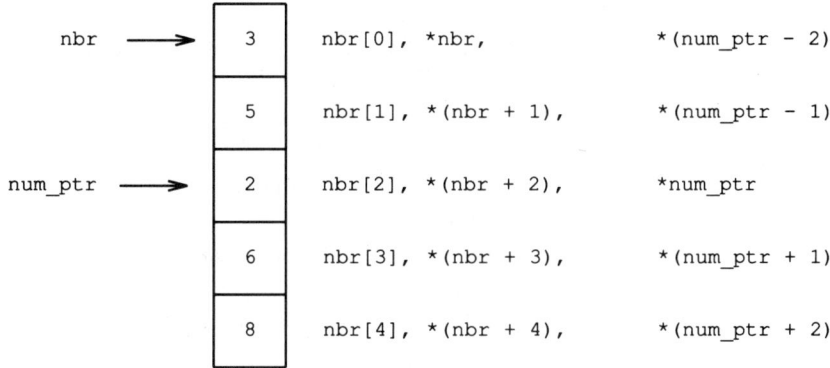

Figure 14-3 Defining an Array with an Alternative Pointer

Now,

```
*num_ptr
```

evaluates to 2, since this is what stored where *num_ptr* points. The expression

```
*num_ptr + 1
```

is 3 (1 added to **num_ptr*) and

```
*(num_ptr + 1)
```

retrieves the **int** following *num_ptr*'s present location, *nbr[3]*, and equates to 6.

To change our point of reference in the *nbr* array, we simply add 1 to *num_ptr*. This can be done with

```
num_ptr++;
```

or

```
++num_ptr;
```

or

```
num_ptr += 1;
```

or

$$\text{num\_ptr = num\_ptr + 1;}$$

All of these statements point *nbr_ptr* to the next **int**. The result is shown in Figure 14-4

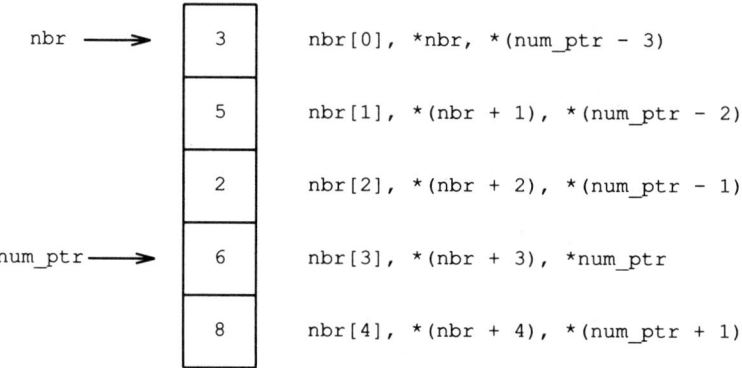

Figure 14-4 Repositioning an Array Pointer

Now, the same set of *num_ptr* expressions refer to different values.

num_ptr is *nbr[3]*, which is 6
num_ptr + 1 is *nbr[3]* + 1, which is 7
(num_ptr + 1) is *nbr[4]*, which is 8

Exercise 14-2 Assume the *nbr* array has been established with Segment 14-1. Now, if

$$\text{num\_ptr = nbr + 1;}$$

evaluate

  a. *num_ptr
  b. *num_ptr * 2
  c. *num_ptr - 1
  d. *(num_ptr + 2)
  e. *(num_ptr + 2) * 2

In Segment 14-4, we referred to each element in the *nbr* array using pointer arithmetic and indirection. Another approach is to establish a second pointer in the array, such as *num_ptr*. Then, we simply increment the pointer to refer to the next array element. Segment 14-3 is the **for** loop that prints cost categories from the **print_pl( )**

Sec. 14.3 The Array Transformation Rule

function. In Segment 14-5, this loop has been rewritten to use an array pointer, *costptr*. Incidentally, this chapter only deals with one-dimensional arrays. Pointers and two-dimensional (or higher) arrays is the subject of the next chapter. Therefore, we will still use array notation with the two-dimensional cost category name array.

```
costptr = cost_amt;   /* point num_ptr at cost_amt[0] */
for (count = 0; count < cost_count; count++, costptr++) {
    printf("%-*s  $%6ld\n", MAX_LEN - 1,
            cost_cat[count], *costptr);
    totalcost += *costptr;
}
```

Segment 14-5 Using Array Pointers to Index an Array

Note that

$$costptr = cost\_amt;$$

assigns one pointer to another.

The array pointer, *costptr*, has to be incremented each time through the **for** loop to keep *costptr* pointing to the correct array element. We also have to increment *count* to ensure that the proper number of cost categories are printed and to index the *cost_cat* array. Recall that we can combine two expressions into one statement using the comma operator, which tells C to evaluate the expression on the left and then the one on the right.

Instead of incrementing *costptr* as part of the loop control commands, we can combine it into the statement

$$total\ +=\ *costptr;$$

by

$$total\ +=\ *costprt++;$$

The expression

$$*costptr++$$

combines two unary operators that have the same precedence. Unary operators associate right to left. Thus, the expression is evaluated as

$$*(costptr++)$$

This means *costptr* is incremented *after* it is fixed in the expression. Thus, the indirection operator retrieves the value stored in the original array element, which then is added to *totalcost*. After the statement is executed, *costptr* is incremented and points to the next element in the array.

Be very careful when combining unary operators in the same expression. They can have unexpected results. If

```
*num_ptr
```

presently evaluates to seven, then

```
++*num_ptr
```

increments the value referenced by *num_ptr* before it is fixed in the expression. Thus, it is evaluated as

```
++(*num_ptr)
```

or the result of the indirection is incremented before it is retrieved. Thus, the expression evaluates to 8 and after the expression is executed, 8 is stored at *num_ptr*. In contrast, the expression

```
*++num_ptr
```

increments *num_ptr* before the indirection, retrieving the next value in memory.

14.4 PASSING ARRAYS AS FUNCTION ARGUMENTS

Treating an array's name as a pointer simplifies the handling of arrays. For example, we can pass an entire array to a function simply by telling the function where the array starts, that is, by passing the array's name as an argument! We actually do this in the **flex-pl** program.

Because a string is nothing more than a character array, a string variable's name must be a pointer to the first character in the string. This is why we can print the string with **printf( )** or read characters into it with **gets( )** by passing only the string's name as an argument.

RULE A string array's name is a pointer to the first character in the string.

Not only do pointers allow us to pass entire arrays to functions, they allow functions to return entire arrays! An example is the **gets( )** function. **gets( )** is declared as a function returning a *pointer* to **char**

```
char *gets();
```

What **gets( )** returns is a pointer to the first character entered. The string read by **gets( )** is stored in the argument sent to the function. This means, **gets( )** returns the pointer passed to it!

Sec. 14.4 Passing Arrays as Function Arguments

This has some usefulness. In the **getlong( )** function, we read a string, convert it to a **long**, and return this value. This code is shown in Segment 14-6.

```
gets(instr);
nbr = atol(instr);
return(nbr);
```

Segment 14-6 Getting and Converting an Integer

We can combine all of these statements into one by using the return values of the **atol( )** and **gets( )** functions

```
return(atol(gets(instr)));
```

gets( ) returns a pointer to *instr* (the string entered), which **atol( )** converts to a **long** which is then returned. Note that we still need the variable *instr* since the string read must actually be stored somewhere.

Another use of the pointer returned by **gets( )** is to test if a string was entered. If the user types a *return* only, the first character in the entry string is **\0**. We can look for this by testing **gets( )** directly. Since **gets( )** returns a pointer, we must use indirection to evaluate the character stored where this pointer points. The expression

```
*gets(instr)
```

is the first character read. It works by executing **gets( )**, which returns a pointer that becomes the operand for the indirection operator. This **if** statement performs the test

```
if (*gets(instr) == '\0')
    printf("No string entered\n");
```

It is common for functions to return pointers. As we shall see, this provides a great deal of flexibility.

The **flex-pl** program contains the **getrev( )**, **getcost( )**, and **print_pl( )** functions, which are sent entire arrays as arguments. Inside each of these functions, the formal parameter representing each array argument is declared with a dummy variable. Recall that dummy variables identify formal parameters that are arrays (including string variables, which are really arrays anyway). Also, recall that dummy variables are denoted by empty brackets in their declaration.

For example, in **flex-pl**, the *rev_amt* array holds the revenue amounts. The *rev_amt* array is passed to the **getrev( )** function. Inside **getrev( )**, *rev_amt* is represented by the formal parameter *cat_amt*, which is declared

```
long cat_amt[];
```

We now know that an array name is nothing more than a pointer to where the array begins. Thus, a dummy variable is nothing more than another way to declare a pointer!

We don't have to pass an entire array to a function. Sending

```
&rev_amt[3]
```

to a function passes a pointer to the subarray starting with the array's fourth element. No changes are required in the function receiving the subarray. It looks like any other pointer.

Transforming the brackets in a dummy variable declaration to their pointer equivalent changes the declaration

```
long cat_amt[];
```

into

```
long *cat_amt;
```

Once a variable (or formal parameter) is declared to be a pointer, any pointer operation is valid on that variable. This includes array references. Since *cat_amt* is a *pointer to* **long**, we can treat *cat_amt* as an array by using

```
cat_nbr[2];
```

C simply converts this expression to its pointer equivalent,

```
*(cat_nbr + 2)
```

and performs the indirection. C does this even if *cat_nbr* is not an array! Be careful when working with pointers. They can cause problems that are *very* hard to find.

14.5 HOW POINTERS AND ARRAYS DIFFER

There are some differences between arrays and pointers. First, a pointer's value can be changed, as can any other variable in C. Array names, on the other hand, must be treated as constants. The pointer represented by the array's name cannot be changed. If

```
double rev_amt[20]
```

then

Sec. 14.5 How Pointers and Arrays Differ

```
            rev_amt++;

            rev_amt = rev_amt + 1;

            rev_amt += 1;

            rev_amt = &value;
```

are illegal statements.

Further, pointers are uninitialized when defined. This means that they must be pointed somewhere before they can be used. In contrast, array names are initialized to point to the first element in the array. If

```
            double rev_amt[20];
```

then

```
            rev_amt = &rev_amt[0];
```

is assumed.

Also, pointers do not store data. Instead, they store a pointer to a location where information can be found. Pointers are of no value without the existence of actual storage to refer to. Unlike pointers, arrays represent both a block of memory large enough to hold all of the elements defined and a pointer to the first element in the block.

Except for the few differences listed here, pointers and arrays are interchangeable. To demonstrate this, let's rewrite the **flex-pl** program to use pointers instead of arrays. Actually, we will only transform the one-dimensional arrays. Both *cost_cat* and *rev_cat* are two-dimensional arrays and, as we mentioned earlier, manipulating two-dimensional arrays with pointer expressions is the subject of the next chapter. Therefore, these array references will not be modified.

Two basic changes are required. First, all the dummy variables become pointers. Second, all array references are changed to expressions using pointers and indirection. The only place in the **flex-pl** program where we still must use array notation is in the array definitions. This is required because we must define the number of elements in each array.

The revised **flex-pl** program is listed as Program 14-1. No changes are required for the **main( )** routine and it isn't shown.

```
/* ***** FLEX-PL *****
 *
 * This program reads the category and amount of a set of
 * revenues and costs and prints a formatted P&L statement.
 * The program reads entries until a Q only is entered
 * as a category name (the quit signal) or until MAX_CAT
 * categories have been read.
```

```
 *
 * Written for Ray Swartz for "Doing Business with C"
 *
 * Modified to use pointers instead of array references.
 * for all one-dimensional array.
 */

#define MAX_LEN 31      /* Length of category name strings */
#define MAX_CAT 20      /* maximum number of category names */

#include "stdio.h"
#include "getcat.c"     /* source code for getcat function */

int printf();

/* main() */

/* ***** GETREV *****
 * This function prompts for and reads revenue categories
 * and amounts.  The category name and amount arrays
 * are passed to the function as arguments.
 *
 * Modified to use pointers instead of array
 *   indexing.
 *
 * Modified to check for a quit signal (Q) and return
 * the number of categories entered.
 *
 * Written by Ray Swartz for "Doing Business with C"
 */

int getrev(cat_name, cat_amt)
char cat_name[][MAX_LEN];   /* category names */
long *cat_amt;              /* amounts */
{
    long getcat();          /* read category and return amount */
    int count;              /* loop counter */

    printf("\nEnter Dollar amounts only -- no cents\n");
    printf("\n\nREVENUES\n\n");
```

Sec. 14.5 How Pointers and Arrays Differ

```c
        for (count = 0; count < MAX_CAT; count++) {
            *(cat_amt + count) = getcat(cat_name[count], "Revenue");
            if (cat_name[count][0] == 'Q' &&
                cat_name[count][1] == '\0')   /* test for quit signal */
                    break;   /* quit signal entered = quit loop */
        }
        return(count);
}

/* ***** GETCOST *****
 *
 * This function prompts for and reads cost categories
 * and amounts.  The category name and amount arrays
 * are passed to the function as arguments, as is
 * the number of categories to enter.
 *
 * Modified to use pointer notation instead of array
 * indexing.
 *
 * Modified to check for a quit signal (Q) and return
 * the number of categories entered.
 *
 * Written by Ray Swartz for "Doing Business with C"
 */

int getcost(cat_name, cat_amt)
long cat_name[] [MAX_LEN];    /* category names */
long *cat_amt;                /* amounts */
{
    long getcat();            /* read category and return amount */
    int count;                /* loop counter */

    printf("\nEnter Dollar amounts only -- no cents\n");
    printf("\n\nCOSTS\n\n");
    for (count = 0; count < MAX_CAT; count++) {
        *(cat_amt + count) = getcat(cat_name[count], "Costs");
        if (cat_name[count][0] == 'Q' &&
            cat_name[count][1] == '\0')   /* test for quit signal */
                break;   /* quit signal entered = quit loop */
    }
    return(count);
}
```

```
/* ***** PRINT_PL *****
 * This function prints a formatted Profit and Loss
 * statement.  It is sent two category name array
 * and two category amount arrays--one set for
 * revenues and one for costs.  The number of entries
 * of each type is sent to the function as arguments, also.
 *
 * Modified to use pointer notation instead of array
 * indexing.
 *
 * Written by Ray Swartz for "Doing Business with C"
 */

void print_pl(rev_cat, rev_amt, rev_count,
              cost_cat, cost_amt, cost_count)
char rev_cat[] [MAX_LEN];   /* revenue category names */
long *rev_amt;              /* revenue amounts */
int rev_count;              /* number of revenue entries */
char cost_cat[] [MAX_LEN];  /* cost category names */
long *cost_amt;             /* cost amounts */
int cost_count;             /* number of cost entries */
{
    int count;              /* loop counter */
    static char co_name[] = "Johnson's Books";  /* company name */
    long totalrev = 0;      /* revenue amounts total */
    long totalcost = 0;     /* cost amounts total */

    printf("\tProfit and Loss for %s\n\n", co_name);
    printf("          REVENUE\n\n");


    /* Loop to print and total the revenue categories */
    for (count = 0; count < rev_count; count++) {
        printf("%-*s  $%6ld\n", MAX_LEN - 1, rev_cat[count],
               *(rev_amt + count));
        totalrev += *(rev_amt + count);
    }
    printf("                                    ------\n");
    printf("         TOTAL REVENUE            $%7ld\n\n\n",
           totalrev);
```

```
    /* Loop to print and total the cost categories */

    for (count = 0; count < cost_count; count++) {
        printf("%-*s   $%6ld\n", MAX_LEN - 1, cost_cat[count],
            *(cost_amt + count));
        totalcost += *(cost_amt + count);
    }
    printf("                              ------\n");
    printf("       TOTAL COST            $%7ld\n\n\n",
        totalcost);
    if (totalrev >= totalcost)
        printf("       PROFIT                $%7ld\n",
            totalrev - totalcost);
    else
        printf("       LOSS                 ($%7ld)\n",
            totalcost - totalrev);
    return;
}
```

Program 14-1 The **flex-pl** Program Using Pointers

Programs 9-1 and 14-1 are two ways of writing the same program. Comparing these listings will give the reader a firm grasp of pointers and arrays. Pointers are an important part of the C language, so make sure you understand these concepts before continuing.

14.6 SUMMARY

1. For an array to exist, the computer must know where the array begins in memory.
2. An array's name is treated as a pointer assigned the address of the first array element.
3. Since an array name is actually a pointer, we can pass an entire array to a function simply by sending the array name.
4. When a pointer and a constant are added together, the constant is promoted to the same data type as the pointer. The promoted constant represents the number of memory locations required to store that many variables of the pointer's data type. This is called pointer arithmetic.
5. The brackets used in an array reference can be replaced by an addition, a set of parentheses, and the indirection operator.
6. Every array reference has an equivalent pointer reference.

7. Instead of maintaining an integer index into an array, we can create a pointer to the array and simply increment the pointer to move through the array.
8. Caution must be exercised when combining the indirection and increment operators with pointers.
9. The **gets( )** function returns a pointer to the first character entered. The expression

```
*gets(instr)
```

evaluates to the first character stored in *instr*.
10. Formal parameters that were declared as dummy variables are actually pointers.
11. An array name must be treated as a constant. A pointer's value can be changed.
12. Pointers are uninitialized when defined, while an array always points to its allocated memory.
13. Pointers are worthless without actual memory to refer to. Arrays always represent allocated memory.
14. But for the differences listed in 11 through 13 above, arrays and pointers are interchangeable.

E X E R C I S E S

14-3. If *nbr* is an array defined with more than four elements, will the reference

```
3[nbr]
```

work properly? Explain.

14-4. Modify the **getcat( )** function to test if only a newline is entered for the category name by testing what **gets( )** returns. If only a newline is entered, store 'Q' and '\0' in the first two characters of the category name (so that **getrev( )** and **getcost( )** don't have to be changed).

14-5. Modify **getcat( )** to return a pointer to the category entered (this means that the number of categories entered will have to be passed back though an argument). Further change the quit signal to entering only a newline for category name and modify **getrev( )** (or **getcost( )** or both) to test what **getcat( )** returns for the quit signal.

14-6. Modify the **print_pl( )** function to index the revenue and cost amount arrays by creating a separate pointer to them and then incrementing that pointer. Remember to use only one pointer variable to do the indexing.

14-7. Rewrite a previous program that uses array-index notation to one that references array elements with a pointer, an addition, and indirection.

15
Pointers and Multidimensional Arrays

From the discussion in Chapter 14, we know that one-dimensional arrays are implemented completely with pointers. Not surprisingly, multidimensional arrays are implemented with pointers as well. However, arrays with multiple dimensions are represented with several pointers; in fact, each element requires one pointer for each array dimension.

The array defined

```
char rev_cat[5][31];
```

can be viewed as five strings of thirty-one characters each. The first index identifies the string and the second refers to a specific character within the string. Thus,

```
rev_cat[2][3]
```

refers to the fourth character in the third string—remember all arrays start with 0 in C:

```
rev_cat[2][3]
         ↑   ↑
       Third Fourth
       string character
```

241

To deal with an entire string as a whole, we use the first index only. For example,

```
count = 2;
gets(rev_cat[count]);
```

stores the entered string (a revenue category name) into the third string in the *rev_cat* array.

The *rev_cat* array, defined above, can be treated as an indexed series of strings all named *rev_cat*. In C, a string is an array of characters. Also, a string's name (like any array name) is actually a pointer to the first character in the string. Thus, if

```
rev_cat[2]
```

is the name of the array's third string, then

```
rev_cat[2]
```

must be a *pointer to* **char** that points to this string's first character. This means

rev_cat[0] points to the first string in the array,

rev_cat[1] points to the second string in the array,

rev_cat[2] points to the third string in the array,

rev_cat[3] points to the fourth string in the array,

rev_cat[4] points to the fifth string in the array.

A diagram of all this may be helpful. If the *rev_cat* array is defined

```
char rev_cat[5][31];
```

then, Figure 15-1 shows how each string is referred to.

Chap. 15   Pointers and Multidimensional Arrays

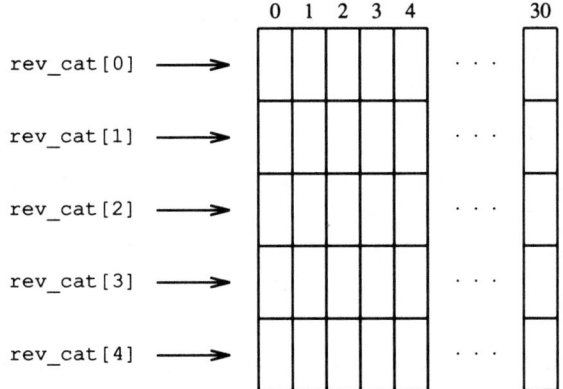

Figure 15-1 A Two-Dimensional Array

Each string's characters are stored in the memory slots numbered 0 to 30. Thus,

```
rev_cat[0][0]
```

is the character in the top left-hand corner and

```
rev_cat[4][30]
```

is in the lower right-hand corner.

In fact, two-dimensional arrays are really two arrays under one name. The first is an array of *pointers* which identify where each string begins. The elements in this array are

```
rev_cat[0]
rev_cat[1]
rev_cat[2]
rev_cat[3]
rev_cat[4]
```

The second array holds the individual characters that make up the strings. These elements are named *rev_cat[0][0]* through *rev_cat[4][30]*.

Each element in the pointer array identifies where the equivalently numbered string begins. When the array is defined, the pointer array is initialized so that

```
rev_cat[0] = &rev_cat[0][0];    /*start of first string */
rev_cat[1] = &rev_cat[1][0];    /*start of second string */
rev_cat[2] = &rev_cat[2][0];    /*start of third string */
rev_cat[3] = &rev_cat[3][0];    /*start of fourth string */
rev_cat[4] = &rev_cat[4][0];    /*start of fifth string */
```

Each string in the *rev_cat* array is 31 characters long. As a result, these statements show what really happens:

```
rev_cat[0] = &rev_cat[0][0];        /* start of first string */
rev_cat[1] = &rev_cat[0][0] + 31;   /* start of second string */
rev_cat[2] = &rev_cat[0][0] + 62;   /* start of third string */
rev_cat[3] = &rev_cat[0][0] + 93;   /* start of fourth string */
rev_cat[4] = &rev_cat[0][0] + 124;  /* start of fifth string */
```

Obviously, the offset required for each string changes when the array is defined with a string length other than thirty-one.

RULE Two-dimensional arrays are really two arrays in one. The first array is a set of pointers that identify where the second arrays begin.

15.1 THE TWO ARRAYS IN A TWO-DIMENSIONAL ARRAY

As we know, every array reference can be rewritten as a pointer combined with indirection. The same is true for *rev_cat*'s string pointers. As an illustration, both

```
rev_cat[2]
```

and

```
*(rev_cat + 2)
```

identify *rev_cat*'s third string. For this to work properly, *rev_cat* (the array name) must point to the first element in the pointer array (which is the beginning of the array, as well). This must be true since *rev_cat* is an array name and array names always point to the array's first element! As a result,

```
*rev_cat            is equivalent to   rev_cat[0]
*(rev_cat + 1)      is equivalent to   rev_cat[1]
*(rev_cat + 2)      is equivalent to   rev_cat[2]
*(rev_cat + 3)      is equivalent to   rev_cat[3]
*(rev_cat + 4)      is equivalent to   rev_cat[4]
```

This is shown graphically in Figure 15-2.

Sec. 15.1   The Two Arrays in a Two-Dimensional Array   245

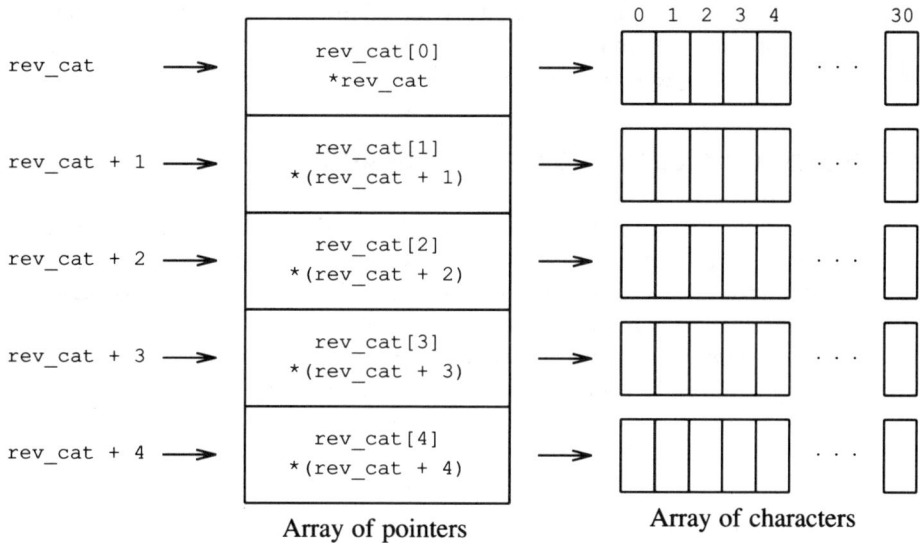

Figure 15-2 The Two Arrays in a Two-Dimensional Array

The *rev_cat* array is defined by

```
char rev_cat[5][31];
```

Since the array stores data type **char**, *rev_cat* is defined as a *pointer to* **char** and then initialized to where the array begins in memory. As a result, the reference

```
rev_cat[1]
```

identifies one *character* location past where *rev_cat* points. This is why the array of pointers is required—so that an entire string (not just a single character) can be referenced using one index only.

Inserting an array of pointers between the array's initial pointer, represented by the array's name, and the characters stored allows us to impose a structure on the array. Now,

```
rev_cat[1]
```

identifies a pointer to where the second string starts.

It is the array of pointers that creates the second dimension. The pointers allow us to break the 155 characters (31 × 5) into five, thirty-one-character strings by identifying the memory location where each string begins. The same structure supports strings of any size! This works because the array of pointers always identifies the first character of each string—no matter what their size.

Pointers provide us with the ability to do indirection. Indirection is required to implement arrays. Two-dimensional arrays require *double indirection*. That is, the first pointer refers to a pointer (the first indirection) which, in turn, identifies where an array element can be found (the second indirection). Incidentally, a three-dimensional array would need triple indirection, and so on.

15.2 TRANSFORMING TWO-DIMENSIONAL ARRAYS

In Chapter 14, we replaced all one-dimensional array references in **flex-pl** with equivalent pointer expressions. The resulting program was listed as Program 14-1. Let's finish the task of removing all array notation from **flex-pl** by converting the two-dimensional array references to pointer expressions.

flex-pl contains two two-dimensional arrays, *rev_cat* and *cost_cat*. We can apply the array transformation rule to these arrays, changing

```
array_name[index]
```

to

```
*(array_name + index)
```

As an example, a **for** loop from the **print_pl( )** function is listed as Segment 15-1.

```
for (count = 0; count < cost_count; count++) {
    printf("%-*s  $%6ld\n", MAX_LEN - 1,
           cost_cat[count], cost_amt[count]);
    totalcost += cost_amt[count];
}
```

Segment 15-1 A **for** Loop with Array References

Segment 15-2 shows the same **for** loop with all array references converted to pointer expressions.

```
for (count = 0; count < cost_count; count++) {
    printf("%-*s  $%6ld\n", MAX_LEN - 1,
           *(cost_cat + count), *(cost_amt + count));
    totalcost += *(cost_amt + count);
}
```

Segment 15-2 Converting Array References to Pointer Expressions

Exercise 15-1 Modify **flex-pl** by transforming all references to string elements in the *rev_cat* and *cost_cat* arrays into pointers. *NOTE*: We haven't yet discussed using pointers to refer to individual characters in a two-dimensional array. However, the correct pointer expression can be created by careful application of the array transformation rule.

Sec. 15.2 Transforming Two-Dimensional Arrays

Converting

```
rev_cat[count]
```

to

```
*(rev_cat + count)
```

is a straightforward transformation. However, to implement the quit signal, both **get_rev( )** and **get_cost( )** must test the first two characters in each category name. This requires us to refer to these characters individually

```
if (cat_name[count][0] == 'Q' &&
    cat_name[count][1] == '\0')
```

cat_name is the formal parameter that represents both the *rev_cat* and *cost_cat* arrays in **get_rev( )** and **get_cost** respectively. How are these transformed into pointer expressions?

The array element

```
cat_name[count][0]
```

is the first character in the string

```
cat_name[count]
```

We can retrieve this character by applying the indirection operator to the pointer to this string's first character

```
*cat_name[count]
```

Recall that

```
cat_name[count]
```

is a pointer to where the string begins.

The expression

```
*cat_name[count]
```

can be transformed further by substituting a pointer expression for the string reference. This results in

```
**(cat_name + count)
```

This looks odd, but it works. The expression inside parentheses,

```
cat_name + count
```

is evaluated first. This identifies the address of this string's pointer. Since the indirection operator associates from right to left, the first indirection,

```
*(cat_name + count)
```

turns this address into the value stored there. The stored value is a pointer to where this string begins. Applying indirection to this pointer

```
**(cat_name + count)
```

evaluates to the first character in the string. Thus, the test

```
cat_name[count][0] == 'Q'
```

and

```
**(cat_name + count) == 'Q'
```

are equivalent.

The second character in the string is located at the address one past the pointer stored in

```
*(cat_name + count)
```

or

```
*(cat_name + count) + 1
```

The character stored there is identified through indirection

```
*(*(cat_name + count) + 1)
```

The parentheses are required to ensure that the additions occur in the proper order. The test

```
if (cat_name[count][0] == 'Q' &&
    cat_name[count][1] == '\0')
```

is the same as

```
if (**(cat_name + count) == 'Q' &&
    *(*(cat_name + count) + 1) == '\0')
```

Sec. 15.2 Transforming Two-Dimensional Arrays

Incidentally, by applying the array transformation rule

$$\text{cat\_name[count][1]}$$

becomes

$$\text{*(cat\_name + count)[1]} \quad \text{/* a legal reference */}$$

which becomes

$$\text{*(*(cat\_name + count) + 1)}$$

Program 15-1 lists a version of the **flex-pl** program that uses only pointer expressions to reference arrays. Note that the only statements containing array indexes are array definitions and formal parameter specifications. **main( )** is unchanged and is not shown here.[1]

```
/* ***** FLEX-PL *****
 * This program reads the category and amount of a set of
 * revenues and costs and prints a formatted Profit and Loss statement.
 * The program reads entries until a Q only is entered
 * as a category name (the quit signal) or until MAX_CAT
 * categories have been read.
 *
 * Written for Ray Swartz for "Doing Business with C"
 *
 * Modified to use pointers for all array references.
 */

#define MAX_LEN 31     /* Length of category name strings */
#define MAX_CAT 20     /* maximum number of category names */

#include "stdio.h"
#include "getcat.c"    /* source code for getcat function */

int printf();

/* main() */
```

---

[1] The array transformations made in the last two chapters are for demonstration purposes. Since array notation is much clearer, the **flex-pl** program that is referred to in the following chapters is the one using array notation.

```
/* ***** GETREV *****
 *
 * This function prompts for and reads revenue categories
 * and amounts.  The category name and amount arrays
 * are passed to the function as arguments.
 *
 * Written by Ray Swartz for "Doing Business with C"
 *
 * Modified to check for a quit signal (Q) and return
 * the number of categories entered.
 *
 * Modified to use pointer notation instead of array
 * indexes
 */

int getrev(cat_name, cat_amt)
char cat_name[][MAX_LEN];   /* category names */
long *cat_amt;              /* amounts */
{
    long getcat();          /* read category and return amount */
    int count;              /* loop counter */

    printf("\nEnter Dollar amounts only -- no cents\n");
    printf("\n\nREVENUES\n\n");
    for (count = 0; count < MAX_CAT; count++) {
        *(cat_amt + count) = getcat(*(cat_name + count), "Revenue");
        if (**(cat_name + count) == 'Q' &&    /* test for quit */
            *(*(cat_name + count) + 1) == '\0')
                break;   /* possible loop exit */
    }
    return(count);
}

/* ***** GETCOST *****
 *
 * This function prompts for and reads cost categories
 * and amounts.  The category name and amount arrays
 * are passed to the function as arguments, as is
 * the number of categories to enter.
 *
 * Written by Ray Swartz for "Doing Business with C"
 *
 * Modified to check for a quit signal (Q) and return
 * the number of categories entered.
 *
 * **Modified to use pointer notation instead of array**
 * **indexes**
 */
```

Sec. 15.2   Transforming Two-Dimensional Arrays

```c
int getcost(cat_name, cat_amt)
long cat_name[] [MAX_LEN]; /* category names */
long *cat_amt;             /* amounts */
{
    long getcat();           /* read category and return amount */
    int count;               /* loop counter */

    printf("\nEnter Dollar amounts only -- no cents\n");
    printf("\n\nCOSTS\n\n");
    for (count = 0; count < MAX_CAT; count++) {
        *(cat_amt + count) = getcat(*(cat_name +count), "Cost");
        if (**(cat_name + count) == 'Q' &&    /* test for quit */
            *(*(cat_name + count) + 1) == '\0')
                break;   /* possible loop exit */
    }
    return(count);
}

/* ***** PRINT_PL *****
 *
 * This function prints a formatted Profit and Loss
 * statement.  It is sent two category name arrays
 * and two category amount arrays--one set for
 * revenues and one for costs.  The number of entries
 * of each type is sent to the function as arguments, also.
 *
 * Written by Ray Swartz for "Doing Business with C"
 *
 * Modified to use pointer notation instead of array
 * indexes
 */

void print_pl(rev_cat, rev_amt, rev_count,
              cost_cat, cost_amt, cost_count)
char rev_cat[] [MAX_LEN];    /* revenue category names */
long *rev_amt;               /* revenue amounts */
int rev_count;               /* number of revenue entries */
char cost_cat[] [MAX_LEN];   /* cost category names */
long *cost_amt;              /* cost amounts */
int cost_count;              /* number of cost entries */
{
    int count;                    /* loop counter */
    static char co_name[] = "Johnson's Books";  /* company name */
    long totalrev = 0;        /* revenue amounts total */
    long totalcost = 0;       /* cost amounts total */

    printf("\tProfit and Loss for %s\n\n", co_name);
    printf("        REVENUE\n\n");
```

```
    /* Loop to print and total the revenue categories */

    for (count = 0; count < rev_count; count++) {
        printf("%-*s  $%6ld\n", MAX_LEN - 1, *(rev_cat + count),
                *(rev_amt + count));
        totalrev += *(rev_amt + count);
    }
    printf("                                   ------\n");
    printf("         TOTAL REVENUE             $%7ld\n\n\n",
            totalrev);

    /* Loop to print and total the cost categories */

    for (count = 0; count < cost_count; count++) {
        printf("%-*s  $%6ld\n", MAX_LEN - 1, *(cost_cat + count),
                *(cost_amt + count));
        totalcost += *(cost_amt + count);
    }
    printf("                                   ------\n");
    printf("         TOTAL COST                $%7ld\n\n\n",
            totalcost);
    if (totalrev >= totalcost)
        printf("         PROFIT                    $%7ld\n",
                totalrev - totalcost);
    else
        printf("         LOSS                     ($%7ld)\n",
                totalcost - totalrev);
    return;
}
```

Program 15-2 The **flex-pl** Program Using Pointer Expressions Only

The three functions **getrev()**, **getcost()**, and **print_pl()**, are passed either the *rev_cat* or *cost_cat* array or both from **main()** as arguments. In **main()**'s function calls, these two-dimensional arrays are listed by name only. Thus, each function receives a pointer to where these arrays begin. However, inside each function, the formal parameter associated with the two-dimensional array(s) is declared as a dummy variable. The formal parameters are specified by

```
        char cat_name[] [MAX_LEN];
```

Why is it necessary to include the string length in this specification?

As we now know, two-dimensional arrays are composed of two one-dimensional arrays. Since the function receives only the beginning pointer, it must be able to align the array's elements properly. That is, the function must know where each string in the array starts. The declaration tells it that

Sec. 15.3   Array Bounds Checking

```
rev_cat[1] = rev_cat + MAX_LEN
rev_cat[2] = rev_cat + 2 * MAX_LEN
rev_cat[3] = rev_cat + 3 * MAX_LEN
rev_cat[4] = rev_cat + 4 * MAX_LEN
```

Without knowing the size of the array's second dimension, C wouldn't know how to set up the pointer array that references the array's elements as strings!

Exercise 15-2   Modify both the **get_rev( )** and **get_cost( )** functions to declare the formal parameter *cat_name* as a pointer to **char** and then to reference each string in the array directly. [HINT: Use the MAX_LEN macro.]

15.3 ARRAY BOUNDS CHECKING

We are not required to declare the first dimension of the array argument for two reasons. First, only the array's second dimension (and higher for arrays with more than two dimensions) is needed for alignment, the beginning of the pointer array is identified by the array name. Second, the C language does not provide any array bounds checking. That is, C does not check if an array's index is outside the bounds of the array itself. As a result, it has no need to know the size of the array's first dimension.

   RULE   C does not perform array bounds checking.

Some people cite C's failure to do array bounds checking as a serious flaw in its design. They argue that the computer should not allow an array index to refer to memory not defined as part of the array. Further, problems caused by such programming errors can be extremely difficult to recognize and correct, since, by definition, an out-of-bounds error only occurs under certain conditions.

C's proponents counter these arguments by pointing out that array bounds checking increases the overhead of every program that uses arrays. To perform array bounds checking requires the computer to store the size of each array (increasing the size of the program) and to verify that *every* array reference is legal before using it (increasing the program's execution time). This makes these programs larger and much slower than the same program written in C. Further, how would bounds checking be done on pointers that are not array names?

In either case, it must be emphasized that C does not complain, in any way, if a program contains an array reference that is outside the array's bounds. As an example, a common mistake is to use an array index that is the size of the array. If

```
double rev_amt[MAX_CAT];
```

then the reference

```
rev_amt[MAX_CAT]
```

is one element past the end of the array. If bounds checking occurred, the program would terminate with an "out-of-bounds" error.

However in C, memory is addressed directly. Thus, the reference

```
rev_amt[MAX_CAT]
```

is converted to its equivalent pointer expression

```
*(rev_amt + MAX_CAT)
```

and evaluated as if a specific memory location is being accessed. Even though it is outside the array's bounds, C allows the reference as long as it evaluates to a legal memory location (i.e., one addressable by the machine).

As a result, one of the most difficult errors to locate in a C program is an out-of-bounds error. If the error occurs while data is being written to memory, the program often will terminate unexpectedly or simply "hang," forcing the machine to be restarted. Should the program not terminate, its behavior can become very erratic. Be forewarned. It is a smart precaution to keep disk backups current when executing C programs for the first time.

When a program does wild things or just terminates for no reason, it strongly suggests that something is wrong. However, an out-of-bounds error that reads a legal memory location causes problems that are not so obvious. Legal memory locations always store some value. While reading some random data from memory may not crash the program, it will make the program's results meaningless.

C's pointers provide us with the power to reach directly inside the computer's memory. As such, we must be careful not to get burned by grabbing the wrong thing!

15.4 SUMMARY

1. Just like arrays with one dimension, higher-dimensioned arrays are implemented with pointers. One pointer is required for each dimension.
2. In a two-dimensional array, the first dimension (represented by the first index) identifies a pointer array that holds the starting addresses of the second dimensions.
3. The name of a two-dimensional array is a pointer to the beginning of the array, which is the first element in the pointer array.
4. Identifying a character in a string array requires double indirection. The first indirection gets the address of the string and the second indirection refers to the individual character in that string.
5. Each of these expressions references the second character in the second string in a string array:

Sec. 15.4 Summary

```
str[1][1]

*(str + 1)[1]

*(*(str + 1) + 1)
```

6. When a multidimensional array is passed to a function as an argument, all the dimensions must be specified except the first. This allows the function to align the address in the first pointer array properly.
7. C does not perform array bounds checking. That is, C does not check to see if an array's index is outside the memory set aside for that array.

EXERCISES

15-3. Write a macro that takes an array name and two integers and then expands to the pointer expression that refers to the element identified by the array name and two indexes.

15-4. Modify **print_pl( )** to declare the revenue and cost category array arguments as *pointers to* **char** (instead of arrays) and then to refer to the elements in these arrays using indirection instead of array index notation.

15-5. In Exercise 15-2, the **get_rev( )** function is rewritten to use the revenue category array as a *pointer to* **char**. Modify the function to directly identify the address of each string using the array name (the argument passed in) and an offset to the first element of each string's memory only.

15-6. Rewrite either Exercise 9-7 or 9-8 to use double indirection instead of array index notation.

PART 6
Strings

16

Strings, Arrays, and Pointers

In C, strings are not a separate data type. Instead, they are represented as character arrays. In addition, C doesn't treat a string any differently than an array, with the exception that strings are terminated with \0, the special EOS (end-of-string) character constant.

Many languages contain special variables and operations for handling strings. C doesn't. As a result, working with strings in C requires practice. This is why we have dedicated an entire chapter to them.

Since strings are actually arrays, we can use pointers to refer to the entire string or parts of it. If a string is defined

```
char co_name[81];
```

then the string's name *co_name* is really a pointer to the string's first character

```
co_name = &co_name[0];
```

Pointers provide a great deal of flexibility in indexing strings. Suppose we want to access the last ten characters stored in *co_name*. We can do this by defining *strptr* to be a pointer to **char** and pointing at the proper spot in *co_name*.

```
    char co_name[81];
    char *strptr;

    strptr = &co_name[70];   /* first one is 0, 80 is last one */
```

We also can accomplish this with pointer arithmetic

```
            strptr = co_name + 70;
```

In addition, this can be done in the definition of *strptr*.

```
        char *strptr = &co_name[70];
```

assuming *co_name* was previously defined.

Even though pointers were just discussed in Part 4, we have been using them in relation to strings since the very beginning. As we now know, C doesn't pass entire arrays as function arguments. Instead, a pointer to the beginning of the array is passed. For example, in this call to **printf( )**,

```
            printf("%s\n", co_name);
```

we are sending **printf** a pointer to the *co_name* string. Another way to pass **printf( )** the *co_name* string is

```
            printf("%s\n", &co_name[0]);
```

However,

```
            printf("%s\n", co_name[0]);
```

does not work properly. This is an error because

```
                  co_name[0]
```

is a character, not a pointer!

If a string can be passed only as a pointer, why does

```
            printf("Enter Company Name: ");
```

work? In C, a string constant is treated as a pointer to the first character in the string, that is, the string is stored exactly as listed and the quoted string itself is treated as a pointer to the first character in the string. Thus, **printf( )** receives a pointer to the string

```
                Enter Company Name:
```

RULE A string constant is treated as a pointer to the first character in the string constant.

Because a string constant is actually stored in memory and accessible via a pointer, we can initialize a *pointer* to **char** with

```
char *prompt = "Enter Company Name: ";
```

or set pointers with

```
char *prompt;

prompt = "Enter Company Name: ";
```

This is merely setting one pointer equal to another. As an extension, we could print a string by

```
char *prompt = "Enter Company Name: "

printf(prompt);
```

though to do so hides what is actually going on and is not recommended.

One perverse side effect of viewing string constants as pointers is that it makes the term *constant* a misnomer. A string constant is like any other *pointer* to **char**. This means we can use indirection and change the characters stored in a string constant! As an illustration, if

```
char *co_name = "Johnson's Books";
```

then

```
*(co_name + 9) = '\0';   /* at the space between the words */
```

shortens the constant to "Johnson's". Needless to say, it is not good programming style to modify string constants.[1]

While a *pointer* to **char** can be assigned a string constant, we cannot do the same thing with a defined string variable (i.e., a **char** array). As an illustration, the following expression is illegal:

```
char co_name[81];

co_name = "Johnson's Books";
```

---

[1] The ANSI standard has made string constants truly constant. However, the standard allows for modifiable string constants as a common extension.

Sec. 16.1 A Careful Look at **chars**

An array name is a constant that cannot be changed (i.e., pointed somewhere else). This demonstrates one of the differences between arrays and pointers.

We can initialize a string when it is defined. One way to store "Johnson's Books" in the string *co_name* is

```
static char co_name[] = "Johnson's Books";
```

The empty brackets in the definition make *co_name* big enough to handle the initializing string.

16.1 A CAREFUL LOOK AT chars

In the United States two character sets are widely used. The most popular is the ASCII code, established by the American National Standards Institute (ANSI). The other code is EBCDIC, created by IBM. Various national and international organizations have published other "standard" character sets. Most, if not all, programs will fail if they are run using character sets other than those with which they were written. Incompatible character sets are one obstacle to program portability that C designers had to solve.

The entire English language uses little more than 100 symbols (fifty-two for upper- and lower-case characters, ten for the digits 0 through 9, and the rest for punctuation!). Thus, a computer's character set need not be very large and, as a rule, character sets usually contain less then 256 symbols. In fact, the ASCII character set only defines 128 different symbols! See Appendix A for a full listing of the ASCII and Appendix B for EBCDIC.

There are two major incompatibilities between character sets. First, they use different numeric codes for the same symbol. For example, the ASCII code for *A* is 65 whereas in EBCDIC it is 193. Second, they don't contain the same symbols. The ASCII code contains 128 characters while EBCDIC has 256.

To shield C programs from these problems, C doesn't rely on any specific character set. Instead, C uses a character constant to represent a specific character's numeric value. When the program is compiled, the appropriate numeric value from the machine's character set is substituted for each character used in the program.

Since a **char** is really an integer, it can be manipulated as such. This causes no problem as long as the values used do not exceed the largest code in the character set. As an example,

```
printf("%c", 'A');
```

will print the letter *A*.

```
printf("%d", 'A');
```

will print the code representing *A* in the character set. If your computer uses ASCII, this would print 65. On the other hand, the results of

```
               printf("%c", 248);
```

are unpredictable since there is no corresponding ASCII code for 248 (there is one in EBCDIC though).[2]

Since **char**s are integers, we can perform arithmetic operations on them. As an illustration,

```
               printf("%d", '1' - '0');
```

will print the difference between the numeric code for the character **'1'** and **'0'** in the computer's character set.

16.2 WRITING STRING FUNCTIONS

As we found out in the last chapter, C doesn't perform array bounds checking. Overwriting an array's bounds, that is, trying to store too much data in it, will make a program fail. What's worse, the program may not stop executing, but continue to run and produce bogus results.

The most common source of overwriting errors is string input. An example is when **gets( )** reads a forty-five-character string but only has a thirty-character string to store it in! Unless we take precautions against this, our programs will eventually fail.

To protect itself, the **flex-pl** program lists the maximum number of characters that can be entered for a category name. However, it does not test if the name read is too long. Unfortunately, telling the user to do something is no guarantee that the request will be obeyed. As a result, all input must be checked against the program's limits. This is especially true where these boundaries mean program failure if surpassed.

RULE   *Never* assume that the user will do what you ask and *always* verify that entered data is within the program's limits.

In addition to printing out the maximum allowable length of a category name, **flex-pl** must check if the string entered is larger than the variable can store. To do this, we must be able to determine a string's length. The first step in fixing the potentially fatal overwrite problem in **flex-pl** is to create a function that is sent a string and returns its length.

This function, let's call it **strlen**( ), is straightforward to write. The key idea is that the length of a string is the number of characters before the **\0**. The algorithm is listed as Algorithm 16-1.

1. Initialize count to 0
2. If str[count] = **'\0'** go to step 5
   else go to step 3.
3. Increment count by 1

---

[2] Many computers offer an "extended" version of ASCII which contains 256 symbols.

Sec. 16.2   Writing String Functions

4. Go to 2.
5. Return count (which holds the length of the string).

Algorithm 16-1   Algorithm for Finding the Length of a String

The function is shown as Function 16-1.

```
/* ***** STRLEN *****
 *
 * Count the number of characters in the string argument
 * not including the terminating \0.
 *
 * Written by Ray Swartz for Doing Business with C.
 */

int strlen(str)
char *str;
{
    int count = 0;    /* initialize counter */

    while(str[count] != '\0')   /* is this the last character? */
        count++;
    return(count);
}
```

Function 16-1   The **strlen( )** Function

It might seem that we can save a statement by moving the incrementing of **count** into the array index

```
while(str[count++] != '\0').
```

However, this gives the wrong answer since **count** is incremented even when \0 is found, resulting in *count* being 1 too big.

Not surprisingly, there are other ways to write **strlen( )**. We are going to look at three of them. First, instead of referencing *str* as an array, we can treat it as a pointer. This requires another statement inside the **while** loop to increment the pointer, *str*, to the next character. The pointer version is shown as Function 16-1a.

```
/* ***** STRLEN *****
 *
 * Count the number of characters in the string argument
 * not including the terminating \0.
 *
```

```
 * Written by Ray Swartz for "Doing Business with C".
 *
 * Modified to use pointers.
 */

int strlen(str)
char *str;
{
    int count = 0;    /* initialize counter */

    while(*str != '\0') {   /* is this the last character? */
        str++;    /* point to the next character */
        count++;
    }
    return(count);
}
```

Function 16-1a The **strlen( )** Function Using Pointers

Incidentally, the argument *str* is local to the **strlen( )** function. As a result, incrementing *str* has no effect on the string represented by *str*. Further, *str* only exists while **strlen( )** is executing. It goes away when the function terminates.

We can shorten Function 16-1a by incrementing the pointer *str* within the **while** test. This is shown as Function 16-1b.

```
/* ***** STRLEN *****
 *
 * Count the number of characters in the string argument
 * not including the terminating \0.
 *
 * Written by Ray Swartz for "Doing Business with C".
 *
 * Modified to use pointers.
 */

int strlen(str)
char *str;
{
    int count = 0;    /* initialize counter */

    while(*str++ != '\0')   /* is this the last character? */
        count++;
    return(count);
}
```

Function 16-1b Another Pointer Version of **strlen( )**

Sec. 16.2   Writing String Functions   263

However, does

$$*str++$$

work properly? Both indirection and increment operators are unary and have the same precedence. Unary operators associate right to left. This means the expression

$$*str++$$

is evaluated as

$$*(str++)$$

The pointer is incremented *after* the indirection occurs (more precisely, after the address currently stored in *str* is fixed in the indirection expression). The result is to check the character currently referenced by *str* and to increment *str* to point at the next character, all in the same expression.

Another approach to the **strlen( )** function is to use the difference between two pointers. If

```
char instr[30];
char *str1 = instr;      /* points at first character */
char *str2 = &instr[10]; /* points at eleventh character */
```

then the expression

$$str2 - str1$$

evaluates to 10, the number of **char**s between the two addresses. This works for **strlen( )** if *str2* points to the **\0** in the string and *str1* points to the beginning. This version of **strlen( )** is shown as Function 16-1*c*.

```
/* ***** STRLEN *****
 *
 * Count the number of characters in the string argument
 * not including the terminating \0.
 *
 * Written by Ray Swartz for "Doing Business with C".
 *
 * Modified to use pointers.
 */
```

```
       int strlen(str)
       char *str;
       {
           char *beg_str = str;   /* beginning of string */

           while(*str != '\0')    /* is this the last character? */
                str++;            /* doesn't increment for \0 */
           return(str - beg_str);
       }
```

Function 16-1c Another Pointer Version of **strlen( )**

These are not the only ways to write the **strlen( )** function. The point of showing these three versions is to demonstrate the variety of approaches found in string functions. Regardless of how **strlen( )** is written, it does the same basic operation—count the number of characters in the string before the \0.

At first glance, it may appear that we can test the length of the entered string in **flex-pl** using the code in Segment 16-1, which is taken from the **getcat( )** function (Function 10-1).

```
       printf("\nEnter a %s Category (%d Character Maximum): ",
                STRING_LEN, class);
       gets(catstr);
       if (strlen(catstr) >= STRING_LEN) /* entered string too long? */
       rest of function
```

Segment 16-1 Testing the Length of an Entered String

If the string stored in *catstr* (which represents the category name variable) is too long, the damage has already been done (i.e., memory has been overwritten) by the time the function tests for it.

Instead, we must know that the string entered will fit into *catstr* before we store it there! This calls for a different approach. First, the entered string is read into a very large string variable, represented by *instr*. We then test the length of the string and if it won't fit into *catstr*, we print an error message and reprompt. If it will fit, we copy the string into *catstr* and continue the function. This is listed as Algorithm 16-2.

1. Read *string* into *instr*.
2. If *strlen(instr)* >= STRING_LEN then go to step 3
     else go to step 5
3. Print "String entered too large"

Sec. 16.2 Writing String Functions

4. Go to step 1
5. Copy *instr* into *catstr*
6. Continue function

Algorithm 16-2 Testing the Length of an Entered String

Before we can implement Algorithm 16-2, we must be able to copy the contents of one string into another. We can't copy a string by assigning one pointer to the other, for instance

```
char str1[20];
char str2[20];

...
str1 = str2;     /* This won't work */
```

This doesn't work for two reasons. First, recall that array names are treated as constants in C and can't appear on the left-hand side of an assignment operator. Second, even if *str1* and *str2* are pointers, assigning the address stored in *str2* to *str1* doesn't copy the characters; it simply points *str1* at a different place. Now, *str1* and *str2* are the *same* variable. By making *str1* and *str2* equal, we lose the memory referenced by *str1* because no variable points to it anymore!

In C, we must actually copy the characters from one string to another. Clearly, this is a common task that should be coded into a general function. The function, called **strcpy()**, is sent two string pointers (or array names, which are the same thing). If **strcpy()** is called

```
strcpy(str1, str2)
```

then *str2* is copied into *str1*. The algorithm for this function is listed as Algorithm 16-3.

1. If *str2 is \0, go to step 5
   else go to step 2
2. Assign: ***str1 = *str2** (the character referenced by *str2* is stored where *str1* points).
3. Increment both *str1* and *str2*
4. Go to step 1
5. Return

Algorithm 16-2 The **strcpy()** Algorithm

strcpy() returns a pointer to the first character in *str1*, the string that results from the copying operation. Although this isn't always useful, we occasionally will want to refer to the string after the copy is made. This is the same idea behind the **gets( )** function returning a pointer to the string entered.

A pointer implementation of **strcpy( )** is shown as Function 16-2.

```
/* ***** STRCPY *****
 * This function copies the character in str2 into
 * str1.
 *
 * Written by Ray Swartz for "Doing Business with C".
 */

char *strcpy(str1, str2)
char *str1;                  /* string where copy is put */
char *str2;                  /* string being copied */
{
   char *begin str1 = str1;   /* return value */

   while((*str1 = *str2) != '\0') { /* \0 copied before test */
       str1++;
       str2++;
   }
   return(begin str1);
}
```

Function 16-2 The **strcpy( )** Function

The expression

$$(\text{*str1} = \text{*str2}) \mathrel{!=} \text{'}\backslash 0\text{'}$$

stores the characters identified by the pointer *str2* in the memory location referenced by *str1*. After the assignment, the character that was assigned is tested against **\0**.

The **strcpy( )** function can be shortened by incrementing the pointers in the assignment expression. This version is shown as Function 16-2*a*.

```
/* ***** STRCPY *****
 * This function copies the character in str2 into
 * str1.
 *
 * Written by Ray Swartz for "Doing Business with C".
 */
```

Sec. 16.2 Writing String Functions

```
    char *strcpy(str1, str2)
    char *str1;
    char *str2;
    {
        char *begin_str1 = str1;

        while((*str1++ = *str2++) != \0)
            ;    /* The \0 is copied before the test */
        return(begin_str1);
    }
```

Function 16-2a The **strcpy( )** Function

The **while** loop in Function 16-2a demonstrates one of the valuable side effects of C's operator usage. The loop performs the required processing by testing its stopping condition. If the character assigned and tested is not **\0**, there is nothing we want to do but test the stopping condition again!

A loop must do *something* if the loop test is true. For this reason, C contains a special statement called the *null* statement. A null statement is represented by a semicolon and does nothing. It is used to complete control statements that require no additional processing. It doesn't matter where the semicolon is placed. To make null statements obvious, they are put on a line by themselves.

RULE   A null statement represents the required statement of a control structure that has no need to process commands inside the structure.

Loops whose bodies are null statements, are called *empty loops*. Empty loops are quite common in C, especially in string processing when copying or comparing a set of characters in a string.

Exercise 16-1   Using an array-index reference, rewrite the **strlen( )** function with an empty **while** loop.

Exercise 16-2   Modify the **strcpy( )** function to take an **int** argument that tells the function how many characters from *str2* to copy into *str1*. If *str2* is shorter than this new argument, the copy should stop at the **\0** in *str2*. In all cases, *str1* should end with **\0**. Call the function **strncpy( )** and write it with an empty loop.

Now that we can determine the length of a string and copy one string into another, we can verify that the category name read by **getcat( )** will fit into the variable that must store it. Algorithm 16-2 (above) listed the steps required to do this. Function 16-3 shows **getcat( )** with these changes included.

```
/* ***** GETCAT *****
 *
 * This function prompts for a revenue or cost category
 * name (depending on the string stored in the argument
 * class), reads the name entered, then calls getlong
 * to read the amount for this category.  The amount entered
 * is returned by getcat.
 *
 * Written by Ray Swartz for "Doing Business with C"
 *
 * Modified to test for the quit signal (Q only)
 * entered as category name.  If the quit signal is
 * found, the function does not prompt for amount.
 *
 * Modified to use a macro (STRING_LEN) for the maximum
 * category name length.
 *
 * Modified to verify the length of the category name
 * is no longer than STRING_LEN.
 */

#include "getlong.c"      /* source code of getlong function */
#include "strlen.c"       /* source code of strlen function */
#include "strcpy.c"       /* source code of strcpy function */

#ifdef MAX_LEN
#define STRING_LEN MAX_LEN - 1   /* Use if MAX_LEN defined */
#else
#define STRING_LEN 30            /* Default value */
#endif

#ifndef BUFSIZ
#define BUFSIZ 512               /* Default buffer size */
#endif

long getcat(catstr, class)
char catstr[];      /* string variable for entered category name */
char class[];       /* category classification (Revenue or Cost) */
{
    char instr[BUFSIZ];     /* input string */
    char *gets();
    char *strcpy();
    int strlen();
    int printf();
    long getlong();         /* prints a prompt and reads long value */
```

Sec. 16.3 String Functions in C's Standard Library

```
        do {
            printf("\nEnter a %s Category (%d Character Maximum): ",
                STRING_LEN, class);
            if(strlen(gets(instr)) > STRING_LEN)
                printf("Name entered too long, only %d characters allowed",
                    STRING_LEN);
        } while (strlen(instr) > STRING_LEN);
        strcpy(catstr, instr);   /* copy name into category variable */
        if (catstr[0] == 'Q' && catstr[1] == '\0')
            return(0);      /* quit signal -- don't prompt for amount */
        else
            return(getlong(catstr));   /* return amount entered */
    }
```

Function 16-3   Checking for Length of Name in **getcat( )**

Function 16-3 assumes that *instr* can hold whatever **gets( )** reads. Most computers store the characters typed at the keyboard in a special buffer until a newline is entered and then the whole line is sent to the program. There is a limit to the number of characters that can be held in this buffer. The computer ignores any characters that would overflow this buffer. As a result, an input string cannot exceed the size of the keyboard buffer.

The macro BUFSIZ represents the number of characters the keyboard buffer can hold. On most systems, BUFSIZ is **#define**d in *stdio.h*. However, to protect ourselves, we use conditional compilation to ensure that it is **#define**d in all circumstances.

16.3 STRING FUNCTIONS IN C'S STANDARD LIBRARY

In reality, we do not have to write a **strlen( )** or **strcpy( )** function because they are part of C's Standard Library. The standard library contains several other *string handling* functions. The most common ones are described below (see Appendix D for a more complete listing of C's standard library). Incidentally, a specific implementation of the C language may offer more than, less than, or different functions.

The standard string functions can be distinguished by what data type they return. Some, like **strlen( )**, return an **int**, while others, like **strcpy( )**, return a *pointer* to **char**.

16.3.1 String Handling Functions That Return an int

Strings are not one of C's "built-in" data types, but are represented by an aggregation of **char**s. For this reason, strings are called an *aggregate* data type. Unfortunately, C's operators only work on the built-in data types. Therefore, if *str1* and *str2* are defined, as below,

```
                char str1[10];
                char str2[10];
```

then

$$\text{str1 == str2}$$

does not determine if the two strings are equal, that is, store the same characters. Instead, it tests if what is stored in *str1* is equal to what is stored in *str2*. Both store pointers to the first character in their respective strings. Thus,

$$\text{str1 == str2}$$

is true only if *str1* and *str2* point to the same memory location. Not quite what we had in mind.

Determining the equality of two strings is done by **strcmp( )**, which is a function that compares the strings, character by character. **strcmp( )** is sent two arguments, both pointers to the characters to be compared. Assume that the first argument is *str1* and the second *str2*. **strcmp( )** returns a value less than 0 if *str1* is *lexicographically* less than *str2*; a 0 if *str1* is equal to *str2*; and a number greater than 0 if *str1* is lexicographically greater than *str2*. Lexicographically, *str1* is less than *str2* if

1. The character code value of the first element in *str1* is less than the corresponding character code in *str2*.
2. Both *str1* and *str2* begin with a series of the same characters and the first element in *str1* different than one in *str2* has a lower code value.
3. *str1* is shorter than *str2* and both contain the same characters up to the length of *str1*. Put another way, a null character is always less than any other.

It is important to note that **strcmp( )** does not return a −1, 0, and +1 only. For reasons of efficiency, **strcmp** returns the difference between the characters that are not equal (∗str1 − ∗str2). This way, the function doesn't have to test the outcome and return a specific value. The sign of the result is good enough.

Exercise 16-3   Write the **strcmp()** function.

As an example of using the **strcmp( )** function, we will rewrite the quit signal test in **getrev( )**. The quit signal is the string **"Q"** entered as a category name. At present, we individually test the first two characters in the category name string:

```
if (cat_name[count][0] == 'Q' &&
    cat_name[count][1] == '\0')
```

This same test can be done by **strcmp( )**:

```
if (strcmp(cat_name[count], "Q") == 0)
```

Because **strcmp( )** compares strings, we sent the *string* constant **"Q"** (note the double quotation marks) as one of the arguments. It is common to send **strcmp( )** constant arguments. Recall that string constants are treated as pointers to the first character in the string.

We don't always want to compare all the characters in two strings. For these cases, the **strncmp( )** function is provided. **strncmp( )** compares two strings just like **strcmp( )** but only compares a specified maximum number of characters. **strncmp( )** is sent three arguments, the two strings, which are pointers to **char**, and the number of characters to compare, which is an **int**. The call to **strncmp( )** is

```
strncmp(str1, str2, nbr)
```

where *nbr* represents how many characters to compare.

Exercise 16-4 Write the **strncmp()** function.

16.3.2 String Handling Functions that Return a Pointer to char

It makes sense for string handling functions that compare two strings or determine string length to express their result as an **int**. However, functions that directly manipulate strings should return pointers to the strings they produce. These pointers allow us to access the resulting strings immediately, which is often desirable.

We've already discussed and demonstrated one function that returns a string pointer, **strcpy( )**. A companion function allows us to specify the number of characters to copy from one string to another. Not surprisingly, it is called **strncpy( )**. A similar function was described in Exercise 16-2.

strncpy( ) copies exactly *nbr* characters from *str2* into *str1*. The call is

```
char *strncpy();

strncpy(str1, str2, nbr)
```

where

```
            char *str1;
            char *str2;
            int nbr;
```

Be careful when using **strncpy( )** because it can create nonterminated strings. If *str2* contains more than *nbr* characters, then *str1* will not be terminated with a \0. If *str2* is shorter than *nbr* characters, *str1* is padded with \0s to ensure that specified number of characters get copied. Also, like **strcpy( )**, whatever is in *str1* is overwritten and a pointer to *str1* is returned.

An operation similar to copying strings is putting one string on the end of another. C provides two functions that do just this, called **strcat( )** and **strncat( )**. **strcat( )**

writes all of *str2*, including the \0, to the end of *str1* and returns a pointer to *str1*. The call is

```
char *strcat();

strcat(str1, str2)
```

where

```
char *str1;
char *str2;
```

It is assumed that *str1* is big enough to hold the resulting string. The original \0 in *str1* is overwritten.

First, **strcat( )** must find the end of *str1*. Then, beginning at the \0 in *str1*, copy *str2* into *str1*. Copying *str2* onto the end of *str1* is equivalent to the **strcpy( )** function. The function returns a pointer to *str1*.

As expected, **strncat( )** appends the first *nbr* characters of *str2* to *str1*. The resulting string is always terminated with a \0. If *str2* contains *nbr* or more characters, **strncat( )** writes *nbr* + 1 characters to the end of *str1*—the number of characters specified and a \0. If *str2* has less than *nbr* characters, *str1* is padded with \0s. A pointer to the new *str1* is returned. The call is

```
char *strncat();

strncat(str1, str2, nbr).
```

where

```
char *str1;
char *str2;
int nbr;
```

The standard library also contains two functions that search for a string for a certain character. These functions are called by two different names, **strchr( )** and **index( )** check your compiler's documentation for the correct one to use. **strchr( )** or **index( )** is passed the string to search and the character to search for. It returns a pointer to the first occurrence of the character in the string. If the string doesn't contain the character, the macro NULL is returned. The function call is

```
char *strchr();

strchr(str, search)
```

where

```
                    char *str;
                    char search;
```

or

```
                    char *index();

                    index(str, search)
```

Suppose we needed to know the *position* of the character's occurrence in *str*. Some implementations have a function called **strpos( )** that does this—returning −1 if the *search* character is not in *str* and numbering the first character as 0. For those that don't, a simple way to solve this problem is to take advantage of pointer arithmetic. As an illustration, say that all our customers have codes beginning with an 'r' for retail and a 'w' for wholesale. To find out which price to charge a particular customer, we would have to know if the customer code began with an 'r'. Consider Segment 16-2.

```
            char *position;
            static char str[] = "r-acme"    /* customer code */
            char *strchr();

            if (position = strchr(str, 'r')) == NULL) {
                /* no 'r' in the code at all */
```

Segment 16-2 Finding A Character's Position in a String

If the test is false, we must discover where 'r' is located. Since *str* is a pointer to the first character and *position* points to the first 'r', then this test determines if 'r' is the first character.

```
                    if(str - position == 0) {
                        /* 'r' is first character */
```

When two pointers are manipulated, remember that C adjusts the result to account for the number of memory locations used by each data type. Also, this works because we know that *str* and *position* are in the same string.

A companion function to **strchr( )** or **index( )** is one that searches for the *last* occurrence of a character in a string. This function is called **strrchr( )** or **rindex( )** and the arguments and return value are the same as for **strchr( )** or **index( )**. The name of this function is derived from the fact that it searches from the right side of the string.

16.4 SUMMARY

1. A string's name is a pointer to the first character in the string.
2. A string constant is treated as a pointer to the first character in the string constant. This allows the perverse result that string constants can be changed!

3. Characters are represented inside the computer as small integers. The mapping of integers onto characters is done by a character set.
4. The standard library function **strlen( )** is passed a string and returns the length of that string.
5. The expression

$$*str++$$

evaluates from right to left. This expression retrieves the character stored where *str* points and then increments the pointer.
6. The result of subtracting one pointer from another pointer of the same data type is the number of data elements between the two.
7. The standard library function **strcpy( )** takes two string arguments and copies the contents of the second into the first one.
8. The macro BUFSIZ represents the largest string that can be stored in the keyboard buffer without a newline.
9. Some standard library string functions return **int** and some return *pointers* to **char**.
10. The standard library function **strcmp( )** takes two string arguments and compares them. It returns an **int** less than zero if the first string is lexicographically less than the second one, an **int** value of 0 if they are equal, and an **int** greater than zero if the first string is greater than the second one.
11. The standard library function **strncpy( )** copies a specified number of characters from its second string argument into its first one. The number to copy is specified in another argument. The function returns a pointer to the beginning of the first string.
12. The standard library function **strcat( )** copies the second string argument onto the end of the first string argument. The function returns a pointer to the beginning of the first string.
13. The standard library function **strncat( )** copies a specified number of characters from the second string argument onto the end of the first string argument. The function returns a pointer to the beginning of the first string.
14. The standard library function **strchr( )** searches a string argument for a character specified as an argument. If found, a pointer to the first occurrence of the character in the string is returned. A companion function, **strrchr( )**, does the same thing except it finds the last occurrence of the specified character.

E X E R C I S E S

16-5. Write a program that reads a string and then reverses it.
16-6. Write a function called **getstr( )** that is sent a string and an **int**. The **int** argument is the

longest string that can be entered. If the string entered is too long, the function should print a message return NULL.

16-7. Modify the function written in Exercise 16-6 to take the prompt to print as an argument (in addition to the two listed in 16-6) and to create the prompt by combining this argument with the maximum size allowed for the entry.

16-8. Write a program that reads a string and then separates that string into words. Assume a word is any non-space set of characters. *Hint*: Use the **strchr( )** function.

16-9. Write a function called **cntchr( )** that counts the number of times a specified character occurs in a string.

16-10. Write a function called **chgchr( )** that changes all of the occurrences of one character into another.

16-11. Write a function called **chkchrs( )** that checks if a string (the first argument) consists of characters other than those listed in a second argument. The function takes two arguments, a string to check and a string holding the legal characters for that string. The function returns a nonzero value if only legal characters are found and zero if at least one nonlegal character is found.

16-12. Modify **getlong( )** to use the **chkchrs( )** function written for Exercise 16-10 to test if the string entered for an amount contains a legal number only. A legal number can contain digits, one decimal point, and a leading + or −.

16.5 ADDENDUM

This addendum lists the source code for the string functions **strncpy( )**, **strcat( )**, **strncat( )**, **strchr( )**, and **strrchr( )**.

```
/* ***** STRNCPY *****
 *
 * This function copies a specified number of characters
 * from str2 into str1.  If str2 contains less than
 * that number of characters, str1 is filled with \0.
 * If str2 contains more than nbr characters, that number
 * of characters is transferred to str1 and str1 is NOT
 * terminated.  A pointer to str1 is returned.
 *
 *  WARNING: this function can return with str1 not
 *           terminated.
 *
 * Written by Ray Swartz for "Doing Business with C".
 */

char *strncpy(str1, str2, nbr)
char *str1;
char *str2;
int nbr;
```

```
    {
        char *s = str1;   /* so pointer to str1 can be returned */
        count = 0;

        while(count++ < nbr) {
            if (*str2 != '\0')
                *str1++ = *str2++;
            else          /* pad str1 with \0s if nbr > length of str2 */
                *str1++ = '\0';
        }
        return(s);
    }

/* ***** STRCAT *****
 *
 * This function copies str2 to the end of str1.  A
 * pointer to str1 is returned.
 *
 * Written by Ray Swartz for "Doing Business with C"
 */

char *strcat(str1, str2)
char *str1;
char *str2;
{
    char *s = str1;   /* return pointer */

    while(*str1++ != '\0')   /* find end of str1 */
        ;
    str1--;           /* get rid of \0 in str1 */
    while((*str1++ = *str2++) != '\0')
        ;             /* copy str2 to end of str1 */
    return(s);
}

    /* ***** STRNCAT *****
     *
     * This function copies the specified number (nbr) of
     * characters from str2 to the end of str1.
     * If str2 contains less than nbr characters, str1 is
     * padded with \0.  If str2 contains more than nbr
     * characters, nbr + 1 characters are written to str1--
     * nbr characters from str2 and a \0.  A pointer
     * to str1 is returned.
     *
```

Sec. 16.5 Addendum

```
 * WARNING: This function may copy more than nbr characters
 *          into str1.
 *
 * Written by Ray Swartz for "Doing Business with C"
 */

char *strncat(str1, str2, nbr)
char *str1;
char *str2;
int nbr;
{
    char *s = str1;   /* return pointer */
    int count = 0;

    while(*str1++ != '\0')   /* find end of str1 */
        ;
    str1--;            /* get rid of \0 in str1 */
    while(count++ < nbr) {   /* move nbr characters at most */
        if (*str2 != '\0')
            *str1++ = *str2++; /* append str2 to str1 */
        else
            *str1++ = '\0';    /* pad str1 with \0s */
    }
    *str1 = '\0';
    return(s);
}

/* ***** STRCHR *****
 *
 * This function searches a string for the first occurrence
 * of a character. If the string does not contain the
 * character, NULL is returned, otherwise a pointer to
 * this character in the string is returned.
 *
 * Written by Ray Swartz for "Doing Business with C"
 */

char *strchr(str, c)
char *str;
char c;
```

```
{
    while(*str != '\0') {
        if(*str == c)         /* character found? */
            return(str);      /* return pointer */
        else
            str++;            /* check next character */
    }
    return(NULL);    /* character not found */
}

/* ***** STRRCHR *****
 *
 * This function searches a string for the last occurrence
 * of a character.  If the string does not contain the
 * character, NULL is returned, otherwise a pointer to
 * this character in the string is returned.
 *
 * Written by Ray Swartz for "Doing Business with C"
 */

char *strrchr(str, c)
char *str;
char c;
{
    int strlen();
    int count;       /* character counter */

    count = strlen(str);
    while(--count >= 0) {
        if(str[count] == c)        /* skip \0 */
            return(str + count);   /* return pointer */
    }
    return(NULL);    /* character not found */
}
```

17

Reading and Writing Strings

To operate, a program needs computer resources. These resources are regulated by the operating system that controls the available hardware. At minimum, a program must be able to read from and print to somewhere.

Virtually every computer handles input and output differently. To run on a specific machine, our programs must perform input and output operations as dictated by that computer's design. Without a general way to deal with the requirements of individual computers, our C programs will not be portable.

To resolve this problem, the C language makes only one assumption about the underlying computer executing a program: The machine provides a place to read input and print output. A C program gets input from the *standard input* device and sends output to the *standard output* device. How a computer implements these devices is of no concern to C. By convention, the standard input is a keyboard and the standard output is the terminal screen connected to that keyboard.

In previous chapters, we have talked about **printf( )** printing to the terminal and **gets( )** reading the keyboard. In reality, **printf( )** sends information to the standard output and **gets( )** reads from the standard input. More will be said about the standard input and output in Part 7, where data files are discussed. For the rest of this chapter, we will assume that the keyboard is used for input and the terminal for output.

The C standard library provides three distinct levels of capability for reading and writing strings. The most primitive functions read and write single characters only. The next higher set of functions handles entire strings, instead of individual characters. The most sophisticated functions can read or write formatted strings.

Because reading and writing strings are complementary tasks, the standard library contains functions that perform both jobs at each level. The lowest-level functions are **getchar( )** and **putchar( )**. **getchar( )** reads the next character from the standard input and **putchar( )** prints a character on the standard output. **gets( )** reads an entire string from the standard input and **puts( )** prints a string to the standard output. Last, **scanf( )**, the input counterpart of **printf( )**, reads the standard input according to a specified format. These are shown in Table 17-1.

TABLE 17-1 Reading and Writing Functions in the Standard Library

	Read	Write
Single characters	**getchar( )**	**putchar( )**
Entire strings	**gets( )**	**puts( )**
Formatted strings	**scanf( )**	**printf( )**

C's input and output functions are designed to isolate the higher-level printing tools from the underlying hardware. Every input function, regardless of its end result, reads a single character at a time from the keyboard. In the same way, output functions are implemented by repeatedly printing a single character at the terminal. This reduces the hardware dependency to two functions—the one that reads a character (**getchar( )**) and the one that writes a character (**putchar( )**).[1]

The end result is that once **getchar( )** and **putchar( )** are implemented for a specific machine, the other input and output functions work without modification! This greatly simplifies transporting C's standard library functions to a new machine and is one of the main reasons C is available for so many computers.

17.1 WRITING INPUT AND OUTPUT FUNCTIONS

In addition to creating string functions that manipulate strings once they have been stored in the computer's memory, we often have to write special input and output routines. Many times, these functions must read or write individual characters. For this reason, we will discuss **getchar( )** and **putchar( )** in detail.

getchar( ) returns the character read from the keyboard. **getchar( )** takes no arguments.

---

[1] In most cases, **getchar( )** and **putchar( )** are written in even lower-level functions, discussed in Part 7.

Sec. 17.1 Writing Input and Output Functions

```
inchar = getchar();
```

In this example, *inchar* is assigned the character read. **putchar()** is sent the character to print as its single argument.

```
putchar(inchar);
```

Here, *inchar* is printed.

At first glance, it may seem that **getchar()** should return data type **char**. However, this makes a limiting assumption about the standard input, that the standard input only returns characters. But, if **getchar()** encounters an error, it must notify the calling routine with a unique return code. If **getchar()** only returned **char**s, all possible return codes would map onto valid characters.

To get around this problem, **getchar()** returns a character, stored as an **int**. In reality, characters are just *small* integers. In C, nothing is lost if characters are treated as integers.

RULE   Characters can be stored in **int** variables without problem.

RULE   The **getchar()** function returns an **int**.

To signify an error, **getchar()** returns the integer macro EOF, which is distinguishable from all characters. The most common input "error" is when no more characters can be read from a device. The EOF macro stands for *end of file*. EOF is what occurs when a data file has been read completely and is at the end of the file. As we shall see, the standard input device is treated as if it is a data file.[2]

Unlike all other C functions, **getchar()** is not declared in our programs. Instead, **getchar()** is declared in the *stdio.h* file. Thus, to use **getchar()** we must put

```
#include "stdio.h"
```

in our programs. The same is true of **putchar()**. Incidentally, the EOF macro also is defined in the *stdio.h* file.

We must do two things to use **getchar()** correctly. First, define an **int** variable to hold the value returned. Second, **#include** *stdio.h* in our program:

---

[2] Many computer systems that run C allow the standard input and output devices to be "redirected", that is, temporarily changed to another device such as a data file. Thus, the standard input and output, even though they are the keyboard and the terminal screen, can generate an EOF. See Part 7 or your computer's documentation for more information.

```
#include "stdio.h"

...

int inchar;

inchar = getchar();
```

RULE **getchar( )** and **putchar( )** are declared in the *stdio.h* file. To use them, we must **#include** this file in our program *before* either function is called.

The call to **putchar( )** is

```
#include "stdio.h"

int inchar;
...
putchar(inchar);
```

putchar( ) returns the character printed or the macro EOF if an error occurs.

As an example of usage, Program 17-1 reads a character from the keyboard and then prints it on the terminal screen after checking for an input error.[3]

```
#include "stdio.h"

main()
{
    int inchar;    /* character read */

    if ((inchar = getchar()) != EOF)
        putchar(inchar);
    exit(0);
}
```

Program 17-1 Reading and Writing with **getchar( )** and **putchar( )**

Unfortunately, Program 17-1 doesn't work exactly as envisioned. Both **getchar( )** and **putchar( )** are *buffered* functions. Recall that buffers, which were discussed in the last chapter, sit between the computer and an input or output device. Buffers speed up input and output operations by holding several characters and reading or printing all of them at once. Typically, terminal and keyboard buffers are *flushed*, or cleared, when a

---

[3] If standard input and output are files, Program 17-1 is a rudimentary file copying program!

Sec. 17.2   How **gets( )** Works

newline character is encountered. As a result, when Program 17-1 is executed, no characters are printed until a newline is entered and then all of them appear![4]

Incidentally, Program 17-1 shows the typical usage of **getchar( )**,

$$(\text{inchar} = \text{getchar}()) \mathrel{!=} \text{EOF})$$

which is reading a character and then testing for an input error. If the test is true (no error was found) *inchar* holds the entered character.

17.2 HOW gets( ) WORKS

To further demonstrate how **getchar( )** is used, let's write the **gets( )** function. As we know, **gets( )** reads a line of input that is terminated by a newline. As characters are typed, **gets( )** stores them in the string sent as an argument. When a newline is read, **gets( )** ends the string with a **\0** and returns a pointer to the string's first character. The algorithm is listed as Algorithm 17-1.

1. Read a character
2. If '**\n**' read, go to 4
    else go to 3
3. Store character in next string slot and increment string counter; loop back to 1
4. Put '**\0**' at next string slot
5. Return pointer to string's first character

Algorithm 17-1   Algorithm for **gets( )**

Function 17-1 shows one version of the **gets( )** function.

```
#include "stdio.h"

/* ***** GETS *****
 * This function reads a line from the terminal, stores it
 * in str (passed in), terminates str with '\0', and returns
 * a pointer to str's first character.
 *
 * Written by Ray Swartz for "Doing Business With C"
 */

char *gets(str)
char *str;
```

---

[4] There are ways around this but it is system-dependent. Consult the system administrator or computer documentation for specific details.

```
{
    int c;          /* input character */
    char *s = str;  /* return pointer */

    while((c = getchar()) != '\n')
        *str++ = c; /* store c in next slot and increment */
    *str = '\0';    /* last increment was inside loop */
    return(s);      /* pointer to first character */
}
```

Function 17-1 The **gets( )** Function

Exercise 17-1 The **gets( )** written in Function 17-1 doesn't handle errors at all. Modify **gets( )** to return NULL if **getchar( )** returns EOF.

The **puts( )** (put string) function prints its string argument on the terminal screen and *then adds a newline*. If *str* is the string to print, the call to **puts( )** is

```
puts(str)
```

puts( ) uses **putchar( )** to write each character in the string to the terminal screen until a \0 is found. It then prints a newline and stops. **puts( )** is an **int** function that returns an EOF if an error occurs and some other value otherwise.

RULE   **puts( )** adds a newline to the string it prints.

Exercise 17-2 Write the **puts( )** function.

Up to now, we have done quite well using **printf( )** to do our printing. Why use **puts( )** at all? The answer lies in using the appropriate function for the task at hand. The **printf( )** function requires a good deal of overhead since it must evaluate the format string and then convert its arguments before printing. **puts( )** is a simpler function, so it requires less code to implement and runs faster than **printf( )**. However, we must be careful to use **puts( )** only when we want a newline added to the string printed. Some people never use **puts( )**, preferring to use **printf( )** instead.

In the same way that **printf( )** converts its arguments into a specified format, the **scanf( )** function reads input and stores it in a list of variables according to codes listed in a format string. Since **scanf( )** stores values inside its arguments, it must be sent pointers to the actual variables. As an example,

```
scanf("%d", &nbr);
```

reads and converts an integer value, storing it in the variable *nbr*.

Sec. 17.2 How **gets( )** Works

RULE scanf( )'s arguments must be pointers.

scanf( ) returns one of three **int** messages, the number of variables successfully assigned (less than or equal to the number of arguments), 0 if none were assigned, and EOF if an error occurs. **scanf( )** uses some of the same formatting codes as **printf( )** (although there are many inconsistencies). Segment 17-1 shows a **scanf( )** call in a programming context.

```
long nbr;
int puts();
int scanf();

printf("Enter this period's revenue: ");  /* no \n is printed */
if (scanf("%ld", &nbr) != 1)   /* test for input error */
    puts("Error on input");
...
```

Segment 17-1 A Sample **scanf( )** Call

In this example, **scanf( )** reads the string entered and converts it into a **long** and stores it in *nbr*. Since we want the changes made by **scanf( )** to be permanent (i.e., not local to **scanf( )**), we must send a pointer to *nbr*. **scanf( )** is a buffered input function. No input conversion is performed until a newline is encountered to release the string from the input buffer.

In addition to **long**s, **scanf( )** converts the input to

int	if %d is listed,
float	if %f is listed,
double	if %lf is listed,
string	if %s is listed, and
char	if %c is listed.

scanf( ) is not limited to reading a single variable. For example, we can tell **scanf( )** to read two **int**s by

```
int nbr1;
int nbr2;
int scanf();

...
if (scanf("%d %d", &nbr1, &nbr2) != 2)
    puts("Error on input");
```

Note the space in the format. This tells **scanf( )** to skip all the "white space" between the two numbers in the input string. White space includes *blanks*, *tabs*, and *newlines*. Thus, **scanf( )** works properly if

                                23   27

or

                                 23 27

or

                                  23

                                  27

is entered. In addition, **scanf( )** skips leading white space unless a **%c** has been specified at the beginning of the format. Like **printf( )**, **scanf( )** has a large number of formatting options.

RULE   Always test **scanf( )**'s return code to ensure that the proper number of variables is entered.

At first glance, **scanf( )** may appear as useful as **printf( )**. However, reading input is much more difficult than printing output. For example, suppose we are getting input with **scanf( )** using the code **%ld** to read a **long** and 32,333 is entered instead of 32333. **scanf( )** will read in 32 stopping at the first nondigit. If our program doesn't fail, the wrong answer is sure to result.

Many working programs fail because of bad input. To do business data processing correctly, we need robust input functions that provide access to the data entered as well as the ability to convert it when necessary. In fact, instead of using **scanf( )**, we have created our own data entry functions.

scanf( ) is a useful tool when we know what the input string will look like. This can be during program testing or when we have written a program that we will use ourselves. However, because of its inflexibility *once a format string has been specified*, **scanf( )** is not recommended for business data processing applications.

RULE   Use **scanf( )** sparingly, if at all.

The standard library contains another set of complimentary string functions, **sprintf( )** (which we have used before) and **sscanf( )**. Recall that **sprintf( )** combines a format and a set of variables and stores the result in a string. **sscanf( )**, just like its namesake **scanf( )**, converts and assigns data according to a specified format. The difference is that **sscanf( )** reads from a string sent as an argument while **scanf( )** gets characters from the standard input. The call to **sscanf( )** is

Sec. 17.3   Writing a Conversion Function

```
int sscanf();

sscanf(str, format, pointer-list);
```

The variables referenced by *pointer-list* are assigned values according to the specifications in *format* and the characters in *str*. Since the assigned values are passed back to the calling routine, pointers to the appropriate variables must be sent to **sscanf( )**. Like **scanf( )**, **sscanf( )** is an **int** function that returns the number of successful assignments made. As an example of usage, the call

```
sscanf(str, "%d %d", &nbr1, &nbr2)
```

reads what is stored in *str* and converts it into two integers, which are assigned to the variables *nbr1* and *nbr2*.

17.3 WRITING A CONVERSION FUNCTION

So far, we've written functions that manipulate strings and functions that read and write them. A third type of string function is one that performs *conversions*. A string conversion program changes character representation of data into its numeric equivalent. Examples are the three conversion functions in the standard library, **atoi( )**, **atol( )**, and **atof( )**.

One important rule of interactive programming is to read data in a format "natural" to the user. Since we are writing business applications that often deal with amounts, numbers that contain commas may be entered. The standard conversion functions assume that this will not happen. In addition, numbers containing commas are converted up to the comma. This causes our programs to print erroneous results. To prevent conversion errors from ruining our programs, we will rewrite the **atol( )** function to ignore commas. This new function is called **catol( )**.

Before we can write **catol( )**, we must know how to convert a string of digits into a number. The conversion process is straightforward. We initialize a **long** variable, *value*, to 0. Reading through the string until a nondigit is found, we multiply *value* by 10 and add the numeric equivalent of the next character to *value*. *value* holds the converted number when the process terminates. To demonstrate, suppose the string "2543" is passed to **catol( )**. The process is shown in Table 17-2.

TABLE 17-2 Converting a String to a Number

	Value	Character	Calculation
(initial)	0	2	0 * 10 + 2 = 2
	2	5	2 * 10 + 5 = 25
	25	4	25 * 10 + 4 = 254
	254	3	254 * 10 + 3 = 2543
(returned)	2543	\0	

Before we write the **catol( )** function, two issues must be resolved. First, how can we test to see if a character is a digit? Second, how do we convert a digit to its equivalent numeric value?

17.4 TESTING AND CONVERTING CHARACTERS

Testing and converting individual characters requires knowledge of the underlying character codes used by the computer. Since no worldwide character set standard exists, the designers of C included macros that perform character testing and converting. The proper macros are **#include**d when the program is compiled.

The macros that test characters all begin with *is*, are passed a character as an argument, and evaluate to true (non-0) or false (0) depending on the outcome of the test. The testing macros are listed and briefly described in Table 17-3.

TABLE 17-3 Character Testing Functions

Macro	Returns true (non-0) if
isalpha(x)	x is a letter
isalnum(x)	x is a letter or a digit
iscntrl(x)	x is a control character
isdigit(x)	x is a digit
isgraph(x)	x is a printable character excluding space
islower(x)	x is a lower-case letter
isprint(x)	x is a printable character including space
ispunct(x)	x is a printable character excluding space, digit, and letter
isspace(x)	x is a white space character
isupper(x)	x is an upper-case letter
isxdigit(x)	x is a hexadecimal digit

A similar set of functions converts their arguments *under certain conditions*. These are listed and briefly described in Table 17-4.

TABLE 17-4 Character Conversion Functions

Macro	Result
tolower(x)	Converts x to lower-case if x is a letter (**isalpha(x)** is true), else nothing
toupper(x)	Converts x to upper-case if x is a letter, else nothing

The character-testing macros are **#define**d in the header file, *ctype.h*. We must **#include** this file in any program that uses character-testing macros. As a result, these

Sec. 17.4   Testing and Converting Characters

macros should not be declared explicitly. Incidentally, character-testing macros and conversion functions return or evaluate to **int**.

We can use the **isdigit( )** macro to test if characters are digits. This solves the first problem with writing **catol( )**. However, none of the character functions discussed so far converts a digit to its integer value. We will have to do this for ourselves.

If our computer uses the ASCII or EBCDIC character sets, converting characters to integers is simple because of how the digits 0 through 9 are represented. Table 17-5 lists these characters and their corresponding ASCII and EBCDIC codes.

TABLE 17-5 ASCII and EBCDIC Codes *for* 0 to 9

Character	ASCII code (decimal)	EBCDIC code (decimal)
0	48	240
1	49	241
2	50	242
3	51	243
4	52	244
5	53	245
6	54	246
7	55	247
8	56	248
9	57	249

Note that differences between codes and their corresponding numeric values are the same

$$'9' - '5' = 57 - 53 = 4 \text{ (ASCII)}$$
$$= 249 - 245 = 4 \text{ (EBCDIC)}.$$

Thus, if *inchar* is a **char** storing a digit (i.e., **isdigit(c)** is true), then

```
inchar - '0'
```

equals the integer represented by *inchar*.

We are now ready to write **catol( )**. The algorithm is listed in Algorithm 17-2. The function is passed the string to convert as *str*.

1. Set *value* to 0
2. If **isdigit(*str)** is true go to 3
   else go to 4
3. *value* = *value* * 10 + c − '0';
   go to 2

4. If *str is a comma go to 2
   else go to 5
5. Return *value*

Algorithm 17-2 catol( ) Algorithm

As written, the algorithm will only handle positive numbers. If the first character is a minus or a plus, the function returns zero. The solution is to add a variable (*sign*) that is assigned −1 if the first character is a minus sign. Then the converted value is multiplied by *sign*. To accomplish this, we must add steps 1*a*, 1*b*, and 1*c* to Algorithm 17-2:

1*a*. Set *sign* to 1
1*b*. If first character is a '−' set factor = −1
1*c*. Else if first character is a '+' skip it

The **catol( )** function is listed as Function 17-2.

```
/* ***** CATOL *****
 *
 * This function converts the string argument into a
 * long integer, ignoring commas in the process.
 * The function checks the first character for a sign
 * and terminates on the first non-digit character
 * (besides a comma).
 *
 * Written by Ray Swartz for "Doing Business with C".
 */

#include "ctype.h"

long catol(str)
char *str;    /* string of digits to convert */
{
    long value = 0;
    int sign = 1;    /* toggle for a negative number */

    if (*str == '-') {    /* converting a negative number */
        sign = -1;
        str++;            /* skip this character */
    }
    else if (*str == '+')    /* simply skip a '+' */
        str++;
```

Sec. 17.4 Testing and Converting Characters

```
            for( ; isdigit(*str) || *str == ','; str++)
                if (isdigit(*str))
                    value = value * 10 + *str - '0';
    value *= sign;      /* set proper sign of number */
    return(value);
}
```

Function 17-2 The **catol**( ) Function

A few points about **catol**( ) are in order. First, it may seem that the body of the **for** loop in **catol**( ) should be enclosed in braces, because it consists of two lines. However, these two lines make up a *single* statement only and braces are not required here. Second, even though the variable *value* appears on both sides of the assignment,

```
            value = value * 10 + *str - '0';
```

we cannot substitute an assignment operator to get

```
            value *= 10 + *str - '0';
```

because this would multiply *value* by the sum

```
            10 + *str - '0';
```

which is incorrect. Last, since the **isdigit**( ) macro evaluates to true or false, we can test the result directly instead of comparing it to 1 or 0. Thus,

```
            if (isdigit(*str))
```

works fine and is more efficient.

Exercise 17-3   **catol**( ) may not work on computers that don't use ASCII or EBCDIC. This means **catol**( ) may not be portable to some computers. To ensure portability, write a special conversion function **ctoi**( ) (character to integer) that doesn't depend on the character set. *Hint*: Use a **switch** statement.

The **catoi**( ) function solves the problem of input that contains commas. However, the same problem exists when printing numbers. A previous rule states "All output must be in a format that the user can understand easily." Up to now, our programs have been printing numbers without commas. This can lead to misunderstood output.

Unfortunately, one shortcoming of the **printf**( ) function is that it will not insert commas into numeric output. The obvious solution is to write a function, which we will call **putlong**( ), that adds commas to the numbers we print, so that

```
            NET PROFIT    $65547
```

becomes

```
            NET PROFIT    $65,547
```

Before we write **putlong( )**, we have to decide how **putlong( )** will pass back the string that holds the formatted number. Several of the string functions in the standard library return *pointers to* **char**. Thus, one approach is to have **putlong( )** return a pointer to the formatted string.

Unfortunately, this can cause problems. All the string functions that return pointers return them to one of their string arguments. However, **putlong( )** would return a pointer to string that is *local* to **putlong( )**. Since local variables disappear when the function terminates, the pointer returned by **putlong( )** may not refer to anything.

This problem is made worse if **putlong( )** is used repeatedly in the same statement, which is likely. For example, we might use this **printf( )** to print two formatted numbers

```
        printf("%s\t%s\n", putlong(value1), putlong(value2));
```

The results of this statement are unpredictable and **putlong( )** should not be designed this way.

Another approach is to send **putlong( )** a destination string as an argument. This not only avoids the problem mentioned above, but is more efficient because **putlong( )** will not have to create a local variable to hold the conversion. Further, since **putlong( )** is passed a string as an argument, it can return a pointer to that string. This allows the previous **printf( )** to work properly! The call to **putlong( )** is

```
        char *putlong(value, dest_str)
        long value;        /* the number to convert */
        char *dest_str;    /* where to store the converted string */
```

The next major design issue is figuring out where to insert the commas. It is tempting to simply add one comma for each three digits. However, we must not put a comma in front of a number or as its last character.

Our approach will make use of C's modulo operator (the %). The modulo operation is like division except the answer is the remainder. For example,

6 % 3 = 0 (read 6 *modulo* 3)
7 % 3 = 1
8 % 3 = 2
9 % 3 = 0

Nothing is left over when six is divided by three; one remains when seven is divided by three, and so on. In the same way,

Sec. 17.4 Testing and Converting Characters

Digits in *value*	Comma after digit
6	3
7	1 and 4
8	2 and 5
9	3 and 6

We insert the first comma

$$\text{(number of digits in } value) \ \% \ 3$$

characters from the beginning (left side) unless the modulo expression evaluates to 0, in which case a comma is inserted three digits from the beginning. We determine how many digits are in *value* by converting it to a string using **sprintf( )**.

Conversion functions must always check for negative numbers and **putlong( )** is no exception. We can do this directly by testing if *value* is negative before we begin converting it to a string. The algorithm for **putlong( )** is listed as Algorithm 17-3.

1. Set *str_pntr* = *dest_str*, and *count* = 0
2. If *value* < 0, set *dest_str = '-', increment *dest_str*, and set *count* = 1
3. Convert *value* to a string with **sprintf( )**; store the result in *numstr*
4. Set *length* to what **sprintf** returns minus 1
5. If *count* <= *length* go to 6
   else 10
6. Store *numstr[count]* in *dest_str and increment *dest_str*
7. If this is the third digit in a group but not the last one in *numstr*, insert a comma in *dest_str* and increment *dest_str*
   [if (length - count) % 3 = 0 && count != length]
8. Increment *count*
9. Go to 5
10. Terminate *dest_str* with \0
11. Return *str_pntr* (pointer to first character in *dest_str*)

Algorithm 17-3 The **putlong( )** Function

It may seem odd that we set the variable *length* to 1 less than the actual length of the converted string (step 4 in Algorithm 17-3). But, because array indexes start at 0, the length of *numstr* (which is stored in *length*) "appears" to be one less than it really is. Without this correction, **putlong( )** puts commas in the wrong spots. The **putlong( )** function is shown as Function 17-3.

```
/* ***** PUTLONG *****
 *
 * This function converts the numeric argument (long) to an
 * equivalent string of digits with commas inserted.
 *
 * Written by Ray Swartz for "Doing Business with C".
 */

char *putlong(value, dest_str)
long value;
char *dest_str;      /* where formatted string is stored */
{
    char numstr[30];    /* holds string conversion of value */
    char *str_pntr = dest_str;  /* pointer returned */
    int sprintf();
    int length;         /* number of digits in value */
    int count = 0;      /* loop counter */

    if (value < 0) {
        *dest_str++ = '-';  /* converting a negative number */
        count = 1;          /* skip first character */
    }
    length = sprintf(numstr, "%ld", value) - 1;
    for( ; count <= length; count++) {
        *dest_str++ = numstr[count];   /* transfer digits */
        if ((length - count) % 3 == 0 && count != length)
            *dest_str++ = ',';
    }
    *dest_str = '\0';
    return(str_pntr);
}
```

Function 17-3 The **putlong( )** Function

String processing is an important aspect of many applications, especially business programs. Part 6 has concentrated on functions that perform string input and output, manipulation, and conversion. These are the three most common types of string functions.

The main purpose of Part 6 has been to introduce the techniques necessary for working with strings and to create general string functions. Without question, C programmers must be able to design and implement string functions to write meaningful applications in C. In fact, most programmers develop their own favorite set of string functions that they use over and over again!

17.5 SUMMARY

1. C makes only one assumption about the underlying hardware executing a C program: It can read from and print to somewhere.
2. Where the program prints to is called standard output and where is reads from is called standard input.
3. C provides three types of input and output functions; character, string, and formatted.
4. The **getchar( )** function returns data type **int**, which allows it to differentiate the end of input from all legal characters.
5. The **scanf( )** function does formatted input. It reads the keyboard (standard input), matches what's read to a format string, and then stores the matched input into one of the listed pointers.
6. Use **scanf( )** sparingly, if at all.
7. C contains a set of character-testing macros. These macros test if a character fits into a certain class, such as digits, lower case characters, and so on.
8. C also contains a set of conversion functions that convert lower-case characters to upper-case and vice versa.
9. A digit can be converted into its corresponding numeric value by subtracting the digit 0 from it (in ASCII or EBCDIC).

E X E R C I S E S

17-4. Integrate the **catol( )** and **putlong( )** functions into **flex-pl**.

17-5. Write a function to take a double value and to insert commas into it.

17-6. Write a function that reads in a dollar and cents amount and converts this to a **long** representing the number of cents in this amount.

17-7. Write a complimentary function to Exercise 17-6 that takes a **long** value representing cents and converts it to a dollars and cents string.

17-8. Integrate the functions in Exercises17-6 and 17-7 into **flex-pl**.

17-9. Write a function that searches for the occurrence of one string in another, and then write a program that tests this function.

17-10. Write a function to read in a date string in the format MM/DD/YY, verifiy that the date is valid, and then store the date in three integers, one each for month, day, and year. These three integers are passed to the function as arguments.

PART 7
Creating New Data Types

18
Data Structures

Although C provides several data types for our use, it also allows us to "create" new data types. We can't actually extend the number and kinds of types offered by C, but we can create new names for them or combine them.

One difficulty with moving a program from one machine to another is the variation that exists amongst computers. Some computers have huge memories while others have small ones. This variety can affect our C programs in a subtle way, by altering the storage capabilities of C's data types.

As an example, consider the three integer data types **short**, **int**, and **long**. Typically, on a smaller computer a **short** and an **int** are treated as the same data type and a **long** is twice their size (in storage capacity). On larger machines, **long** and **int** are the same and **short** is half of their size.[1] Moreover, on some computers, **short**, **int**, and **long** are all different sizes. A program that uses **int** variables may act differently on a "large **int**" machine than it does on a "small **int**" machine.

---

[1] On smaller machines, **short** and **int** are usually 16 bits and a **long** is stored in 32. On larger machines, **int** and **long** are 32 bits and a **short** is 16.

18.1 typedef

C has a feature that can minimize the effect of data types that may change from one machine to the next. It is the **typedef** mechanism. Using **typedef**, we can identify variables that are "data-type sensitive" and modify all of them by changing a single **typedef** statement. In effect, **typedef** allows us to "create" new data types.

The **typedef** command equates any valid data type with another name. For example, **flex-pl** uses **long** integers to store the category amounts. With a **typedef**, we can identify *AMOUNT* as a data type name representing **long** by

```
typedef long AMOUNT;
```

Substituting AMOUNT for **long** we can define

```
AMOUNT revenue[30];
AMOUNT cost[30];
```

Now, to change the data type of *revenue* and *cost* requires rewriting the **typedef** only!

A **typedef** is just like a variable definition. We list the data type followed by the type name. All this is preceded by the keyword **typedef**.

Another example of **typedef** substitutions is

```
typedef char STRING;
typedef int LOOP_CNT;
typedef char *STR_PTR;   /* char * is the data type */
typedef float REAL
```

Now, instead of defining

```
char rev_cat[MAX_CAT][MAX_LEN];
```

we can use

```
STRING rev_cat[MAX_CAT][MAX_LEN];
```

where MAX_CAT and MAX_LEN are defined as integer constants.

In addition, we can **typedef** a name to represent an array definition. Thus,

```
typedef char CATEGORY[MAX_LEN];
```

says *CATEGORY* symbolizes a **char** array MAX_LEN elements long. With this **typedef** in force, we can define

```
CATEGORY name;
```

This defines *name* as a character string of MAX_LEN size. In addition,

```
CATEGORY rev_cat[MAX_CAT];
```

creates an array of MAX_CAT strings each MAX_LEN in size.

Further, **typedef**s can be used to modify one another. Previously we set

```
typedef char STRING;
typedef char CATEGORY[MAX_LEN];
```

We could have defined CATEGORY in terms of STRING:

```
typedef char STRING;
typedef STRING CATEGORY[MAX_LEN];
```

Segment 18-1 demonstrates **typedef** usage.

```
#include "stdio.h"

#define MAX_LEN 31

typedef char STRING;         /* these have file scope */
typedef STRING CATEGORY[MAX_LEN];

main()
{
    CATEGORY name;

    printf("Enter category name: ");
    gets(name);
    ...
}
```

Segment 18-1 Using **typedef**

typedefs are treated like regular variable definitions, with the exception that a **typedef** defines a data type name and not a variable. **typedef**s must appear in the same program block where they are referenced and must be defined before they are used. Note that the **typedef**s in Segment 18-1 have file scope. This is common because **typedef**s tend to be used throughout an entire program.

It may seem that **typedef**s offer little more than the **#define** facility. In fact, this **typedef** statement

```
typedef char STRING;
```

Sec. 18.2   Data Structures

and this **#define** substitution

```
#define STRING char
```

have the same results. The main difference is that **typedef** is processed by the compiler and **#define** is handled by the preprocessor. **#define** tokens are substituted by the preprocessor without regard for possible errors. **typedef**s are checked for consistency by the compiler. In addition, **typedef**s can be used on aggregate types.

Because of these features, we will use **typedef**s when we are dealing with data types and **#define** macros to provide text substitution. Further, all **typedef** names, as well as **#define** macros, will be shown in upper-case characters, for consistent style.

The main goal of using **typedef**s is to increase the readability and portability of our programs. We can better document our work by defining related variables in the same way. For example, this sequence defines *revenue* and *cost* to be **int**s and alerts anyone looking at the code that these variables may be related.

```
typedef int AMOUNT;

AMOUNT revenue;
AMOUNT cost;
```

Besides adjusting data types of a set of variables and making our programs easier to understand, **typedef**s are used to extend an older C compiler to conform to newer versions of the language. For example, the **void** data type is a recent addition to the C language. As a result, some compilers do not recognize **void**. To maintain compatibility, we can define

```
typedef int void;
```

in our program. Now, our **void** functions are treated as type **int** by the compiler. When we move this code to a compiler that allows **void**, we simply delete the **typedef**.

18.2 DATA STRUCTURES

Arrays provide one important kind of data structuring, grouping together a number of elements *with the same data type*. Arrays allow us to write generalized application programs that can handle different amounts of data defined as one of C's allowed data types.

Unfortunately, arrays have a serious limitation: Each element in an array must be the same data type. The problem is that not all the information we deal with can be represented by one of C's basic data types. As an example, each revenue or cost entry in the **flex-pl** program is comprised of two variables with *different* data types, a character string for the entry's category and a **long** for the dollar amount. To represent them, we use two arrays, a string array for category names and a **long** array for amounts, and relate the variables by index number. The first revenue's category and amount are stored in element 0 of their respective arrays.

The data required by most meaningful business applications are too complex to be stored in a variable of one data type. As a result, we must represent such data as a collection of several individual variables. For example, to process payroll records we must store data on employees. Some of the information needed in a payroll record might be stored in

```
char emp_name[NAME_LEN];      /* name */
char job_code[CODE_LEN];      /* job */
char ssn[12];                 /* social sec. # */
float payrate;                /* hourly pay */
float hours_wked;             /* hours worked */
int deductions;               /* for income taxes */
```

With so many variables representing an employee, the data manipulation gets quite complicated. If **print_check( )** is a function that prints an employee's pay check and a payroll report, the function call is

```
print_check(emp_name, job_code, ssn, payrate,
            hours_wked, deductions);
```

This is a nightmare for program documentation and maintenance.

C provides a way to represent complex data in a straightforward manner by allowing us to group a set of variables together to form a larger construct, called a *structure*. A structure is an aggregation of related variables that has a name. Thus, instead of accessing a set of variables individually, we can address them all at once with a structure.

As an example, consider a revenue entry from the **flex-pl** program. It uses a thirty-one-character (MAX_LEN) string for the category name and a **long** for the corresponding amount.

```
char rev_cat[MAX_LEN];
long rev_amt;
```

Without knowing how the program works, we would not know that these two variables had anything in common. In this case, even **typedef** isn't much help. By using a data structure, however, we can create a single variable that represents both parts of a revenue entry!

Creating a data structure is a two-step process. First, we have to *declare* the structure by identifying what variables make up the structure. That is, we must tell the compiler that the structure exists and what constitutes it. Second, we have to *define* a variable to represent an instance of the structure.

Two steps are required to create a structure because each structure contains different variables and, essentially, is a new data type. Thus, we must tell the compiler

Sec. 18.2 Data Structures

what this structure contains before we can use it. Once we have declared the structure, we can use it to define variables that can store the data contained in that structure.

A data structure is declared by using the keyword **struct** and listing the variables that make up that structure. Segment 18-2 declares *rev_entry* to be a structure comprised of a string with MAX_LEN characters and a **long**. The variables *rev_cat* and *rev_amt* are called *members* of the *rev_entry* structure.

```
struct rev_entry {
    char rev_cat[MAX_LEN];    /* category name */
    long rev_amt;             /* category amount */
};
```

Segment 18-2 Declaring a Structure

Note the keyword **struct**, the beginning and ending braces, and the terminating semicolon; all these are required for a structure declaration.

rev_entry is the name that identifies this structure and is called a *structure tag*. We can now refer to this structure as we would any other data type, such as **int** or a **float**. A *rev_entry* structure contains the listed members, *rev_cat* and *rev_amt*.

RULE Declaring a data structure identifies what members make up the structure.

rev_entry cannot store information. It only identifies what that particular structure contains. To store data in a structure, we must *define* a variable to represent a *rev_entry* structure. To do so requires

```
struct rev_entry revenue;
```

Note that we used both the keyword **struct** and the structure tag *rev_entry* to define *revenue*. The definition allocates enough memory to hold all the structure's members. Thus, *revenue* can store a string with MAX_LEN characters and a **long**. Segment 18-3 repeats the *rev_entry* structure declaration followed by *revenue*'s definition.

```
struct rev_entry {          /* Declaration */
    char rev_cat[31];
    long rev_amt;
};

struct rev_entry revenue;   /* Definition */
```

Segment 18-3 Declaring and Defining a Structure

We don't have to use separate statements to declare a structure and to define a variable to store the structure. We can combine the declaration and definition into one statement by listing the variables to define immediately after the declaration's closing brace. This is shown in Segment 18-4.

```
struct rev_entry {         /* declaration */
    char rev_cat[31];
    long rev_amt;
} revenue;                 /* definition */
```

Segment 18-4 Declaring and Defining a Structure in the Same Statement

Structure tags are not always necessary. We can define a variable to store a structure with the listed members without naming the structure with a tag. In this case, we simply remove the structure tag. An example is shown in Segment 18-5.

```
struct {
    char rev_cat[31];
    long rev_amt;
} revenue;
```

Segment 18-5 Defining a Structure Variable

revenue is defined as a structure containing the listed members. Since this structure is not tagged, to define another variable like *revenue* would require listing the structure members again. Clearly, structure tags are useful if we must refer to a structure more than once, as is generally the case.

Exercise 18-1 Write a structure declaration that represents a bank check and a date (with 3 characters for the name of the month).

In addition to structure tags, we can use **typedef** with a structure declaration. Recall that **typedef** provides alternative names for C's data types. In the same way, we can **typedef** a structure declaration, in place of using a structure tag. Segment 18-6 shows an example.

```
typedef struct {
    char rev_cat[MAX_LEN];
    long rev_amt;
} REV;
```

Segment 18-6 Using **typedef** with a Structure Declaration

Now,

```
REV revenue;
```

defines *revenue* to be a structure variable. The only difference between the declaration in Segment 18-3 and Segment 18-6 is how a variable is defined. When a **typedef** is used, we don't put the keyword **struct** in the definition. Incidentally,

Sec. 18.3   The Member Operator (.)   303

```
                    REV rev88, rev89;
```

defines two REV structures.

18.3 THE MEMBER OPERATOR (.)

A data structure stores information in its members. The structure *rev88*, defined above, holds a MAX_LEN character string in its *rev_cat* member and a **long** in the *rev_amt* member. The same is true of the structure named *rev89*.

RULE   The data stored in a structure is stored in the members.

To access the information in a structure, we must identify the appropriate member of a specific structure variable that holds the data we want. As a result, there are two parts to a structure reference, the name of a structure variable and one of the members in that structure. C contains a special operator to perform the processing required to get what is stored in structure members.

The structure member operator is represented by a period. Thus,

```
                    revenue.rev_cat
```

is the legal name for the category string in the *revenue* structure and

```
                    revenue.rev_amt
```

is the name of the **long** value. These can be used like any other variable names. For example,

```
                    revenue.rev_amt = 10;
```

stores 10 in the *rev_amt* member of the *revenue* structure.

```
                rev_total = revenue.rev_amt * 3;
```

multiplies the value stored in *revenue.rev_amt* by three and assigns the result to *rev_total*.

Since

```
                    revenue.rev_cat
```

represents a string, it really is a pointer to **char** that refers to a MAX_LEN character array. As an example,

```
                    gets(revenue.rev_cat);
```

reads a category name into the *revenue* structure's *rev_cat* member.

Above, we used

> REV rev88, rev89;

to define two REV structure variables. Information stored in one of these structures can be referred to only if that structure's name is listed. Both

> rev88.rev_amt

and

> rev89.rev_amt

evaluate to the *rev_amt* member of a REV structure. However, these two expressions identify *different* storage locations (different variables). *rev88* and *rev89* are similar, in that they both represent a REV structure, but they are two separate instances of such a structure.

The structure member operator has highest precedence, along with parentheses and brackets. This insures that members don't get separated from their structures and guarantees that structure member expressions are always evaluated as a single construct.

RULE Structure member expressions are always evaluated as a single construct.

Like ( ) and [ ], the . associates from left to right. As an example,

> revenue.rev_cat[0]

refers to the first character in the category name stored in the revenue structure. Since the operators in this expression have the same precedence, they are evaluated from left to right. The subscript indexes the structure member.

For completeness, converting this array reference to pointer format results in

> *revenue.rev_cat

This, too, identifies the first character in the *rev_cat* member. The member operator has higher precedence then the indirection operator. Again, the structure member expression is treated as a single variable reference, which in this case is a **char** pointer. This means the expression

> revenue.rev_cat[3]

which is the fourth character in the *rev_cat* string, can also be written as

> *(revenue.rev_cat + 3)

Sec. 18.4   Handling Structures

Segment 18-6 demonstrates the use of structures to prompt for and read a revenue entry.

```
main()
{
    struct rev_entry {
        char rev_cat[MAX_LEN];
        long rev_amt;
    } revenue;

    int printf();
    char *gets();
    long getlong();

    printf("Enter Revenue category (%d characters max): ",
           MAX_LEN - 1);
    gets(revenue.rev_cat);
    revenue.rev_amt = getvalue(revenue.rev_cat);
    ...
```

Segment 18-6   Using Structures

18.4 HANDLING STRUCTURES

Although the C language has been quite stable since it was first introduced in 1978, some changes have occurred. One of the major extensions involves handling structures. Originally, only two operations were allowed on structures, referring to a structure member with the member operator and finding the structure's location in memory with the address operator. If

```
struct rev_entry {
    char rev_cat[MAX_LEN];
    long rev_amt;
} revenue;
```

then

&revenue

evaluates to the address where the structure's members are stored.

It was *not* possible to pass a structure to a function as an argument, have a function return a structure, or assign one (entire) structure to another in a single assignment operation.

In later versions of the C language, these restrictions have been lifted. However, the extensions have been made to individual compilers and it is not uncommon to find compilers that enforce the original structure rules. This is especially true of microcomputer C compilers. To ensure portability, we will observe the limitations stated in the original language.[2]

For example, to copy the information in one structure variable to another, we will individually assign each member. If

```
struct rev_entry rev1, rev2;
```

then

```
strcpy(rev2.rev_cat, rev1.rev_cat);
rev2.rev_amt = rev1.rev_amt;
```

copies the contents of *rev1* into *rev2*. Since the *rev_cat* member is a string, we must use the **strcpy( )** function to assign the characters in *rev1.rev_cat* to *rev2.rev_cat*.[3]

One of the most useful features of a data structure is the ability to send an entire structure to a function by passing only a single argument. For example, the **getrev( )** function in the **flex-pl** program prompts for and reads a revenue category name and the associated amount. At present, **getrev( )** is passed two variables, one for the category name and one for the amount (actually it is sent two *arrays*, but this description is true enough for the time being). If we store all of this information in a *rev_entry* structure, we can send the string for the category name and the **long** to hold the amount by passing one variable—the structure.

Instead of sending the structure as an argument, which may not be fully portable, we will pass a *pointer* to the structure. To pass **getrev( )** a structure pointer requires the use of the address operator

```
struct rev_entry revenue;
...
getrev(&revenue);
```

We will see how to handle this argument in **getrev( )** shortly.

18.5 POINTERS TO STRUCTURES

As we know, a pointer is nothing more than a memory address. This is true of structure pointers as well. How do we refer to members from a structure that is identified only by a pointer?

---

[2] The ANSI standard allows structures to be handled like any other variable. See Appendix C for more information.

[3] On systems that allow structures to be treated like any other variable, we can assign one structure to another using the assignment operator. In this case, *rev1* is copied into *rev2* by

```
rev2 = rev1;
```

Sec. 18.5 Pointers to Structures

To define *rev_ptr* as a pointer to a *rev_entry* structure requires[4]

```
struct rev_entry *rev_ptr;
```

Like all pointers, *rev_ptr* must be initialized (with a structure variable's address) before it can be used. Here again, the address operator is utilized. This example points *rev_ptr* at *revenue*. Note that *revenue* and *rev_ptr* are the same structure type.

```
struct rev_entry revenue;
struct rev_entry *rev_ptr = &revenue;
```

Figure 18-1 shows the relationship of *rev_ptr* to *revenue*.

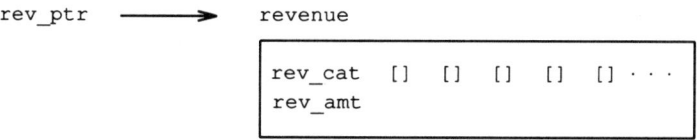

Figure 18-1 Structures and Structure Pointers

The expression

```
revenue.rev_amt
```

identifies a specific member of the *revenue* structure. However (assuming *rev_ptr* points at *revenue*), the expression

```
rev_ptr.rev_amt
```

is *illegal* because *rev_ptr* is a pointer, not a structure. To refer to one of *revenue*'s members using *rev_ptr* requires indirection to locate the actual structure in memory *before* we can get information out of that structure. At first, it may seem that we apply indirection to *rev_ptr* this way:

```
*rev_ptr.rev_amt
```

However, the member operator has higher precedence than the indirection operator. Thus, the expression evaluates as

```
*(rev_ptr.rev_amt)
```

---

[4] *rev_ptr* can be defined by

```
REV *rev_ptr;
```

as well.

which again is incorrect because *rev_ptr* is not a structure and doesn't contain a *rev_cat* member! In fact, the C compiler will identify this as a syntax error.

To access a structure using a structure pointer requires that we perform the indirection (which locates the structure in memory) before we retrieve the specified structure member. To do this, we put parentheses around the indirection:

```
(*rev_ptr).rev_amt
```

Now, this expression is evaluated properly. The structure is located (*rev_ptr*) before we try to extract one of its members.

Incidentally, in the expression

```
(*rev_ptr).rev_amt
```

the indirection is done first *not* because parentheses have highest precedence (they don't; parentheses and the structure member operator have equal precedence); instead, it is the left-to-right associativity of these operators that dictates what's inside the parentheses be done first.

The designers of C felt this syntax was too cumbersome and included a special *structure pointer* operator that is a "shorthand" way to reference members using a structure pointer. The structure pointer operator is denoted by two characters, a dash and a greater-than sign, used together:

```
->
```

This means the expressions

```
(*rev_ptr).rev_amt
```

and

```
rev_ptr->rev_amt
```

are equivalent. The structure pointer operator has the same precedence (highest) as the structure member operator.

Exercise 18-2   Write a code segment that copies the contents of one *rev_entry* structure into another when both are referenced by structure pointers. Assume *rev_ptr1* identifies the first and *rev_ptr2* the second one.

Earlier, we showed how to send the **getrev( )** function a structure pointer as an argument. To demonstrate the structure pointer operator, let's rewrite the **getrev( )**

Sec. 18.5 Pointers to Structures

function to take a structure pointer argument. Before we can modify **getrev( )**, however, we must insure that the *rev_entry* structure is declared properly.

Since a *rev_entry* structure pointer is being passed to the **getrev( )** function, the argument must be declared:

```
int getrev(rev_ptr)
struct rev_entry *rev_ptr;
```

In order for us to declare *rev_ptr* properly, the declaration of the *rev_entry* structure must be visible to **getrev( )**. Declaring the *rev_entry* structure inside the **main( )** routine does not work because the structure declaration would be *local* (have block scope) to **main( )**.

One solution is to declare the *rev_entry* structure globally. Recall that global declarations are visible in a source code file from where they appear down to the end of the file. *rev_entry* can be given file scope by declaring it outside of any function. This is shown in Segment 18-7.

```
#define MAX_LEN 31
#define MAX_CAT 20

#include "stdio.h"
#include "getcat.c"

struct rev_entry { /* file scope */
    char rev_cat[MAX_CAT];
    long rev_amt;
};

main()
{
    ...
```

Segment 18-7 Declaring the *rev_entry* Structure Globally

Now, we can define a *rev_entry* structure pointer simply by putting

```
struct rev_entry *rev_ptr;
```

in the appropriate function.

Exercise 18-3 Another solution is using a global **typedef**. Rewrite Segment 18-7 to define a such a **typedef**.

A **getrev( )** function that takes a structure pointer as an argument is listed as Function 18-1. The previous version of **getrev( )** reads in up to MAX_CAT number of entries (or until "Q" is entered). Function 18-1 is a modified version of **getrev( )** that only reads a single revenue entry and then returns. This distinction will be removed later in this chapter.[5] In addition, Function 18-1 assumes the *rev_entry* structure has been globally declared (without **typedef**).

```
/* ***** GETREV *****
*
* This function prompts for and reads a revenue
* category and amount.  The category name and amount
* are passed to the function inside a structure.
* If a "Q" only is entered, the function returns
* QUIT, else YES is returned.
*
* Written by Ray Swartz for "Doing Business with C"
*
* Modified to use a (global) structure: rev_entry.
*
* ASSUME: printf function is declared globally.
*/

int getrev(rev_ptr)
struct rev_entry *rev_ptr;
{
   char getcat();

   rev_ptr->rev_amt = getcat(rev_ptr->rev_cat, "Revenue");
   if (strcmp(rev_ptr->rev_cat, "Q") == 0)
      return(QUIT);
   else
      return(YES);
}
```

Function 18-1 A Modified Version of **getrev( )** Using a Structure Pointer

Two new operators have been introduced in this chapter, the structure member and the structure pointer operators. An updated precedence table is listed as Table 18-1.

---

[5] We must introduce structure arrays before we can exactly duplicate the **getrev( )** function.

Sec. 18.6 Arrays of Structures

TABLE 18-1 An Updated Precedence Table

Operator	Associativity
( ) [ ] . ->	Left to right
++ -- (type) ! * & -	Right to left
* / %	Left to right
+ -	Left to right
< <= >= >	Left to right
== !=	Left to right
&&	Left to right
||	Left to right
= += -= *= /= %=	Right to left
,	Left to right

18.6 ARRAYS OF STRUCTURES

Data structures allows us to combine variables together, but what if our application needs to store a number of similar structures that must be indexed like an array? An example is the **flex-pl** program, which requires enough storage for all the revenue and cost entries before it can format the P&L report.

C allows *data structure arrays*. Data structure arrays are very similar to arrays of other data types. The main exception is that a structure must be declared before we can define an array to be of that structure type. Assuming the *rev_entry* structure has been declared,

```
struct rev_entry revenue[5];
```

defines *revenue* to be a five-element *rev_entry* structure array. As with all other arrays, we must use brackets when defining or referencing structure arrays. If the structure was declared with a **typedef** (REV), the array would be defined

```
REV revenue[5];
```

Structure arrays have the same attributes as other C arrays. Thus, the first structure in the *revenue* array is named

```
revenue[0]
```

To refer to members in one of *revenue*'s elements, we first have to identify the proper structure in the array (using an index), and then specify the member within that structure (using the member operator). For example,

```
revenue[2].rev_amt
```

is the *rev_amt* member of the third structure in the *revenue* array. This expression works properly because both the brackets and the member operators have the same precedence and associate left to right. This means that

```
revenue[2].rev_cat[3]
```

identifies the fourth character in the *rev_cat* string in the third *revenue* structure.

RULE   Structure arrays are just like other C arrays.

Like other arrays, the name of a structure array is really a pointer to the first (structure) element. This means that

*revenue	is the same as	*revenue[0]*
*(revenue + 1)	is the same as	*revenue[1]*
	and so on.	

As a result,

(*revenue).rev_amt	is the same as	*revenue[0].rev_amt*
(*(revenue + 1)).rev_amt	is the same as	*revenue[1].rev_amt*
	and so on.	

The double set of parentheses is required so that the indirection (to locate the structure) is done first.

Note that the member operator is used in the expression

```
(*revenue).rev_amt
```

Since *revenue* is a pointer, the result of the indirection is the structure itself. Further, we can use the structure pointer operator with array elements replacing

```
(*(revenue + 1)).rev_amt
```

with

```
(revenue + 1)->rev_amt
```

As with other arrays, we can index through a structure array by incrementing a pointer. If

```
struct rev_entry revenue[5];
struct rev_entry *rev_ptr = revenue;   /* both pointers */
```

Sec. 18.6 Arrays of Structures

then we can index through the *revenue* array by incrementing *rev_ptr*:

```
rev_ptr++
```

After each increment, *rev_ptr* refers to the next *revenue* element. As an illustration, Segment 18-8 shows a **for** loop that adds up the amounts stored in the *revenue* array using *rev_ptr* to index each element.

```
/* assuming the declarations

struct rev_entry revenue[5];
struct rev_entry *rev_ptr = revenue;

have been made */

totalrev = 0;        /* initialize accumulator */
for (count = 0; count < 5; count++) {
    totalrev += rev_ptr->rev_amt;
    rev_ptr++;       /* next array element */
}
```

Segment 18-8 Indexing a Structure Array with a Structure Pointer

Using structure pointers to index through a structure array is common in functions that are passed a pointer to a structure array.

In Segment 18-8, we increment *rev_ptr* with

```
rev_ptr++;
```

even though the previous statement uses *rev_ptr* only once. In this case, we should be able to combine the increment operator with the structure reference. However, we must be careful because the increment operator has lower precedence than the structure pointer operator. The correct expression is

```
(rev_ptr++)->rev_amt
```

and the assignment statement becomes[6]

```
totalrev += (rev_ptr++)->rev_amt;
```

---

[6] The author tested this expression without the parentheses and found that two separate compilers interpreted the statement correctly. That is, the expression

```
rev_ptr++->rev_amt
```

compiled and executed correctly.

18.7 ADDING STRUCTURES TO THE flex-pl PROGRAM

To add structures to the **flex-pl** program requires us to rewrite every reference to a category name and amount. The first step is to declare a structure called *pl_entry*:

```
struct pl_entry {          /* can handle both revenues and costs */
    char category[MAX_LEN];   /* category name */
    long amount;              /* category amount */
};
```

Next, we must modify **main( )** to define two *pl_entry* arrays, one for revenues and one for costs. Also, **main( )** must pass a pointer to the beginning of these arrays as arguments to the **get_rev( )**, **get_cost( )**, and **print_pl( )** functions. The new **main( )** is listed as Program 18-1.

```
/* ***** FLEX-PL *****
 *
 * This program reads the category and amount of a set of
 * revenues and costs and prints a formatted P&L statement.
 * The program reads entries until a Q only is entered
 * as a category name (the quit signal) or until MAX_CAT
 * categories have been read.
 *
 * Written by Ray Swartz for "Doing Business with C"
 *
 * Modified to use structures for both revenue and
 * cost data.
 */

#define MAX_LEN 31      /* maximum length of category names */
#define MAX_CAT 20      /* maximum number of categories */

#include "stdio.h"
#include "getcat.c"     /* the getcat function */

int printf();

struct pl_entry {             /* file scope declaration */
    char category[MAX_LEN];   /* category name */
    long amount;              /* category amount */
};
```

Sec. 18.7 Adding Structures to the flex-pl Program

```
main()
{
    struct pl_entry revenue[MAX_CAT];   /* block scope definition */
    struct pl_entry cost[MAX_CAT];
    int rev_count;           /* number of revenue categories */
    int cost_count;          /* number of cost categories */
    int getrev();            /* read all revenue entries */
    int getcost();           /* read all cost entries */
    void print_pl();         /* print the P&L statement */

    rev_count = getrev(revenue);      /* get revenues */
    cost_count = getcost(cost);       /* get costs */
    print_pl(revenue, rev_count, cost, cost_count);
    exit(0);
}
```

Program 18-1 The *flex-pl* **main( )** Using Structures

Since *revenue* and *cost* are structure arrays, a pointer to their first elements is passed by referencing their name only.

All three functions called by **main( )** must be modified to take a structure pointer as an argument and then to store data in the structure's members. In general, every reference to a category or amount variable must be rewritten as a structure pointer expression. Also, the formal parameter representing the structure pointer must be incremented to move through the array. Function 18-2 shows **getrev( )**, Function 18-3 shows **getcost( )**, and Function 18-4 lists **print_pl( )**.

```
/* ***** GETREV *****
 *
 * This function prompts for and reads revenue categories
 * and amounts.  The category name and amount arrays
 * are passed to the function inside a structure.
 * The function returns the number of categories entered.
 * If "Q" is entered, data entry terminates.
 *
 * Written by Ray Swartz for "Doing Business with C"
 *
 * Modified to use structures.
 */

int getrev(entry)
struct pl_entry *entry;       /* an array of structures */
{
    long getcat();            /* read category and return amount */
    int count;                /* loop counter */
```

```
        printf("\nEnter Dollar amounts only -- no cents\n");
        printf("\n\nREVENUES\n\n");
        for (count = 0; count < MAX_CAT; count++) {
            entry->amount = getcat(entry->category, "Revenue");
            if (entry->category[0] == 'Q' &&
                entry->category[1] == '\0')
                    break;     /* possible loop exit */
            entry++;           /* go to the next structure element */
        }
        return(count);
    }
```

Function 18-2 The **getrev( )** Function Using Structures

```
/* ***** GETCOST *****
 *
 * This function prompts for and reads cost categories
 * and amounts.  The category name and amount arrays
 * are passed to the function inside a structure.  The
 * function returns the number of categories entered.
 * If "Q" is entered, data entry terminates.
 *
 * Written by Ray Swartz for "Doing Business with C"
 *
 * Modified to use structures.
 */

int getcost(entry)
struct pl_entry *entry;    /* an array of structures */
{
    long getcat();         /* read category and return amount */
    int count;             /* loop counter */

    printf("\nEnter Dollar amounts only -- no cents\n");
    printf("\n\nCOSTS\n\n");
    for (count = 0; count < MAX_CAT; count++) {
        entry->amount = getcat(entry->category, "Cost");
        if (entry->category[0] == 'Q' &&
            entry->category[1] == '\0')
                break;     /* possible loop exit */
        entry++;           /* go to the next structure element */
    }
    return(count);
}
```

Function 18-3 The **getcost( )** Function Using Structures

Sec. 18.7 Adding Structures to the flex-pl Program

```
/* ***** PRINT_PL *****
 *
 * This function prints a formatted Profit and Loss
 * statement.  It is sent category names and amounts
 * inside two structure arrays.  The number of entries
 * of each type is sent to the function as arguments, also.
 *
 * Written by Ray Swartz for "Doing Business with C"
 *
 * Modified to use structures.
 */

void print_pl(revenue, rev_count, cost, cost_count)
struct pl_entry *revenue;  /* revenue entries */
int rev_count;             /* number of revenue entries */
struct pl_entry *cost;     /* cost entries */
int cost_count;            /* number of cost entries */
{
    int count;             /* loop counter */
    static char co_name[] = "Johnson's Books";  /* company name */
    long totalrev = 0;     /* revenue amounts total */
    long totalcost = 0;    /* cost amounts total */

    printf("\tProfit and Loss for %s\n\n", co_name);
    printf("         REVENUE\n\n");

    /* Loop to print and total the revenue categories */

    for (count = 0; count < rev_count; count++) {
        printf("%-*s   $%6ld\n", MAX_LEN - 1,
            revenue->category, revenue->amount);
        totalrev += (revenue++)->amount;   /* increment structure */
    }
    printf("                              ------\n");
    printf("        TOTAL REVENUE         $%7ld\n\n\n",
        totalrev);

    /* Loop to print and total the cost categories */

    for (count = 0; count < cost_count; count++) {
        printf("%-*s   $%6ld\n", MAX_LEN - 1,
            cost->category, cost->amount);
        totalcost += (cost++)->amount;   /* increment structure */
    }
```

```
            printf("                                   ------\n");
            printf("          TOTAL COST                $%7ld\n\n\n",
                totalcost);
        if (totalrev >= totalcost)
            printf("          PROFIT                    $%7ld\n",
                totalrev - totalcost);
        else
            printf("          LOSS                     ($%7ld)\n",
                totalcost - totalrev);
        return;
    }
```

Function 18-4 The **print_pl( )** Function Using Structures

In Functions 18-2 and 18-3, the structure array pointer argument, named *entry* in both functions, is incremented as the last line of a **for** loop. This increment can be performed as part of the loop control statements by using the comma operator:

```
        for (count = 0; count < MAX_CAT; count++, entry++) {
        ...
```

In Function 18-4, the structure pointer is incremented as part of the expression that totals the reports revenues and costs:

$$totalrev\mathrel{+}= (revenue\mathrm{++})\mathrm{-}\mathrm{>}.amount;$$

18.8 STRUCTURES AS STRUCTURE MEMBERS

A data structure can contain any legal C data type as a member, including another data structure. This flexibility extends the usefulness of C's structures even further.

As an example, consider the *check* structure:

```
        struct check {
            char name[41];     /* receiver of check */
            char date[20];     /* date check written */
            double amount;     /* amount of check */
            int chk_nbr;       /* check number */
        };
```

We might use this structure in a program that prints checks to pay our bills. *check* contains a member called *date* that holds a twenty-character string. Although this approach works fine, it makes verifying the date difficult. We don't want our program writing checks with invalid dates!

Another approach is to represent the date as a structure:

Sec. 18.8 Structures as Structure Members

```
struct date {
    char month[10];    /* month's full name */
    int day;
    int year;
};
```

This not only provides a specific format for entering and printing dates, it also makes the functions that perform these tasks easier to write.

Exercise 18-4 Write a function, called **getdate**( ), that prompts, reads and verifies a date that is entered by the function. A verified date is returned in the structure that is passed in as an argument.

Once the *date* structure has been declared, it can be a member of another structure. As an example, let's make *date* a member of the *check* structure:

```
struct date {
    char month[10];    /* month's full name */
    int day;
    int year;
};

struct check {
    char name[41];          /* receiver of check */
    struct date chk_date;   /* date check written */
    double amount;          /* amount of check */
    int chk_nbr;            /* check number */
};

struct check payment;
```

Note that we have defined a *date* structure variable as a member (named *chk_date*). This is required because each member in a structure must be capable of storing information.

How do we access the date of a check? Since the structure member operator associates left to right, the expression

```
payment.chk_date.day
```

refers to the *day* member of the *chk_date* structure, which is a member of the *payment* structure.

As an example of usage, the code in Segment 18-9 assigns May 3, 1988 (the author's birthday) to *chk_date*.

```
                struct check payment;

                strcpy(payment.chk_date.month, "May");
                payment.chk_date.day = 3;
                payment.chk_date.year = 1988;
```

Segment 18-9   Referring to a Structure That Is a Structure Member

Incidentally, the second character stored in the *month* member of the *chk_date* structure is referred to as follows:

```
                payment.chk_date.month[1];
```

18.9 INITIALIZING A STRUCTURE

Structure variables that have **static** storage can be initialized when they are *defined*.[7] The procedure is similar to the initialization of arrays. The beginning member values are listed inside braces and separated by commas.

For example, to assign a date to a *date* structure requires

```
            static struct date birthday = { "May", 3, 1988};
```

A structure array can be initialized by enclosing each element's values in braces (separated by commas) and then enclosing the entire set of initializers in braces. As an illustration, to establish a range of dates, we might use a two-element *date* structure array with the first member initialized to the first valid date and the second one to the last date:

```
              static struct date date_range[2] =
                    { {"January", 1, 1988}, {"December", 31, 1988} };
```

The braces surrounding each element's values are optional. Thus,

```
              static struct date date_range[2] =
                    { "January", 1, 1988, "December", 31, 1988 };
```

is acceptable. However, it is better to use inner braces to delimit each element's initializers. Also, if the list of initial values does not contain enough entries to assign all of the structure's members, the remaining members are set to 0.

Incidentally, a common error is to attempt initialization inside a structure *declaration*:

---

[7] The restriction on initializing automatic structures is removed in the ANSI standard.

Sec. 18.10   Summary   321

```
struct date {
    char month[10] = "January";
    int day = 1;
    int year = 1988;
};
```

However, a structure declaration only specifies the members of the *date* structure. Since a structure declaration doesn't allocate space, it makes no sense to initialize the members inside one. The compiler will report this as an error.

Initializing structures which contain structure members is done in a similar way. Suppose we wanted to define *payment* as a *check* structure with the initial values of

Name:	Barbara Williams
Date:	May 21, 1988
Check Amount:	358.94
Check Number:	265

The initializing definition of *payment* is

```
static struct check payment =
    { "Barbara Williams", "May", 21, 1988, 358.94, 265 };
```

18.10 SUMMARY

1. The **typedef** mechanism allows us to rename any data type.
2. **typedef** can be used to identify a type name as an array with a specified number of elements.
3. A **typedef** definition is just like a variable definition in that the name follows the data type.
4. A **typedef** has block scope. This means it is only visible in the program block were it is defined.
5. **typedef**s allow related variables to be made more obvious and make it easy to change the data types used in a program.
6. Data structures can hold variables of different data under one name.
7. To create a data structure we must first declare what the structure "looks" like, that is, what member make up that structure. The keyword **struct** is used when declaring a structure.
8. When a structure is declared, it can be given a name which refers to the listing of structure members. This name is called a structure tag.
9. After a structure "template" has been declared, variables of that structure type can be defined, which actually allocates storage for the structure's members.
10. The information stored in a structure is actually held in the structure's member variables.

11. To access a structure member requires the structure member operator, the period.
12. The structure member operator has highest precedence, along with parentheses and brackets. This insures that a structure member is never separated from its structure.
13. In the original specification of C only two operations could be performed on a structure, accessing a structure member (the . operator) and taking a structure address (the & operator).
14. Since structure pointers are common in C, a special operator was created to represent the relationship between a structure pointer and one of the members in the structure referenced by that pointer. It is the structure pointer operator which is represented by ->.
15. The structure pointer operator has the same precedence as the structure member operator.
16. C allows data structure arrays.
17. Structure arrays are defined using brackets like all other C arrays. To refer to a member in an element in a structure array, the programmer puts the brackets identifying the structure element before the structure member operator:

```
revenue[2].rev_amt
```

18. A data structure can contain any C data type as a member. This includes other structures as well.
19. A **static** structure variable can be initialized. The members are assigned values from a list of initializers in the order they are listed (from top to bottom) in the structure declaration.

E X E R C I S E S

18-5. Rewrite **flex-pl** to use the **typedef** REV.

18-6. Modify the *pl_entry* structure to include a member that holds either "Revenue" or "Cost" and rewrite **getcat( )** to extract this information from the structure instead of taking it as an argument.

18-7. Write a program that prompts for and reads enough information to write a check. Store the check in a structure.

18-8. Write a program to balance a check book.

18-9. Rewrite Exercise 9-7 (creating a daily sales report) to use data structures.

18-10. Rewrite Exercise 9-8 (creating an invoice) to use data structures.

19

Dynamic Storage

In the **flex-pl** program, we use the MAX_CAT macro to define the category array sizes. As a result, there is a preset maximum number of revenue or cost categories that can be entered. Although it is true that we only have to modify a single value (and recompile) to adjust this limitation, anyone who needs to enter more categories than allowed by MAX_CAT is out of luck.

Hard-coded limits (i.e., constants) should be avoided in programs if at all possible. This is especially true for data entry programs where a preset maximum might mean the program can't handle the task at hand.

The only reason we use MAX_CAT is because we want to store the entered data in an array and C requires that an array's dimensions be defined with an integer. To allocate the proper amount of memory, the compiler must know the exact number of memory locations required by the array.

To be executable, a compiled program must be smaller than the memory available to the computer. This means a compiled program leaves some of the computer's memory unused. If there was a way to access this unallocated memory, then we could expand an array if it became necessary to do so. Further, entire arrays could be created by the program while it was running, if there were enough unallocated memory.

In C, any part of memory can be accessed by a pointer set to the appropriate address. Thus, our programs can use unallocated memory if we can find a way to point at it. Access lies in the C standard library!

Memory that isn't specifically set aside by the compiler is called *unallocated storage*. To allocate memory while the program is running, we must know how much memory is needed. C's data types require different amounts of memory. Further, different computers store the same data types in different amounts of memory. Thus, the real challenge is to access the correct amount of memory in a *machine-independent* way.

19.1 THE sizeof( ) OPERATOR

As usual, C's solution is simple yet elegant. C has a special operator that evaluates to the number of memory locations required by a data type. This operator is named **sizeof**. **sizeof** is a unary operator that reports the "size of" its operand.

If the operand is a data type, **sizeof** evaluates to the number of memory locations used to store a variable of that data type. For example,

```
sizeof(double)
```

reports the amount of memory needed to store a **double** variable. Thus, an array of ten **double**s requires

```
10 * sizeof(double)
```

memory locations. Although the amount of memory used to represent a ten-element **double** array may vary from one computer to another, the expression

```
10 * sizeof(double)
```

will always identify how much memory any particular machine uses for such an array.

As a larger illustration, Program 19-1 prints the storage requirements for C's data types.

```
main()
{
    int printf();

    printf("Length of CHAR is %d\n", sizeof(char));
    printf("Length of INT is %d\n", sizeof(int));
    printf("Length of LONG is %d\n", sizeof(long));
    printf("Length of FLOAT is %d\n", sizeof(float));
    printf("Length of DOUBLE is %d\n", sizeof(double));
    printf("Length of CHAR * is %d\n", sizeof(char *));
    exit(0);
}
```

Program 19-1 Using the **sizeof** Operator

Sec. 19.1   The **sizeof( )** Operator   **325**

The output of Program 19-1, run on the author's home computer, is shown in Output 19-1.

```
Length of CHAR is 1
Length of INT is 2
Length of LONG is 4
Length of FLOAT is 4
Length of DOUBLE is 8
Length of CHAR * is 2
```

Output 19-1

What constitutes a single memory location varies among computers. For **sizeof** to work in a portable way, there must be a point of reference across all machines. C requires that the

```
sizeof(char)
```

equate to 1. Thus, **sizeof** actually reports the number of **char**-sized memory locations required to store the listed data type![1]

In addition to data types, **sizeof** can determine the amount of space required for structures or arrays. If **sizeof**'s operand is an array name, structure name, or a structure variable, the expression reports the number of memory locations assigned to that array or structure.

For example, the structure *pl_entry*, used in the **flex-pl** program in Chapter 18, contains

```
struct pl_entry {
    char category[MAX_LEN];
    long amount;
} revenue;
```

where

```
#define MAX_LEN 31
```

The expression

```
sizeof(revenue)
```

equates to

```
31 + sizeof(long)
```

---

[1] Note specifically that sizeof(char) is *not* defined to be a byte.

Given the values in Output 19-1, this is 35. If

$$\text{double percent[30];}$$

then

$$\text{sizeof(percent)}$$

evaluates to

$$30 \text{ * sizeof(double)}$$

Again, using the values in Output 19-1, this is 240 memory locations.

Be careful here. A common error is to treat the result of a **sizeof** expression as the number of elements in the array. Instead, the number of elements in an array is

$$\text{sizeof(array)/sizeof(}\textit{array data type}\text{)}$$

Finally, if an expression is sent to **sizeof**, the amount of memory required to *store* the result is reported. If

```
double tax_pct;
long profit;
```

then

$$\text{sizeof(tax\_pct * profit)}$$

is the same as

$$\text{sizeof(double)}$$

since the expression is treated as the multiplication of two **double**s.

Unlike other operators that are evaluated during program execution, **sizeof**'s result is calculated by the compiler. Thus, **sizeof** should be treated as a *constant*. This means an expression listed as **sizeof**'s operand will *not* be evaluated. As an illustration, if

$$\text{int count = 0;}$$

then

$$\text{sizeof(count++);}$$

Sec. 19.2 Allocating Memory

reports the memory required to store an **int** but *does not perform the increment*. This makes sense, given the fact that when the compiler evaluates **sizeof**, the variable *count* doesn't exist![2]

RULE   **sizeof** is evaluated by the compiler and should be treated as a constant. An expression listed as a **sizeof** operand is not evaluated when the program is run.

Exercise 19-1   Run Program 19-1 on your computer and then try to figure out what these **sizeof** expressions equal.

> A. `double count = 0;`
> `double *pntr = &count;`
>
> `sizeof(*pntr)`
>
> B. `long payrate[30][51];`
>
> `sizeof(payrate)`

19.2 ALLOCATING MEMORY

Several standard library functions provide access to unallocated memory. These functions are told how much memory is needed and return a pointer to that much memory. If the specified amount of unused memory isn't available, they return the macro NULL.

The simplest allocation function is **malloc( )**. **malloc( )** is passed an *unsigned int* argument that is the number of memory locations required. **malloc( )** returns a **char *** to the requested amount of *contiguous* memory. Since it returns a pointer, **malloc( )** must be declared

```
char *malloc();
```

If

```
char *catstr;
char *malloc();
```

then

```
catstr = malloc(10);
```

---

[2] *count* won't store a value until the program is executed.

points *catstr* at enough memory to store a nine-character string (don't forget the \0). The memory allocated by **malloc( )** is uninitialized. Now, *catstr* can be treated as if the definition

```
char catstr[10];
```

occurred in the program.

RULE   **malloc( )** is sent an **unsigned int** as an argument.

RULE   The memory allocated by **malloc( )** is uninitialized.

If **malloc( )** can't locate enough contiguous memory to service our request, it returns NULL (a null pointer). Since memory is being allocated as the program is executing, there is a very real possibility that a call to **malloc( )** will fail. To use **malloc( )** properly, its return value must be tested for NULL. A typical call to **malloc( )** is

```
if ((catstr = malloc(10)) == NULL) {
    printf(error message);
    ...
}
```

Here, the value returned by **malloc( )** is stored in *catstr* and then tested. This insures that *catstr* is a valid pointer before we use it! Segment 19-1 provides an example that reads in a category and then creates enough space to store it.

```
char *catstr;         /* will hold category name entered */
char malloc();
char instr[BUFSIZ];   /* maximum size input string */
char *gets();
char *strcpy();
int strlen();

do {
    printf("Enter category name: ");
    gets(instr);
    if ((catstr = malloc(strlen(instr) + 1)) == NULL)
        printf("Not enough memory to store name.  Re-enter\n");
    else
        strcpy(catstr, instr); /* put string in allocated memory */
} while (catstr == NULL);    /* loop on error */
...
```

Segment 19-1   Using **malloc( )**

There are two points to notice in Segment 19-1. First, we determine how much memory is needed by reading in the string to store and then use its length in the call to

Sec. 19.2   Allocating Memory

malloc( ). Second, the **strlen( )** function only reports how many characters are in the entered string. We must add one to the value returned by **strlen( )** to make room for the **\0**.

When we define a string variable inside a program, we have to "guess" how big to make the variable. In almost all cases, this wastes memory since we must define strings to be large enough to handle any input the user is likely to enter. When we use **malloc( )**, we are allocating space *after* the string has been entered and its size is known. As a result, there is no "wasted" space, and our programs are more efficient!

In Segment 19-1, only a single category name can be entered because just one pointer is defined. In **flex-pl**, several category names are entered. To dynamically create storage for an array of strings, we define an array of pointers. As each category name is entered, we use **malloc( )** to allocate enough room for them, storing the pointer in the next array element in this **char** pointer array.

For example, the **flex-pl** program allows up to MAX_CAT revenue and cost categories to be entered. Instead of defining *rev_cat* and *cost_cat* to be string arrays, we can define them as arrays of character pointers:

```
char *rev_cat[MAX_CAT];
char *cost_cat[MAX_CAT];
```

and then use **malloc( )** to allocate enough space to hold each category name after it is entered. Segment 19-2 shows how this is done.

```
char *rev_cat[MAX_CAT];    /* will hold revenue categories */
char malloc();
char instr[BUFSIZ];        /* input string */
char *gets();
char *strcpy();
int strlen();
int count;

for (count = 0; count < MAX_CAT; count++) {
   do {
      printf("Enter revenue category: ");
      gets(instr);    /* should test for quit signal here */
      if ((rev_cat[count] = malloc(strlen(instr) + 1)) == NULL)
         printf("Not enough memory to store name.  Re-enter\n");
      else
         strcpy(rev_cat[count], instr);
   } while (rev_cat[count] == NULL);   /* loop on error */
}
...
```

Segment 19-2   Using **malloc( )** with String Arrays

In Segment 19-2, the revenue categories use no more memory than is exactly required for them.

Up to now, **malloc( )** has only allocated space for character strings. But what if we need to allocate memory to store a numeric value? Since **malloc( )** returns a character pointer, assigning the **char** pointer **malloc( )** returns to a numeric pointer will cause data alignment problems. Using the **sizeof** operator insures that **malloc( )** retrieves enough space to store a **double**. However, when we refer to the value stored in *amount*, the program may fetch the wrong data because a character pointer is being used to refer to a **double**.

Does this mean we have to have a separate allocation function for each data type? Not at all. We can correct the alignment problem with another C operator, the *type cast*. Recall that we can temporarily change a value's data type by casting it to another type. The same thing can be done with the pointer returned by **malloc( )**! To allocate space for a **double** we use **malloc( )** to find the memory and then cast the returned **char** pointer into a **double** pointer before assigning it to *amount*.

```
amount = (double *) malloc(sizeof(double));
```

We must remember that *amount* is a pointer to this newly allocated memory. The indirection operator is required to assign or reference *amount*'s data:

```
*amount = 2.345;
```

or

```
total = *amount + sub_total;
```

In most instances, we want to allocate enough memory for an array of data elements. We can do this with **malloc( )** by multiplying a basic data type by the number of elements we want. For example, we can create a ten-element **double** array with

```
double *amount;
char *malloc();

amount = (double *) malloc( 10 * sizeof(double));
```

Now, *amount* is just like an array, that is, the array's name is a pointer to the memory that stores the array's elements. Further, because of the array transformation rule, we even can refer to *amount*'s elements using array notation. Now,

```
amount[0] = 2.345;
```

and

```
total = amount[count] + subtotal;
```

are legal statements, as are

Sec. 19.2 Allocating Memory

```
                    *amount = 2.345;
```

and

```
                    total = *(amount + count) + subtotal;
```

Using **malloc( )** to create numeric arrays causes an inconvenience. The data **malloc( )** delivers to us is uninitialized. In many applications, this won't be a problem. However, in programs where we want to use the array elements for accumulation or counting, we must write a set of initializing statements every time we use **malloc( )**.

A better solution is to use another of the allocation functions, which provides us with initialized memory. This function is named **calloc( )** and it returns memory that is set to 0 (if numeric) and \0 if **char**. **calloc( )** takes two arguments. The first one tells it how many elements and the second one the size of each element. The total amount of memory allocated is the first argument multiplied by the second. Both arguments are unsigned **int**s. Like **malloc( )**, **calloc( )** returns a pointer to **char**. As an example,

```
            double *amount;
            char *calloc();

            amount = (double *) calloc(10, sizeof(double));
```

does the same thing the previous **malloc( )** did: create a ten-element **double** array called *amount*. However, all 10 elements are set to 0.

calloc( ) acts just like **malloc( )** if there isn't enough free memory to fulfill the request: The macro NULL is returned. The value returned by **calloc( )** should always be tested for NULL before continuing with the program.

In addition to using C's basic data types, we can use the allocation functions to create space for data structure variables. In fact, everything we've said about using **malloc( )** and **calloc( )** with basic data types and arrays is true for creating structure variables.

For example, if

```
            typedef struct pl_entry {
                char category[MAX_LEN];
                long amount;
            } PL;
```

then

```
            PL *revenue;    /* structure pointer */
            char *malloc();

            revenue = (PL *) malloc(sizeof(PL));
```

allocates enough space for one *PL* structure and assigns its location to the variable *revenue*. Since *revenue* is a pointer, we must use the structure pointer operator to refer to *revenue*'s members. Both

```
gets(revenue->category);
```

and

```
revenue->amount = getcat(revenue->category, "Revenue");
```

are legal statements. Incidentally, the cast

```
(PL *)
```

is valid once *PL* is defined as a **typedef** to a structure.

As an example, let's modify the **getrev( )** function (Function 18-2) to take a structure pointer as an argument and then to allocate the memory required for a structure array. One significant change is required to make **getrev( )** allocate space for the entered revenue entries. Instead of returning the number of entries read, **getrev( )** must now return a pointer to the beginning of the newly allocated structure array.

At first glance, it may seem that we can assign the pointer returned by **calloc( )** directly to the structure pointer argument passed to **getrev( )**. Segment 19-3 shows what such a code would look like.

```
int getrev(entry)
PL *entry;
{                          /* assume PL defined with file scope */
    long getcat();         /* read category and return amount */
    int count;             /* loop counter */

    printf("\nEnter Dollar amounts only -- no cents\n");
    printf("\n\nREVENUES\n\n");
    entry = (PL *) calloc(MAX_CAT, sizeof(PL));  /* problem here */
    if (entry == NULL)
        printf("Out of memory in getrev function\n");
```

Segment 19-3 Assigning Space to a Pointer That Is a Function Argument

However, the code in Segment 19-3 *won't work*. The problem is how C passes function arguments. Recall that a variable's *value* (in **getrev( )**, a copy of the pointer stored in *entry*) is what is passed to a function as an argument and that any changes that occur inside the function are made to that copy only. As a result, the assignment

```
entry = (PL *) calloc(MAX_CAT, sizeof(PL));
```

Sec. 19.2 Allocating Memory

is valid only so long as the **getrev( )** function is executing. When **getrev( )** terminates, so does our assignment of the array. This leads to the perverse effect that the structure array exists, we just can't find it!

To make the array assignment permanent, the function must return the address where the structure begins (i.e., the pointer returned by **calloc( )**). This requires significant modifications in **getrev( )**. First, we must change **getrev( )**'s data type from **int** to pointer to *PL*. In addition, we must find another way to pass back the number of revenue entries entered. Previously, the number of entries was returned by **getrev( )**. Instead, we will pass this value back to the calling routine through an argument. That is, a pointer to the revenue counting variable is sent to **getrev( )** and when data entry terminates the number of entries entered is stored in this variable. With these changes, **getrev( )** is declared:

```
PL *getrev(num)
int *num;      /* number of revenue categories entered */
```

In the previous version (Function 18-2), **getrev( )** used its structure pointer argument to index through the structure array, incrementing the pointer after each entry. We must be careful in the allocation version of **getrev( )**, because the structure pointer refers to the beginning of the array. If we increment this pointer, we will lose data. A simple solution is to use two pointers, one to index the array and one to pass back to the calling routine. The indexing pointer is incremented and the other one is left alone. Function 19-1 shows the **getrev( )** function that allocates memory for the revenue structure array.

```
PL *getrev(num)
int *num;
{
    PL *revptr;             /* indexing pointer */
    PL *beginptr;           /* returned pointer */
    char *calloc();
    long getcat();          /* read category and return amount */
    int count;              /* loop counter */

    printf("\nEnter Dollar amounts only -- no cents\n");
    printf("\n\nREVENUES\n\n");
    beginptr = revptr = (PL *) calloc(MAX_CAT, sizeof(PL));
    if (revptr == NULL)
        return(NULL);       /* not enough memory */
    for (count = 0; count < MAX_CAT; count++, revptr++) {
        revptr->amount = getcat(revptr->category, "Revenue");
        if (revptr->category[0] == 'Q' &&
            revptr->category[1] == '\0')
                break;      /* possible loop exit */
    }
```

```
        *num = count;        /* number entered */
        return(beginptr);    /* return pointer to PL array */
}
```

Function 19-1 Memory Allocating **getrev**( ) Function

When we modify how the **getrev**( ) function is called and what it returns, we must also change the routine that calls **getrev**( ). In **flex-pl**, it is **main**( ) that calls **getrev**( ). **main**( ) must declare **getrev**( ) as function returning a pointer to *PL*. In addition, **getrev**( ) must be sent the address of the variable that stores the count of revenue entries. Since the **getrev**( ) function is similar to the **getcost**( ) function, Program 19-2 shows the changes necessary to integrate both of them into **main**( ).

```
main()
{
    PL *revenue;          /* points to array of revenue entries */
    PL *cost;             /* points to array of cost entries */
    PL *getrev();         /* read all revenue entries */
    PL *getcost();        /* read all cost entries */
    int rev_count;        /* number of revenue categories */
    int cost_count;       /* number of cost categories */
    void print_pl();      /* print the P&L statement */

    if ((revenue = getrev(&rev_count)) == NULL) {
        printf("Not enough memory for revenue entries\n");
        exit(1);
    }
    if ((cost = getcost(&cost_count)) == NULL) {
        printf("Not enough memory for cost entries\n");
        exit(1);
    }
    print_pl(revenue, rev_count, cost, cost_count);
    exit(0);
}
```

Program 19-2 The **main**( ) for Storage Allocation **flex-pl**

There are two points to note in Program 19-2. First, if either **getcost**( ) or **getrev**( ) returns NULL, the program must terminate. Should either function return NULL, **main**( ) prints an error message and exits with a code of 1. This can be used to inform the operating systems that the program failed. Second, the only changes we've made to the program have been made where spaces for the structure arrays are allocated. We haven't altered the format of the arrays at all. As a result, no changes are required in the **print_pl**( ) function.

In addition to functions that allocate unused memory, the standard library contains a function that *deallocates* memory. The computer's memory is a limited resource. Many times, our programs will allocate memory that is used for a short time only.

When we are done with this memory, it should be returned to the "unused" state. That is, made part of the pool of memory available for allocation by **malloc( )** and **calloc( )**. This is done with the **free( )** library function.

free( ) can deallocate memory that was allocated by a function such as **malloc( )** or **calloc( )**. **free( )** is passed a pointer to the memory to be added back to the unused memory pool. For example, if *memptr* is a pointer to memory allocated by **malloc( )**, then

```
free(memptr)
```

frees this memory. **free** expects a pointer to **char** and to be on the safe side, a cast should be used with all non-**char** pointers, such as

```
free( (char *) memptr);
```

19.3 THE realloc( ) FUNCTION

Arrays are useful in a wide variety of application programs. Unfortunately, arrays limit the expandability of our programs because they must be defined with a preset number of elements. Even when we use the allocation functions to create them, we get an amount of memory specified by a certain number of elements, each of a set size. What happens if we need more memory?

By using another one of the standard allocation functions, we can *resize* a block of memory created by **malloc( )** or **calloc( )**. The reallocation function, **realloc( )**, is passed two arguments, a pointer to a previously allocated region of memory and a new size for that region. The new size is listed as the number of memory locations needed.[3] For example, suppose our program defines

```
PL *revenue;
char *calloc();
```

and allocates space for *revenue* by

```
revenue = (PL *) calloc(MAX_CAT, sizeof(PL));
```

Should the user want to enter more than MAX_CAT entries, the program can reallocate the size of the *revenue* array to accept another MAX_CAT entry:

---

[3] Some compilers don't provide a **realloc( )** function. For this reason, a version of **realloc( )** has been provided as an addendum to this chapter.

```
char *realloc();

revenue = (PL *) realloc((char *) revenue,
                2 * MAX_CAT * sizeof(PL));
```

Like its relatives **malloc( )** and **calloc( )**, **realloc( )** returns NULL if the request can't be satisfied. If the new size is larger than the present one, a new section of memory is allocated and the contents of the presently allocated memory are moved into this newly created section. If the requested size is smaller than the present size, then the data stored at the end of the present region will be lost.

As written, the **getrev( )** function allows us to enter MAX_CAT entries. After the final entry, the function returns without giving the user any chance to enter more categories. This is necessary because there is no more allocated storage space. However, with **realloc( )** we can resize the structure array to hold more data. This means that **getrev( )** will get data until the user enters the quit signal or the computer runs out of memory, whichever comes first!

To implement reallocating the category name array as more entries are entered requires us to rewrite the **getrev( )** function, last shown as Function 19-1. The main issue is how to allocate space properly. To minimize the use of **realloc( )**, we will allocate space in a set number at a time, represented by the ALLOC_NBR macro. When ALLOC_NBR entries have been entered, we use **realloc( )** to increase the size of the revenue array to handle another ALLOC_NBR entries.

If

```
int count = 0;      /* counter for revenue entries */
int alloc_cnt = 1;  /* number of times realloc used */
```

then we need to allocate more space when

```
count + 1 >= alloc_cnt * ALLOC_NBR
```

Since array elements begin at 0, the number of entries is actually 1 more than *count*. Incidentally, the logical test could be redone as == only, but our experience tells us that >= should be used in these instances to make sure!

Recall that **realloc( )** is sent two arguments, a pointer to the memory being reallocated (cast to a **char ***) and the new size expressed in memory locations. The amount of memory needed is the number of entries (ALLOC_NBR) times the size of each entry (**sizeof**(PL)) times one plus the number of times we have reallocated the array:

```
++alloc_cnt * ALLOC_NBR * sizeof(PL)
```

If

```
char *revptr;    /* pointer to revenue array */
```

Sec. 19.3 The realloc( ) Function

then the call to **realloc( )** is

```
(PL *) realloc( (char *) revptr,
        ++alloc_count * ALLOC_NBR * sizeof(PL));
```

At first glance, it may seem that we can assign the pointer returned by **realloc( )** directly back into *revptr*. However, this is an error since **realloc( )** returns NULL if not enough free memory exists to service the request. If NULL is stored in *revptr* then we would lose all the entries made up to this point!

A better approach is to use a second pointer to hold what **realloc( )** returns, test this value, and assign it to *revptr* only after it has been tested for NULL. Segment 19-4 shows the code that implements array resizing.

```
if (count + 1 >= alloc_count * ALLOC_NBR) {
    beginptr = (PL *) realloc( (char *) revptr,
            ++alloc_count * ALLOC_NBR * sizeof(PL));
    if (beginptr == NULL) {
        printf("Out of memory\n");
        break;   /* memory error - exit loop */
    }
    revptr = beginptr;  /* reassign the array pointer */
}
```

Segment 19-4 Resizing an Array

The entire reallocating **getrev( )** function is shown as Function 19-2.

```
PL *getrev(num)
int *num;      /* number of revenue categories entered */
{
    PL *revptr;             /* array pointer */
    PL *beginptr;           /* returned pointer */
    long getcat();
    char *calloc();
    char *realloc();
    char *gets();
    int count = 0;          /* counter for revenue entries */
    int alloc_cnt = 1;      /* number of times memory allocated */
    int quit_flag = 0;      /* loop control */

    printf("\nEnter Dollar amounts only -- no cents\n");
    printf("\n\nREVENUES\n\n");
    revptr = (PL *) calloc(ALLOC_NBR, sizeof(PL));
    if (revptr == NULL)
        return(NULL);    /* not enough memory */
    while (! quit_flag) {
        revptr[count].amount = getcat(revptr[count].category,
                    "Revenue");
```

```
            if (revptr[count].category[0] == 'Q' &&
                revptr[count].category[1] == '\0') {
                quit_flag = 1;
                continue;  /* initiates loop exit */
            }
            if (count + 1 >= alloc_count * ALLOC_NBR) {
                beginptr = (PL *) realloc( (char *) revptr,
                        ++alloc_count * ALLOC_NBR * sizeof(PL));
                if (beginptr == NULL) {
                    printf("Can't enter any more - memory full\n");
                    break;  /* memory error = exit loop */
                }
                revptr = beginptr;  /* reassign the array pointer */
            }
            count++;
        }
        if (quit_flag)
            *num = count - 1;  /* don't count quit entry */
        return(revptr);
    }
```

Function 19-2 The Allocating **getrev( )** Function

In **getrev( )**, we use array notation to refer to the structures in the *revptr* array instead of incrementing *revptr*. We do this to preserve the value assigned to *revptr* (where the array starts), which is required for **realloc( )** to work properly. Also, recall that the **continue** command tells C to skip the rest of a loop's commands and immediately retest the loop's stopping condition. In **getrev( )**, **continue** is used to terminate data entry when the quit signal is found.

Program 19-3 shows the **flex-pl** program that allocates space for both revenue and cost entries as needed. The **print_pl( )** function is not listed since it has not been changed.

```
/* ***** FLEX-PL *****
 *
 * This program reads the category and amount of a set of
 * revenues and costs and prints a formatted P&L statement.
 * The program reads entries until a Q only is entered
 * as a category name.
 *
 * Written for Ray Swartz for "Doing Business with C"
 *
 * Modified to use structures for both revenue and
 * cost data.
 *
 * Modified to allocate space for the revenue and cost
 * entries.
 */
```

Sec. 19.3   The realloc() Function

```
#define MAX_LEN 31        /* maximum length of a category entry */
#define ALLOC_NBR 5       /* number of entries allocated */

#include "stdio.h"
#include "getcat.c"       /* source code for getcat function */

int printf();

typedef struct {          /* can handle both revenues and costs */
    char category[MAX_LEN];   /* category name */
    long amount;              /* category amount */
} PL;

main()
{
    PL *revenue;          /* points to array of revenue entries */
    PL *cost;             /* points to array of cost entries */
    PL *getrev();         /* read all revenue entries */
    PL *getcost();        /* read all cost entries */
    int rev_count;        /* number of revenue categories */
    int cost_count;       /* number of cost categories */
    void print_pl();      /* print the P&L statement */

    if ((revenue = getrev(&rev_count)) == NULL) {
        printf("Not enough memory for revenue entries\n");
        exit(1);
    }
    if ((cost = getcost(&cost_count)) == NULL) {
        printf("Not enough memory for cost entries\n");
        exit(1);
    }
    print_pl(revenue, rev_count, cost, cost_count);
    exit(0);
}

/* ***** GETREV *****
 *
 * This function prompts for and reads revenue categories
 * and amounts.  A pointer to the variable that holds
 * the number of revenue categories entered is passed to
 * the function (num).  The function returns a pointer
 * to the revenue entry structure array.
 * If "Q" is entered, data entry terminates.
 *
```

```
 * Written by Ray Swartz for "Doing Business with C"
 *
 * Modified to use structures.
 *
 * Modified to allocate space for ALLOC_NBR revenue
 * entries with malloc().  When this number has been
 * entered, realloc() is called to allocate ALLOC_NBR
 * more entries.
 */

PL *getrev(num)
int *num;       /* number of revenue categories entered */
{
    PL *revptr;            /* array pointer */
    PL *beginptr;          /* returned pointer */
    char *calloc();
    char *realloc();
    char *gets();
    long getcat();
    int count = 0;         /* counter for revenue entries */
    int alloc_cnt = 1;     /* number of times memory allocated */
    int quit_flag = 0;     /* loop control */

    printf("\nEnter Dollar amounts only -- no cents\n");
    printf("\n\nREVENUES\n\n");
    revptr = (PL *) calloc(ALLOC_NBR, sizeof(PL));
    if (revptr == NULL)
        return(NULL);      /* not enough memory */
    while (! quit_flag) {
        revptr[count].amount = getcat(revptr[count].category,
                        "Revenue");
        if (revptr[count].category[0] == 'Q' &&
           revptr[count].category[1] == '\0') {
               quit_flag = 1;
               continue;   /* initiates loop exit */
        }
        if (count + 1 >= alloc_count * ALLOC_NBR) {
            beginptr = (PL *) realloc( (char *) revptr,
                    ++alloc_count * ALLOC_NBR * sizeof(PL));
            if (beginptr == NULL) {
                printf("Can't enter any more - memory full\n");
                break;  /* memory error = exit loop */
            }
            revptr = beginptr;  /* reassign the array pointer */
        }
        count++;
    }
```

Sec. 19.3   The **realloc( )** Function

```
        if (quit_flag)
            *num = count - 1;    /* don't count quit entry */
        return(revptr);
}

/* ***** GETCOST *****
 *
 * This function prompts for and reads cost categories
 * and amounts.  A pointer to the variable that holds
 * the number of cost categories entered is passed to
 * the function (num).  The function returns a pointer
 * to the cost entry structure array.
 * If "Q" is entered, data entry terminates.
 *
 * Written by Ray Swartz for "Doing Business with C"
 *
 * Modified to use structures.
 *
 * Modified to allocate space for ALLOC_NBR revenue
 * entries with malloc().  When this number has been
 * entered, realloc() is called to allocate ALLOC_NBR
 * more entries.
 */

PL *getcost(num)
int *num;        /* number of cost categories entered */
{
    PL *costptr;            /* array pointer */
    PL *beginptr;           /* returned pointer */
    char *calloc();
    char *realloc();
    char *gets();
    int count = 0;          /* counter for cost entries */
    int alloc_cnt = 1;      /* number of times memory allocated */
    int quit_flag = 0;      /* loop control */

    printf("\nEnter Dollar amounts only -- no cents\n");
    printf("\n\nCOSTS\n\n");
    costptr = (PL *) calloc(ALLOC_NBR, sizeof(PL));
    if (costptr == NULL)
        return(NULL);    /* not enough memory */
    while (! quit_flag) {
        costptr[count].amount = getcat(costptr[count].category,
                            "Cost");
        if (costptr[count].category[0] == 'Q' &&
            costptr[count].category[1] == '\0') {
                quit_flag = 1;
                continue;   /* initiates loop exit */
        }
```

```
            if (count + 1 >= alloc_count * ALLOC_NBR) {
                beginptr = (PL *) realloc( (char *) costptr,
                         ++alloc_count * ALLOC_NBR * sizeof(PL));
                if (beginptr == NULL) {
                    printf("Can't enter any more - memory full\n");
                    break;     /* memory error = exit loop */
                }
                costptr = beginptr;    /* reassign the array pointer */
            }
            count++;
        }
        if (quit_flag)
            *num = count - 1;   /* don't count quit entry */
        return(costptr);
    }
```

Program 19-3 The Storage Allocation **flex-pl**

19.4 SUMMARY

1. Hard-coded limits (represented by constants) in programs should be avoided if at all possible.

2. C provides a set of functions to allocate memory not used by the executable program.

3. To determine how much memory is required by a particular data type, C provides the **sizeof( )** operator. **sizeof( )** evaluates to the number of **char**-sized memory locations a listed data type requires. If an array or structure name is evaluated by **sizeof( )**, the number of memory locations needed to store all of the array elements or structure members results.

4. C provides a set of memory allocation functions that go into unallocated memory and retrieve a pointer to and allocate the requested number of memory locations.

5. The **malloc( )** function is sent a single argument and returns a **char** pointer to that many memory locations. The macro NULL is returned if the request cannot be fulfilled. To allocate space for other data types, the pointer returned by **malloc( )** can be cast to point to the proper data type.

6. The **calloc( )** function is sent two arguments, the number of memory locations in this data type and how many to allocate. **calloc( )** returns a **char** pointer to the allocated memory or NULL if the request cannot be fulfilled.

7. The **realloc( )** function resizes memory allocated with **malloc( )** or **calloc( )**. **realloc( )** is sent a **char** pointer to the allocated memory and the number of memory locations this memory to hold. **realloc( )** returns a pointer to this resized memory or NULL if the request cannot be fulfilled.

Sec. 19.5 Addendum 343

EXERCISES

19-2. Run Program 19-1 on your computer system to see how many memory locations C's data types require.

19-3. Rewrite Exercise 9-7 (creating a daily sales report) to allocate space as needed.

19-4. Rewrite Exercise 9-8 (creating an invoice) to allocate space as needed.

19-5. Write a function called **get_name( )** that prompts for, reads, and verifies the company name to print on the P&L statement. The function should allocate the space for the name entered and return a pointer to the allocated memory.

19-6. Create a structure that holds the company name and the date of the P&L statement. Write functions to enter this information (Exercise 19-5 is fine) and then modify **print-pl( )** to take a pointer to this structure as an argument and print this information on the P&L statement.

19-7. Implement the **ralloc( )** function described in the addendum to this chapter on your computer system.

19-8. Rewrite **flex-pl** to use the **ralloc( )** function described in the addendum to this chapter.

19.5 ADDENDUM

19.5.1 A realloc( ) Function

Even though **realloc( )** is considered a standard library function, some compilers don't provide a **realloc( )** function in their libraries. Thus, for the changes made to **flex-pl** in Chapter 19 to work with these compilers, we have to write a function that performs **realloc( )**'s task.

realloc( ) does three things. First, it allocates the amount of memory requested in the second argument. Next, it moves the data in the memory referenced by the function's first argument into the newly allocated memory. Last, it returns a pointer to the new memory. The function we write, which will be called **ralloc( )**, must offer all these services.

Examining the arguments sent to **realloc( )** in light of what the function does leaves a question. To move the memory referred to by the pointer argument, **realloc( )** must know how much memory is allocated to this pointer, but this size is not sent as an argument. How does **realloc( )** get this information? The answer is that this information is stored as part of the storage allocated by the memory by the allocation functions themselves.[4]

Unfortunately, our function won't have access to this allocation data and we must devise a way for **ralloc( )** to determine the amount of memory assigned to the old pointer. The simplest way to figure something out is to keep track of it as we go along.

---

[4] **sizeof( )** is evaluated at compile-time and dynamic memory allocated at run-time. This means that **sizeof( )** cannot be used to determine the size of an array allocated with one of the allocation functions.

This is what **ralloc( )** will expect the calling routines to do. As a result, **ralloc( )** is passed the number of elements referred to by the old pointer and the size of those elements. Further, **ralloc( )** assumes that the new pointer will contain elements that are the same size.

ralloc( ) needs two more arguments, a pointer (cast as a **char ***) to the existing memory, and the number of elements the new memory is to hold. This version of **ralloc( )** assumes that the memory being allocated is larger than that referred to by the existing pointer. The call to **ralloc( )** is listed in Segment 19A-1.

```
char *ralloc(ptr, count, new_size, length)
char *ptr;      /* pointer to existing memory allocation */
int count;      /* number of elements referenced by ptr */
int new_size;   /* number of elements desired */
int length;     /* size of the elements being allocated */
```

Segment 19A-1 Call to **ralloc( )**

Moving the contents of memory from one section to another is done with a loop that simply assigns one location to another:

```
limit = count * length;
for (loop_count = 0; loop_count < limit; loop_count++)
    *(new_ptr + loop_count) = *(ptr + loop_count);
```

new_ptr points to the newly allocated memory. The **ralloc( )** function is listed in Function 19A-1.

```
/* ***** RALLOC *****
 *
 * This function implements the realloc function for
 * compilers that don't contain one.  The function
 * is sent a pointer to allocated memory, the
 * number of elements allocated, the new size
 * to be allocated, and the length of each
 * element.  It returns a pointer to the
 * new memory and frees the memory associated
 * with the original pointer.
 *
 * Written by Ray Swartz for "Doing Business with C"
 *
 */
```

---

[5] There is some chance that this loop won't work if the memory segments are too large. Check the compiler's documentation for the appropriate limits.

Sec. 19.5   Addendum

```
char *ralloc(ptr, count, new_size, length)
char *ptr;      /* pointer to existing memory allocation */
int count;      /* number of elements referenced by ptr */
int new_size;   /* number of elements desired */
int length;     /* size of the elements being allocated */
{
    char *calloc();
    long loop_count;    /* used in memory moving loop */
    char *new_ptr;      /* pointer to new memory */
    long limit;         /* memory allocated to ptr */

    if (count > new_size)
        return(NULL);           /* new memory less than old memory */
    limit = count * length;
    new_ptr = calloc(new_size, length);
    if (new_ptr != NULL) {  /* check for calloc failure */
        for (loop_count = 0; loop_count < limit; loop_count++)
            *(new_ptr + loop_count) = *(ptr + loop_count);
    }
    return(new_ptr);            /* NULL if calloc fails */
}
```

Function 19A-1   The **ralloc( )** Function

PART 8
Working with Data Files

20

Working with Data Files in C

Although C was designed to be a portable programming language, C programs must be executed on specific machines, often having unique characteristics. To provide continuity between a general (i.e., portable) language and an individual computer, a C programming *environment* was developed. Based on elementary aspects of the UNIX operating system, this environment supplies a basic computer interface between our C programs and the underlying machine. To run C programs, a computer needs to provide only the services required by this environment!

20.1 THE C PROGRAMMING ENVIRONMENT

A C program gets input from the standard input device and sends output to the standard output device.[1] The default source for standard input is the keyboard and the default destination for standard output is the terminal screen connected to that keyboard.

All of the input functions we have used so far, **getchar( )**, **gets( )**, and **scanf( )**, read the standard input. Likewise, the output routines **putchar( )**, **puts( )**, and **printf( )** all print to the standard output.

---

[1] In C parlance, standard input is called *standard in* or abbreviated *stdin*; standard output is called *standard out* or just *stdout*.

Sec. 20.2   Redirecting Standard Input and Output

C doesn't set the destination of standard input and standard output; it simply assumes they exist. They may be assigned by the operating system, as on UNIX or MS-DOS, or by a special interface (generally provided by the compiler) between our C programs and the computer operating system. Because standard input and standard output are set outside our programs, we can change where these standard destinations get or send data without modifying our programs. This is called *redirecting* standard input and standard output.

20.2 REDIRECTING STANDARD INPUT AND OUTPUT

By convention, the symbols < and > are used to redirect standard input and standard output respectively. As an example, suppose we wanted to store the results of a profit and loss statement in a file called *pl-stmt.88*. We can do this by redirecting the standard output of the **flex-pl** program into the file *pl-stmt.88*:

```
flex-pl > pl-stmt.88
```

Now, when the program's **printf( )**s print to the standard output, the information is directed into the file *pl-stmt.88* and *not* displayed on the terminal. Further, suppose we created an input file, called *rev-cost.88*, with all the information needed by the **flex-pl** program in exactly the required order. Using input redirection, we can tell **flex-pl** to read from *rev-cost.88* instead of the keyboard by:

```
flex-pl < rev-cost.88
```

Now, when **gets( )** reads from the standard input, it reads the next line in the *rev-cost.88* file. However, redirecting the standard input doesn't affect the standard output. As a result, the program prints prompts on the terminal screen regardless of where input is coming from. We can redirect both standard input and standard output by[2]

```
flex-pl < rev-cost.88 > pl-stmt.88
```

Redirecting the standard output changes where *every* **printf( )** prints. The data entry prompts end up in the *rev-cost.88* file, too! In addition, if we redirect standard input but not standard output, the program will still print prompts on the terminal screen (the standard output) even though we are not entering anything from the keyboard.

While redirection provides flexibility, it is a two-edged feature. Our programs work as designed for the default conditions, but may produce unintended results in other circumstances (e.g., printing prompts into the data file).

How does our program know if it is reading a file or getting characters typed at a keyboard? It doesn't. C views all input and output, regardless of its source and

---

[2] If you aren't working on a UNIX or MS-DOS system, it is possible that these redirections won't work. Check with your system administrator or documentation if you aren't sure.

destination, as a *stream* of individual characters. A file is simply a stream stored on a disk or tape. The keyboard creates a stream of characters as we type on it. A terminal or printer are devices that display a stream. It is this orientation that allows the concept of I/O redirection to work.

We can now understand why **getchar( )** and the other standard input functions check for an end of file (EOF) condition. Otherwise, redirecting standard input to a data file would cause serious problems when EOF was reached. In fact, since the keyboard is viewed as a stream, it can generate an EOF condition, too. On UNIX, this is done by typing a *control-D* as the first character on a line. Other systems may use other characters to do this. Again, check your system's documentation for specifics.

As an example of the power of redirection, Program 20-1 is a rudimentary file-copying program.

```
#include "stdio.h"

main()
{
    int inchar;     /* character read */

    while ((inchar = getchar()) != EOF)
        putchar(inchar);
    exit(0);
}
```

Program 20-1   Rudimentary File-Copying Program

Since **getchar( )** reads the standard input and **putchar( )** prints to the standard output, Program 20-1 can copy a file if both input and output are redirected. Assuming that Program 20-1 is called **ez-copy**, then

```
ez-copy <file1 >file2
```

copies the contents of *file1* into *file2*. Further, Program 20-1 lists the contents of a file only if standard input is redirected, such as

```
ez-copy < file1
```

20.3 ACCESSING FILES

Before a program can directly access data stored in a file, the file has to be *opened*. This tells the operating system of the program's intention to use the file so the necessary resources can be allocated. It is actually the operating system that will locate and prepare the file, (even create it, if necessary) for use by our program.

Sec. 20.3   Accessing Files

The devices that store files and the operating systems that drive these devices are very different from one computer to the next. To increase portability, C uses a special **typedef** called FILE that contains all of the computer specific information needed to work with a file on a specific machine.[3] For example,

```
FILE *infile;
```

defines *infile* to be a pointer to type FILE (this definition only allocates space for a FILE pointer variable, it does *not* open the file).

To open a file, we must use the standard library function **fopen( )** and tell the operating system the file's name and how we intend to *use* the file. A file must be opened in a specific *mode*. There are three file modes, *read*, *write*, and *append*.

Opening a file in read mode requires that the file exist. If it doesn't already exist in the file system, **fopen( )** fails and returns NULL to denote an error condition. If **fopen( )** finds the file, it is opened and positioned at the beginning of the file. **fopen( )** then returns a FILE pointer to represent this now open file.

```
infile = fopen("datafile", "r") /* represents read mode */
```

A file opened in read mode can only be read by the program.

RULE   A file opened in read mode can only be read by the program.

Opening a file in write mode tells **fopen( )** to create the file, whether it presently exists or not. If the file exists it is effectively erased. In either case, the file is opened and positioned at the beginning of the file. **fopen( )** then returns a FILE pointer for the file. If **fopen( )** can't create the file (this would happen if there is no more space on the floppy disk), it returns NULL to denote an error condition.

Opening a file in append mode tells **fopen( )** to search for the named file and, if it is found, to open it and position the file pointer at the *end* of the file. This allows a program to add information at the end of a file without erasing the file. Appending doesn't erase the data presently in the file. If the file doesn't exist, **fopen( )** creates it. In either case, **fopen( )** returns a FILE pointer if it succeeds and NULL if an error occurs during the opening procedure. File opening information is displayed in Table 20-1.

TABLE 20-1   fopen( ) Modes

Open mode	Create file?	Position
"r"	No	Beginning
"w"	Yes	Beginning
"a"	No if file exists Yes otherwise	End

---

[3] FILE represents a data structure that contains the variables used to store the information on an open file. You can see what this data structure contains by looking in *stdio.h*.

fopen( ) is sent two arguments. The first is the name of the file to open. **fopen( )** expects a pointer to a string containing the filename. The second argument specifies the file opening mode. This is the *string* **"r"** for reading, **"w"** for writing, and **"a"** for append.

RULE   **fopen( )** modes are identified by a string (double quotation marks) not a character (single quotation marks).

Since **fopen( )** returns a pointer to FILE, it must be declared

```
FILE *fopen();
```

before it can be used properly. As an example, suppose we want to read the information in the file *rev-cost.88*. First, we must open the file in read mode. This is done in Segment 20-1.

```
#include "stdio.h"

main()
{
    FILE *fopen();
    FILE *infile;      /* input file pointer */
    int printf();

    if ((infile = fopen("rev-cost.88","r")) == NULL) {
        printf("Can't open rev-cost.88 file\n");
        exit(1)
    }
    /* file opened and ready */
    ...
}
```

Segment 20-1   Opening a File in Read Mode

To open *pl-stmt.88* in write mode (say, to write the results of **flex-pl** to a file), the **fopen( )** call is

```
fopen("pl-stmt.88", "w");
```

To open the file in append mode, the **fopen( )** call is

```
fopen("pl-stmt.88","a");
```

In the above **fopen( )** calls, we used a string constant for the file name argument. We also can use string variables. As an illustration, this will work too:

Sec. 20.4 What Is Opened Should Be Closed

```
            static char name[15] = "pl-stmt.88";

            fopen(name, "a");
```

Many versions of C contain additional **fopen( )** modes. One popular set allows for *updating* files. That is opening a file in a combined read and write mode. Update mode allows a program to read information in a file, as well as change or add to it.

Typically, there are three update modes denoted "r+" (read/update), "w+" (write/update), and "a+" (append/update). A file opened in "r+" mode, only opens existing files for updating. The "w+" mode creates a file upon opening it (erases existing files). The "a+" mode opens an existing file at the end or creates one if it doesn't exist. Table 20-1 has been amended in Table 20-2 to show these additional file modes.

TABLE 20-2 Additional **fopen( )** Modes

Open mode	Create file?	Position
"r"	No	Beginning
"w"	Yes	Beginning
"a"	No if file exists Yes otherwise	End
"r+"	No	Beginning
"w+"	Yes	Beginning
"a+"	No if file exists Yes otherwise	End

20.4 WHAT IS OPENED SHOULD BE CLOSED

Opening a file reserves system resources that are used as we work with the file. When we no longer need to access the file, these resources should be returned to the system for use elsewhere. In programming parlance, this is called *closing* a file. This not only frees the reserved resources but tells the computer to perform whatever clean-up is required, such as writing out any "left-over" characters and updating directory entries. C contains a standard library function, called **fclose( )**, which is used to close files. **fclose( )** is an **int** function. It is sent the FILE pointer, which identifies the file to close. Should any error occur, **fclose( )** returns EOF; otherwise, 0 is returned. To close the file opened in Segment 20-1, the **fclose( )** call is

```
            fclose(infile);    /* infile is a FILE * */
```

fclose( ) is used to close all files no matter what mode the files were opened in.

All open files are closed when a program terminates normally (i.e., when **exit( )** is called). It is not uncommon for C programmers to open files without explicitly closing them with **fclose( )**, waiting instead for the system to do it at program completion. Waiting for the system to close files can cause unforseen problems should the program fail unexpectedly. If the program fails before the file is closed, it is likely that the data in the file will be corrupted. We will always explicitly close files opened by our programs.

RULE   Every file opened in a program should be closed with **fclose( )**.

20.5 STANDARD FILE I/O FUNCTIONS

Once a file is open, we can *get* characters from it or *put* characters to it. In Chapter 17, we discussed the standard library functions **getchar( )**, **gets( )**, **scanf( )**, **putchar( )**, **puts( )**, and **printf( )**. Unfortunately, these functions only work with the standard input and standard output destinations.

The standard library contains an equivalent set of functions that perform the same tasks as the six standard I/O functions, except they operate on open files. Table 20-3 lists these functions.

TABLE 20-3   Standard File I/O Functions

	Read standard input	Write standard output	Read open file	Write open file
Single characters	**getchar( )**	**putchar( )**	**getc( )**	**putc( )**
Entire strings	**gets( )**	**puts( )**	**fgets( )**	**fputs( )**
Formatted text	**scanf( )**	**printf( )**	**fscanf( )**	**fprintf( )**

The functions listed in the right two columns of Table 20-3 closely resemble those in the left two columns. The main difference is that the functions on the right work with data files and those on the left assume that standard input and standard output are their destinations.

In most cases, the functions that read from or write to a file do the same things as their counterparts that work with standard input or output. In the following discussion, it is assumed the definition

```
FILE *filep;
```

is in scope and that *filep* points to a file opened in the appropriate mode.

Sec. 20.6   The **getc( )** and **putc( )** Functions

20.6 THE getc( ) AND putc( ) FUNCTIONS

getc( ) and **putc( )** read and write single characters. They are just like **getchar( )** and **putchar( )**, except **getc( )** reads from a file and **putc( )** writes to one. The file being read from or written to is identified by a FILE pointer sent to the functions as an argument. The expression

```
inchar = getc(filep)
```

returns the next character in the file *filep* and assigns it to *inchar* (an **int**). If there are no more characters available from the file, **getc( )** returns EOF. The **putc( )** function is sent two arguments, the character to write and the file to write it to. For example,

```
putc(outc, filep);
```

prints the character stored in *putc* to *filep*. **putc( )** returns the character printed or EOF if an error occurs (e.g., trying to write to a file opened in read mode). **getc( )** and **putc( )** are both **int** functions.

In Chapter 17, we wrote a simple program that read a character from the standard input and wrote it on standard output:

```
#include "stdio.h"

main()
{
    int inc;   /* character read from standard input */

    while ((inc = getchar()) != EOF)
        putchar(inc);
}
```

If we substitute **getc( )** for **getchar( )** and **putc( )** for **putchar( )**, we have a simple file-copying program. The only thing we have to add is a way to open and refer to the file being copied. This program is listed as Program 20-2. As an example of usage, Program 20-2 uses the **scanf( )** function to read the names of the files.

```
#include "stdio.h"

/* ***** File Copying Utility *****
 *
 * This program copies one file (infile) to another (outfile).
 *
 * Written by Ray Swartz for "Doing Business with C"
 */
```

```
main()
{
    FILE *infile;        /* File pointer of file being copied */
    FILE *outfile;       /* File pointer of new (copy) file */
    FILE *fopen();
    char filename[15];   /* file name variable */
    int inc;             /* input variable */
    int fclose();
    int scanf();
    int printf();
    int getc();
    int putc();

    printf("Enter name of file to be copied: ");
    scanf("%14s", filename);  /* limit name to size of variable */
    if ((infile = fopen(filename, "r")) == NULL) {
        printf("Can't open %s\n", filename);
        exit(1);  /* error in opening file */
    }
    printf("Enter name of file to hold copy: ");
    scanf("%14s", filename);  /* limit name to size of variable */
    if ((outfile = fopen(filename, "w")) == NULL) {
        printf("Can't open %s\n", filename);
        exit(1);  /* error in opening file */
    }
    while ((inc = getc(infile)) != EOF)   /* file copying loop */
        putc(inc, outfile);
    fclose(infile);
    fclose(outfile);
    exit(0);
}
```

Program 20-2 A Program to Copy Files

20.5 THE fgets( ) FUNCTION

Reading entire strings from a file is done with the **fgets( )** function. To read a string from an open file, the call to **fgets( )** is

fgets(str, nbr, filep);

where *str* is a pointer to a character array that will store what is read, *nbr* is an **int** that is the maximum number of characters to be stored in *str* (including the \0), and *filep* is a FILE pointer that identifies the file being read.

fgets( ) reads characters from the specified file until a *newline* is encountered or *nbr* − 1 characters have been read from the file. If a newline is read, it is stored in *str*.

Sec. 20.6   The **fputs( )** Function   355

In either case, *str* is terminated with \0. **fgets( )** returns *str* (a pointer to **char**) if all goes well and **fgets( )** is declared

```
char *fgets();
```

If an error occurs during the read, such as trying to read *past* the end of the file, **fgets( )** returns NULL.

RULE   If **fgets( )** reads a newline from a file the newline is stored in the string argument sent to **fgets( )**.

RULE   **fgets( )** returns NULL if any reading error occurs, including trying to read past the end of file.

The key to using **fgets( )** is realizing that *nbr* represents the maximum number of characters that can be *stored* in *str*. Since *str* must be terminated with '\0', **fgets( )** reads, at most, *nbr* − 1 characters.

There are two mistakes to avoid when using **fgets( )**. A common error is to send **fgets( )** a maximum that is 1 too small. Another common error is to test for reaching the end of the file by

```
if (fgets(str, nbr, filep) == EOF)
```

fgets( ) returns NULL to signify *any read error*, which includes reaching EOF.

RULE   **fgets( )** reads one less character than the number sent as the second argument.

20.6 THE fputs( ) FUNCTION

Writing entire strings to a file is done with the **fputs( )** function. To write a string to a file, the call is

```
fputs(str, filep);
```

where *str* is a pointer to the null-terminated string to be written and *filep* is a FILE pointer that identifies the destination file. Characters are written to the specified file until a \0 is found in *str*. The \0 is *not* written to the file. Unlike **puts( )**, **fputs( )** does *not* add a newline to its output. **fputs( )** is an **int** function that returns a value other than EOF if successful. Should any error occur, **fputs( )** returns EOF.

The file I/O functions **fgets( )** and **fputs( )** perform differently than the related **gets( )** and **puts( )** functions that work with the standard input and output. Because **gets( )** reads the standard input, which is commonly a keyboard, it assumes that a newline is the line terminating character. In the same way, **puts( )** writes to the standard output, usually a terminal screen, and adds a newline to the printed string for cursor control.

On the other hand, **fgets( )** reads files. To *accurately* report what is in the file, **fgets( )** returns all characters read, including *newlines*. For compatibility, **fputs( )** only writes exactly what is listed in its first argument, adding nothing.

20.7 THE fprintf( ) AND fscanf( ) FUNCTIONS

The **fprintf( )** function provides the same formatting capabilities as **printf( )** with the extension that **fprintf( )** writes to a file. In the same way, the **fscanf( )** function extends **scanf( )** to read from a file. Both **fprintf( )** and **fscanf( )** employ the same formatting conventions as their standard input and output relatives.

Both **fprintf( )** and **fscanf( )** must be sent a FILE pointer that identifies the open file to use. This **fprintf( )** call

```
co_name = "Acme Inc."      /* co_name is a pointer to char */
fprintf(filep, "Profit and Loss Statement for %s\n", co_name);
```

writes the string

```
Profit and Loss Statement for Acme Inc.
```

to the file identified by *filep*.

Exercise 20-1 Rewrite the **print_pl( )** function to write a P&L statement to a file called *pl-stmt*.

This **fscanf( )** call

```
fscanf(filep, "%s %ld", category, &amount);
```

reads a string of characters and a **long** value from the file represented by *filep*. The string is stored in the memory referred to by *category*, which must be a pointer to **char** with enough space to store the characters read (although this is not checked by **fscanf( )**). The **long** value read is stored in *amount*, which must be defined as a **long**. Note that a pointer to *amount* is passed to the function.

The space between the **%s** and the **%ld** in the format string tells **fscanf( )** to ignore any number of *white-space* characters in the file between the string and the numeric value read. Recall that whitespace is a space, tab, or newline. As an example, the **fscanf( )** call reads in this line

```
Sales          38987
```

this line

Sec. 20.8   The **feof( )** Macro   357

```
                          Sales
                          38987
```

or this one

```
                          Sales

                          38987
```

fprintf( ) and **fscanf( )** are both **int** functions. **fprintf( )** returns an EOF if an error occurs during output; otherwise, some other value is returned. In some implementations, **fprintf( )** returns the number of characters printed. **fscanf( )** returns the number of successful assignments performed or EOF if the end of the input file is read *before* the first assignment is made.

20.8 THE feof( ) MACRO

Reading information from a file can be tricky business. If an error occurs during the reading process, our programs must act accordingly. The problem is being able to differentiate between finding the end of the file and a true file error (e.g., a full disk or some hardware failure). All three file reading functions return a single value (NULL or EOF) if the end of file is found *or* an error has taken place.

For example, in Program 20-1, the file copy utility, the actual file copying is done in the loop:

```
            while ((inc = getc(infile)) != EOF)
                putc(inc, outfile);
```

An assumption is made in this program that when **getc( )** reports EOF, it has reached the end of the file and the copy is complete. However, **getc( )** also reports EOF if an error has occurred. At present, our program ignores this second possibility. In reality, there is little else we can do given the ambiguity of the **getc( )** return code.

To differentiate between reaching the end of a file and a reading error requires the use of a special macro called **feof( )**. The **feof( )** macro is defined in *stdio.h*. **feof( )** evaluates to true if an attempt has been made to read *past* the end of a file. Otherwise, it returns false.

By using **feof( )** in conjunction with **getc( )**, **fgets( )**, and **fscanf( )**, we can isolate the times when these functions are reporting an error when they return EOF or NULL. A read error has occurred when **feof( )** evaluates to false after a file input function returns an EOF or NULL. Segment 20-2 shows the copying loop from Program 20-1 changed to accommodate **feof( )**.

```
        while((inc = getc(infile)) != EOF)
            putc(inc, outfile); /* copying loop */
        if ( ! feof(infile)) {  /* false means not at EOF */
            printf("Read error on input file\n");
        fclose(infile);
```

Segment 20-2   Error Detection in File Copy Utility Program

Note that **feof( )** was tested *after* EOF is returned by **getc( )**. This is required because **feof( )** checks for attempts to read past the end of the file. This means **feof( )** returns false if the file is at the end but no attempt has been made to read past it.

RULE   The macro **feof( )** should be tested only after a file input function has returned EOF or NULL.

20.9 MAKING A STATEMENT

The current **flex-pl** program requires the user to enter all the revenue and cost information each time the program is run. If another copy of the profit and loss statement is needed, the data must be reentered We can simplify this process by storing the entered revenue and cost information in a data file. Then, if another statement is needed, the entries can be read from the file.

To implement reading and writing to files, the **flex-pl** will be split into two programs. The first, **get-pl**, gets the data from the keyboard and writes the revenue data into the file *revenue.dat* and the cost data into *cost.dat*. The second, **make-pl**, reads the data in *revenue.dat* and *cost.dat* and prints the profit and loss statement.

The two programs, **get-pl** and **make-pl**, do *not* have to be written from scratch. Instead, they can be created by modifying the **flex-pl** program. You can get **get-pl** from **flex-pl** by replacing the **print-pl( )** function with one that creates the *revenue.dat* and *cost.dat* data files. **make-pl** requires only that **getrev( )** and **getcost( )** be modified to read from a file, not the keyboard.

We designed the **flex-pl** program to use functions that perform the individual tasks required by the program. Now that we have changed the requirements of **flex-pl**, we see the value of this approach. We can make significant changes in how the program operates without having to rewrite the program. The design remains constant, we simply have to replace one function with another!

20.10 THE get-pl PROGRAM

We will start with the **get-pl** program because a data file must be created before it can be read. The first step in designing a program that writes into a file is to determine how the data will be stored in the file. Since what is written to the *revenue.dat* and *cost.dat* files must be read into a program later, we end each data line with a newline. This

Sec. 20.10 The **get-pl** Program

allows us to read the data easily with **fgets( )**. Further, each category entry will take up two lines—one for the category name and one for the amount. As an example, the data

```
                Sales: 38987
```

is stored as

```
                Sales
                38987
```

The function that creates the revenue and cost data file is called **mkfile( )**. **mkfile( )** will open a file in write mode, loop through the data structures writing each entry to the file, and then close the file when it is done. These steps must be done for both the revenue and cost entries.

We know how to open and close a file. Assuming the revenue structure is represented by the pointer *revenue* (passed in as an argument), the number of revenue entries by *rev_count*, and the output file by *outfile*, Segment 20-3 shows the loop that prints the data into the file.

```
        for (count = 0; count < rev_count; count++)
            fprintf(outfile, "%s\n%ld\n", revenue[count].category,
                    revenue[count].amount);
```

Segment 20-3   A Loop to Write Data to a File

The entire **mkfile** function is listed as Function 20-1.

```
/* ***** MKFILE *****
 *
 * This function creates the revenue.dat and cost.dat
 * files from structure arrays passed in as arguments.
 * The file format is for each entry to be listed on
 * two lines with the category name on the first
 * line.
 *
 * Written by Ray Swartz for "Doing Business with C"
 */
void mkfile(revenue, rev_count, cost, cost_count)
PL *revenue;          /* revenue entry array */
PL *cost;             /* cost entry array */
int rev_count;        /* number or revenue entries */
int cost_count;       /* number of cost entries */
{
    FILE *fopen();
    FILE *outfile;    /* open revenue or cost file */
    int count;        /* loop counter */
```

```
            int fprintf();
            int fclose();

            if ((outfile = fopen("revenue.dat", "w")) == NULL) {
               printf("Can't create revenue.dat file\n");
               return;
            }
            for (count = 0; count < rev_count; count++)
               fprintf(outfile, "%s\n%ld\n", revenue[count].category,
                       revenue[count].amount);
            fclose(outfile);
            if ((outfile = fopen("cost.dat", "w")) == NULL) {
               printf("Can't create cost.dat file\n");
               return;
            }
            for (count = 0; count < cost_count; count++)
               fprintf(outfile, "%s\n%ld\n", cost[count].category,
                       cost[count].amount);
            fclose(outfile);
            return;
      }
```

Function 20-1 The **mkfile( )** Function

Exercise 20-2 Function 20-1 doesn't check for write errors. Modify it to do so.

To change **flex-pl** into **get-pl** requires only two changes to **main( )**. The call to **print_pl( )** is replaced by

```
            mkfile(revenue, rev_count, cost, cost_count);
```

and **mkfile( )** must be declared

```
                  void mkfile();
```

20.11 THE make-pl PROGRAM

The **make-pl** program is created in much the same way as **get-pl**. We begin with **flex-pl** and exchange the two functions **getrev( )** and **getcost( )** with a single function that reads data from the appropriate file, **read_pl( )**. The reason we wrote separate functions to read the entered revenue and cost data was to allow each function to print what type of information was being entered. **getrev( )** asked for "Revenues" and **getcost( )** asked for "Costs".

Sec. 20.11   The **make-pl** Program

In **make-pl**, there is no interaction with the user and therefore no reason to have two input functions. We simply can call **read-pl( )** twice. We pass **read_pl( )** the filename to read and a counting variable. Like **getrev( )** and **getcost( )**, **read_pl( )** returns a pointer to type PL that is a pointer to the structure array holding the data read. **read_pl( )** is listed as Function 20-2.

```
/* ***** READ_PL *****
 *
 * This function reads revenue and cost entries from
 * a file whose name is passed to the function. The
 * number of entries read is stored in a variable
 * that is passed to the function as a pointer.
 * The function returns a pointer to a PL structure array.
 * Storage for the data read is created by calloc
 * and enlarged by realloc if necessary. The
 * #define macro ALLOC_NBR regulates the number
 * elements allocated each time.
 *
 * Written by Ray Swartz for "Doing Business with C"
 *
 */

PL *read_pl(filename, nbr)
char *filename;   /* data file to read */
int *num;         /* number of revenue categories entered */
{
    FILE *fopen();
    FILE *infile;          /* open file being read */
    PL *revptr;            /* returned pointer */
    PL *beginptr;          /* array pointer */
    char instr[BUFSIZ];    /* used to read amount string */
    char *calloc();
    char *realloc();
    char *strcpy();
    char *fgets();
    long atol();
    int strlen();
    int count = 0;         /* counter for revenue entries */
    int alloc_cnt = 1;     /* number of times memory allocated */

    if ((infile = fopen(filename, "r")) == NULL) {
        printf("Can't open file: %s\n", filename);
        return(NULL);
    }
    revptr = (PL *) calloc(ALLOC_NBR, sizeof(PL));
    if (revptr == NULL)
        return(NULL);      /* not enough memory */
```

```
      while (fgets(instr, BUFSIZ, infile) != NULL) {
        if (strlen(instr) >= MAX_LEN) { /* test category name length */
           printf("File error on file: %s\n", filename);
           printf("   Category name is too long\n");
           break;
        }
        strcpy(revptr[count].category, instr);
        if (fgets(instr, BUFSIZ, infile) == NULL) {
           printf("File error on file: %s\n", filename);
           printf("   Category name read without an amount\n");
           break;
        }
        revptr[count].amount = atol(instr);   /* convert amount */
        if (count + 1 >= alloc_count * ALLOC_NBR) {
           beginptr = (PL *) realloc( (char *) revptr,
                       ++alloc_count * ALLOC_NBR * sizeof(PL));
           if (beginptr == NULL) {
              printf("Out of memory reading file: %s\n", filename);
              break;
           }
           revptr = beginptr;   /* reassign array pointer */
        }
        count++;
      } /* end of reading while loop */
      if ( ! feof(infile)) {  /* check for file error */
         printf("Error has occurred reading file: %s\n", filename);
         return(NULL);
      }
      *num = count - 1;   /* don't count last (NULL) entry */
      return(revptr);
}
```

Function 20-2 The **read_pl( )** Function

The function checks for reading errors throughout and it may display multiple error messages. For example, if a non-EOF reading error occurs after a category is read, the message

```
              File error on file: filename
              Category name read without an amount
```

is printed. In addition, because the **feof( )** macro evaluates to false,

```
              Error has occurred reading file: filename
```

is displayed as well. In this case, too much is better than nothing at all!

In addition, we test to insure that the category name in the file will fit into a *category* structure member. Although we tested for this in **get-pl** before the data was

Sec. 20.11 The **make-pl** Program

written into the file, we retest here to make sure the data are correct. Because of the file format, someone could have changed the file with a text editor.

Unfortunately, there is a bug in Function 20-2. Recall that if **fgets( )** reads a newline in the file, it stores the newline in the string. This means that each category name has a newline at the end, which will cause formatting problems in the P&L statement. In addition, the newline makes each name one character longer which could cause a category name length error when, in fact, the name is the correct size.

The solution is to remove the newline from the input string before it is assigned into the structure. We can erase the newline by placing a \0 on top of it. Since the newline ends the string, it must be stored at

```
strlen(instr) - 1
```

We can remove the newline by

```
instr[strlen(instr) - 1] = '\0';
```

which should be added to **read_pl** just before the **strcpy** command.

To create **make-pl** from **flex-pl**, we have to make two changes to the **main( )** routine. First, **getrev( )** and **getcost( )** must be replaced by two calls to **read_pl( )**.

```
if ((revenue = read_pl("revenue.dat"; &rev_count)) == NULL) {
```

and

```
if ((cost = read_pl("cost.dat"; &cost_count)) == NULL) {
```

Second, **read_pl( )** must be declared:

```
PL *read_pl();
```

Program 20-3 lists the **get-pl** program and Program 20-4 lists **make-pl**. Only the functions that have been modified are shown.

```
/* ***** GET-PL *****
 *
 * This program reads the category and amount of a
 * set of revenues and costs and stores them in a
 * file for use later.  The revenues are stored in
 * revenue.dat and the costs in cost.dat.  An entry
 * is stored on two lines in a file with the category
 * name stored first.
 *
 * Written by Ray Swartz for "Doing Business with C"
 *
 */
```

```c
#define MAX_LEN 31        /* maximum length of a category entry */
#define ALLOC_NBR 5       /* number of entries allocated */

#include "stdio.h"
#include "getcat.c"       /* source code for getcat function */

int printf();

typedef struct {          /* can handle both revenue and costs */
    char category[MAX_LEN];  /* category name */
    long amount;             /* category amount */
} PL;

main()
{
    PL *revenue;          /* points to an array of revenue entries */
    PL *cost;             /* prints to an array of cost entries */
    PL *getrev();         /* read all revenue entries */
    PL *getcost();        /* read all cost entries */
    int rev_count;        /* number of revenue categories */
    int cost_count;       /* number of cost categories */
    void mkfile();        /* print the entered data to file */

    if ((revenue = getrev(&rev_count)) == NULL) {
        printf("Not enough memory for revenue entries\n");
        exit(1);
    }
    if ((cost = getcost(&cost_count)) == NULL) {
        printf("Not enough memory for cost entries\n");
        exit(1);
    }
    mkfile(revenue, rev_count, cost, cost_count);
    exit(0);
}

/* The getrev() and getcost() function are unchanged */

#include "getrev.c"
#include "getcost.c"

/* ***** MKFILE *****
 *
 * This function creates the revenue.dat and cost.dat
 * files from structures passed in as arguments.
 * The file format is for each entry to be listed in
 * two lines with the category name on the first line.
 *
 * Written by Ray Swartz for "Doing Business with C"
 */
```

Sec. 20.11 The make-pl Program

```c
void mkfile(revenue, rev_count, cost, cost_count)
PL *revenue;       /* structure array for revenue entries */
PL *cost;          /* structure array for cost entries */
int rev_count;     /* number of revenue entries */
int cost_count;    /* number of cost entries */
{
    FILE *fopen();
    FILE *outfile;    /* open revenue or cost file */
    int count;        /* loop counter */
    int fprintf();
    int fclose();

    if ((outfile = fopen("revenue.dat", "w")) == NULL) {
        printf("Can't open revenue.dat file\n");
        return;
    }
    for (count = 0; count < rev_count; count++)
        fprintf(outfile, "%s\n%ld\n", revenue[count].category,
                revenue[count].amount);
    fclose(outfile);
    if ((outfile = fopen("cost.dat", "w")) == NULL) {
        printf("Can't open cost.dat\n");
        return;
    }

    for (count = 0; count < cost_count; count++) {
        fprintf(outfile, "%s\n%ld\n", cost[count].category,
                cost[count].amount);
    fclose(outfile);
    return;
}
```

Program 20-3 The get-pl Program

```c
/* ***** MAKE-PL *****
 *
 * This program reads the category and amount of a
 * set of revenues and costs from the revenue.dat
 * and cost.dat files respectively, and prints a
 * profit and loss statement from them.  An entry
 * is stored on two lines in a file with the category
 * name stored first.
 *
 * Written by Ray Swartz for "Doing Business with C"
 */

#define MAX_LEN 31      /* maximum length of a category entry */
#define ALLOC_NBR 5     /* number of entries allocated */

#include "stdio.h"

int printf();
```

```c
typedef struct {         /* can handle both revenue and costs */
    char category[MAX_LEN];  /* category name */
    long amount;             /* category amount */
} PL;

main()
{
    PL *revenue;         /* points to an array of revenue entries */
    PL *cost;            /* prints to an array of cost entries */
    PL *read_pl();       /* read entries from data file */
    int rev_count;       /* number of revenue categories */
    int cost_count;      /* number of cost categories */
    void print_pl();     /* print the P&L statement */

    if ((revenue = read_pl("revenue.dat", &rev_count)) == NULL) {
        printf("Not enough memory for revenue entries\n");
        exit(1);
    }
    if ((cost = read_pl("cost.dat", &cost_count)) == NULL) {
        printf("Not enough memory for cost entries\n");
        exit(1);
    }
    print_pl(revenue, rev_count, cost, cost_count);
    exit(0);
}

/* ***** READ_PL *****
 *
 * This function reads revenue and cost entries from
 * a file whose name is passed to the function.  The
 * number of entries read is stored in a variable that
 * is passed to the function as a pointer.  The function
 * returns a pointer to a PL structure array.  Storage
 * for the data read is created by malloc and enlarged
 * by realloc, if necessary.  The #define macro ALLOC_NBR
 * regulates the number of element allocated each time.
 *
 * Written by Ray Swartz for "Doing Business with C"
 */

PL *read_pl(filename, nbr)
char *filename;    /* data file to read */
int *num;          /* number of revenue categories entered */
{
    FILE *fopen();
    FILE *infile;          /* open file being read */
    PL *revptr;            /* array pointer */
    PL *beginptr;          /* returned pointer */
    char instr[BUFSIZ];    /* used to read amount string */
```

Sec. 20.11 The make-pl Program

```c
    char *calloc();
    char *realloc();
    char *strcpy();
    char *fgets();
    long atol();
    int  strlen();
    int  count = 0;        /* counter for revenue entries */
    int  alloc_cnt = 1;    /* number of times memory allocated */

    if ((infile = fopen(filename, "r")) == NULL) {
        printf("Can't open file: %s\n", filename);
        return(NULL);
    }
    revptr = (PL *) calloc(ALLOC_NBR, sizeof(PL));
    if (revptr == NULL)
        return(NULL);      /* not enough memory */
    while (fgets(instr, BUFSIZ, infile) != NULL) {
        instr[strlen(instr) - 1] = '\0';  /* remove newline */
        if (strlen(instr) >= MAX_LEN) { /* test name length */
            printf("File error on file: %s\n", filename);
            printf("   Category name is too long\n");
            break;
        }
        strcpy(revptr[count].category, instr);
        if (fgets(instr, BUFSIZ, infile) == NULL) {
            printf("File error on file: %s\n", filename);
            printf("   Category name read without an amount\n");
            break;
        }
        revptr[count].amount = atol(instr);  /* convert amount */
        if (count + 1 >= alloc_count * ALLOC_NBR) {
            beginptr = (PL *) realloc( (char *) revptr,
                    ++alloc_count * ALLOC_NBR * sizeof(PL));
            if (beginptr == NULL) {
                printf("Out of memory reading file: %s\n", filename);
                break;
            }
            revptr = beginptr;  /* reassign array pointer */
        }
        count++;
    }
```

```
        if ( ! feof(infile)) {    /* check for file error */
            printf("Error has occurred reading file: %s\n", filename);
            return(NULL);     /* possible function return */
        }
        *num = count - 1;     /* don't count last (NULL) entry */
        return(revptr);
}

/* The print_pl program is unchanged */
```

Program 20-4   The make_pl( ) Program

20.12 SUMMARY

1. C provides a programming environment that guarantees a device exists to send the program input and to take the program's output.
2. Typically, C's environment allows redirection of the standard input and standard output devices.
3. To access a data file, that file must be opened by the program.
4. A data file is represented inside a program by a variable defined as a pointer to type FILE.
5. The **fopen( )** function opens a file, named in the function's first argument, for access in a specific mode. **fopen( )** returns a pointer to FILE.
6. The file opening modes are reading, writing, or appending. The file opening mode is specified as **fopen( )**'s second argument.
7. The standard library provides six functions to read from and write to files. These functions read and write a single character, whole lines, and formatted lines.
8. The character reading function is **getc( )** and the character writing function is **putc( )**.
9. The string reading function is **fgets( )** and the string writing function is **fputs( )**.
10. The formatted reading function is **fscanf( )** and the formatted writing function is **fprintf( )**.
11. The **fclose( )** tells the system a file is no longer needed by a program. Every open file should be closed with **fclose( )**.
12. The file reading functions return a single value if the end of the file has been read or an error has occurred during reading. To distinguish these two conditions, the **feof( )** macro is supplied. **feof( )** returns false if the file is not past EOF (error occurred) and returns true if an attempt has been made to read past the EOF.

EXERCISES

20-3. Modify both **get-pl** and **make-pl** to prompt for the names of the files that hold the revenue and cost data.

20-4. At present, the revenue and cost entries are stored in different files. Modify both **get-pl** and **make-pl** so that revenue and cost entries are stored in a single file.

20-5. Modify **flex-pl** to allow the user to write the data entered into a file, if desired. The program should print a P&L statement on the standard output in either case.

20-6. Write a single P&L printing program that asks the user whether the revenue and cost data will be entered from the keyboard or from a file. The program should prompt if reading from the keyboard and get the file name and read from the file otherwise. In essence, this program will combine the **flex-pl** and **make-pl** programs.

20-7. Write a program that reads the information required to write a series of checks. This data should be written to a file. Be sure to verify the information entered for each check.

20-8. Write a program that reads the file created by Exercise 20-7. This program should list a check on the terminal screen, ask the user if this check should be printed, and then print the check on a printer (use a file if a printer is not available). *NOTE*: Check with the system administrator or the system documentation to find out how to open the printer as a file. Once opened, the printer can be treated as any other file.

21

Command Line Arguments

All the programs we have written so far have prompted for data or read it from a file. C contains another way to pass information to a program, command line arguments. In addition to redirecting standard input and output, another feature of the C programming environment is providing access to whatever is typed on the command line. Command line information is sent to our programs in much the same way arguments are passed to a function.

Before we can refer to command line arguments, we must declare to **main()** that we intend to use them.

The information on the command line is passed to **main** in a two-dimensional character array. The operating system creates the command line arguments by separating the command line at whitespace (space and tab) characters. The operating system also sends **main()** the argument count.

21.1 argv AND argc

Up to now, we have always labeled a **main()** routine with empty parentheses, for example,

```
main()
```

Sec. 21.1 **argv** and **argc**

To receive command line information, we must declare that 2 arguments will be passed to **main( )**: a two-dimensional character array, *argv*, and an argument count, *argc*.

```
main(argc, argv)
int argc;        /* number of command line arguments */
char *argv[];    /* the actual command line arguments */
```

argv is declared as an array of pointers to **char**. Each pointer in the *argv* array points to one of the command line arguments stored as a string.

As an illustration, consider Program 20-2, which copies the contents of one file to another. As written, this program, which we will call **copy**, reads the names of the files from *stdin* (after prompting on *stdout*). Another way to design the program is to have it read the filenames from the command line. The first argument is the source file (one being copied) and the second one the destination. To copy *pldata.87* to the file *pl87.bak*, as a backup, the command line is

```
copy pldata.87 pl87.bak
```

Note that the arguments are separated by white space.

When **copy** is invoked, all the information entered on the command line is stored in the *argv* array. The program name is always stored in *argv*'s first element (*argv[0]*). Thus, for every program, *argc* (the argument counter) will be at least 1 (the program name). Figure 21-1 shows the contents of *argv* and *argc* after the above command line call to **copy**.

```
argc: 3

argv[0]: copy
argv[1]: pldata.87
argv[2]: pl87.bak
```

Figure 21-1 *argv* and *argc* Status

In reality, *argv* holds pointers to the listed strings.
In Program 20-2, we read the name of the source file into the variable *filename* and opened the file with

```
if ((infile = fopen(filename, "r")) == NULL)
```

In our command line version, we open the source file with

```
if ((infile = fopen(argv[1], "r")) == NULL)
```

and the destination file with

```
                if ((outfile = fopen(argv[2], "w")) == NULL)
```

Before we do this, however, we must insure that two filenames were listed on the command line. Otherwise, we are sending random (i.e., unallocated) pointers to the **fopen( )** function and our program will fail. This is where *argc* comes in. We should only try to open the files using *argv*'s elements if *argc* equals 3. Otherwise, the user has sent the wrong number of arguments to **copy**. Thus, before opening the files we must test

```
        if (argc != 3) {
            printf("Usage: copy source-file destination-file\n");
            exit(1);
        }
```

The error message is simply a reminder of proper usage. The command line **copy** program is listed as Program 21-1.

```
/* ***** File Copying Utility *****
 *
 * This program copies one file (infile) to another (outfile)
 * taking the filenames off the command line.
 *
 * Written by Ray Swartz for "Doing Business with C"
 */

#include "stdio.h"

main(argc, argv)
int argc;
char *argv[];
{
    FILE *infile;       /* File pointer of file being copied */
    FILE *outfile;      /* File pointer of new file (copy) */
    FILE *fopen();
    int inchar;         /* input variable */
    int fclose();
    int printf();
    int getc();
    int putc();

    if (argc != 3) { /* command line args in error */
        printf("Usage: copy source-file destination-file\n");
        exit(1);
    }
    if ((infile = fopen(argv[1], "r")) == NULL) {
        printf("Can't open %s\n", argv[1]);
        exit(1);    /* error in opening file */
    }
```

Sec. 21.1   argv and argc

```
        if ((outfile = fopen(argv[2], "w")) == NULL) {
            printf("Can't open %s\n", argv[2]);
            exit(1);   /* error in opening file */
        }
        while ((inchar = getc(infile)) != EOF)   /* file copying loop */
            putc(inchar, outfile);
        fclose(infile);
        fclose(outfile);
        exit(0);
    }
```

Program 21-1   Copy Program that Reads Command Line

Exercise 21-1   Modify the **flex-pl** program to take the name of the revenue and cost input files off the command line.

Program 21-1 uses constants to reference the *argv* array elements. We can also treat *argv* as a pointer, incrementing it to step through the command line arguments. *argv* points to the beginning of an array of char pointers. These pointers, in turn, locate the actual arguments. This means that

```
                            *argv
```

can be substituted for

```
                            argv[0].
```

Unfortunately, we don't usually care about *argv*'s first element (the program name). To access the first command line argument (*argv[1]*), we must increment *argv* to point to it. We can do this by

```
                        argv = argv + 1;

                        argv += 1;
```

or

```
                            argv++;
```

However, it is common to use a prefix operator in the first reference to *argv*:

```
        if ((infile = fopen(*++argv, "r")) == NULL)
```

The expression

```
                            *++argv
```

increments the pointer before performing the indirection (unary operators associate right to left).

21.2 READING ARGUMENTS FROM THE COMMAND LINE

One problem with the **copy** program is that it provides no overwriting protection. If the destination file exists, the file's contents are replaced by **copy**. Overwriting files is one way valuable information gets lost.

We don't want to stop **copy** from overwriting files since this is a legitimate copying operation. Instead, we should add an argument that tells **copy** to check if the destination file exists *before* it performs the copy. If the argument does not appear on the command line, the copy is made regardless of the existence of the destination file.

The "checking" argument must be distinguishable from the filename arguments. By convention, options listed on the command line start with a -. The argument we will send to **copy** will be a **-x**. Also, to make implementing this option easier, we will require that the **-x** appear as the first argument only.

Determining if a file exists is done by trying to open the file in read mode. Recall that **fopen( )** fails if an attempt is made to open a nonexistent file in read mode. This extended **copy** program is listed as Program 21-2.

```
/* ***** File Copying Utility *****
 *
 * This program copies one file (infile) to another (outfile)
 * taking the filenames off the command line.
 * In addition, if a -x appears as the first argument,
 * the program checks if the destination file exists.
 * If the file exists, the command terminates without
 * performing the copy.
 *
 * Written by Ray Swartz for "Doing Business with C"
 */

#include "stdio.h"

#define YES 1
#define NO 0

main(argc, argv)
int argc;
char *argv[];
```

Sec. 21.2   Reading Arguments from the Commmand Line

```
    {
        FILE *infile;           /* source file */
        FILE *outfile;          /* destination file */
        FILE *fopen();
        int inchar;             /* input variable */
        int fclose();
        int printf();
        int getc();
        int putc();
        int exist_flag = NO;    /* YES if -x on command line */

        if (argc < 3 || argc > 4) { /* command line args in error */
            printf("Usage: copy [-x] source-file destination-file\n");
            exit(1);
        }
            if (strcmp(*++argv, "-x") == 0) { /* test first argument */
                exist_flag = YES;
                argv++;  /* go to next argument */
            }
        if ((infile = fopen(*argv, "r")) == NULL) {
            printf("Can't open %s\n", *argv);
            exit(1);  /* error in opening file */
        }
            argv++;       /* next argument is destination file */
            if (exist_flag == YES) {
                if (fopen(*argv, "r") != NULL) {
                    printf("Copying error: %s exists\n", *argv);
                    printf("File copy not made");
                    exit(2); /* distinguish from open error */
                }
            }
        if ((outfile = fopen(*argv, "w")) == NULL) {
            printf("Can't open %s\n", *argv);
            exit(1);  /* error in opening file */
        }
        while ((inchar = getc(infile)) != EOF)
            putc(inchar, outfile);  /* file copying loop */
        fclose(infile);
        fclose(outfile);
        exit(0);
```

Program 21-2 File-Checking Copy Program

In Program 21-2, the command line arguments are referenced by pointer indirection. This is required since the first argument might be **-x** or the source file's name. Thus, when we open the source file, we use the location referenced by *argv*. If **-x** is the first argument, we increment past it after doing the required processing.

Exercise 21-2 At present, Program 21-2 terminates if the destination file exists and the **-x**-option is listed. Modify Program 21-2 to inform the user if the destination file exists (and the **-x**-option is listed) and then ask if the copy should be made anyway.

Incrementing *argv* is possible because it is a local variable. This approach is valuable for programs that don't know the order of their command line arguments and must search through the list.

Program 21-2 contains a small error. The error message printed if the wrong number of arguments is listed on the command line is

```
printf("Usage: copy [-x] source-file destination-file\n");
```

This assumes the name of the program is **copy**. If the program has been renamed, this message is no longer accurate. Instead, it is better to use the name listed on the command line. Recall that the program name is stored in *argv[0]*. The correct error message is

```
printf("Usage: %s [-x] source-file destination-file\n", argv[0]);
```

21.3 SUMMARY

1. A C program can read the information typed on the command line when the program is invoked.
2. This information is passed to the **main( )** routine as two arguments, an **int** that is the number of arguments passed and a pointer to an array of **char** pointers that reference the actual argument strings.
3. By convention, *argc* is used to represent the argument count and *argv* the **char** pointer array.
4. Every program is passed at least one argument, which is the program name.
5. The command line arguments can be referred to in a number of ways.
6. In situations where we don't know the order of the command line arguments, we can increment the local variable *argv* to step through them.

E X E R C I S E S

21-3. At present, we can only use **copy** to make a single copy of a file. Modify it to also print a copy to the standard output if a **-s** is entered on the command line. For simplicity, assume that **-s** must be the first argument if it is to be used at all and that the **-x** is not allowed.

21-4. Extend the program written in Exercise 21-3 to allow the **-x** option as well as **-s** and that either option can anywhere on the command line.

21-5. Modify the **make-pl** program to read the filenames of the revenue and cost input files from the command line. If no filenames are listed on the command line, have the program prompt the user for them.

21-6. Modify **make-pl** to read more than one file holding revenue or cost data. The category names of all the entries in the second or more revenue or cost data files are checked against those already read in. If a match is found, for example, if two files both have a Sales Income category, these categories are combined into one. The data files are to be specified on the command line with '**-r**' preceding a revenue filename and '**-c**' a cost filename. Thus, the command

```
make-pl -rrev.1-88 -rrev.2-88 -ccost.1-88 -ccost.2-88
```

will create a P&L statement for the first 2 months of 1988.

PART 9
Additional Language Features

22

Additional C Features

22.1 NUMERIC CONSTANTS

All the numeric constants used in this book are treated as decimal values. C also allows numeric constants to be listed in octal or hexadecimal. To specify an octal constant, a zero is put in front of the number. For example,

```
0177
```

is the octal constant 177 (127 in decimal).

A hexadecimal constant is specified by putting a zero and an 'x' in front of the value. For example,

```
0x2a
```

is the hexadecimal constant 2a (42 in decimal).

Octal and hexadecimal constants are treated the same as decimal constants. They can be assigned to variables and printed by **printf( )**. The **printf( )** formatting code for printing an octal value is **%o**. The **printf( )** formatting code for printing a hexadecimal value is **%x**. Both of these codes are for **unsigned** integers. For printing **unsigned long** values, use **%lo** for octal and **%lx** for hexadecimal.

22.2 POINTERS TO FUNCTIONS

Along with pointers to data, C also allows *pointers to functions*. Pointers to functions are not conventional pointers but instead represent all the information required to invoke a specific function.

Function pointers are created by the compiler whenever a function's name is used in a way that is *not a function call*, that is, the reference to the function's name doesn't contain parentheses. Function pointers can be manipulated or stored in an appropriately defined variable, array element, or structure member.

Defining a variable to be a pointer to a function is similar to defining other pointers. The data type of such a variable is the type returned by the function. For example, to define the variable *functptr* to be a pointer to a function returning an **int** requires

```
int (*functptr)();   /* pointer to function return int */
```

The parentheses are required because without them the compiler would think we were declaring a function returning a pointer to **int**, for instance,

```
int *functptr();    /* function returning pointer to int */
```

C treats function names much the same as array names, that is, the function name by itself is evaluated as a pointer to the function. Thus, we can point *functptr* at the function **atoi( )** by

```
functptr = atoi;   /* no parentheses makes atoi a pointer */
```

atoi( ) must be declared as a function before we can reference it in this manner.

Once *functptr* is equated to **atoi( )**, we can use it to convert a string into an integer. The call to **atoi( )** is

```
atoi(str);
```

The equivalent call to *functptr* is

```
(*functptr)(str);
```

We can assign what the function returns by

```
value = (*functptr)(str);
```

22.3 ENUMERATION TYPES

In Chapter 7, we wrote a program called **chk-inv** which reads in a series of book purchases, calculates the amount of discount this customer receives, and then prints the invoice total. **chk-inv** recognizes five types of customers:

High volume retail
Wholesale
High volume wholesale
Mail order company
High volume mail order

To represent these inside a program, we might use this set of macros

```
#define HV_RETAIL 1
#define WHOLESALE 2
#define HV_WHOLESALE 3
#define MAIL_ORDER 4
#define HV_MAIL_ORDER 5
int cust_type;    /* type of customer */
```

In essence, we are trying to create a type of data that has only a few specifically *enumerated* values. Although defining macros is one way to do this, it has a serious shortcoming. If we mistakenly assign the wrong value to *cust_type* (6 or larger), neither the preprocessor nor the compiler will complain. This can be a very difficult error to find.

Other programming languages, notably PASCAL and ADA, provide a way to define a special data type whose values can be explicitly identified. Then, if a value outside this permissible range is assigned to a variable of this data type, the compiler flags it as an error. In this way, their proper use is enforced by the compiler.

A similar feature has recently been added to the C language. These special data types are called *enumerated types* and the keyword **enum** was introduced to identify such constructs.

Enumerated types are declared by listing all possible values. Once the data type is declared, we have to define variables to be of that type.

Declaring an **enum** is similar to the declaration of a structure where the structure's members resemble the enumerated values. Also, as with structures, enumerated types can be given an optional tag. This tag identifies the now declared data type for use in defining variables.

As an example,

```
enum customer {hvr, wh, hvw, mo, hvmo};
```

declares *customer*, the tag, to be an enumerated type consisting of five *enumerators*: *hvr, wh, hvw, mo, hvmo*. The braces and terminating semicolon are required. This only

Sec. 22.3   Enumeration Types

declares a template. To use it, we must define variables to be of type *customer*.

```
enum customer cust_type;
```

Note that the keyword **enum** (like **struct**) is required when defining variables that are an **enum** type. As with structures, we can combine the **enum** declaration with the variable definition.

```
enum customer {hvr, wh, hvw, mo, hvmo} cust_type;
```

In addition, enumerated variables can be defined without tagging the enumerated type, for instance,

```
enum {hvr, wh, hvw, mo, hvmo} cust_type;
```

This prevents us, however, from defining other variables of this type.

Once *cust_type* is defined to be of type *customer*, it can only be assigned the values *hvr*, *wh*, *hvw*, *mo*, and *hvmo*. *cust_type* can also be tested for being equal to any of the values in its enumeration list. As an example, once the *customer* type has been declared and *cust_type* is defined to be of that type, this assignment is legal:

```
cust_type = hvwh;
```

This test, and those similar, is legal also:

```
if(cust_type == hvr)
```

The scope of enumerated variables is the same as any other variable—the block where it is defined. As such, enumerated variables can have external, static, register, or automatic storage.

Enumerators are treated as integer constants. Unless otherwise specified, the first enumerator in an enumeration list is assigned the value 0. The following enumerators are given values incremented by 1 through the list. In the *customer* type, *whr* is assigned 0, *wh* is assigned 1, etc. This can be changed by assigning a different integer value to one or more of the enumerators. For example, this declaration sets *wh* to 6 and *mo* to 10:

```
enum {hvr, wh = 6, hvw, mo = 10, hvmo} cust_type;
```

Now, *hvw* is assigned the *wh* value incremented 1 (7) and *hvmo* is assigned 11.

This has a perverse effect. Once established, the enumeration list can be bypassed entirely through the direct use of their integer values. Thus,

```
customer = 0;
```

instead of

```
              customer = hwr;
```

is accepted by the compiler. However, if this is done, it is questionable whether **enum**s should be used at all.

Not all compilers have implemented **enum** types. Of those that have, not all perform the necessary type checks whenever **enum**s variables are assigned a value. For this reason, caution is advised when using enumerated variables.

22.4 UNIONS

In the **flex-pl** program, we used data type **long** to represent the category amounts. Some amounts may need to be stored exactly to the penny. One way to do this is to use **double** variables. Unfortunately, this requires us to use two variables to store one value. C offers another way to do this.

By using a special construct called a *union*, we can create a variable that can store *both* a **long** and a **double** using only one variable! Conceptually, a union is similar to a structure. It has members which must be declared in the same way as a structure's members. The only difference is in the use of the keyword **union** instead of **struct**.

The one important distinction between unions and structures is that a structure's members are all stored in *separate* memory locations whereas a union puts all of its members in the *same* storage space. As a result, a union can represent any one of its members; however, it can only store one of them at a time! It is usage that determines which one is being referenced.

As an example, let's create a union for the category amount variable that can handle a **long**, as well as a **double**. The declaration is

```
              union cat_amt {
                  long l_amt;
                  double d_amt;
              };
```

Once this union is declared, we can define a variable to be of this type by

```
              union cat_amt amount;
```

As expected, these two steps can be combined into one.

To access the information stored in *amount*, we must specify which format is to be used, **long** or **double**. This is done with the member operator (also familiar from structures). To refer to *amount* as a **long** requires

```
              amount.l_amt
```

If a **double** is necessary

```
              amount.d_amt
```

is used.

Sec. 22.4   Unions

Once declared as part of a union, both members coexist in the same piece of memory. We can refer to either member, even interchange them, as the program progresses. C makes no attempt to enforce consistency of usage and it is up to the programmer to ensure that information stored in a union is referred to in the proper format.

A union can contain as many members as needed and the compiler allocates enough storage to hold the largest member. In addition, pointers to members can be defined. When in doubt, check the syntax and usage rules of structures for guidance.

As a final union illustration, Segment 22-1 shows what the *PL* **typedef** would look like if *amount* is a union.

```
union pl_amt {
    long l_amt;
    double d_amt;
};

typedef struct {
    char category[MAX_LEN];
    union pl_amt amount;
} PL;
```

Segment 22-1   PL Declaration with a Union

In most cases, an additional variable is required so the program can determine what type of data is stored in the union variable. For example, we might define

```
int amt_type;
```

which is set to either

```
#define LONG 0
```

or

```
#define DOUBLE 1
```

To use a union with the **getlong( )** function requires some rewriting. Recall that **getlong( )** returns the amount entered as a **long**. To allow the function to handle both **long**s and **double**s, it must be changed to store the entered amount in the appropriate structure or (union) member. Otherwise, the function would have to return different data types and this isn't allowed.

Let's assume that we have created a function called **l_or_d( )** which returns the macro **LONG** if its string argument doesn't contain a decimal point and **DOUBLE** if it does. Further, suppose that the *PL* structure being entered is referred to by *revptr*, which is defined *PL* ∗. Inside **getlong( )** this code could be used to perform the proper conversion

```
        if (l_to_d(instr) == LONG)
            revptr->amount.l_amt = atol(instr);
        else
            revptr->amount.d_amt = atof(instr);
```

Caution should be exercised when using unions. Neither the compiler nor the program will complain if we retrieve a **long** value from *amount* even though a **double** was just stored there. In addition, unions are hard to document because their use is context sensitive.

22.5 THE goto STATEMENT AND LINE LABELS

Although C is considered to be a structured language, it does contain three nonstructured commands. All three cause an *unconditional* jump to a specific spot in a program. The **break** and **continue** commands are used within loops (and, in the case of **break**, with the **switch** command) to skip over certain parts of the loop's body. These have been demonstrated previously.

The third member of this trio is the **goto** statement. When executed, it jumps to a specified statement somewhere in *the present function block* regardless of structure boundaries. The target statement is identified through the use of a *line label*.

Line labels are like variable names followed by a colon. As an example, the label *end_fnct* identifies a **return** statement:

```
            end_fnct: return;
```

Line labels need not be declared before use and can occur before they are referred to.

A **goto** statement includes the keyword **goto** and a location label. This command

```
                goto end_fnct;
```

would cause the function to return immediately by jumping to *end_fnct* and executing **return**.

RULE   **goto** commands can only transfer control to a line within the same function.

One of the underlying tenets of structured programming is that all computer programs can be written without using **goto** statements. For this reason, no demonstration of this statement will be shown in the text and it is recommended that the **goto** command *never* be used. It is included here for the purposes of completeness only.

Unlike the unrestricted **goto**, which can jump into, out of, or over any and all structure that exists in a function, the **break** and **continue** commands have tightly defined usage whose scope covers a single structure only. However, they too are unconditional jumps. Should they ever be used? Some say all three commands should not be put in a C program under any condition. Others suggest that clearly documented

break, **continue**, and **goto** statements can make programming easier. Again, choose a style and be consistent in its application.

22.6 RECURSION

In C, a function can be called by any other function, but can a function be called by itself? As we know, in C every function call is a local event. A function has its own set of variables that are local to that instance of the function. In addition, arguments are passed by value and can be considered "private" copies, as well. It is because of this isolation that functions can call themselves. Functions that do so are referred to as *recursive*.

It may seem odd that a recursive function can do anything valuable. Wouldn't it simply keep calling itself creating an infinite loop? This is a real danger with these types of functions, which dictates a general design consideration: All recursive functions must have an explicit stopping rule, usually called a *base case*. Recursive functions are useful when the problem at hand can be solved by successive applications of a simple algorithm to a decreasing data set.

In business application programming, recursive functions are rarely, if ever, needed. As a result, recursive programming techniques will not be explained further. Recursion is mentioned for the sake of completeness only.[1]

22.7 BITWISE OPERATORS

At the very lowest level, the data stored inside a computer, no matter what its purpose, is encoded as a series of ones and zeros. This mimics the on/off nature of underlying electric impulses that actually move through the machine.

Because only two digits are used, this encoding is called the *binary numbering system* and each piece of storage holds a *binary digit*. In computer parlance, a binary digit is called a *bit*. These basic units are used at the machine language level.

In most cases, all this detail is hidden from us by the compiler. On occasion, however, it is useful to have access to the individual bits that make up a memory location, for example when manipulating the attributes of characters on the display screen (e.g., colors on the terminal), sending information out a hardware port, or performing other machine-specific actions. In addition, we may need to use smaller units of storage than provided by C's data types.

As a rule, the smallest chunk of memory available to C programmers is a **char**, which generally contains at least eight bits. This means that we must use at least eight bits to store binary information such as true or false. Moreover, using an **int** would cost us more memory. Although this is wasteful, we don't get charged by the bit. Generally there is more than enough memory in the computer to handle our needs; some

---

[1] For a full discussion of creating recursive C functions see "A Book on C" by Al Kelley and Ira Pohl, Benjamin-Cummings, 1984.

applications, however, require huge tables of true/false data. Using **int**s for these tables can mean running out of memory while the program is executing.

Again, the designers of C provided an insightful solution to the problem. They included a set of special operators that can manipulate individual bits in C's integer data types, **int, short, long, unsigned** and **char**. These are called *bitwise operators*.

For people doing system programming, machine interfacing, or simply playing around in the operating system, these operators provide the memory access needed without forcing them to write machine language code. However, in everyday business usage, the need for these operators is rare.

Bitwise operators, like most of C's operators, represent single machine language instructions available on virtually all modern computers. In addition, they fall into two categories, logical operators and shift operators. The symbols and names of all bitwise operators are listed in Table 22-1.

TABLE 22-1 C's Bitwise Operators

Name	Symbol
One's complement	~
Logical AND	&
Logical OR	|
Exclusive OR	^
Left shift	<<
Right shift	>>

Table 22-2 shows an updated precedence table.

TABLE 22-2 Precedence Table Including Bitwise Operators

Operator	Associativity
() [] . ->	Left to right
++ -- (type) ~ * & ! sizeof	Right to left
* / %	Left to right
+ -	Left to right
<< >>	Left to right
< <= >= >	Left to right
&	Left to right
^	Left to right
|	Left to right
&&	Left to right
||	Left to right
== !=	Left to right
= += -= *= *etc.*	Right to left
,	Left to right

22.8 ONE'S COMPLEMENT OPERATOR

C has a special operator, the one's complement operator, that converts a value into its one's complement representation. It is symbolized by ~ (tilde) and is a unary operator with the attendant precedence and associativity. It can be used on any **int** constant or expression. Thus,

~ 1

and

~ (value - 6)

are both valid expressions, as long as *value* is an **int**.

Incidentally, taking the one's complement of a binary number, say

00100101   (37 in base 10)

is accomplished by changing all 0s to 1s and visa versa. The outcome would be

11011010   (218 in base 10)

22.9 BITWISE LOGICAL OPERATORS

Logical operations have only two results, true or false, which can be implemented in binary notation by representing 1 as true and 0 as false. This means that an **int** stored in memory can be seen as a string of true and false values.

C provides operators to manipulate memory in such a way through the use of *bitwise logical operators*. The three operations available are *logical and*, *logical or*, and *exclusive or*. These are binary operators requiring **int** operands which are evaluated bit by bit to an **int** result. The symbols used are

Logical AND	&
Logical OR	|
Exclusive OR	^

The most common way to show the effects of these actions is by tables. The *logical and* evaluates to 1 (true) only if both operands are 1:

Logical AND

0 & 0 = 0
0 & 1 = 0
1 & 0 = 0
1 & 1 = 1

The *logical or* is 1 if at least one operand is 1:

Logical OR

0 & 0 = 0
0 & 1 = 1
1 & 0 = 1
1 & 1 = 1

The *exclusive or* is 1 *only if one* of the operands is 1:

Exclusive OR

0 & 0 = 0
0 & 1 = 1
1 & 0 = 1
1 & 1 = 0

The most common use of these operators is in *masking* bits in stored values. An **int** variable can hold a series of 1/0 flags instead of a numeric value. We use the *logical and* operator to extract the condition of a flag in the variable and the *logical or* to set a flag. As an example, Segment 22-2 lists some macros that might be used as masks to test flags.

```
#define HV_RETAIL 1         /* high volume retail */
#define WHOLESALE 2
#define HV_WHOLESALE 4      /* high volume wholesale */
#define MAIL_ORDER 8
#define HV_MAIL_ORDER 16    /* high volume mail order */
```

Segment 22-2 Sample Masking Values

The masks listed in Segment 22-2 could be used to identify the status of a customer. As Table 22-3 shows, the macros take values that are powers of two. Each mask macro has been assigned to one of the right-most five bits in an **int**.

Sec. 22.9   Bitwise Logical Operators   389

TABLE 22-3 Mask Macros Listed Numerically

Macro	Binary	Decimal
HV_RETAIL	1	1
WHOLESALE	10	2
HV_WHOLESALE	100	4
MAIL_ORDER	1000	8
HV_MAIL_ORDER	10000	16

Masks work by isolating an individual bit in a memory location. Recall that any non-0 value will be evaluated as true in C. Thus, the expression

```
if (cust_type & HV_RETAIL)
```

will evaluate to true if *cust_type* has a 1 in the digits (right-most) spot and false otherwise. No other bits are tested because HV_RETAIL is represented by

```
...0000001
```

and the *logical and* is 0 if at least one bit is 0. The other masks in Segment 22-2 work in a similar fashion. Note that the test

```
if (cust_type & WHOLESALE)
```

works because if *cust_type* has a 0 in the spot being tested the result of the operation is 0 (false). If it had a 1 there, it would evaluate to true. By the way, this works too:

```
if ((cust_type & WHOLESALE) == WHOLESALE)
```

It will only be true if the proper bit in *cust_type* is set to 1.

In the same way, a bit can be set in a flag variable by the *logical or* operator. This expression

```
cust_type | HV_RETAIL
```

evaluates to the numeric value that turns on the HV_RETAIL bit, although it doesn't store the value anywhere. Again, the only bit affected is the one opposite the 1 in the mask. Any bit set to 1 in *cust_type* will remain set.

All binary bitwise operators have equivalent assignment operators. As a result, the statement that sets the HV_RETAIL flag and stores the result back in *cust_type* can be written

```
cust_type = cust_type | HV_RETAIL;
```

or

```
                    cust_type |= HV_RETAIL;
```

For obvious reasons, it is vitally important that the bitwise operators, **&** and **|**, and the logical operators, **&&** and **||**, not be confused. This is a common cause of many programming errors.

22.10 SHIFTING OPERATORS

Implementing multiplication and division on a computer using the binary numbering system can be complicated. However, by using the right operations it can be done fairly easily.

Dividing or multiplying by 10 is done simply by moving the decimal point around. To multiply by 10 we shift the number left once and add a 0 on the right as we do this. Division by 10 is done by shifting the digits once to the right while keeping the decimal point in the same place. To multiply or divide by 100, the same thing is done twice.

This works because 10 is the base, or *radix*, of our numbering system. These operations can be performed this way whenever we use the *radix* of a number system. Thus, in a binary system, multiplying or dividing by 2 can be done by shifting.

C provides operators for shifting bits both left and right in memory. The symbols used for each are

| Shift left | << |
| Shift right | >> |

These are binary operators requiring the **int** variable to be shifted and the number of shifts to perform. The expression

```
                         nbr >> 3
```

evaluates to the value that results when bits in *nbr* are shifted to the right three times.

In a left shift, 0s are "shifted" in and the bits on the left (high order bits) are lost for good. In a right shift, the bits on the right (low-order bits) are lost and, depending on how the specific machine works, either 1s or 0s will be shifted into the left hand bits. The shift operation is also referred to as *rotating* left and right.

22.11 BIT FIELDS

When we are working with the individual bits inside a variable, we can directly manipulate them with shifting and logical operators. This is relatively easy if we are working with single bits flags only. However, we may choose to combine several bits into a single value. This would allow us to represent something with more than two values.

Sec. 22.11 Bit Fields

As an example, suppose we wanted to make sure that each invoice was within the customer's credit limit. Instead of using a separate variable for this information, we can store it in the unused bits of the *cust_type* variable. The customer type masks only use the five right-most bits in *cust_type*. Assuming *cust_type* is a thirty-two-bit integer (a machine dependent assumption), we have twenty-seven bits of storage for the credit limit. Twenty-seven bits can hold up to 128 million. Figure 22-1 shows how *cust_type* is allocated.

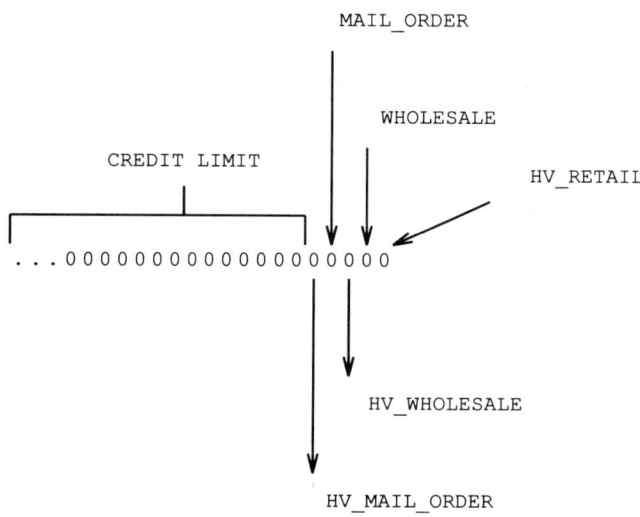

Figure 22-1 Individual Bit Usage in *cust_type*

C has a structure-like construct, called *bit fields*, which allows us to define a variable as a series of individual bits. As an illustration, Segment 22-3 defines *cust_type* as a bit field variable.

```
struct cust {
    unsigned int hv_retail:1;
    unsigned int wholesale:1;
    unsigned int hv_wholesale:1;
    unsigned int mail_order:1;
    unsigned int hv_mail_order:1;
    unsigned int credit_limit:27;
} cust_type;
```

Segment 22-3 Declaring Bit Fields

The length of the bit field assigned to each member is declared after a colon. Further, *cust* is the structure tag and can be used to define additional variables of this type. Here we have declared the bit field structure and defined *cust_type* to be of that type. Bit fields can be any *int* data type. *unsigned* is used to avoid the assignment of a sign bit.

The members of a bit field are referenced just like those in any other structure. We can use either the member operator:

```
cust_type.hv_retail = 1;
```

or the structure pointer operator:

```
cust_ptr->credit_limit = 234543;
```

Also, assignments of values larger than can be stored by the declared number of bits are undefined. Other data types can be intermingled with a structure that has bit fields in it.

There are some things that are not allowed. We cannot declare bit field arrays inside a single structure. Also, pointers to individual bit fields and trying to find their addresses is not legal.

It cannot be emphasized strongly enough that all operations on bits are machine-dependent and not portable. For this reason, they should only be used in applications where absolutely necessary and those which will not be moved, or better yet, not at all.

RULE   All bitwise operators should be treated as machine-dependent operations.

22.12 SUMMARY

1. Pointers to functions allow functions to be treated like data.
2. Enumeration types allow a data type to be declared that specifically lists all the elements that can be represented.
3. Elements in an enumerated type are given names that represent integer values.
4. Unions provide a way to combine variables in the same memory location. Unions are declared and defined just like structures. However, unions can store only one of its members at a time.
5. The compiler doesn't keep track of what data type is stored in a union at present. It is up to the programmer to refer to the data properly.
6. The **goto** statement allows program control to be unconditionally transferred to a line label anywhere in the current function.
7. Since a function call is a local event, a C function can call itself. Such a function is called recursive.
8. C provides several operators that can directly manipulate bits, the individual binary digits that are stored inside the computer.
9. C also allows structures to have members made from a set number of bits. These members are called bit fields.

A

The ASCII Character Set

Character	Octal	Decimal	Hexadecimal
nul	0	0	0
soh	1	1	1
stx	2	2	2
etx	3	3	3
eot	4	4	4
enq	5	5	5
ack	6	6	6
bel	7	7	7
bs	10	8	8
ht	11	9	9
nl	12	10	a
vt	13	11	b
np	14	12	c
cr	15	13	d
so	16	14	e
si	17	15	f
dle	20	16	10
dc1	21	17	11
dc2	22	18	12
dc3	23	19	13

Character	Octal	Decimal	Hexadecimal
dc4	24	20	14
nak	25	21	15
syn	26	22	16
etb	27	23	17
can	30	24	18
em	31	25	19
sub	32	26	1a
esc	33	27	1b
fs	34	28	1c
gs	35	29	1d
rs	36	30	1e
us	37	31	1f
space	40	32	20
!	41	33	21
"	42	34	22
#	43	35	23
$	44	36	24
%	45	37	25
&	46	38	26
'	47	39	27
(	50	40	28
)	51	41	29
*	52	42	2a
+	53	43	2b
,	54	44	2c
-	55	45	2d
/	57	47	2f
0	60	48	30
1	61	49	31
2	62	50	32
3	63	51	33
4	64	52	34
5	65	53	35
6	66	54	36
7	67	55	37
8	70	56	38
9	71	57	39
:	72	58	3a
;	73	59	3b
<	74	60	3c
=	75	61	3d
>	76	62	3e
?	77	63	3f
@	100	64	40
A	101	65	41
B	102	66	42
C	103	67	43
D	104	68	44
E	105	69	45

Appendix A

Character	Octal	Decimal	Hexadecimal
F	106	70	46
G	107	71	47
H	110	72	48
I	111	73	49
J	112	74	4a
K	113	75	4b
L	114	76	4c
M	115	77	4d
N	116	78	4e
O	117	79	4f
P	120	80	50
Q	121	81	51
R	122	82	52
S	123	83	53
T	124	84	54
U	125	85	55
V	126	86	56
W	127	87	57
X	130	88	58
Y	131	89	59
Z	132	90	5a
[	133	91	5b
\	134	92	5c
]	135	93	5d
^	136	94	5e
_	137	95	5f
`	140	96	60
a	141	97	61
b	142	98	62
c	143	99	63
d	144	100	64
e	145	101	65
f	146	102	66
g	147	103	67
h	150	104	68
i	151	105	69
j	152	106	6a
k	153	107	6b
l	154	108	6c
m	155	109	6d
n	156	110	6e
o	157	111	6f
p	160	112	70
q	161	113	71
r	162	114	72
s	163	115	73
t	164	116	74
u	165	117	75
v	166	118	76

Character	Octal	Decimal	Hexadecimal
w	167	119	77
x	170	120	78
y	171	121	79
z	172	122	7a
{	173	123	7b
|	174	124	7c
}	175	125	7d
~	176	126	7e
del	177	127	7f

B

The EBCDIC Character Set

Character	Octal	Decimal	Hexadecimal
nul	0	0	0
soh	1	1	1
stx	2	2	2
etx	3	3	3
pf	4	4	4
ht	5	5	5
lc	6	6	6
del	7	7	7
smm	12	10	a
vt	13	11	b
ff	14	12	c
cr	15	13	d
so	16	14	e
si	17	15	f
dle	20	16	10
dc1	21	17	11
dc2	22	18	12
tm	23	19	13
res	24	20	14

Character	Octal	Decimal	Hexadecimal
nl	25	21	15
bs	26	22	16
il	27	23	17
can	30	24	18
em	31	25	19
cc	32	26	1a
cu1	33	27	1b
ifs	34	28	1c
igs	35	29	1d
irs	36	30	1e
ius	37	31	1f
ds	40	32	20
sos	41	33	21
fs	42	34	22
byp	44	36	24
lf	45	37	25
etb	46	38	26
esc	47	39	27
sm	52	42	2a
cu2	53	43	2b
enq	55	45	2d
ack	56	46	2e
bel	57	47	2f
syn	62	50	32
pn	64	52	34
rs	65	53	35
uc	66	54	36
eot	67	55	37
cu3	73	59	3b
dc4	74	60	3c
nak	75	61	3d
sub	77	63	3f
space	100	64	40
¢	112	74	4a
<	114	76	4c
(	115	77	4d
+	116	78	4e
|	117	79	4f
&	120	80	50
!	132	90	5a
$	133	91	5b
*	134	92	5c
)	135	93	5d
;	136	94	5e
¬	137	95	5f
-	140	96	60
/	141	97	61
,	153	107	6b

Appendix B

Character	Octal	Decimal	Hexadecimal
%	154	108	6c
–	155	109	6d
>	156	110	6e
?	157	111	6f
:	172	122	7a
#	173	123	7b
@	174	124	7c
=	176	126	7e
"	177	127	7f
a	201	129	81
b	202	130	82
c	203	131	83
d	204	132	84
e	205	133	85
f	206	134	86
g	207	135	87
h	210	136	88
i	211	137	89
j	221	145	91
k	222	146	92
l	223	147	93
m	224	148	94
n	225	149	95
o	226	150	96
p	227	151	97
q	230	152	98
r	231	153	99
s	242	162	a2
t	243	163	a3
u	244	164	a4
v	245	165	a5
w	246	166	a6
x	247	167	a7
y	250	168	a8
z	251	169	a9
A	301	193	c1
B	302	194	c2
C	303	195	c3
D	304	196	c4
E	305	197	c5
F	306	198	c6
G	307	199	c7
H	310	200	c8
I	311	201	c9
J	321	209	d1
K	322	210	d2
L	323	211	d3
M	324	212	d4

Character	Octal	Decimal	Hexadecimal
N	325	213	d5
O	326	214	d6
P	327	215	d7
Q	330	216	d8
R	331	217	d9
S	342	226	e2
T	343	227	e3
U	344	228	e4
V	345	229	e5
W	346	230	e6
X	347	231	e7
Y	350	232	e8
Z	351	233	e9
0	360	240	f0
1	361	241	f1
2	362	242	f2
3	363	243	f3
4	364	244	f4
5	365	245	f5
6	366	246	f6
7	367	247	f7
8	370	248	f8
9	371	249	f9

C

The ANSI C Standard

C was first introduced to the world in 1978 by the book *The C Programming Language* by Brian Kernighan and Dennis Ritchie. Since this book was published, C has been implemented on a number of computers. For the most part, these implementations are faithful to the language specification contained in the Kernighan and Ritchie book.

As C has become a very popular programming language, the demand for C compilers has grown. In the years since 1978, several extensions have been added to C and some problems have arisen as C is implemented on machines that offer more or less functionality than required by C's basic assumptions.

In the summer of 1983, the ANSI (American National Standards Institute) X3J11 committee met for the first time to begin the process of specifying a C standard. The committee's purpose was first to codify existing practice where possible and to clarify areas where there were incompatibilities between implementations. Second, in areas where there was no clear existing practice, the committee's job was to establish clear and unambiguous rules consistent with the rest of the language.

The committee established a set of working rules to insure that the standard would appeal to a wide audience. One problem faced by the committee was the large body of C code already written, installed, and working. First, the committee wanted to "break" as little existing C code as possible. Further, the committee wanted to provide programmers with an opportunity to write portable programs (but not force them to!). Last, the committee wanted to preserve the "spirit" of C, which they felt was expressed in these statements:

> Trust the programmer.
>
> Don't prevent the programmer from doing what needs to be done.
>
> Keep the language small and simple.
>
> Make it fast even if it isn't guaranteed to be portable.

As of this writing (March, 1987), the X3J11 committee has published a draft standard for public comment, one of the last steps before final acceptance of the standard by ANSI. It is expected that the committee's work will become an official ANSI standard by 1989.

Most of what is covered in this book is part of standard C. However, a number of changes and extensions have been made. The purpose of the appendix is to explain the key features of the ANSI C standard.

C.1 FUNCTION PROTOTYPES

One of the easiest mistakes to make in a C program is to call a function with improper arguments. We might send too many or too few arguments or arguments of the wrong data type. A program containing such an error will compile successfully but fail in some unpredictable way. As a result, this error must be located by the programmer (or some debugging aid) and can be very hard to find.

The standard committee wanted to shift the burden of finding function-calling errors from the programmer to the compiler. To do this, the committee added *function prototypes* to the language. A function prototype is a function declaration that includes number, type, and order of the function's arguments, how many arguments the function will be passed, and each argument's data type.

For example, in the text, the **getcat( )** function is defined with

```
long getcat(catstr, class)
char *catstr;      /* holds entered category name */
char *class;       /* Revenue or Cost */
```

To define **getcat( )** with a function prototype definition (a function definition contains the source code of the function) requires combining the data types of the formal parameters with their names inside the parentheses after the function's name, for instance,

```
long getcat(char *catstr, char *class)
```

Note that the parameters no longer are declared under the function name.

A similar change is required for function declarations. Function prototype declarations include the number of arguments listed in the proper calling order, as well as each argument's data type. For example, the function prototype for **getcat( )** is

Sec. C.1 Function Prototypes

```
long getcat(char *, char *)
```

If desired, a prototype declaration can contain "dummy" parameter names, such as

```
long getcat(char *category_var, char *revenue_str)
```

Parameter names appearing in prototype declarations have very limited scope (to the end of the prototype declaration only) and are used for documentation purposes only.

If a function prototype is in scope for a function and that function is called with an argument list that doesn't contain the proper number of arguments, the compiler will report an error. If a function argument is the wrong data type, it is converted *as if through assignment* to the declared type. However, the data type of the argument and data type specified in the prototype must be assignment compatible.

As an example, the **print_pl( )** function would be declared

```
void print_pl(char rev_cat[] [MAX_LEN], long *rev_amt,
          int rev_count, char cost_cat[] [MAX_LEN],
          long *cost_amt, int cost_count);
```

Now, no matter what the data type of the arguments sent for *rev_count* or *cost_count*, the values received by the function will be **int**s (subject to assignment compatibility). The conversion to **int** is as if the arguments listed are assigned to *rev_count* and *cost_count* before the function is called.

Declaring function prototypes for the functions we create is straightforward. However, what about declaring functions from the standard library? Specifically, what about functions that take no arguments and those that take a variable number of arguments? Functions that take no arguments are identified by an argument list of **void** only, for example,

```
int getchar(void);
```

Functions that take a variable number of arguments must contain the notation ... (an ellipsis) where any number of arguments might be listed. For example, the **printf( )** function always has at least one argument, the format string. Depending on what is being printed, a **printf( )** call may have several additional parameters. To declare this fact, **printf( )** is declared

```
int printf(char *, ...);
```

Before function prototypes could be incorporated into C, the standard committee had to solve a serious problem. If prototypes were required, all present C programs would break (since none of them contain prototypes).

The committee's solution is to continue to allow "old-style" function definitions and have the compiler create a function prototype from them. The compiler will do this if a prototype declaration is in scope for the function defined in the old style. The key to this solution is using global function prototype declarations contained in header files.

Thus, if the file *stdio.h* lists prototype declarations for each function in the standard library (or **#include**s files that do), recompiling a program with an ANSI standard compiler works![1]

If no function prototype declaration exists for a function, as is currently the case for existing C programs, the compiler will create one from the function call. For example, if a function is called by

```
funct ("test", a, 3.46);
```

and no prototype is in scope for **funct( )**, the compiler uses

```
int funct (char *, long, double);
```

as the prototype (assuming the data type of *a* is **long**).

A function has no prototype if it is undeclared (auto-type **int**) or if the function is declared with a data type and empty parentheses, as in

```
long getcat( );
```

The Standard sets additional rules for functions without prototype declarations. First, the Standard requires that such functions contain a fixed number of arguments only. Second, default widening rules apply, converting arguments into **int**, **long**, or **double**. Third, the compiler will not check for data type or argument count agreement between the function call and the function definition.

C.2 REMOVING RESTRICTIONS

Originally, the C language contained two restrictions on arrays, structures, and unions. Automatic arrays, structures, and unions could not be initialized when defined. Second, only two operations could be performed on a structure, referring to a member (the . operator) and finding its address (the **&** operator).

The ANSI Standard removes both of these restrictions. Automatic arrays and structures can be initialized just like their **static** and global counterparts. Also, structures can be assigned to one another (providing they are the same type), sent to functions as arguments, and returned by a function. One operation *not* allowed is the comparison of two structures, even if they are the same data type.

C.3 NEW ARITHMETIC FEATURES

A new data type, **long double** and a new type modifier, **signed**, were added to C. **signed** represents an integer type. The major application of the keyword **signed** is in

---

[1] Refer to Appendix D to see what files need to be **#include**d for each standard library function.

Sec. C.3 New Arithmetic Features

dealing with **char**s. Some computers use **signed char**s and the **signed** data type provides the ability to represent them exactly.

long double is a third floating-point data type along with **float** and **double**. Some computers can represent more than two floating-point types and **long double** was introduced to provide more flexibility for programmers of those machines.

The type **long double** is useful only if the machine at hand can represent data in a format that offers more precision than data type **double**. Otherwise, **long double** refers to the same size data as **double**. This is much the same as with **int** and **long**.

Previously, C allowed only integer, **long**, and **double** constants. To provide more flexibility, the standard committee expanded this to include **float, long double**, and **unsigned** constants. Recall that any integer constant followed by **l** or **L** is stored as a **long** value. In the same way, any integer constant followed by **u** or **U** is stored as an **unsigned int**. A floating-point constant is stored as **float** if followed by **f** or **F** and **long double** is followed by **l** or **L**. For example,

```
23U                       /* an unsigned constant */

648292736UL               /* an unsigned long constant */

14.554F                   /* a float constant */

1.23832873625272L         /* a long double constant */
```

C has long been criticized for the way it handles arithmetic. Previously, all calculations are performed as **int**, **long**, or **double**. Thus, the expression

```
float value1 = 2.0 ;
float value2 = 2.0 ;
float total;

total = value1 * value2;    /* in essence 2 * 2 */
```

would be carried out in **double** precision. With the addition of **float** constants and the **long double** data type, the standard committee decided to have C perform arithmetic operations in either of the floating-point data types, *so long as the answer would be the same in all three*. This allows programmers concerned with execution speed to use **float** while programmers concerned with precision can use **long double**.

Up to now, the numeric characteristics of the compiler, such as the largest number representable or integer size, were found in the documentation, if at all. To further aid numerical analysis in C, the committee established two special header files, *float.h* and *limits.h*. The macros in these header files define the numerical environment of a C compiler. The *float.h* file contains macros that define the floating-point characteristics of the compiler. As an example, *float.h* contains macros that represent the largest and smallest number that can be stored in a **float, double** and **long double**, among many others. *limits.h* contains similar information for the integers and character data types.

C.4 TWO NEW KEYWORDS HELP PUT DATA IN ITS PROPER PLACE

The C language described by Kernighan and Ritchie stored string constants like any other character array. This means quoted strings are not really constants but can be modified! Further, some of today's computers have special "read only" sections of memory that not only guarantee that constants remain constants but also speed up references to such data.

The handling of string constants in a C program was addressed in two ways by the standard committee. First (after a great deal of debate), they decided that string constants could not be modified. Second, two new keywords were added to specify how certain kinds of data are to be handled by the computer.

Making string constants truly constant breaks existing code. To provide relief for programmers who modify string constants in their already working code, the committee said that a common extension is to allow string constants to be modifiable.

Another change was made in the handling of string constants. To make string substitution easier, the standard instructs compilers to concatenate string constants that are adjacent, that is, if two string constants are next to one another, the compiler will make one string out of them. As an example, if

```
#define CO_NAME "Acme, Inc."
```

then the statement that results from

```
printf("Profit and Loss Statement for " CO_NAME);
```

is

```
printf("Profit and Loss Statement for " "Acme, Inc.");
```

which becomes

```
printf("Profit and Loss Statement for Acme, Inc.");
```

A new keyword, **const**, was introduced to identify variables that are not to be modified. **const** is a *type modifier*, not a distinct data type. However, a variable defined as **const** only is assigned a data type of **int**. A variable defined

```
const float value = 5.21;
```

cannot be modified in the program. Note that **const** variables can be initialized. In fact, that's the only way they can be assigned a value!

All data types can be specified as **const**. Further, specific members within a structure or union can be identified as **const**, as well.

Sec. C.4   Two New Keywords Help Put Data in Its Proper Place

The committee also allowed non-**const** pointers to **const** variables and **const** pointers to non-**const** variables. Unfortunately, the syntax of these definitions can be confusing.

```
const int *pntr_to_const;
```

defines *pntr_to_const* to be a pointer to **const int** (note that **const** is to the left of **int**). This means the pointer *pntr_to_const* can be modified but that the memory location (or locations) it refers to cannot be modified.

```
int *const const_pntr;
```

defines *const_pntr* to be a constant pointer to a changeable **int** variable (note **const** is to the left of the variable name). Thus,

```
*const_pntr = 5;
```

is legal since it is assigning a value to the memory location where the (constant) pointer points.

A non-**const** pointer *cannot* be assigned a pointer to a **const** variable without an explicit cast. For example,

```
int *const const_pntr;
int *ptr;

ptr = const_pntr;          /* not legal */
ptr = (int *) const_pntr;  /* required */
```

Undoubtedly, it is possible to create a bizarre set of declarations and definitions involving **typedef**s, **const** pointers, and pointers to **const** that could get around the intent of the **const** specifier. The standard does *not* require that a compiler find every attempt to modify memory defined to be **const**. However, a quality compiler will try to find as many as it can.

Since C was created, computer technology has advanced in giant leaps. A portable program may be used in a completely different environment than the one it was originally written for. As an example, many of today's computers can perform more than one task concurrently and provide segments of memory that can be shared by two or more of these concurrently executing programs. In such an environment, memory locations referred to by variables in one program could be changed by actions taken by another program with access to the same (shared) memory!

As an example, consider this code segment:

```
while (wait_flag == 0)
    ;
```

This **while** loop is infinite if *wait_flag* equals 0 and never performed if it doesn't. However, suppose that *wait_flag* is a shared memory variable and that this loop is used to synchronize this program with another one currently running. Then, the purpose of this loop is to wait until the other program changes the value stored in *wait_flag*.

A "smart" compiler might issue a warning or an error if the above code segment is encountered. Worse yet, the compiler might even "optimize" this code and remove the loop entirely!

To handle these situations, a new keyword, **volatile**, was added to C. Like **const**, **volatile** is a type modifier. Variables defined to be **volatile** are identified as referring to memory locations whose contents may change independently of the operation of this program. Any operation on a **volatile** variable must be performed exactly as stated in the program. No optimization is to be done on what may appear to be programming errors or inefficiencies.

Note that **const** variables or pointers can also be **volatile**

```
volatile const long flag = 0 ;
```

Further, assigning a **volatile** pointer to a non-**volatile** pointer requires a cast. By the way, the definition says that *flag* is a constant in this program but refers to memory that may be changed by some other program.

C.5 POINTERS

Computers use many different methods for referring to memory. This may cause a portability problem whenever a pointer to one data type has to be assigned to a pointer of another type. On one machine, these two pointers may be compatible and on another they may not be.

To solve this problem, the standard committee introduced the concept of a **void** pointer (**void***). Also, the committee stated that pointers to different data types are not *assignment compatible*, that is, an explicit cast must be used every time a pointer is assigned a value other than a pointer to the same data type.

The purpose of the **void** pointer is to allow pointers to be moved around without fear of creating assignment errors. A pointer can be assigned to a **void** pointer and back again without error. If

```
int *nbr;
char *word;
void *vptr;
```

then these assignments are legal

Sec. C.6   New Preprocessor Features   409

```
                    vptr = word;
                    word = vptr;
                    word = (char *) nbr;
                    nbr = (int *) word;
```

and these assignments are *illegal*

```
        vptr = nbr;
        word = vtpr;    /* legal but result uncertain */

        word = nbr;     /* cast required */

        nbr = word;     /* cast required */
```

The macro NULL is used to represent an uninitialized pointer or a pointer that doesn't reference an actual memory location. As a result of the changes in pointer compatibility, NULL has been redefined as

```
                            (void *) 0
```

Another pointer portability problem is how to universally represent the difference between two pointers. A common C programming approach is to subtract one pointer from another to determine their relative position in an array or how many elements are in a segment of an array.

The data type of this result depends on the data type used to specify pointers on a particular system. To make the data type of the difference of two pointers portable, the committee introduced the *prtdiff_t* data type. This **typedef** is defined in the *stddef.h* header file. As an example, in

```
                    prtdiff_t size;
                    char *str1, *str2;

                    size = str1 - str2;
```

prtdiff_t is defined as a signed integral type (i.e., an **int** or **long**).

C.6 NEW PREPROCESSOR FEATURES

Several additional features were added to the C preprocessor. First, taking advantage of the new string concatenation rule (two adjacent string constants are concatenated into one string constant), the standard adds two new string creating capabilities. Both of these features can be used when defining a macro that takes arguments.

If the character # is listed before one of the macro's arguments in the macro definition, then that argument is converted into a string constant. For example, if

```
#define pr(a) printf("Company Name: " # a)
```

then

```
pr("Acme, Inc.);
```

results in

```
printf("Company Name: Acme, Inc.");
```

The same operation can be performed to paste together variables. When two non-quoted strings are separated by ## in a macro definition, those two strings are pasted together to form a single variable name. For example, if

```
#define prx(a) printf("x" # a " = %d\n", x ## a)
```

then

```
prx(1);
```

results in

```
printf("x1 = %d\n", x1);
```

Two new preprocessor directives, **#error** and **#pragma**, were also added. **#error** instructs the compiler to produce a message that includes the text following **#error**. This directive is useful in trying to identify where compilation errors are occurring.

The second directive, **#pragma**, provides a way to extend the power of the compiler in a standard, through a compiler-defined way. The line following **#pragma** causes the compiler to perform whatever operation those tokens specify for this compiler. If the **#pragma** line is not recognized by the compiler, it is treated as a comment.

A preprocessor that conforms to the standard will allow *benign redefinition* of macros. Previously, if a macro appeared in more than one **#define** directive within the same scope (i.e., source code file), the compiler would most likely fail with a macro redefinition error. Benign redefinition occurs when a macro appears in more than one **#define** directive but it is always defined the same way. As an example, if

```
#define MAX_CAT 30
```

appeared in the header file, *pl.h*, and

```
#define MAX_CAT 30
```

appeared in the source code file, then if *pl.h* is **#include**d in the source code, benign redefinition occurs. This is now allowed by the standard.

Sec. C.7 Additional Features

How can a programmer write quality code without knowing if the compiler conforms to the standard? To answer this question, the standard uses predefined macros. One of these predefined macros is **_STDC_** (two underscores on each side). If this equates to 1, the compiler conforms to the standard. This allows conditional compilation to account for differences between standard and non-standard compilers.

```
#ifdef _STDC_
        double getdbl(char *);

#else
        double getdbl();

#endif
```

There are four other predefined names. They are

LINE	Current source code line number (number)
FILE	Current source code file name (string)
DATE	Date this file was compiled (mmm dd yyyy)
TIME	Time this file was compiled (hh:mm:ss)

C.7 ADDITIONAL FEATURES

In addition to the above, the standard added a special character constant to represent an alarm. This character constant is \a, which causes either an audible (a beep) or visible (a blink) alarm. In addition, a hexadecimal constant can now be explicitly defined with \x###, where ### represent the digits 0–9, and the letters a–f and A–F.

The data type that the **sizeof** operator evaluates to dictates the maximum size of an array. To insure portability, a special **typedef** is defined by each compiler that identifies the unsigned integral data type of the **sizeof** operator. This **typedef** is **size_t** and it is **#define**d in the header file *stddef.h*

Also in the *stddef.h* file is the macro **offsetof( )**. The **offsetof( )** macro evaluates to the number of bytes from the beginning of a structure that a member is stored. The first argument is the name of the structure and the second argument is the name of the member in question. Thus,

```
offsetof(revenue, REV)
```

is the number of bytes from the beginning of the REV structure that the variable *revenue* is stored.

For the standard to be international, it must handle problems of international languages and customs. As an example, different countries represent the date and time in different formats. Further, languages contain different characters that sort in less than obvious ways.

The standard specifies a set of functions and structures that handle these international problems in a portable way. A special header file, *locale.h*, was created to hold a set of "locale-specific" macros:

LC_ALL	All locale-specific characteristics
LC_COLLATE	The local collating sequence
LC_CTYPE	Designates *ctype.h* characteristics
LC_NUMERIC	Identifies decimal point character
LC_TIME	Identifies time and date format

These macros are used as arguments to the **setlocale( )** function.

setlocale( ) is called with one of the locale macros and a string that identifies the locale being set. The default locale (English) is represented by **"C"**. Thus, when a program is started, it's as if

```
setlocale(LC_ALL, "C");
```

is called. If an empty string is sent to **setlocale( )**, the locale is set to a compiler-defined native environment:

```
setlocale(LC_ALL, "");
```

The purpose of setting a locale is to allow numbers, time, and dates to be represented in a locale-specific way. In the header file *time.h*, a structure *tm* is declared which contains the members

```
int tm_sec;     /* number of seconds [0 to 59] */
int tm_min;     /* number of minutes [0 to 59] */
int tm_hour;    /* hours since midnight [0 to 23] */
int tm_mday;    /* day of the month [1 to 31] */
int tm_mon;     /* months since January [1 to 11] */
int tm_year;    /* years since 1900 */
int tm_wday;    /* day; Sunday = 0 [0 to 6] */
int tm_yday;    /* days since January 1 [0 to 365] */
int tm_isdst;   /* positive if daylight savings in effect, 0 otherwise */
```

In addition, two **typedef**s are defined, **clock_t** and **time_t**. These are types capable of representing times that can be manipulated arithmetically.

Several functions are provided for retrieving and manipulating numbers, times, and dates. These are briefly described below and identified by their prototypes.

```
double difftime(time_t time1, time_t time2)
```

difftime( ) returns the difference between *time1* and *time2* expressed in seconds.

```
time_t mktime(struct tm *timeptr)
```

Sec. C.7 Additional Features

mktime( ) returns the time and day stored in *timeptr* encoded as a value of type *time_t*.

```
time_t time(time_t *timer)
```

time( ) returns the current calendar time.

```
char *asctime(struct tm *timeptr)
```

asctime( ) returns a pointer to a string that is the data in *timeptr* (a date represented by the members in *struct tm*) in the format:

```
day month day time year\n\0
```

The first of January, 1988 at noon is

```
Fri Jan 1 12:00:00 1988\n\0

char *ctime(time_t *timer)
```

ctime( ) converts the calendar time represented by *timer* into a string expressing local time in the format returned by **asctime( )**.

```
struct tm *gmtime(time_t *timer)
```

gmtime( ) converts the calendar into the equivalent Greenwich Mean Time (stored as *struct tm* members).

```
struct tm *localtime(time_t *timer)
```

localtime( ) converts the calendar time (referred to by *timer*) into a local time stored as members of *struct tm*.

```
size_t strftime(char *s, size_t maxsize, char *format,
         struct tm *timeptr)
```

strftime( ) takes a format string similar to **printf( )** and converts the locale-specific format of time and date into the requested string. The format string takes formatting codes that begin with %. This function assumes that Sunday is the beginning of the week, unless specifically stated otherwise.

%a	Abbreviated weekday name
%A	Full weekday name
%b	Abbreviated month name
%B	Full month name
%c	Approximate date and time representation

%d   Month day as a decimal number [0 to 31]
%H   The hour as a decimal number [00 to 24]
%I   The hour as a decimal number [00 to 12]
%j   The day of the year as a decimal number [001 to 366]
%m   The month as a decimal number [01 to 12]
%M   The minute as a decimal number [00 to 59]
%p   Locale's equivalent of **AM** and **PM**
%S   The second as a decimal number [00 to 59]
%U   The week number of the year as a decimal number [00 to 52]
%w   The weekday as a decimal number [0 to 6]
%W   The week number of the year as a decimal number [00 to 52] (assumes that Monday is the first day of the week)
%x   Locale's appropriate date representation
%X   Locale's appropriate time representation
%y   The last two digits of the year [00 to 99]
%Y   The complete year as a decimal number
%Z   The time zone name, if one exists (empty otherwise)
%%   The percent sign

Other characters are passed as is to the formatted string. All of these time functions require that *time.h* be **#include**d for them to work.

Two additional string functions were added to handle comparing strings in a locale-specific manner, that is, to take local alphabets into account.

```
size_t strxfrm(char *to, char *from, size_t maxsize)
```

strxfrm( ) converts the string represented by *from* into a locale-specific version that can be used for sorting. *maxsize* is the maximum number of characters that *to* can hold.

```
int strcoll(char *s1, char *s2)
```

strcoll( ) operates just like **strcmp( )** except the strings are compared in a locale-specific manner.

C.8 CAVEAT PROGRAMMER—LET THE PROGRAMMER BEWARE

The information listed here is accurate as of this writing (December 1987). However, at this time the standard has not been officially approved and is still subject to change. One area of caution is the international section of the standard. Not only is this the newest section, but other organizations are working on similar issues. It is likely that some changes will be made in this section of the standard.

Sec. C.8　Caveat Programmer—Let the Programmer Beware

As a result, it is highly recommended that the information listed in this appendix be verified before being relied upon. Undoubtedly, many books on the standard will be published as soon as the standard becomes official. One magazine dedicated to covering the C language and which focuses on the standard is the *The C Users Journal*, published by C Users Group, Box 97, McPherson, KS, 67460. A copy of the current version of the ANSI standard (be it draft or official) can be purchased by calling Global Engineering Documents at 800-854-7179.

D

A C Standard Library Reference

Program transportability was one of the design objectives of the C Language. To achieve this goal, C's designers split the language into two parts. The language specification includes data types, control structures, and operators. The second part is a library of functions that, among other things, provides the interface between C and the underlying hardware. By moving source code from one computer to another and then compiling it on the new machine, we link in the interfaces needed for the target computer through the standard library.

The aim of this appendix is to provide a quick reference for commonly used standard library functions. It is possible that a particular system won't provide some of the functions listed here, and, almost certainly, many others will be available. In all cases, check with a specific system's documentation to be certain of the contents of the standard library.

To conform to the ANSI C standard (see Appendix C), the functions listed in this appendix are prototypes, that is, each function's formal parameters are declared as part of the function's name. For example, **fopen( )** is listed as

```
FILE *fopen(char *filename, char *mode)
```

instead of

Sec. D.1 Character Functions   417

```
FILE *fopen(filename, mode)
char *filename;
char *mode;
```

For a full discussion of function prototypes, see Appendix C.

The functions are categorized by general operation to allow for easy scanning of related routines. Within each section, the functions are listed alphabetically. Those functions listed in bold typeface have *not* been discussed in the text.

D.1 CHARACTER FUNCTIONS

isalnum	ispunct
isalpha	isspace
iscntrl	isupper
isdigit	isxdigit
isgraph	tolower
islower	toupper
isprint	

Except for **tolower( )** and **toupper( )**, these functions test the character argument for belonging to a certain group of characters. The header file *ctype.h* must be **#include**d

```
#include "ctype.h"
```

before any of them can be used. *NOTE*: All the functions beginning with **is** may be implemented as macros.

Each test function (those starting with **is**) returns a **true** (non-0) value if the character argument is part of the group or a **false** (0) value if not. In the table below, *ch* represents any single character.

Name	Group tested
isalnum(int ch)	Alphanumeric characters (A–Z, a–z, 0–9)
isalpha(int ch)	Alphabetic characters (A–Z, a–z)
iscntrl(int ch)	Control characters (0 – 31, 127 in ASCII) (any nonprinting character)
isdigit(int ch)	Decimal digits (0–9)
isgraph(int ch)	Any "printing" character other than space (in ASCII: 33 – 126)
islower(int ch)	Any lower-case character (a–z)
ispunct(int ch)	Any punctuation character including space (all except alphanumeric and control characters)
isspace(int ch)	Any white-space character (space, tab, newline, vertical tab, form feed, and carriage return)
isupper(int ch)	Any upper-case character (A–Z)
isxdigit(int ch)	Any hexadecimal digit (0–9, A–F, a–f)

The functions **tolower( )** and **toupper( )** convert the character from one group into a character from a corresponding group. If the character argument (represented by *ch*) is not a member of the initial group, no conversion occurs and *ch* is returned unchanged. Otherwise, the character returned is the converted value. For example

```
int tolower(int ch)
```

returns the lower-case equivalent of *ch* if *ch* is an upper-case character. If *ch* is not an upper-case character, *ch* is returned without change. Further,

```
int toupper(int ch)
```

returns the upper-case equivalent of *ch* if *ch* is a lower-case character. If *ch* is not a lower-case character, *ch* is returned without change.

D.2 FILE-HANDLING FUNCTIONS

clearerr	**fseek**
fclose	**ftell**
feof	**remove**
ferror	**rename**
fflush	**rewind**
fopen	

The functions in this section are used to manipulate files. They do not perform input and output (see "Input and Output Functions"). Instead, they implement basic file operations such as opening, closing, and repositioning files.

The inner workings of file systems are inherently machine-dependent. To fit a computer's file system into C's standard library requires the definition of a special structure with the **typedef** FILE. This **typedef** is declared in the header file *stdio.h*. Before any of the functions listed in this section can be used, the preprocessor directive

```
#include "stdio.h"
```

must appear.

```
void clearerr(FILE *filep)
```

Any existing error indication on the open file represented by *filep* is cleared. See the related function *ferror*. This function may be implemented as a macro.

```
int fclose(FILE *filep)
```

Sec. D.2   File-Handling Functions   419

The open file represented by *filep* is closed. Any data presently stored in this file's buffer is written to disk. A zero is returned if the file is closed successfully. EOF is returned if an error occurs.

```
int feof(FILE *filep)
```

The open file represented by *filep* is checked for being past the EOF. A non-0 (true) value is returned if the file is past the EOF. Otherwise, 0 (false) is returned. *NOTE*: **feof( )** returns true only if an attempt has been made to read *past* the EOF. **feof( )** returns 0 (false) if all the characters in the file have been read (the file is technically at the EOF) but no attempt has been made to read further. This function may be implemented as a macro.

```
int ferror(FILE *filep)
```

The open file represented by *filep* is checked for an error condition. A non-0 (true) value is returned if an error has occurred on the file and 0 (false) otherwise. **ferror( )** doesn't affect the error condition of the file and repeated calls to **FERROR( )** will return the same value. The **clearerr( )** function must be used to clear errors discovered by **ferror( )**. See the related function **clearerr( )**. This function may be implemented as a macro.

```
int fflush(FILE *filep)
```

The buffer of the open file represented by *filep* is written to disk (flushed).

```
FILE *fopen(char *filename, char *mode)
```

This function prepares the data file *filename* for access by a program. A file must be opened in a specific mode. *mode* is a string (double quotation marks required for a constant) that identifies the file opening mode. **fopen( )** uses the mode to determine if the file can be accessed in the specified mode and, if so, where to position it once opened. There are three basic file access modes: *read*, *write*, and *append*. A file opened in *read* mode can only be read. A file opened for *write* or *append* can only be written. Only existing files can be opened with *read* access. A file opened with *write* access will be created, whether it presently exists or not. A file opened with *append* access will be created if it doesn't exist otherwise it is opened and positioned at the very end of the file. Unlike *write* mode, *append* mode doesn't delete what is presently in the file. Both *read* and *write* modes position the file at the beginning. A file opened in *append* mode cannot overwrite any information presently in the file.

String arguments are used to denote the mode desired:

"r"   *read* mode
"w"   *write* mode
"a"   *append* mode

Some systems allow three additional modes that open a file for both reading and writing. They are called *update* modes and are denoted by

"r+"	*read update* mode
"w+"	*write update* mode
"a+"	*append update* mode

The same opening and creating rules apply as in the regular modes.

A pointer to FILE is returned if the file is opened successfully. Otherwise, the token NULL is returned.

```
int fseek(FILE *filep, long offset, int location)
```

This function repositions the open file represented by *filep*. The file is reset according to the values in *offset* and *location*. The file's new position is determined by moving *offset* number of bytes from the specified location.

Location	Where *offset* is measured from
seek_set	Beginning of file
seek_cur	Present position
seek_end	End of file

If successful, **fseek()** returns 0; otherwise, a non-0 value is returned. *NOTE*: The *offset* argument is a **long** and can be a negative value. Further, the *seek_set*, *seek_cur*, and *seek_end* are ANSI defined macros. On non-ANSI systems use 0, 1, and 2, respectively.

```
long ftell(FILE *filep)
```

This function reports the character position of the file represented by *filep*. The value returned by **ftell()** can be used as the second argument to **fseek()**.

```
int remove(char *filename)
```

This function removes the unopened file named *filename* from the file system. If successful, 0 is returned; otherwise, a non-0 value is returned. Removing an opened file results in uncertain behavior.

```
int rename(char *old, char *new)
```

This function renames the file presently named *old* to *new*. **rename()** returns 0 if successful; otherwise, a non-0 value is returned.

Sec. D.3 Input and Output (I/O) Functions

```
void rewind(FILE *filep)
```

The open file represented by *filep* is positioned at the beginning of the file. *NOTE*: This is the same as **fseek (filep, 0L, seek_set)**.

D.3 INPUT AND OUTPUT (I/O) FUNCTIONS

fgetc	printf
fgets	putc
fprintf	putchar
fputc	puts
fputs	scanf
fscanf	sprintf
getc	sscanf
getchar	**ungetc**
gets	

These functions are used by programs to read data in and write it out. These functions require

```
#include "stdio.h"
```

Those functions that aren't passed a pointer to FILE as an argument read the standard input and write to the standard output. These two destinations can be referenced by the *stdin* and *stdout* macros.

```
int fgetc(FILE *filep)
```

This function reads the next character from the open file represented by *filep*. The character read is returned by **fgets( )** as an **int**. If an error occurs or the end of file is found, EOF is returned.

```
char *fgets(char *str, int nbr, FILE *filep)
```

This function reads characters from the open file represented by *filep* until a newline is encountered or *nbr*−1 characters have been read. All characters read are stored in *str*, including a newline (if read). *nbr* is sent to limit how many characters are placed into *str* if a newline is *not* found. In either case, *str* is terminated with \0. If at least one character is read, a pointer to *str* is returned by **fgets( )**. If an error occurs or end of file is found before any characters are read, NULL is returned.

```
int fprintf(FILE *filep, char *format, ...)
```

The result of combining the *format* string with the variables in the argument list (declared by ...) is written to the open file represented by *filep*. The *format* string can contain **printf**( ) formatting codes. These codes are described in detail in Appendix E. The variables in the argument-list must match the data types specified by formatting codes in *format*. The number of characters actually written is returned if successful. Otherwise, a negative **int** is returned. *NOTE*: **fprintf**( ) outputs only characters. All numeric values are printed as character digits.

```
int fputc(char ch, FILE *filep)
```

This function writes its character argument to the open file represented by *filep*. If successful, *ch* is returned. On error, EOF is returned.

```
int fputs(char *str, FILE *filep)
```

This function writes the characters in *str* to the open file represented by *filep*. Characters are written until \0 is found in *str*. The \0 is *not* written to the file. Unlike **puts**( ), a newline is *not* appended to *str* unless there is one in the string. On error, EOF is returned.

```
int fscanf(FILE *filep, char *format, ...)
```

This function reads the open file represented by *filep* and assigns the data read into the variables referred to in the argument list (declared by the ... in the function prototype) according to the specifications in *format*. There must be a pointer for each formatting code in *format* and their data types must agree. The same format conventions used by **scanf**( ) are available to **fscanf**( ) (these are different than those used by **printf**( )). **fscanf**( ) terminates if all the codes in *format* are successfully matched by input data, if an item read cannot be correctly matched to the next format code, or if EOF is reached during input. **fscanf**( ) returns the number of items (as numbered by the codes in *format*) successfully matched, otherwise EOF is returned. *NOTE*: EOF is returned if end of file is found before an item is matched or the first item cannot be matched by the input.

```
int getc(FILE *filep)
```

This function reads the next character in the open file represented by *filep*. The character read is returned as an **int**. If no more characters are available from *filep* or an error occurs, EOF is returned.

```
int getchar(void)
```

This function reads the next character from the standard input and returns that character as an **int**. If *stdio.h* is **#included**, **getchar**( ) may be implemented as a macro. **getchar**( ) is the same as **getc(stdin)**. On error or end of file, EOF is returned.

```
char *gets(char *str)
```

Sec. D.3 Input and Output (I/O) Functions

This function reads characters into *str* from standard input until a newline is encountered. The newline is not stored in *str*, which is terminated by \0. If successful, a pointer to the first character in *str* is returned. If an error occurs, end of file is found, or no characters are read, NULL is returned.

```
int printf(char *format, ...)
```

The result of combining the *format* string with the variables in the argument list (represented by ... in the function prototype) is written to the standard output. The *format* string can contain formatting codes intermingled with regular text. The formatting codes are described in detail in Appendix E. The variables listed in the argument list must match the data types specified by formatting codes in *format*. If no formatting codes are included in *format*, no variables need follow. The number of characters actually written is returned if successful; otherwise, a negative **int** is returned. *NOTE*: **printf( )** outputs characters only. All numeric values are printed as character digits.

```
int putc(char ch, FILE *filep)
```

This function prints the character *ch* to the open file represented by *filep*. If successful, *ch* is returned; otherwise, EOF is returned.

```
int putchar(char ch)
```

This function writes the character *ch* to the standard output. If *stdio.h* is **#include**d, **putchar( )** may be implemented as a macro. **putchar( )** is the same as **putc(stdout)**. On error, EOF is returned.

```
int puts(char *str)
```

This function writes *str* followed by a newline to the standard output. On error, EOF is returned.

```
int scanf(char *format, ...)
```

This function reads the standard input and assigns the data read into the variables referred to by the pointer in the argument list (represented by ... in the function prototype) according to the specifications in *format*. There must be a pointer for each formatting code in *format* and their data types must agree. The format conventions used by **scanf( )** are different than those used by **printf( )**. **scanf( )** terminates if all the codes in *format* are successfully matched by input data, if an item read cannot be correctly matched to the next format code, or if EOF is reached during input. **scanf( )** returns the number of items (as numbered by the codes in *format*) successfully matched; otherwise, EOF is returned. *NOTE*: EOF is returned if end of file is found before an item is matched or the first item cannot be matched by the input.

```
int sprintf(char *str, char *format, ...)
```

The result of combining the *format* string with the variables in the argument list (represented in the function prototype by **...**) is stored in *str*. *str* is terminated with **\0**. The *format* string can contain **printf( )** formatting codes. These codes are described in detail in Appendix E. The variables listed in the argument list must match the data types specified by formatting codes in *format*. If no formatting codes are included in *format*, no variables need follow. The number of characters actually written is returned if successful; otherwise, a negative **int** is returned. *NOTE*: **sprintf( )** doesn't check if *str* is large enough to hold the formatted result.

```
int sscanf(char *str, char *format, ...)
```

This function reads through *str* and assigns the data read into the variables referenced by pointers in argument list (represented by **...** in the function prototype) according to the specifications in *format*. There must be a pointer for each formatting code in *format* and their data types must agree. The same format conventions used by **scanf( )** are available to **sscanf( )** (these are different than those used by **printf( )**). **sscanf( )** terminates if all the codes in *format* are successfully matched in *str*, if an item read cannot be correctly matched to the next format code, or if **\0** is found in *str* before *format* is completed. **sscanf( )** returns the number of items (as numbered by the codes in *format*) successfully matched; otherwise, 0 is returned. *NOTE*: Zero is returned if **\0** is found before an item is matched or the first item cannot be matched by *str*.

```
int ungetc(char ch, FILE *filep)
```

This function writes the character *ch* "back" onto the open file represented by *filep*. The file must be open in input mode for *ungetc* to operate properly. *ungetc* only works on buffered files and actually puts the character *ch* into the file buffer as the next character to be read. After a call to **ungetc( )**, **getc( )** will return the character *ch*. If at least one character has been read from the file, one character can be "pushed back." Some implementations allow more than one character to be pushed onto the file. Others require that the file be read between calls to **ungetc( )**. Check specific system documentation for exact details.

D.4 MEMORY ALLOCATION FUNCTIONS

calloc
free
malloc
realloc

In virtually all cases, a compiled program does not require all a computer's available memory. The functions in this section allow a program to access this unused memory to allocate storage for variables during program execution. This is generally

Sec. D.4   Memory Allocation Functions

called *dynamic memory allocation*. Also included is a function to release memory allocated in this way.

These functions must be told how much memory to set aside, and they return a pointer to that much memory. This is a primary use of the **sizeof** operator. For the program to treat this memory properly, we have to **cast** the pointer returned to the appropriate data type. The **sizeof** and **cast** operators are commonly used with the functions listed below.

Because there may not always be enough memory to satisfy our demands, we should always test to ensure that these functions have executed successfully. This is especially important for programs that will be transported to different types and sizes of computers. To use these functions,

```
#include "stdlib.h"
```

must appear in the source code file (*ansi*).

If the compiler is not ANSI standard, the system will probably not have a file called *stdlib.h*, and this header file should not be **#include**d. Also, instead of using *size_t* as a data type for the arguments passed to **calloc()**, **malloc()** and **realloc()**, check the system's documentation for the data type to declare the integer arguments to these functions (probably **unsigned int** or **unsigned long**).

```
char *calloc(size_t nbr, size_t size)
```

This function allocates a contiguous block of memory large enough to store *nbr* objects where each object is *size* bytes in length. If successful, **calloc()** returns a **char** pointer to this now allocated memory, which is completely initialized to 0s (\0). **calloc()** returns NULL if the request cannot be fulfilled.

```
void free(char * pntr)
```

This function frees a region of memory, referred to by *pntr*, that was previously allocated dynamically (by a call to **calloc()** or **malloc()**). Memory released by **free()** is returned to the available memory pool and can be reallocated.

```
char *malloc(size_t size)
```

This function allocates a contiguous block of memory large enough to store an object *size* bytes in length. If successful, **malloc()** returns a **char** pointer to this now allocated memory. NULL is returned if the request cannot be fulfilled.

```
char realloc(char *pntr, size_t size)
```

This function resizes memory previously allocated by one of the allocation functions. *pntr* points to the memory being resized and *size* is the number of characters *pntr* is to refer to after resizing. If *size* is larger than the current capacity of *pntr*, the contents of *pntr* are copied to a new memory region and a pointer to that memory is returned. The extra memory is uninitialized. If *size* is smaller than the current capacity of *pntr*, the current memory region is truncated to *size*. If a new memory region is referenced by *pntr* as a result of a call to **realloc( )**, the old memory region is deallocated. If the request cannot be fulfilled, NULL is returned.

D.5 STRING CONVERSION FUNCTIONS

    atof

    atoi

    atol

The functions in this section convert a string of characters into their equivalent numeric value.

```
double atof(char *str)
```

This function converts the characters in *str* into their representative **double** value. **atof( )** terminates conversion when a invalid character is encountered. **atof( )** accepts a beginning plus or minus, followed by a string of digits or a period. The period may come after digits and be followed by more digits. Leading white space is ignored. The converted **double** value is returned. If no valid characters are found, 0 is returned.

```
int atoi(char *str)
```

This function converts the characters in *str* into their true integer value. **atoi( )** terminates conversion when a nonnumeric character is encountered. **atoi( )** accepts a leading plus or minus sign followed by a string of digits. All leading white space is ignored. The converted **int** value is returned. If no valid characters are found, 0 is returned.

```
long atol (char *str)
```

This function converts the characters in *str* into their true **long** value. **atol( )** terminates conversion when a nonnumeric character is encountered. **atol( )** accepts a leading plus or minus sign followed by a string of digits. All leading white space is ignored. The converted **long** value is returned. If no valid characters are found, 0 is returned.

D.6 STRING MANIPULATION FUNCTIONS

strcat	strncat
strchr	strncmp
strcmp	strncpy
strcpy	strrchr
strlen	

The functions in this section work with strings as a singular unit. Some functions return **char** pointers while others return **int** values. None of these functions test if destination strings are large enough to hold the characters being stored in them.

The prototypes for these functions are declared in the header file *string.h* and the directive

```
#include "string.h"
```

must appear in programs that use them (*ansi*).

```
char *strcat(char *str1, char *str2)
```

This function appends *str2* to the end of *str1*. The **\0** in *str1* is overwritten by the first character in *str2*. The characters from *str2* are appended until a **\0** is encountered. The **\0** is added to the end of *str1* as well. A pointer to *str1* is returned.

```
char *strchr(char *str, char ch)
```

This function searches *str* for the first occurrence of the character *ch*. If a match is found, **strchr( )** returns a pointer to this character in *str*. If not, NULL is returned. In some library implementations, this function is called **index( )**.

```
int strcmp(char *str1, char *str2)
```

This function compares *str1* to *str2 lexicographically*. If *str1* is less than *str2*, a negative number is returned; if they are equal, zero is returned; otherwise, a positive value is returned. *NOTE*: A common error is to only look for −1, 0, or +1 as **strcmp( )**'s return value.

```
char *strcpy(char *str1, char *str2)
```

This function copies all the characters of *str2* into *str1*. *str2* must be terminated with a **\0**, which is also copied. **strcpy( )** returns a pointer to *str1*.

```
                int strlen(char *str)
```

This function counts the characters in *str* before the \0. This count is returned.

```
        char *strncat(char *str1, char *str2, int nbr)
```

This function appends *nbr* characters from *str2* onto the end of *str1*. The \0 that terminates *str1* is overwritten by the first character in *str2*. If *str2* is less than *nbr* characters in length, only that number of characters are added (including the \0). If *str2* is longer than *nbr* characters, *nbr* characters are appended to *str1* and a terminating \0 is added (*nbr* + 1 characters are appended to *str1*). If *nbr* is 0, no changes occur. A pointer to *str1* is returned.

```
        int strncmp(char *str1, char *str2, int nbr)
```

This function compares the first *nbr* characters in *str1* with *str2* lexicographically. A negative number is returned if these characters from *str1* are less than the corresponding characters in *str2*; 0 if they are equal; and positive otherwise. If either string contains less than *nbr* characters, the entire string is used. If *nbr* is 0, 0 is returned.

```
        char *strncpy(char *str1, char *str2, int nbr)
```

This function copies *nbr* characters from *str2* into *str1*. If *str2* contains fewer than *nbr* characters, *str1* is padded with \0 until *nbr* characters have been copied into *str1*. If *str2* contains more than *nbr* characters, only *nbr* of them are copied into *str1*. **strncpy( )** returns a pointer to *str1*. NOTE: *str1* is terminated with \0 only if a \0 from *str2* is copied into it.

```
            char *strrchr(char *str, char ch)
```

This function searches *str* for the last occurrence of the character *ch*. A pointer to this character in *str* is returned if one is found; otherwise, NULL is returned. In some library versions, this function is called **rindex( )**.

E

printf( ) Formatting Codes

In the text, we noted that **printf**( ) is a very flexible printing function. Not every **printf**( ) feature was demonstrated and the purpose of this appendix is to show exactly what **printf**( ) can do.

The information listed in this appendix is taken from the ANSI C standard draft proposal. Some of the information will not apply to nonstandard compilers. The ANSI specific information will be specifically identified.

A **printf**( ) formatting code can contain the following specifications:

```
%[flag][field width][precision][size][conversion][%]
```

The brackets denote that these specifications are optional. However, at minimum, either a *conversion* or a percent sign must follow a percent sign.

A *flag* specifier identifies whether the field will be left justified (a minus sign), have a plus or minus sign to denote the sign of the number converted (a plus sign), preceeded by a single space or a minus sign (a space), padded to the left by 0s (a 0), or specifically formatted to match the numeric type used (a #). By default, a field is right justified (padded on the left with spaces).

If the conversion is to octal (conversion: o), a # flag means to preceed the value by 0. For hexadecimal conversion (conversions: x, X), the # flag means to preceed the value by "0x" (conversions: x) or "0X" (for conversions: X). For floating-point conversion (conversions: e, E, f, g, G), the **#** flag means that the value will always have a decimal point, even if no digits follow the decimal point. Further, for conversions g and G, trailing 0s are not removed.

A *field width* specifier is an integer that is the minimum number of spaces that the converted value is to fit into. If the value converted is smaller than the field width specifier, by default the field is right justified (padded with spaces on the left), although this can be changed by the *flag* specifier. If the value converted is larger than the field width specifier, the field is expanded to accomodate the value.

A *precision* specifier is denoted by a period followed by an optional integer. If the integer is omitted, it is assumed to be 0. If the conversion is a string (conversion: s), the precision specifier identifies how many characters from the (front of the) string are to be printed. If the conversion is an integer (conversions: d, i, o, u, x, X), the precision specifies the minimum number of digits to be printed. For floating-point numbers (conversions: e, E, f), the precision specifies the number of digits to appear after the decimal point. For the conversions g or G, the precision specifies the maximum number of significant digits to print. The amount of padding or digits called for by the precision specifier overrides the field width specifier.

The *size* specifier is either an h, l, or L. The h (ANSI) specifies that a converted value is a **short int** (conversion: d, i, o, x, or X) or an **unsigned short int** (conversion: u). The **l** (the letter "el") specifies that a converted value is a **long int** (conversion: d, i, o, x, or X) or an **unsigned long int** (conversion: u). The **L** (ANSI) specifies that a converted value is a **long double** (conversion: e, E, f, g, or G).

The *conversion* specifier is either: d, i, o, u, x, X, f, e, E, g, G, c, s, p, or n. Each one (or set if all refer to the same kind of conversion) is described below.

The codes: d, i, o, u, x, X specify an integer conversion. The d or i (ANSI) specifies a signed **int** (decimal) conversion. The o specifies an unsigned octal conversion. The u specifies an unsigned **int** conversion. The x and X both specify an unsigned hexadecimal conversion. With x, the digits a–f (lower case) are used. With X, the digits A-F (upper case) are used.

In integer conversion, the precision, if listed, specifies the minimum number of digits to print. If the value contains less than the precision calls for, leading 0s are added to the value. The default precision is 1 and if zero precision is stated and the value being printed is 0, no characters are printed.

The codes: f, e, E, g, and G specify a **double** conversion. **float**s are converted to **double** when sent to **printf( )** as an argument. So these codes work for **float** conversion as well.

The code f specifies a conversion in the form [-]###.###. If a precision is listed, exactly that many digits are printed to the right of the decimal point, even if they are all 0s. If the precision is listed as zero, no decimal point appears. If no precision is stated, the precision is six digits to the right of the decimal point. If a decimal point is printed, at least one digit appears to the left of it. In all cases, the value printed is rounded to the appropriate decimal place, if necessary.

The codes e and E specify a conversion of the type [-]#.##[eE][+-]##. There is always one digit to the left of the decimal point. The number of digits to the right of the decimal point is equal to the precision. If no precision is stated, six digits are printed after the decimal point. If the precision is zero, no decimal point is printed. If the code is E, then a number with E before the exponent is printed. If the code is e, then a number with e before the exponent is printed. The exponent always contains at least two digits; more are listed if necessary.

The codes g and G specify that either the f or e format be used, depending on the number being printed. The precision specifies the number of significant digits to be printed. If the value being printed requires an exponent less than −4 or greater than the precision, the e format is used (E is used if the code is G). Otherwise, the f format is used. A decimal point is printed only if it is followed by a digit.

The codes c and s specify that **char** data be printed. Code c prints single characters. Code s prints a string of characters. The precision is not relevant for the c conversion. However, for s conversion, the precision specifies how many characters from the beginning of the string are to be printed. If no precision is listed, the entire string (up to the first null character) is printed.

Two additional codes are part of the **printf( )** specification in the C standard, p and n. The code p specifies that a pointer value is to be printed. The value of the pointer is converted into printable characters in a manner defined by the implementation. The code n tells **printf( )** to store the number of characters printed so far into the appropriate argument in the argument list. This argument must be a pointer to **int**.

The code % specifies that a percent sign be printed. To print a percent sign, the **printf( )** specification is %%.

The C standard requires that these conversion codes be available. However, the standard allows an implementation to offer more conversion codes if desired.

The **printf( )** function returns the number of characters printed or a negative value if an error occurred.

F

General Reference Section

This section contains general information that is intended for quick reference. Even after we have become proficient in C, there often is a need to check specific details. The tables and other information listed here are not designed to be complete, only useful. In fact, several blank pages have been added at the end to provide room for expansion as the need arises.

F.1 KEYWORDS IN C

auto	double	int	struct
break	else	long	switch
case	enum	register	typedef
char	extern	return	union
const (ANSI)	float	short	signed
continue	for	signed	void
default	goto	sizeof	volatile (ANSI)
do	if	static	while

F.2 PRECEDENCE TABLE

Operator	Associativity	Name
() [] . ->	Left to right	(Grouping)
++ -- (type) ! * & - sizeof ~	Right to left	(Unary)
* / %	Left to right	(Arithmetic)
+ -	Left to right	(Arithmetic)
<< >>	Left to right	(Shift)
< <= >= >	Left to right	(Relational)
== !=	Left to right	(Equality)
&	Left to right	(Bitwise)
^	Left to right	(Bitwise)
|	Left to right	(Bitwise)
&&	Left to right	(Logical)
||	Left to right	(Logical)
?:	Left to right	(Conditional)
= += -= *= /= %= &= ^= |= <<= >>=	Right to left	(Assignment)
,	Left to right	(Comma)

F.3 SPECIAL CHARACTER CONSTANTS

\a	Alarm (ANSI)
\b	Backspace
\f	Formfeed
\n	Newline
\r	Carriage return
\t	Horizontal tab
\v	Vertical tab
\\	Backslash character
\"	Double quotation mark character
\'	Single quotation mark character

F.4 EQUIVALENT POINTER AND ARRAY EXPRESSIONS

array represents an array

index and *nbr* are integers

*array = array[0]

*(array + index) = array[index]

**array = *array[0] = array[0][0]

((array + index)) = *array[index] = array[index][0]

((array + index) + nbr) = *(array[index] + nbr) = array[index][nbr]

General Rule of Thumb The notation

```
array[index]
```

is equivalent to

```
*(array + index).
```

We can trade one for the other to create equivalent expressions. Thus, if *array3* is a three dimensional array, then

```
***(array3 + index)
```

can be transformed into

```
array3[index][0][0]
```

by successive applications of the general rule of thumb. As another example,

```
*(*(*(array3 + index) + nbr) + count)
```

can be represented as any of the following

```
*(*(array3[index] + nbr) + count)
```

```
*(array3[index][nbr] + count)
```

```
array3[index][nbr][count]
```

Solutions to In-Chapter Exercises

1-1. If the initial test is true, a **while** loop is selected for execution. Otherwise, a second test is performed, and if it is true, a **do-while** loop is executed; otherwise, the sequence is chosen.

3-1.

    a. 6 + 2 / 4 * 2 = 6 + .5 * 2 = 6 + 1 = 7
    b. 6 / 2 * (4 / 2) = 6 / 2 * 2 = 6
    c. 48 / (2 * 4) / 6 = 48 / 8 / 6 = 1
    d. 6 % 4 / 2 = 2 / 2 = 1

3-2. It would first print a newline, then a tab, then the line

                    Total PROFIT this year is $10000

It would finish with two more newlines.

4-1. The line

                      Total PROFIT this year is $1111

then a newline.

4-2.

```
main()
{
    float revenue;
    float cost;
    int printf();

    revenue = 25098;
    cost = 23987;
    printf("Total profit this year is $%f\n", revenue - cost);
    exit(0);
}
```

4-3.
  a. 5 <= 5 is true so **logical_value** = 1.
  b. The multiply has higher precedence and is done first. 25 == 5 is false so **logical_value** = 0.
  c. The relational operator is done first since it is enclosed in parentheses. 5 < 5 is false and **logical_value** = 5 * 0.
  d. The relational operator has higher precedence so 5 < 6 is 1 (true) and 5 == 1 is false so **logical_value** = 0.

4-4.

```
printf("Total profit this year $%d\nTotal revenue this year $%d\n",
       revenue - cost, revenue);

printf("Total loss this year ($%d)\nTotal costs this year $%d\n",
       cost - revenue, cost);
```

5-1.

```
char co_name[81];    /* leave space for \0 */
char *gets();
int printf();

printf("Enter Company Name (80 characters maximum): ");
gets(co_name);
```
rest of program

5-2.

```
/* A program to read, convert, and display a floating point
 * number.
 *
 * Written by Ray Swartz for "Doing Business with C"
 */
```

Solutions to In-Chapter Exercises

```c
main()
{
    char instr[81];    /* input string */
    char *gets();
    double nbr;        /* holds converted value */
    double atof();
    int printf();

    printf("Enter a Number: ");
    gets(instr);
    nbr = atof(instr);
    printf("The number you entered is %f\n", nbr);
    exit(0);
}
```

5-3.

```c
/*                ***** PL-REPT *****
 * This program prompts the user for revenue and costs
 * (both double) and prints profit if revenue > cost
 * or loss if cost > revenue or a breakeven message if
 * neither.
 *
 * Written by Ray Swartz for "Doing Business with C"
 *
 * Modified to print dollars and cents.
 */
#include "stdio.h"
main()
{
    double revenue;    /* holds total revenue - entered by user */
    double cost;       /* holds total cost - entered by user */
    double atof();
    char instr[81];    /* input string */
    char *gets();
    int printf();

    printf("Enter this year's REVENUE: ");
    gets(instr);                    /* Read revenue */
    revenue = atof(instr);          /* Convert revenue to double */
    printf("\n\nEnter this year's COSTS: ");
    gets(instr);                    /* Read costs */
    cost = atof(instr);             /* Convert costs to double */
    if (revenue > cost)             /* Test for profit */
        printf("\nTotal profit this year $%.2f\n", revenue - cost);
    else if (cost > revenue)        /* Test for loss */
        printf("\nTotal loss this year ($%.2f)\n", cost - revenue);
```

```
        else                         /* Neither profit or loss */
            printf("\nRevenues equal costs for this year\n");
        exit(0);
    }
```

5-4.

```
/*              ***** PL-REPT *****
 * This program prompts the user for revenue and costs
 * (both longs) and prints profit if revenue > cost
 * or loss if cost > revenue or a breakeven message if
 * neither.
 *
 * Written by Ray Swartz for "Doing Business with C"
 *
 * Modified to use longs.
 */
#include "stdio.h"
main()
{
    long revenue;    /* holds total revenue - entered by user */
    long cost;       /* holds total cost - entered by user */
    long atol();
    char instr[81]; /* input string */
    char *gets();
    int printf();

    printf("Enter this year's REVENUE: ");
    gets(instr);                 /* Read revenue */
    revenue = atol(instr);       /* Convert revenue to double */
    printf("\n\nEnter this year's COSTS: ");
    gets(instr);                 /* Read costs */
    cost = atol(instr);          /* Convert costs to double */
    if (revenue > cost)          /* Test for profit */
        printf("\nTotal profit this year $%10ld\n", revenue - cost);
    else if (cost > revenue)     /* Test for loss */
        printf("\nTotal loss this year ($%10ld)\n", cost - revenue);
    else                         /* Neither profit or loss */
        printf("\nRevenues equal costs for this year\n");
    exit(0);
}
```

6-1.

```
/* ***** PL-REPT2 *****
 * This program prompts the user for revenue and cost
 * components and builds a Profit and Loss statement
 * from them.
 *
```

Solutions to In-Chapter Exercises

```c
 *  Written by Ray Swartz for "Doing Business with C"
 *
 *  Modified to use getlong.
 *
 *  Modified to split revenues into mail-order and
 *   retail sales.
 */
#include "stdio.h"
main()
{
    int printf();
    long getlong();      /* prompt and return value entered */
    long mail_order;     /* mail order sales */
    long retail_sales;   /* total retail sales */
    long rebates;        /* total rebates */
    long cgs;            /* cost of goods sold */
    long wages;          /* total wages paid */
    long rent;           /* total store rent paid */
    long ads;            /* total advertising expense */
    long misc;           /* total miscellaneous expense */
    long revenue;        /* total revenue */
    long cost;           /* total cost */

    /* Get revenues first */

    printf("\nRevenue for Johnson's Books\n\n");
    printf("\nEnter dollar amounts only - no cents\n\n");
    retail_sales = getlong("Enter Total Retail Sales");
    mail_order = getlong("Enter Total Mail-Order Sales");
    rebates = getlong("Enter Total Rebates Received");

    /* Now get costs */

    printf("\n\nCosts\n\n");
    cgs = getlong("Enter Cost of Goods Sold");
    wages = getlong("Enter Total Wages Paid");
    rent = getlong("Enter Total Store Rent Paid");
    ads = getlong("Enter Total Advertising Expense");
    misc = getlong("Enter Total Miscellaneous Expenses");
    /* print P&L report */
    printf("\n\tProfit and Loss Statement for Johnson's Books\n\n");
    printf("          REVENUES\n\n");
    printf("          Retail Sales            $%6ld\n", retail_sales);
    printf("          Mail-Order Sales        $%6ld\n", mail_order);
    printf("          Rebates                 $%6ld\n", rebates);
    printf("                                  ------\n");
    revenue = sales + rebates;   /* total revenue */
    printf("          TOTAL REVENUE                   $%7ld\n",
        revenue);
```

```
        printf("\n\n");
        printf("        COSTS\n\n");
        printf("        Cost of Goods Sold     $%6ld\n", cgs);
        printf("        Wages                  $%6ld\n", wages);
        printf("        Rent                   $%6ld\n", rent);
        printf("        Advertising            $%6ld\n", ads);
        printf("        Miscellaneous Expenses $%6ld\n", misc);
        printf("                               ------\n");
        cost = cgs + wages + rent + ads + misc;  /* total costs */
        printf("        TOTAL COST                 $%7ld\n\n",
               cost);
        if (revenue >= cost)
            printf("        PROFIT                     $%7ld\n",
                   revenue - cost);
        else
            printf("        LOSS                      ($%7ld)\n",
                   cost - revenue);
        exit(0);
}

long getlong(prompt)   /* print prompt and read in a long */
char prompt[];
{
    char instr[81];    /* input string */
    char *gets();
    int printf();
    long atol();
    long nbr;          /* converted value */

    printf("%s: ",prompt);
    gets(instr);
    nbr = atol(instr);
    return(nbr);
}
```

7-1.

```
/*      *****  DISC-TBL  *****
 *
 *   This program prints a table with retail prices
 *   for the rows and discount percentages as the
 *   columns.  The prices range from 15.95 to 39.95
 *   and the discounts are 9%, 12%, 15%, 18.5%, 22%
 *
 *   Written by Ray Swartz for "Doing Business with C"
 *
 *   Modified to use the round() function.
 */
#include "stdio.h"
```

Solutions to In-Chapter Exercises 441

```
    main()
    {
        double retail;     /* retail price being discounted */
        double round();
        int printf();

        printf("Retail             Discount Percentage\n");
        printf("Price        9%%     12%%    15%%    18.5%%    22%%\n");
        printf("-------------------------------------------\n");
        retail = 15.95;    /* first value in table */
        while (retail < 39.95) {
            printf("%.2f    %.2f   %.2f   %.2f    %.2f    %.2f\n",
                    round(low_retail),
                    round(low_retail * .91),
                    round(low_retail * .88),
                    round(low_retail * .85),
                    round(low_retail * .815),
                    round(low_retail * .78));
        }
        exit(0);
    }
```

7-2.

```
    /*       *****  DISC-TBL  *****
     *
     *    This program prints a table with retail prices
     *    for the rows and discount percentages as the
     *    columns.  The prices range from 15.95 to 39.95
     *    and the discounts are 9%, 12%, 15%, 18.5%, 22%
     *
     *    Written by Ray Swartz for "Doing Business with C"
     *
     *    Modified to prompt for and read beginning
     *    and ending dollar amounts.
     */
    #include "stdio.h"
    main()
    {
        double low_retail;     /* retail price that begins table */
        double high_retail;    /* retail price that ends table */
        double atof();
        char *gets();
        char instr[50];        /* input string */
        int printf();

        printf("Enter lowest retail price to discount: ");
        gets(instr);
        low_retail = atof(instr);
```

```
        printf("Enter highest retail price to discount: ");
        gets(instr);
        high_retail = atof(instr);
        printf("Retail           Discount Percentage\n");
        printf("Price       9%%     12%%    15%%    18.5%%    22%%\n");
        printf("---------------------------------------------\n");
        while (low_retail <= high_retail) {
            printf("%.2f    %.2f   %.2f   %.2f   %.2f   %.2f\n",
                    low_retail,
                    low_retail * .91,
                    low_retail * .88,
                    low_retail * .85,
                    low_retail * .815,
                    low_retail * .78);
            low_retail = low_retail + 1.0;
        }
        exit(0);
    }
```

8-1.

```
    long getcat(catstr, class, limit)
    char catstr[];      /* string variable for entered category */
    char class[];       /* category classification (Revenue or Cost) */
    int limit;          /* maximum length of category name (catstr) */
    {
        char *gets();
        int printf();
        long getlong();     /* prints a prompt and reads long */

        printf("\nEnter a %s Category (%d Character Maximum): ",
                class, limit);
        gets(catstr);                   /* read category name */
        return(getlong(catstr));        /* return amount entered */
    }
```

8-2.

```
/*  ***** GNRL-PL *****
 *
 * This program formats a profit and loss statement
 * with 3 revenue and 5 cost categories.  The user
 * enters both the category name and the amount.
 *
 * Written by Ray Swartz for "Doing Business with C"
 *
 * Modified to use arrays for amounts.
 */
```

Solutions to In-Chapter Exercises

```
#include "stdio.h"
main()
{
    int printf();
    char rv_cat1[31];      /* revenue category 1 */
    char rv_cat2[31];      /* revenue category 2 */
    char rv_cat3[31];      /* revenue category 3 */
    char cs_cat1[31];      /* cost category 1 */
    char cs_cat2[31];      /* cost category 2 */
    char cs_cat3[31];      /* cost category 3 */
    char cs_cat4[31];      /* cost category 4 */
    char cs_cat5[31];      /* cost category 5 */
    long getcat();         /* read in category name and amount */
    long rev_amt[3];       /* revenue categories */
    long cost[5];          /* cost categories */
    long totalrev;         /* total revenue on P&L report */
    long totalcost;        /* total cost on P&L report */

    printf("Enter Dollars amounts only -- no cents\n");
    printf("\n\nREVENUES\n\n");
    rev_amt[0] = getcat(rv_cat1, "Revenue");
    rev_amt[1] = getcat(rv_cat2, "Revenue");
    rev_amt[2] = getcat(re_cat3, "Revenue");
    printf("\n\nCOSTS\n\n");
    cost_amt[0] = getcat(cs_cat1, "Cost");
    cost_amt[1] = getcat(cs_cat2, "Cost");
    cost_amt[2] = getcat(cs_cat3, "Cost");
    cost_amt[3] = getcat(cs_cat4, "Cost");
    cost_amt[4] = getcat(cs_cat5, "Cost");
    report printing section
```

9-1.

```
/* **** GETCAT ****
 * This function reads a category name and an amount for
 *   that category (using getlong).
 *
 * Modified to ask for dollars only, no cents
 *
 * Written by Ray Swartz for "Doing Business with C"
 *
 */
long getcat(catstr, class)
char catstr[];       /* string variable for entered category */
char class[];        /* category classification (Revenue or Cost) */
```

```
{
    char prompt[81];   /* holds getlong's prompt */
    char *gets();
    int sprintf();
    int printf();
    long getlong();    /* prints a prompt and reads long */

    printf("\nEnter a %s Category (%d Character Maximum): ",
           class);
    gets(catstr);                      /* read category name */
    sprintf(prompt, "%s (enter dollars only)", catstr);
    return(getlong(prompt));   /* return amount entered */
}
```

9-2.

```
/* ***** GETENT *****
 *
 * This function prompts for and reads categories
 * and amounts.  The category name and amount arrays
 * are passed to the function as arguments, as is
 * the number of categories to enter.
 *
 * Written by Ray Swartz for "Doing Business with C"
 */
void getent(cat_name, cat_amt, cat_nbr, cat_type)
char cat_name[][31];       /* category names */
long cat_amt[];            /* amounts */
int cat_nbr;               /* number of categories to enter */
char cat_type[];           /* Revenue or Cost */
{
    int printf();
    int getcat();          /* read category and return amount */
    int count;             /* loop counter */
    printf("Enter Dollar amounts only -- no cents\n");
    printf("\n\n%s\n\n", cat_type);
    for (count = 0; count < cat_nbr; count = count + 1)
        cat_amt[count] = getcat(cat_name[count], cat_type);
    return;
}
```

9-3.

```
/* **** GETCAT ****
 * This function reads a category name and an amount for
 * that category (using getlong).
 *
```

Solutions to In-Chapter Exercises 445

```
 * Modified to check for Q as category name and to
 *    return without calling getlong if found.
 *
 * Written by Ray Swartz for "Doing Business with C"
 *
 */
long getcat(catstr, class)
char catstr[];      /* string variable for entered category */
char class[];       /* category classification (Revenue or Cost) */
{
    char prompt[81];    /* holds getlong's prompt */
    char *gets();
    int printf();
    long getlong();     /* prints a prompt and reads long */

    printf("\nEnter a %s Category (%d Character Maximum): ",
            class);
    gets(catstr);                   /* read category name */
    if (catstr[0] == 'Q' && catstr[1] == '\0')
       return(0);       /* quit signal entered */
    else
       return(getlong(prompt));    /* return amount entered */
}
```

10-1.

```
                #define MAX_CAT_LEN 31
                char rev_cat[MAX_CATEGORIES] [31];
                char cost_cat[MAX_CATEGORIES] [31];
                char cost_cat[MAX_CATEGORIES] [MAX_CAT_LEN];
```

Also, don't forget the prompt in *getcat( )*:

```
printf("\nEnter a %s Category (30 Character Maximum): ", class);
```

the prompt still tells the user that they can enter up to thirty characters for a category name. To use MAX_CAT_LEN in *getcat( )* requires the rewriting of the prompting *printf( )*. We must send *printf( )* the category length maximum as an argument:

```
printf("\nEnter a %s Category (%d Character Maximum): ", class,
        MAX_CAT_LEN - 1);
```

We have to subtract 1 to account for the \0 at the end of the entered string.

The name MAX_CAT_LEN must be defined when the preprocessor reads through *getcat( )* during compilation. This means the directive

```
                #define MAX_CAT_LEN 31
```

must appear before the source code for *getcat( )* is included in the *flex-pl* program:

```
#define MAX_CAT_LEN 31
#include "stdio.h"
#include "getcat.h"
#include "getint.h"
```

10-2.

```
#define PRd(VAR) printf("%d\n", VAR)
```

10-3.

```
#define PRINT_RESULT(result, total1, total2) \
printf("          %s                 $%7ld\n", result, \
total1- total2)

/* ***** PRINT_PL *****
 *
 * This function prints a formatted Profit and Loss
 * statement.  It is sent two category name arrays
 * and two category amount arrays--one set for revenues
 * and one for costs.  The number of entries
 * of each type is sent to the function as arguments, also.
 *
 * Written by Ray Swartz for "Doing Business with C"
 *
 * Modified to use the PRINT_RESULT macro
 */

void print_pl(revenue, rev_count, cost, cost_count)
char rev_cat[] [31];       /* revenue category names */
long rev_amt[];            /* revenue amounts */
int rev_count;             /* number of revenue entries */
char cost_cat[] [31];      /* cost category names */
long cost_amt[];           /* cost amounts */
int cost_count;            /* number of cost entries */
{
    int printf();
    int count;             /* loop counter */
    long totalrev;         /* revenue amounts total */
    long totalcost;        /* cost amounts total */

    printf("\tProfit and Loss for %s\n\n", co_name);
    printf("          REVENUE\n\n");

    /* Loop to print and total the revenue categories */
```

Solutions to In-Chapter Exercises

```
            totalrev = 0;
            for (count = 0; count < rev_count; count++) {
                printf("%-30s    $%6ld\n", revenue->category, revenue->amount);
                totalrev += (revenue++)->amount;
            }
            printf("                                      ------\n");
            printf("          TOTAL REVENUE            $%7ld\n\n\n",
                    totalrev);

            /* Loop to print and total the cost categories */

            totalcost = 0;
            for (count = 0; count < cost_count; count++) {
                printf("%-30s    $%6ld\n", cost->category, cost->amount);
                totalcost += (cost++)->amount;
            }
            printf("                                      ------\n");
            printf("          TOTAL COST               $%7ld\n\n\n",
                    totalcost);
            if (totalrev >= totalcost)
                PRINT_RESULT("PROFIT", totalrev, totalcost);
            else
                PRINT_RESULT("LOSS", totalcost, totalrev);
            return;
        }
```

10-4.

```
        #define PRINT_CAT(name, amt)    printf("%-30s    $%6ld\n", name, amt)
```

11-1. The loop prints from 1 to 9 because **count** is incremented before the logical expression is evaluated. Thus, the first value tested is one and when **count** is 10 (just after the tax for $9 is printed), the test is false and the loop exits before printing the value for 10.

11-2.

```
        count = -1;
        while(++count < cost_count) {
            printf("%-30s    $%6ld\n", cost_cat[count], cost_amt[count]);
            totalcost += cost_amt[count];
        }
```

11-3. **result** is assigned the positive difference between **totalrev** and **totalcost** and the *printf( )* statement then prints either "PROFIT" or "LOSS" depending on the outcome of the test

```
                    totalrev >= totalcost
```

as well as the value stored in result.

11-4.

```
if (v1 > v2 && v2 > 0)
    v3 = v2;
else if (v1 > v2 && v2 <= 0)
    v3 = 0;
else if (v1 > 1)       /* v1 must <= v2 or can't get here */
    v3 = v2;
else
    v3 = v1;
```

14-1.

a) *nbr + 5 evaluates to nbr[0] + 5 which is 8.
b) *(nbr + 2 * 2) evaluates to nbr[4] which is 8.
c) (*nbr + 3) * 2 evaluates to nbr[3] * 2 which is 6.
d) *(nbr + nbr[2]) evaluates to nbr[2] which is 2.
e) *(nbr + *nbr) evaluates to nbr[3] which is 6.
f) *(nbr + *(nbr + 2)) evaluates to (d) which is 2.

14-2.

a) *num_ptr   (nbr[1] = 5)
b) *num_ptr * 2   (nbr[1] * 2 = 10)
c) *num_ptr - 1   (nbr[1] - 1 = 4)
d) *(num_ptr + 2) (nbr[3] = 6)
e) *(num_ptr + 2) * 2 (nbr[3] * 2 = 12)

15-1. The pointer *flex-p1* program is listed as program 15-2.

15-2.

```
/* ***** GETREV *****
 *
 * This function prompts for and reads revenue categories
 *  and amounts.  The category name and amount arrays are
 *  passed to the function as arguments.
 *
 * Written by Ray Swartz for "Doing Business with C"
 *
 * Modified to reference strings using pointers.
 */
int getrev(cat_name, cat_amt)
char *cat_name;            /* pointer to 1ST category string */
long *cat_amt;             /* amounts */
```

Solutions to In-Chapter Exercises 449

```
    {
        long getcat();         /* read category and return amount */
        int count;             /* loop counter */
        char *strptr;          /* pointer to each string */

        printf("\nEnter Dollar amounts only -- no cents\n");
        printf("\n\nREVENUES\n\n");
        for (count = 0; count < MAX_CAT; count++) {
            strptr = *(cat_name + count * MAX_LEN);
            *(cat_amt + count) = getcat(*strptr, "Revenue");
            if (*strptr == 'Q' && *(strptr + 1) == '\0')
                   break;      /* possible loop exit */
        }
        return(count);
    }
```

The same changes are required in *get_cost( )*.

16-1.

```
/* ***** STRLEN *****
 *
 * Count the number of characters in the string argument
 *   not including the terminating \0.
 *
 * Written by Ray Swartz for "Doing Business with C"
 */
int strlen(str)
char *str;
{
    int count = -1;

    while(str[++count] != '\0')
        ;
    return(count);
}
```

or

```
int strlen(str)
char *str;
{
    int count = 0;

    while(str[count++] != '\0')
        ;
    return(--count);   /* the \0 is counted too */
}
```

16-2.

```
/* ***** STRNCPY *****
 *
 * This function copies nbr characters from str2 into str1.
 *   Less than nbr characters is copied if str2 has fewer
 *   than nbr characters.
 *
 * Written by Ray Swartz for "Doing Business with C"
 */
char *strncpy(str1, str2, nbr)
char *str1;
char *str2;
int nbr;
{
    int count = 0;
    char *beginstr1 = str1;    /* return pointer */

    while(count++ < nbr && (*str1++ = *str2++) != '\0')
        ;
    *str1 = '\0';  /* be sure str1 is terminated */
    return(beginstr1);
}
```

16-3.

```
/* ***** STRCMP *****
 * This function compares the two string argument and
 * returns a negative number if str1 is less than str2,
 * 0 if it is equal, and a positive number if str1 is greater
 * than str2.
 *
 * Written by Ray Swartz for "Doing Business with C".
 */

int strcmp(str1, str2)
char *str1;
char *str2;
{
    while(*str1 == *str2 && *str1 != '\0') {
        str1++;
        str2++;
    }
    return(*str1 - *str2);  /* returns 0 is strings equal */
}
```

Solutions to In-Chapter Exercises

16-4.

```
/* ***** STRNCMP *****
 * This function compares the first nbr characters of the
 * two string arguments and returns a negative number if
 * str1 is less than str2, 0 if it is equal, and a positive
 * number if str1 is greater than str2.
 *
 * Written by Ray Swartz for "Doing Business with C".
 */

strncmp(str1, str2, nbr)
char *str1;
char *str2;
int nbr;    /* number of characters to compare */
{
    int count = 1;    /* number of character being compared */

    while(*str1 == *str2 && *str1 != '\0' && count++ = nbr) {
        str1++;
        str2++;
    }
    return(*str1 - *str2);
}
```

17-1.

```
/* ***** GETS *****
 *
 * This function reads a line from the terminal, stores it
 *  in str (passed in), terminates str with '\0', and returns
 *  a pointer to str's first character.  If EOF is returned by
 *  getchar(), the function returns NULL.
 *
 * Written by Ray Swartz for "Doing Business with C"
 */

#include "stdio.h"

char *gets(str)
char *str;
{
    int c;
    char *s = str;  /* needed to return pointer to 1st char */

    while((c = getchar()) != '\n') {
        if (c == EOF)
            return(NULL);  /* input error */
```

```
        else
            *str++ = c;    /* store c in next slot and increment */
    }
    *str = '\0';
    return(s);             /* return pointer to first character  */
}
```

17-2.

```
/* ***** PUTS *****
 *
 * This function prints it string argument and then
 * a newline.
 *
 * Written by Ray Swartz for "Doing Business with C"
 *
 */

#include "stdio.h"

int puts(str)
char *str;
{
    while(*str != '\0') {
        if (putchar(*str++) == EOF)
            return(EOF);
    }
    return(putchar('\n'));
}
```

17-3.

```
/* ***** CTOI *****
 *
 * This function returns the equivalent integer value
 *  of a numeric character.  A -1 is returned if the
 *  character passed does not store a digit.
 *
 * Written by Ray Swartz for "Doing Business with C"
 */

int ctoi(c)
int c;
```

Solutions to In-Chapter Exercises

```
        {
            switch(c) {
                case '0': return(0);
                case '1': return(1);
                case '2': return(2);
                case '3': return(3);
                case '4': return(4);
                case '5': return(5);
                case '6': return(6);
                case '7': return(7);
                case '8': return(8);
                case '9': return(9);
                default: return(-1);    /* error */
            }
        }
```

18-1.

    a.

```
            struct check {
                char name[41];   /* receiver of check */
                char date[20];   /* date check written */
                double amount;   /* amount of check */
            };
```

    b.

```
            struct date {
                char month[4];   /* one for \0 */
                int day;
                int year;
            };
```

18-2.

```
            strcpy(rev_ptr2->rev_cat, rev_ptr1->rev_cat);
            rev2->rev_amt = rev1->rev_amt;
```

18-3.

```
                    #define MAX_LEN 31
                    #define MAX_CAT 20

                    #include "stdio.h"
                    #include "getcat.c"
```

```
                    typedef struct {
                        char rev_cat[MAX_CAT];
                        long rev_amt;
                    } REV

                    main()
                    {
                        ...
```

18-4.

```
/* ***** GETDATE *****
 *
 * This function is passed a date structure and then prompts for
 *  and reads a date and then verifies that the date is valid.
 *
 * Written by Ray Swartz for "Doing Business with C"
 *
 */
void getdate(date_entry)
struct date *date_entry;
{
    char *gets();
    char *strcpy();
    char instr[81];    /* input string */
    static char month_name[][10] = { "January",
                                     "February",
                                     "March",
                                     "April",
                                     "May",
                                     "June",
                                     "July",
                                     "August",
                                     "September",
                                     "October",
                                     "November",
                                     "December"};
    int printf();
    int strlen();
    int atoi();
    int loop_flag = 0;    /* 1 if month name correct */
    int month_nbr;        /* loop counter */

    do {
        printf("\nEnter month's full name: ");
        gets(instr);
```

Solutions to In-Chapter Exercises

```c
            if (strlen(instr) >= 10)
                printf("Name too long\n");
            else {
                for (month_nbr = 0; month_nbr < 12; month_nbr++) {
                    if (strcmp(instr, month_name[month_nbr]) == 0) {
                        loop_flag = 1;
                        break;    /* month found */
                    }
                }
            }
        } while (! loop_flag);
        strcpy(date_entry->name, instr);
        do {
            printf("\nEnter year: ");
            date_entry->year = atoi(gets(instr));
            if (date_entry->year < 1988)
                printf("Enter full year (all 4 digits)\n");
        } while (date_entry->year < 1988);
        do {
            printf("\nEnter day of month: ");
            date_entry->day = atoi(gets(instr));
            switch (month_nbr + 1) {
                /* leap is every four year except that every century
                   year is not a leap year.  However, every 400
                   years, the century year is a leap year.  This
                   means the year 2000 is a leap year and no test
                   is necessary for century */
                case 2: if (date_entry->year % 4) /* leap year = false */
                            loop_flag = date_entry->day > 28;
                        else
                            loop_flag = date_entry->day > 29;
                        break;
                case 4:
                case 6:
                case 9:
                case 11: loop_flag = date_entry->day > 30;
                         break;
                case 1:
                case 3:
                case 5:
                case 7:
                case 8:
                case 10:
                case 12: loop_flag = date_entry->day > 31;
                         break;
```

```
                    default: printf("Enter 1 through 12 only\n");
              }
        } while (loop_flag);
        return;
  }
```

19-1.

a.

$$\text{sizeof(double)}$$

This is 2 given the values in Output 19-1.

b.

$$30 * 51 * \text{sizeof(long)}$$

This is 6120 given the values in Output 19-1.

20-1.

```
/* ***** PRINT_PL *****
 *
 * This function prints a formatted Profit and Loss
 * statement.  It is sent category name and amounts
 * inside two structure arrays.  The number of entries
 * of each type is sent to the function as arguments, also.
 *
 * Written by Ray Swartz for "Doing Business with C"
 *
 * Modified to print the statement into the file
 * pl-stmt instead of to the screen (stdout).
 */
void print_pl(revenue, rev_count, cost, cost_count)
struct pl_entry *revenue;   /* revenue entries */
int rev_count;              /* number of revenue entries */
struct pl_entry *cost;      /* cost entries */
int cost_count;             /* number of cost entries */
{
    FILE *fopen();
    FILE *outfile;          /* the output file */
    int count;              /* loop counter */
    static char co_name[] = "Johnson's Books";  /* company name */
    static char filename[] = "pl-stmt";
    long totalrev = 0;      /* revenue amounts total */
    long totalcost = 0;     /* cost amounts total */
```

Solutions to In-Chapter Exercises

```c
        if ((outfile = fopen(filename, "w")) == NULL) {
            printf("Can't open the statement file %s\n", filename);
            exit(1);
        }
        fprintf(outfile, "\tProfit and Loss for %s\n\n", co_name);
        fprintf(outfile, "             REVENUE\n\n");

        /* Loop to print and total the revenue categories */

        for (count = 0; count < rev_count; count++) {
            fprintf(outfile, "%-*s   $%6ld\n", MAX_LEN - 1,
                    revenue->category, revenue->amount);
            totalrev += (revenue++)->amount;
        }
        fprintf(outfile, "                               ------\n");
        fprintf(outfile, "            TOTAL REVENUE          $%71d\n\n\n",
                totalrev);

        /* Loop to print and total the cost categories */

        for (count = 0; count < cost_count; count++) {
            fprintf(outfile, "%-*s   $%6ld\n", MAX_LEN - 1,
                    cost->category, cost->amount);
            totalcost += (cost++)->amount;
        }
        fprintf(outfile, "                               ------\n");
        fprintf(outfile, "            TOTAL COST             $%71d\n\n\n",
                totalcost);
        if (totalrev >= totalcost)
            fprintf(outfile, "           PROFIT              $%71d\n",
                    totalrev - totalcost);
        else
            fprintf(outfile, "            LOSS              ($%71d)\n",
                    totalcost - totalrev);
        fclose(outfile);
        return;
}
```

20-2.

```c
/* ***** MKFILE *****
 *
 * This function creates the revenue.dat and cost.dat
 *   files from structures passed in as arguments.
 *   The file format is for each entry to be listed
 *   two lines with the category name on the first
 *   line.
 *
 * Written by Ray Swartz for "Doing Business with C"
```

```
 * Modified to check for write errors.
 */

void mkfile(revenue, rev_count, cost, cost_count)
ENTRY *revenue;
ENTRY *cost;
int rev_count;
int cost_count;
{
    FILE *fopen();
    FILE *outfile;    /* open revenue or cost file */
    int count;
    int fprintf();
    int fclose();

    if ((outfile = fopen("revenue.dat", "w")) == NULL) {
       printf("Can't open revenue.dat file\n");
       return;
    }
    for (count = 0; count < rev_count; count++) {
        if (fprintf(outfile, "%s\n%ld\n", revenue[count].category,
               revenue[count].amount); == EOF) {
            printf("File error: copy not completed\n");
            exit(1);
        }
    }
    fclose(outfile);
    if ((outfile = fopen("cost.dat", "w")) == NULL) {
       printf("Can't open cost.dat file\n");
       return;
    }
    for (count = 0; count < cost_count; count++) {
        if (fprintf(outfile, "%s\n%ld\n", cost[count].category,
                cost[count].amount) == EOF) {
            printf("File error: copy not completed\n");
            exit(1);
        }
    }
    fclose(outfile);
    return;
}
```

21-1. See Program 21-2.

21-2.

```
/* ***** File Copying Utility *****
 *
 * This program copies one file (infile) to another (outfile)
 * taking the filenames off the command line.
```

Solutions to In-Chapter Exercises

```
 *    In addition, if a -x appears as the first argument,
 *    the program checks if the destination file exists.
 *
 * Modified to ask if the user to continue the copy if
 *   -x is specified and the file exists.
 *
 * Written by Ray Swartz for "Doing Business with C"
 */

#include "stdio.h"

#define YES 1
#define NO  0

main(argc, argv)
int argc;
char *argv[];
{
    FILE *infile;           /* source file */
    FILE *outfile;          /* destination file */
    FILE *fopen();
    int inchar;             /* input variable */
    int fclose();
    int printf();
    int getc();             /* sometimes declared as macro */
    int putc();             /* sometimes declared as macro */
    int exist_flag = NO;    /* YES if -x on command line */

    if (argc < 3 || argc > 4) { /* command line args in error */
        printf("Usage: copy [-x] source-file destination-file\n");
        exit(1);
    }
    if (strcmp(*++argv, "-x") == 0) {
        exist_flag = YES;
        argv++;  /* go to next argument */
    }
    if ((infile = fopen(*argv, "r")) == NULL) {
        printf("Can't open %s\n", *argv);
        exit(1);  /* error in opening file */
    }
    argv++;      /* next argument is destination file */
    if (exist_flag == YES) {
        if ((outfile = fopen(*argv, "r")) != NULL) {
            do {
                printf("File: %s exists.  Make copy anyway? (y/n)\n",
                        *argv);
                gets(instr);
```

```
                    if (*instr == 'N' || *instr == 'n')
                        exit(2); /* distinguish from open error */
                } while (*instr != 'Y' && *instr != 'y');
            } /* loop until get Y, y, n, or N */
        }
        fclose(outfile);   /* opened for read access above */
        if ((outfile = fopen(*argv, "w")) == NULL) {
            printf("Can't open %s\n", *argv);
            exit(1);   /* error in opening file */
        }
        while ((inchar = getc(infile)) != EOF)
            putc(inchar, outfile);   /* file copying loop */
        fclose(infile);
        fclose(outfile);
        exit(0);
    }
```

Index

& (as address operator), 210
* (asterisk), pointers and, 212, 213
\\ (backslash), 23–24, 433
{ } (braces), 31
[ ] (brackets), order of precedence, 114
\'' (double quotation marks), 23–24, 433
== (equal to), 35–41
^ (exclusive OR), 386–88
\> (greater than), 35–41
\>= (greater than or equal to), 35–41
<< (left shift), 386
< (less than), 35–41
<= (less than or equal to), 35–41
&& (logical AND), 35–41, 386–88
! (logical NOT), 35–41
ll (logical OR), 35–41, 386–88
!= (not equal to), 35–41
(octothorpe), 141
~ (one's complement), 386–87
\>> (right shift), 386
\' (single quotation mark), 23–24, 433

\a (alarm), 23–24, 411, 433
Accessing files, 348–52
Ada language, 380
Address, 209–10
   arrays and, 222–23
Address operator, 210–11
   arrays and, 228
   function arguments and, 218
   order of precedence, 215
Aggregate data type, 269
Alarm (\a), 23–24, 411, 433
ALGOL, 3, 7
Algorithms, 4–7
American National Standards Institute
   C standard, 401–15
      arithmetic features, 404–5
      features, 411–14
      function prototypes, 402–4
      keywords, 406–8
      pointers, 408–9
      preprocessor features, 409–11
      removing restrictions, 404
   X3J11 committee, 4, 401

ANSI; *see* American National Standards
      Institute
Argc, 370–74
Arguments, command line, 370–77
  argc, 370–74
  argv, 370–74
  reading, 374–76
Argv, 370–74
Arithmetic
  features, 404–5
  operators, 17–20
    order of evaluation in, 18, 38
  pointer, 224–25
Arrays, 256–78
  bounds checking, 253–54
  character, string variables and, 116
  data, 111–14
  data structures and, 299–13
  element, 111
  index, 111
    increment operators in, 166–69
  initializing, 200–5
  multidimensional, 128
    pointers and, 241–55
  order of precedence, 225
  pointers and, 221–40
    addresses and, 222–23
    array transformation rule, 225–32, 330, 433–34
    differences with arrays, 234–39
    function arguments and, 232–34
    pointer arithmetic, 224–25
  realloc( ), 335–42
  rules of promotion, 223
  sizeof( ), 325
  string, 117–26
    defining formal parameter, 129
    definition of, 118
    passing as argument, 129
    referencing within function, 129
  transformation rule, 225–32, 330, 433–34
  two-dimensional, 244–53
    transformation, 246–53
ASCII character set, 393–96
ASCII code, 259
Asctime( ), 413
Assignment operators, 169–70
  order of precedence, 170
Assignment variables, 199
Associativity, 19
Asterisk (*), pointers and, 212, 213
Atof( ), 50–52, 287, 426
Atoi( ), 50–52, 287, 426
Atol( ), 50–52, 287, 426

Auto keyword, 182, 432
Automatic storage, 182–83

\b (backspace), 23–24, 433
B programming language, 4
Backslash (\\), 23–24, 433
Backspace (\b), 23–24, 433
Base case, 385
BCPL (British Combined Programming Language), 4
Bell Laboratories, 3
Benign redefinition, 410
Binary arithmetic operators, 169
Binary digit, 385
Binary numbering system, 385
Bit, 385
Bit fields, 390–92
  definition of, 391
Bitwise operators, 385–90
  exclusive OR, 386
  left shift, 386
  logical AND, 386
  logical OR, 386
  one's complement, 386
  order of precedence, 386
  right shift, 386
Braces ({ }), 31
Brackets ([]), order of precedence and, 114
Break keyword, 432
Break command, 136–39
  structured programming and, 137
  switch statement and, 99
British Combined Programming Language (BCPL), 4
Buffers, 282, 285

C program creation, 10–11, 30–42
  conditional statements in, 34–41
  using compiler in, 11
C programming language
  algorithms in, 4–7
  as concise language, 2
  as flexible language, 2
  history of, 3–4
  if-else statements and, 40
  as language of UNIX operating system, 3
  as portable language, 1–2
  programming environment of, 346–47
  structured programming in, 4–7
The C Programming Language, 4, 401

Index

C Users Group, 415
The C Users Journal, 415
Calloc( ), 331, 424–25
Carriage return (\r), 433
Case keyword, 432
Casts, 74–76, 408
    rounding and, 84
Changing program; *See* Modifying program
Char
    data type, 13, 259–60, 405
    keyword, 432
Character
    arrays, string variables and, 116
    constants, 22–24
        special, 23–24, 433
    converting, 288–94
    functions, 417–18
    set
        ASCII, 393–96
        EBCDIC, 397–400
    strings; *see* Strings
    testing, 288–94
Clearerr( ), 418
Clock_t typedef, 412
Closing files, 351–52
Command line arguments, 370–77
    argc, 370–74
    argv, 370–74
    reading, 374–76
Commands
    creating, 66–78
        changing data types in, 73–76
        function data types in, 70–71
        homemade functions in, 71–73
        void data type in, 70–71
        writing functions in, 67–70
    looping; *see* Looping commands
Comments, 53–54
Compilation, conditional, 149–53
Compiler, 11
    directives, 44
Computer dependence, 43–44
Concatenation, 271–72
Conditional operator, 171–74
    macros and, 172
    nesting, 172–74
    order of precedence, 172
Conditional statements, 34–41
Const keyword, 406–8, 432
Constants, 142
    character, 22–24
        special, 23–24, 433
    definition of, 22
    hexadecimal, 378, 411

    numeric, 378
    octal, 378
Continue keyword, 432
Control D, 348
Control structures, 4–8
Conversion functions, 50–52
    writing, 287–88
Converting characters, 288–94
Copying strings, 265–69, 271
Cost, 33–34
    if-else statement and, 34–41
    profit and loss statement and, 57–63
Cost-of-goods
    if-else statement and, 37, 38
    profit and loss statement and, 57–63
Ctime( ), 413
Ctype.h, 288

Data, directly accessing, 208–20
    address operator and, 210–11
    indirection operator and, 213–14
    initializing pointers and, 215
    pointer data type and, 211–13
    pointers as function arguments and, 217–19
Data arrays, 111–14
Data files, 346–69
    accessing, 348–51
    append mode, 349
    C programming environment, 346–47
    closing, 351–52
    creating, 349
    feof( ) macro, 357–58
    fgets( ), 354–55
    fprintf( ), 356–57
    fputs( ), 355–56
    fscanf( ), 356–57
    getc( ), 353–54
    input and output functions, 352
    opening, 348–51
    program termination and, 351–52
    putc( ), 353–54
    read mode, 349
    redirection, 347–48
    standard input as, 281
    system resources, 351–52
    write mode, 349
Data structures, 296–22
    arrays and, 299–13
        indirection, 312
    bit fields and, 391
    dynamic storage and, 331–34
    initialization and, 320–21

Data structures (*cont.*)
  sizeof( ), 325
  as structure members, 318–20
  typedef, 297–99
  variables, 331
Data types, 13–14, 404–5
  aggregate, 269
  casts, 74–76, 408
    rounding and, 84
  changing, 73–76
    casts and, 74–76
    promotion and, 74–76
  char, 13, 259–60, 405
  creating, 296–99
  double, 13, 405
  enumeration, 380–82
  float, 13, 405
  in functions, 70–71
  int, 13, 405, 432
  long, 13, 405
  modifier, 406, 408
  pointer, 211–13
  prtdiff_t, 409
  short, 13
  tag, 380
  unsigned, 13, 405
_DATE, 411
Debugging, 149
Declaration, 370–71
  by inclusion, 187
Decrement operators, 161–69
  in array indexes, 166–69
Default keyword, 432
Difftime( ), 412
#Define, 142–45, 150
  definition of, 143
  typedef and, 298–99
Defining a variable, 13
Do keyword, 432
Do while loop, 86–88
Double
  data type, 13, 405
  keyword, 432
Double quotation marks (\"), 23–24, 433
Dummy variable, 69, 107
Dynamic storage, 323–45
  allocating memory, 327–34
  realloc( ), 335–42
  size of( ) operator, 324–27

EBCDIC, 259
EBCDIC character set, 397–400
#Elif, 151–52
#Else, 151–52
Else keyword, 432
Empty loops, 267
End of file (EOF)
  getchar( ) and, 281
  standard input functions and, 348
End of string (EOS), 46
#Endif, 149–52
Enum keyword, 380–81, 432
Enumerated variables, scope of, 381
Enumeration types, 380–82
EOF (End of file), 281, 348
EOS (End of string), 46
Equal to (==), 35–41
Equality operators, 35–41
#Error, 410
Exclusive OR operator (^), 386–88
Exercises, solutions to, 435–60
Exit( ), 31–32
Expenses, if-else statement and, 38
Expressions, 16–17
  mixing operators in, 94
Extern keyword, 187, 190, 432
External variables, 187, 190–91

\f (formfeed), 23–24, 433
Fclose( ), 351–52, 418
Feof( ) macro, 357–58, 418–19
Ferror( ), 418–19
Fflush( ), 418–19
Fgetc( ), 421
Fgets( ), 352, 354–55, 421
_FILE, 411
File-handling functions, 418–21
Files, data, 346–69
  accessing, 348–51
  append mode, 349
  C programming environment, 346–47
  closing, 351–52
  creation, 349
  feof( ) macro, 357–58
  fgets( ), 354–55
  fprintf( ), 356–57
  fputs( ), 355–56
  fscanf( ), 356–57
  getc( ), 353–54
  input and output functions, 352
  opening, 348–51
  program termination and, 351–52
  putc( ), 353–54
  read mode, 349
  redirection, 347–48

Index

system resources, 351–52
write mode, 349
Flags, 388
Flex-pl program, 314–18
Float
   data type, 13, 405
   keyword, 432
Float.h, 405
Fopen( ), 418–20
   modes, 349–50
For keyword, 432
For loop, 88–91
   commas and, 90
Formal parameter
   modification of, 107
   name, 68
Format string, 422–24
   strftime( ) and, 413–14
Formatted printing, 21–22
Formatting codes, 423
   printf( ) and, 378, 429–31
   scanf( ) and, 285
Formatting specifications, 22
Formfeed (\f), 23–24, 433
Fprintf( ), 352, 356–57, 421
Fputc( ), 421, 422
Fputs( ), 352, 355–56
Free( ), 335, 424–25
Fscanf( ), 352, 356–57, 421–22
Fseek( ), 418, 420
Ftell( ), 418, 420
Function arguments
   arrays and, 232–34
   pointers and, 217–19
Function library, 66–76; *see also* Standard library
Functions
   buffered, 282
   buffered input, 285
   characters, 417–18
      macros and, 417
   conversion, 287–88
   data types of, 70–71
   declaring, 26–27
   defining, 67–70
   definition of, 25
   description of, 67–68
   fgets( ), 352, 354–55
   file-handling, 418–21
   fprintf( ), 352, 356–57
   fputs( ), 352, 355–56
   fscanf( ), 352, 356–57
   getc( ), 352, 353–54
   homemade, 71–73
   input and output, 280–83, 352, 421–24

memory allocation, 424–26
mode, 419–20
parameters, scope of, 195–97
pointers to, 379
prototypes, 402–4
putc( ), 352, 353–54
realloc( ), 335–42
recursion, 385
scope of, 193–94
setlocal( ), 412
static, 191–93
string, 260–69
   conversion, 426
   manipulation, 427–28
   pointers and, 261–69
structured programming with, 25–26
test, 417
writing, 67–70
Fundamentals, 12–29
   arithmetic operators, 17–20
   character constants, 22–24
      special, 23–24
   character strings, 24–25
   data types, 13–14
   declaring functions, 26–27
   expressions, 16–17
   operands, 16–17
   operators, 16–17
   printing, 21–22
   statement format, 15–16
   structured programming with functions, 25–26
   variable names, 14–15

Getc( ), 352–54, 421–22
Getchar( ), 280–83, 421–22
Getlong( ), 67
Get-pl program, 358–60
Gets( ), 283–87, 421–23
   reading strings and, 49, 280
Global scope, 187–91
   static, 191–93
Global variables, 187–91
   initialization, 189
   limiting scope, 191–93
   portability, 197
   static, 191–93
   use of, 190
Gmtime( ), 413
Goto statement, 384–85
   keyword, 432
Greater than (>), 35–41
Greater than or equal to (>=), 35–41

Header file, 44
Hexadecimal constant, 378
History of C, 3-4
Horizontal tab (\t), 23-24, 433

#If, 149-52
If keyword, 432
If-else, 34-41
#Ifdef, 149-52
#Ifndef, 149-52
#Include, 44, 45, 141
   nesting of, 121
Increment operators, 161-69
   in array indexes, 166-69
Index( ), 272-73, 427
Indexing error, 48
Indexing strings, 47-48
Indirection
   concept of, 209
   memory locations and, 217
   operator, 213-14, 330
      order of precedence and, 215
Infinite loop, 91
Initializing variables, 199-200
In-line comments, 31, 53-54
In-line functions, 147
Input, standard; *see* Standard input
Input and output (I/O) functions, 352, 421-24
   writing, 280-83
Int
   data type, 13, 405
   keyword, 432
Integer limits, 14
Interactive programming, 43-65
   definition of, 45
   numeric formatting with printf( ) in, 55-56
   reading numeric data in, 50-54
   reading strings in, 48-50
   round-off error in, 56-57
   standard function library in, 43-44
   standard library header file in, 44-45
   stepwise refinement in, 59-63
   string variables in, 45-48
I/O (Input and output) functions, 352, 421-24
   writing, 280-83
Isalnum( ), 288, 417
Isalpha( ), 288, 417
Iscntrl( ), 288, 417
Isdigit( ), 288-89, 417
Isgraph( ), 288, 417
Islower( ), 288, 417
Isprint( ), 288, 417

Ispunct( ), 288, 417
Isspace( ), 288, 417
Isupper( ), 288, 417
Isxdigit( ), 288, 417

Jump, unconditional, 384
Justification, right, 110

Kernighan, Brian, 4, 401
Kernighan and Ritchie C language, 4
Keywords
   const, 406-8
   enum, 380-81
   listing of, 432
   union, 382
   volatile, 408, 432

Labels, line, 384-85
LC_ALL, 412
LC_COLLATE, 412
LC_CTYPE, 412
LC_NUMERIC, 412
LC_TIME, 412
Left shift operator (<<), 386
Legal expression, definition of, 17
Less than (<), 35-41
Less than or equal to (<=), 35-41
Library, Standard; *see* Standard library
Limits.h, 405
_LINE, 411
Line labels, 384-85
Local scope, 181-82
Localtime( ), 413
Local variables, 182
   modification of, 107
Logical AND, 35-41, 386-88
Logical OR, 35-41, 386-88
Logical operators, 35-41, 386-88
   order of evaluation in, 38
Long
   data type, 13, 405
   keyword, 432
Long double data type, 404-5
Looping structure, 79-82, 86-102
   definition of, 6
   empty, 267
   termination of
      break command and, 136
      quit signal and, 134

Index

commands, 79–104
  designing programs with, 91–98
  do while, 86–88
  for, 88–91
  round( ), 82–86
  while, 80–82

Machine dependence, 43–44
Machine language, 10
Macros
  arguments
    processing, 146–49
    syntax, 146–47
  benign redefinition, 410
  DATE, 411
  definition of, 144
  feof( ), 357–58, 418–19
  FILE, 411
  LC_ALL, 412
  LC_COLLATE, 412
  LC_CTYPE, 412
  LC_NUMERIC, 412
  LC_TIME, 412
  Line, 411
  nesting, 144
  offsetof( ), 411
  printf( ) and, 153–59
  STDC, 411
  substitution, 142–49
    exceptions in, 144
  TIME, 411
Main( ), 31
  purpose of, 92
Make-pl program, 360–68
Malloc( ), 327–31, 424–25
  arrays and, 329
  declaration, 327
  string arrays and, 329
Masking, 388
Memory, 209–10
  address, 12
  allocation, 327–35
    dynamic, 425
    functions, 424–26
  deallocation, 334–42
  unallocated, 323
  variables, 209–10
Mktime( ), 413
Modifier data types, 406, 408
Modifying program, 105–15
  data arrays in, 111–14
Modulo operator, 17

Multidimensional arrays, 128
  pointers and, 241–55
    bounds checking, 253–54
    two-dimensional, 244–53

\n (newline), 433
Names, variables, 14–15
Nesting, 121
Newline (\n), 433
Not (!), 35–41
Not equal to (!=), 35–41
NULL
  calloc( ) and, 331
  definition of, 267, 409
  fopen( ) and, 349
  malloc( ) and, 327–28
  #undef and, 152
Numerics
  constants, 378
  conversion, 378
  data, reading, 50–54
  formatting, with printf( ), 55–56

Octal constant, 378
Octothorpe (#), 141
Offsetof( ), 411
One's complement operator (~), 386–87
Operands, 16–17
Operators, 16–17
  address, 210–11
    arrays and, 228
    function arguments and, 218
    order of precedence, 215
  arithmetic, 17–20
    order of evaluation in, 18, 38
  assignment, 169–70
    order of precedence, 170
  binary arithmetic, 169
  bitwise, 385–90
    exclusive OR, 386, 387–88
    left shift, 386
    logical AND, 386, 387–88
    logical OR, 386, 387–88
    one's complement, 386
    order of precedence, 386
    right shift, 386
  conditional, 171–74
    nesting, 172–74
    order of precedence, 172
  decrement, 161–69

Operators (*cont.*)
    in array indexes, 166–69
    equality, 35–41
    equivalent assignment, 389
    exclusive OR, 386–88
    increment, 161–69
        array indexes and, 166–69
    indirection, 213–14, 330
        order of precedence, 215
    left shift, 386
    logical, 35–41, 386–88
        order of precedence in, 38
    modulo, 17
    one's complement, 386–87
    order of precedence, 433
        address, 215
        arithmetic, 18, 38
        assignment, 170
        bitwise, 386
        conditional, 172
        indirection, 215
        logical, 38
        relational, 38
        unary minus, 174
    postfix, 165
    prefix, 165
    relational, 35–41
        order of precedence in, 38
    right shift, 386
    shifting, 390
    sizeof( ), 324–27, 411, 425
    type cast, 330
    unary, 16, 164
        address operator as, 210, 214
        indirection operator as, 214
        sizeof( ) as, 324
    unary minus, 174–78
        order of precedence, 174
Optimization, 197–99
Order of precedence, 433
    address, 215
    arithmetic, 18, 38
    assignment, 170
    bitwise, 386
    conditional, 172
    indirection, 215
    logical, 38
    relational, 38
    unary minus, 174
Output functions, 352, 421–24
    writing, 280–83
Output, standard; *see* Standard output
Overwriting error, 49

Pascal language, 380
Passing arguments, 25
P&L (Profit and loss) statement, 57–63
    expanding, 57–59
Pl.h, 410
Pointers, 256–78, 408–9
    alternative, 227
    arithmetic, 224–25
    arrays and, 221–40
        addresses and, 222–23
        differences, 234–39
        function arguments, 232–34
        pointer arithmetic, 224–25
        transformation rule, 225–32, 433–34
    data type casts, 408
    data types and, 211–13
    definition of, 212–13
    function arguments and, 217–19
    to functions, 379
    initialization, 215
    memory locations and, 219
    multidimensional arrays and, 241–55
        bounds checking, 253–54
        two-dimensional, 244–53
    strings and, 48
        constants, 257
        functions, 261–69
    variables, 212
    void, 408
Portability, 1–2
    global variables and, 197
Postfix operators, 165
#Pragma, 410
Precedence; *see* Order of precedence
Prefix operators, 165
Preprocessor, 141–60, 409–11
    conditional compilation in, 149–53
    #define directive, 142–45
    directives, 141, 410
    macro arguments and, 146–49
    printf( ) with macros in, 153–59
Printf( )
    arguments and, 153
    definition of, 21–22, 421, 423
    formatting codes, 378, 429–31
    macros and, 153–59
    numeric formatting with, 55–56
    reading strings and, 49
    returned variable and, 27
    rounding and, 82
    scanf( ) and, 280, 284
    special formatting in, 73
Printing, 21–22; *see also* Printf( ); Standard output
Profit, 30–34

Index

Profit and loss statement, 57–63
   expanding, 57–59
Program maintenance, 131
Programming
   interactive; *see* Interactive programming
   structured, 4–7
      functions and, 25–26
Promotion rules in arrays, 223
Prompt, 45
Prtdiff_t typedef, 409
Putc( ), 352–54, 421, 423
Putchar( ), 280–83, 421, 423
Puts( ), 280, 284, 421, 423

Quit signal, 133–35
Quotation marks
   double (\"), 23–24, 433
   single (\'), 23–24, 433

\r (carriage return), 433
Reading and writing strings; *see* Strings, reading and writing
Realloc( ), 335–45, 424–26
Records; *see* Data structures
Recursion, 385
Redefinition, benign, 410
Register keyword, 432
Register storage, 198–99
Relational operators, 35–41
   order of evaluation in, 38
Remove( ), 418, 420
Rename( ), 418, 420
Repetition structures; *see* Looping structures
Return( ), 69
Return, carriage (\r), 433
Return keyword, 432
Revenue, 33–34
   if-else statement and, 34–41
   profit and loss statement and, 57–63
Rewind( ), 418, 421
Right shift operator (>>), 386
Rindex( ), 273
Ritchie, Dennis, 3, 4, 401
Round( ), 82–86
Round-off error, 56–57
Rules of promotion in arrays, 223

Sales
   if-else statement and, 37

profit and loss statement and, 57–63
Scanf( )
   definition of, 421, 423
   return code, 286
   standard input and, 280, 284–87
Scope, 181–82, 403
   conflict of, 187
   file, 190
   of functions, 193–94
      limiting, 194
      parameters, 195–97
   global, 187–91
      static, 191–93
   local, 181–82
   static global, 191–93
Searching strings, 272–73
Selection structure, 5
Sequence structure, 5
Setlocal( ), 412
Shifting operators, 390
Short
   data type, 13
   keyword, 432
Signed keyword, 404–5, 432
Signed chars, 405
Single quotation mark (\'), 23–24, 433
Size_t typedef, 411
Sizeof keyword, 432
Sizeof( ) operator, 324–27, 411, 425
Solution to exercises, 435–60
Special characters, 433
Sprintf( ), 127–33, 421, 423–24
Sscanf( ), 286–87, 421, 424
Standard function library; *see* Standard library
Standard input, 279
   device, 346
   redirection, 347–48, 370
Standard library, 43–44, 416–28
   character functions, 417–18
   file-handling functions, 418–21
   input and output functions, 421–24
   memory allocation functions, 424–26
   string functions, 269–73, 280
      conversion, 426
      manipulation, 427–28
   unallocated memory and, 323, 327
Standard library header file, 44–45
Standard output, 279
   device, 346
   redirection, 347–48, 370
Statement format, 15–16
Static global scope, 191–93
Static keyword, 432
Static storage, 183–87

STDC, 411
Stddef.h, 409, 411
Stdio.h
    definition of, 44,
    EOF macro and, 281
    function prototypes and, 404
    input and output functions and, 421
    string manipulation functions and, 427
    typedef and, 418
Stdlib.h, 425
Stepwise refinement, 59–63
Storage
    automatic, 182–83
    classes, 182–87, 198–99
    default, 182
    dynamic, 323–45
        allocating memory, 327–34
        realloc( ), 335–42
        sizeof( ) operator, 324–27
    initialization, 183, 185
    register, 198–99
    speed and, 197–99
    static, 183–87
        appropriate uses, 186
    temporary, 182
    unallocated, 324
Strcat( ), 271–72, 427
    source code for, 276
Strchr( ), 272–73, 427
    source code for, 277–78
Strcmp( ), 270–71, 427
Strcoll( ), 414
Strcpy( ), 427
Strftime( ), 413–14
Strings, 116–33, 256–78
    arrays, 117–26
        defining formal parameter, 129
        definition of, 118
        passing as argument, 129
        referencing within function, 129
    chars, 259–60
    concatenation, 271–72
    copying, 265–69, 271
    definition of, 24–25
    equality of, 270
    format, 422, 423, 424
    functions
        manipulation, 427–28
        return int, 269–71
        return pointer to char, 271–73
        sprintf( ), 127–33
        standard library, 269–73, 280
    indexing, 47–48
    manipulation functions, 427–28
    reading and writing, 48–50, 260–69, 279–95
        conversion function, 287–88, 426
        converting characters, 288–94
        gets( ), 283–87
        input and output functions, 280–83
        testing characters, 288–94
    searching, 272–73
    sprintf( ) function in, 127–33
    standard library, 269–73
    variables in, 45–48
        character arrays and, 116
        declaration of, 46
        definition of, 116
Strlen( ), 427–28
Strncat( ), 271–72, 427–28
    source code for, 276–77
Strncmp( ), 271, 427–28
Strncpy( ), 271, 427–28
    source code for, 275–76
Strpos( ), 273
Strrchr( ), 273, 427–28
Struct keyword, 301, 432
Structure, declaring, 301
Structured programming, 4–7
    with functions, 25–26
Strxfrm( ), 414
Switch keyword, 432
Switch-case statement, 98–102
    integer constant and, 100

\t (horizontal tab), 23–24, 433
Tab
    horizontal (\t), 23–24, 433
    vertical (\v), 23–24, 433
Tag data type, 380
Testing characters, 288–94
Thompson, Ken, 4
_TIME, 411
Time( ), 413
Time_t typedef, 412
Tolower( ), 288, 417
Toupper( ), 288, 417
Transformation
    rule, in arrays, 225–32, 330
    two-dimensional arrays, 246–53
Truncation, 83
Two-dimensional arrays, 244–53
    transformation, 246–53
Type cast operator, 330
Typedef
    clock_t, 412
    definition of, 297–99

FILE, 349, 418
  keyword, 432
  prtdiff_t, 409
  scope, 298
  size_t, 411
  time_t, 412

Unary minus operators, 174–78
Unary operators, 16, 164
  address operator as, 210, 214
  indirection operator as, 214
  sizeof( ) as, 324
#Undef, 152–53
Ungetc( ), 421, 424
Unions, 382–84
  keyword, 432
UNIX operating system, 3
Unsigned data type, 13, 405
User functions, 66–76

\v (vertical tab), 23–24, 433
Variables
  assignment, 199
  data structure, 331
  definition of, 12
  enumerated, scope of, 381
  external, 187, 190–91
  global, 187–91
    initialization, 189
    limiting scope, 191–93
    portability, 197
    static, 191–93
    use of, 190
  initializing, 199–200
  local, 182
    modification of, 107
  memory, 209–10
  names, 14–15
  pointer, 212
  static global, 191–93
  in strings, 45–48
    character arrays and, 116
    declaration of, 46
    definition of, 116
Vertical tab (\v), 23–24, 433
Void
  compilers and, 299
  data type, 70–71
  definition of, 27
  keyword, 432
Volatile keyword, 408, 432

While keyword, 432
While loop, 80–82
  format of, 80

Disk Order Form

Please send me _____ copies, at $24.95 each, of the listing in *Doing Business with C* on PC format floppy diskettes.

Name _____
Company Name _____
Street Address _____
City _____ State _____ Zipcode _____
Phone _____

Disk Size _____ 5.25" _____ 3.5"

Send check or money order in U.S. funds.

Foreign orders add US$5.00 for shipping and handling.

Send order form to:

Berkeley Decision/Systems
P.O. Box 2528
Santa Cruz, CA 95063